THE
TOP
10
OF EVERYTHING
1999

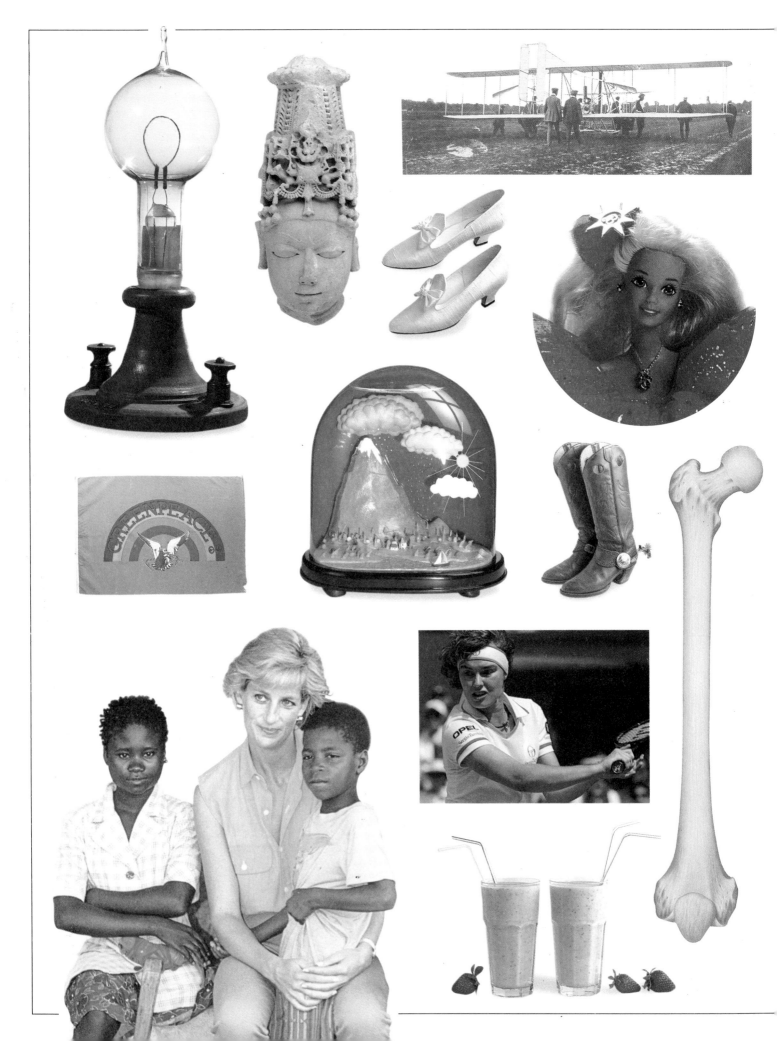

Project Editor Adèle Hayward
US Editors Iris Rosoff, Michael Wise
Managing Editor Stephanie Jackson
Managing Art Editor Nigel Duffield
Production Controller Silvia La Greca

Produced by GLS Editorial and Design,
Garden Studios, 11–15 Betterton Street,
London, WC2H 9BP
Designers Donna Askem, Ian Merrill,
Sue Caws, Jamie Hanson, Harvey de Roemer
Editors Claire Calman, Fergus Day, Helen Ridge
Design director Ruth Shane
Editorial director Jane Laing

First American Edition, 1998
24681097531

Published in the United States by
DK Publishing, Inc.
95 Madison Avenue
New York, New York 10016

Material in this edition is also published in Top 10
of Everything from Covent Garden Books

Visit us on the World Wide Web at http://www.dk.com

Library of Congress Cataloging-in-Publication Data
Ash, Russell.
The top 10 of everything, 1999 / by Russell Ash. -- 1st American ed.
p. cm.
Includes index.
ISBN 0-7894-3523-3 (pb: alk.paper). -- ISBN 0-7894-3524-1 (hc:
alk. paper)
1. Curiosities and wonders. 2. World records – Miscellanea. I. Title.
AG243. A717 1998
031.02 – dc21   98–16593
                                                      CIP

Reproduction by HBM Print Ltd, Singapore.
Printed and bound in the United States by R. R. Donnelley &
Sons Company.

CONTENTS

THE
TOP
10
OF EVERYTHING
1999

RUSSELL ASH

DK PUBLISHING, INC.

INTRODUCTION

Welcome to No. 10! This edition of *The Top 10 of Everything* is, appropriately, the 10th. When it was first published in 1988, no one – including me – imagined that it would be published annually, but such has been its success that it has been issued every year since then. It has also appeared in many national editions and in a variety of languages around the world, and given rise to a range of spin-off publications.

TOP 10 LISTS

For the benefit of newcomers to the book, I should explain that *The Top 10 of Everything* does not contain any "bests" or favorites, but exclusively quantifiable rankings. Some are "worsts," as in the case of murder and disaster victims, which are, sadly, measurable. It focuses on superlatives in numerous categories – tallest, fastest, richest, and so on – but also contains a variety of "firsts" or "latests," which recognize, for instance, the first 10 holders of the Land Speed Record. "Latests," as in the case of award winners, are the most recent 10 achievers in a field of endeavor.

WHAT'S NEW?

In an attempt to squeeze a quart into a pint, and thereby increase the total number of featured lists to over the 1,000 mark for the first time, certain lists have been compacted. Those lists marked with stars are new to this edition, but even those without a star are new in the sense that although the subject may have appeared previously, the entries within the list have been fully updated. Another new feature this year is the introduction of certain "Then & Now" lists, which juxtapose today's listing with that of a decade ago, resulting in often revealing comparisons. Occasional "Snap Facts," another innovation, provide extra morsels of information on the subjects of the adjacent lists.

INFORMATION SOURCES

In response to readers who have asked that sources be included, you will find that these appear below certain lists. By default, those lists that do not have credits result from work especially undertaken for the book by myself or by specialists in various fields, using multiple sources of information. Lists on topics ranging from accidents to place names can be compiled only by extensive research among diverse sources, and through constant monitoring for changes. Most lists contain the latest available information at the time the book went to press, or, if based on annual statistics, for the latest available year. The latter is usually the last calendar year. The exceptions are generally those that are based on "official," or government, figures, which often – despite such technological advances as electronic publishing and the internet – follow a tortuous route from their source to public availability. Consequently, those lists may be a couple of years old. However, without wishing to excuse the slow workings of the statistical world, I would suggest that one of the things *The Top 10 of Everything* attempts to do is to take such figures, which are more often than not issued in dense (and expensive) publications, and present them in a form that is accessible. Regrettably, the demands of our production schedule make it impossible to update some lists beyond a certain cutoff point – frustratingly, certain sports and other events, such as World Cup soccer and various annual awards ceremonies, have a habit of taking place while the book is being finalized, so they sometimes don't make it in time.

THANK YOU!

From the very first year, the book has remained a personal endeavor, but one that could not be compiled without the help of the many individuals and organizations who have kindly supplied information, and whose contributions are acknowledged at the end. I would also like to thank those readers who have taken the trouble to write or e-mail me with their helpful comments and suggestions. Whenever possible, I have responded to them, but the pressures inherent in producing a book of this kind mean that I have sometimes not had the time to do so. I hope they will accept this as my special "thank you."

SUGGESTIONS AND CORRECTIONS

If you wish to present either, you can contact me on our World Wide Web site at http://www.dk.com (where you will find more Top 10 lists and information about other DK books), e-mail me direct at ash@pavilion.co.uk, or write to me c/o the publishers.

Watch out for the next – the millennium – edition of *The Top 10 of Everything*!

SPECIAL FEATURES FOR THIS EDITION

• More than 1,000 lists give you the most comprehensive
Top 10 of Everything ever.

• Stars highlight lists that are new to this edition.

• Then & Now lists pinpoint specific changes over the last decade.

• Snap Fact panels supplement the lists on many pages, providing
additional nuggets of intriguing and unusual information.

• Anniversary panels are distributed throughout the book, recalling
fascinating events that occurred 50, 100, or even 200 years ago.

• Caption lists are appended to many pictures to provide extra
tidbits of data.

THE UNIVERSE & THE EARTH

TOP 10

BRIGHTEST STARS*

	Star	Constellation	Distance#	Apparent magnitude
1	Sirius	Canis Major	8.64	−1.46
2	Canopus	Carina	1,200	−0.73
3	Alpha Centauri	Centaurus	4.35	−0.27
4	Arcturus	Boötes	34	−0.04
5	Vega	Lyra	26	+0.03
6	Capella	Auriga	45	+0.08
7	Rigel	Orion	900	+0.12
8	Procyon	Canis Minor	11.4	+0.38
9	Achernar	Eridanus	85	+0.46
10	Beta Centauri	Cantaurus	460	+0.61

* *Excluding the Sun*

\# *From Earth in light-years, unless otherwise stated*

Based on apparent visual magnitude as viewed from Earth – the lower the number, the brighter the star. At its brightest, the star Betelgeuse is brighter than some of these, but as it is variable its average brightness disqualifies it from the Top 10.

TOP 10

STARS NEAREST THE EARTH*

	Star	Light-years#	Distance from Earth km (millions)	miles (millions)
1	Proxima Centauri	4.22	39,923,310	24,792,500
2	Alpha Centauri	4.35	41,153,175	25,556,250
3	Barnard's Star	5.98	56,573,790	35,132,500
4	Wolf 359	7.75	73,318,875	45,531,250
5	Lalande 21185	8.22	77,765,310	48,292,500
6	Luyten 726-8	8.43	79,752,015	49,526,250
7	Sirius	8.64	81,833,325	50,818,750
8	Ross 154	9.45	89,401,725	55,518,750
9	Ross 248	10.40	98,389,200	61,100,000
10	Epsilon Eridani	10.80	102,173,400	63,450,000

* *Excluding the Sun*

\# *One light-year = 5,878,812,000 miles/9,460,528,404,000 km*

A spaceship traveling at a speed of 25,000 mph/40,237 km/h – which is faster than any human (as opposed to unmanned probes) has yet achieved in space – would take more than 113,200 years to reach Earth's closest star, Proxima Centauri.

TYPES OF STARS

T H E   1 0

Type	Maximum surface temperature °F
1 W	144,000
2 O	72,000
3 B	45,000
4 A	18,000
5 F	13,500
6 G	10,800
7 K	9,000
8 M	6,000
9 = C (formerly R & N)	4,700
= S	4,700

Stars are classified by type according to their spectra – the colors by which they appear when viewed with a spectroscope. These vary according to the star's surface temperature. A letter is assigned to each type – although there are some variations, Type C sometimes being divided into R and N. Using this code, one mnemonic for remembering the sequence in the correct order takes the initial letters of the words in the phrase "Wow! O Be A Fine Girl Kiss Me Right Now Sweetie." Within these types, there are sub-types, with dwarfs generally hotter than giants. Most stars fall in the mid-range (B to M), with those at the extreme ends being comparatively rare.

SNAP FACTS

• The Andromeda Galaxy is 2,200,000 light-years away from the Milky Way, contains 300 billion stars, and is 180,000 light-years in diameter. It is the most distant thing in the universe the unaided human eye can see.

• Andromeda is a rotating spiral nebula 2,309,000 light-years from Earth (13 million trillion miles). Its light left there just after the first humans appeared on Earth, and comes from billions of stars – no individual one can be made out.

• More than half of all stars are binary stars – two or more stars that orbit one another. They range in size from giants up to 40 times the mass of the Sun to dwarfs down to 1/10 the mass of the Sun.

GALAXIES NEAREST THE EARTH

T O P   1 0

	Galaxy	Distance (light-years)
1	Large Cloud of Magellan	169,000
2	Small Cloud of Magellan	190,000
3	Ursa Minor dwarf	250,000
4	Draco dwarf	260,000
5	Sculptor dwarf	280,000
6	Fornax dwarf	420,000
7 =	Leo I dwarf	750,000
=	Leo II dwarf	750,000
9	Barnard's Galaxy	1,700,000
10	Andromeda Spiral	2,200,000

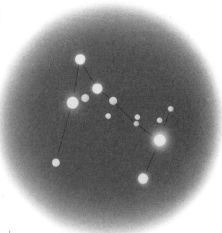

THE MILKY WAY
Often referred to as just "the Galaxy," the Milky Way is a giant spiral made up of several billion stars, including our Sun. Its true nature has been discovered only in the 20th century.

LARGEST REFLECTING TELESCOPES IN THE WORLD

T O P   1 0

	Telescope name	Location	Opened*	Aperture (m)
1	Keck I and II Telescopes	Mauna Kea Observatory, Hawaii	1992/96	10.82
2	Bolshoi Teleskop Azimutal'ny	Special Astrophysical Observatory of the Russian Academy of Sciences, Mount Pastukhov, Russia	1976	6.0
3	Hale Telescope	Palomar Observatory, California	1948	5.0
4	William Herschel Telescope	Observatorio del Roque de los Muchachos, La Palma, Canary Islands	1987	4.2
5 =	Mayall Telescope#	Kitt Peak National Observatory, Arizona	1973	4.0
=	4-meter Telescope#	Cerro Tololo Inter-American Observatory, Chile	1976	4.0
7	Anglo-Australian Telescope	Siding Spring Observatory, New South Wales, Australia	1974	3.9
8 =	ESO 3.6-meter Telescope	European Southern Observatory, La Silla, Chile	1975	3.6
=	Canada-France-Hawaii Telescope	Mauna Kea Observatory, Hawaii	1970	3.6
=	United Kingdom Infrared Telescope	Mauna Kea Observatory, Hawaii	1979	3.6

* *Dedicated or regular use commenced*

\# *Northern/southern hemisphere "twin" telescopes*

THE SOLAR SYSTEM

TOP 10
LARGEST PLANETARY MOONS IN THE SOLAR SYSTEM

	Moon	Planet	Diameter km	Diameter miles
1	Ganymede	Jupiter	5,269	3,274

Discovered by Galileo in 1609–10, Ganymede is thought to have a surface of thick ice.

2	Titan	Saturn	5,150	3,200

The Dutch astronomer Christian Huygens discovered Titan in 1655. It has a dense atmosphere rich in nitrogen and ethane.

3	Callisto	Jupiter	4,820	2,995

Similar in composition to Ganymede, Callisto is heavily pitted with craters.

4	Io	Jupiter	3,632	2,257

Io has a crust of solid sulfur with volcanic eruptions hurling material far into space.

5	Moon	Earth	3,475	2,159

Our own satellite is a quarter of the size of Earth and the 5th largest in the Solar System.

6	Europa	Jupiter	3,126	1,942

Europa's ice-covered surface is crossed with mysterious black lines resembling canals.

7	Triton	Neptune	2,750	1,708

Discovered by British amateur astronomer William Lassell in 1846, Triton has nitrogen and methane glaciers on its surface.

8	Titania	Uranus	1,580	982

Titania was discovered by William Herschel in 1787 and has a snowball-like surface of ice.

9	Rhea	Saturn	1,530	951

Saturn's second largest moon was discovered by 17th-century French astronomer Giovanni Cassini. Its icy surface is pitted with craters.

10	Oberon	Uranus	1,516	942

Discovered by Herschel, Oberon was named after the fairy husband of Titania in Shakespeare's A Midsummer Night's Dream.

TOP 10
LARGEST METEORITES EVER FOUND

	Location	Estimated weight (tons)
1	Hoba West, Grootfontein, South Africa	60.0
2	Ahnighito ("The Tent"), Cape York, West Greenland	34.1
3	Bacuberito, Mexico	29.8
4	Mbosi, Tanganyika	28.7
5	Agpalik, Cape York, West Greenland	22.2
6	Armanti, Western Mongolia	22.0
7	Mundrabilla, Western Australia	17.6
8=	Willamette, Oregon	15.4
=	Chupaderos, Mexico	15.4
10	Campo del Cielo, Argentina	14.3

It is calculated that about 500 meteorites strike the surface of Earth every year, although many fall in the ocean and in unpopulated areas. The actual risk of being struck by a falling meteorite has also been estimated, and for citizens of the US placed at one occurrence every 9,300 years.

TOP 10
MOST FREQUENTLY SEEN COMETS

	Comet	Period (years)
1	Encke	3.302
2	Grigg-Skjellerup	4.908
3	Honda-Mrkós-Pajdusáková	5.210
4	Tempel 2	5.259
5	Neujmin 2	5.437
6	Brorsen	5.463
7	Tuttle-Giacobini-Kresák	5.489
8	Tempel-L. Swift	5.681
9	Tempel 1	5.982
10	Pons-Winnecke	6.125

HALLEY'S COMET
Returning every 76 years, its next appearance will be in 2061.

TOP 10
BODIES FARTHEST FROM THE SUN*

	Body	Average distance from Sun '000 km	Average distance from Sun '000 miles
1	Pluto	5,914,000	3,675,000
2	Neptune	4,497,000	2,794,000
3	Uranus	2,871,000	1,784,000
4	Chiron	2,800,000	1,740,000
5	Saturn	1,427,000	887,000
6	Jupiter	778,300	483,600
7	Mars	227,900	141,600
8	Earth	149,600	92,900
9	Venus	108,200	67,200
10	Mercury	57,900	36,000

* In the Solar System, excluding satellites and asteroids

Chiron, a "mystery object" that may be either a comet or an asteroid, was discovered on November 1, 1977 by American astronomer Charles Kowal. It measures 124–186 miles/200–300 km in diameter and orbits between Saturn and Uranus. A so-called "Planet X" is believed by some to orbit beyond Pluto.

TOP 10
LONGEST DAYS IN THE SOLAR SYSTEM

	Body	days	Length of day* hours	Length of day* mins
1	Venus	244	0	0
2	Mercury	58	14	0
3	Sun	25#	0	0
4	Pluto	6	9	0
5	Mars		24	37
6	Earth		23	56
7	Uranus		17	14
8	Neptune		16	7
9	Saturn		10	39
10	Jupiter		9	55

* Period of rotation, based on Earth day
 # Variable

SURFACE OF MARS

TOP 10 LARGEST BODIES IN THE SOLAR SYSTEM

❶ Sun (865,036 miles/
1,392,140 km) ❷ Jupiter (88,846 miles/
142,984 km) ❸ Saturn (74,898 miles/
120,536 km) ❹ Uranus (31,763 miles/
51,118 km) ❺ Neptune (30,778 miles/
49,532 km) ❻ Earth (7,926 miles/
12,756 km) ❼ Venus (7,520 miles/
12,103 km) ❽ Mars (4,222 miles/6,794 km)
❾ Ganymede (3,274 miles/5,269 km)
❿ Titan (3,200 miles/5,150 km)

TOP 10

LARGEST ASTEROIDS IN THE SOLAR SYSTEM

	Asteroid	Year discovered	Diameter km	miles
1	Ceres	1801	936	582
2	Pallas	1802	607	377
3	Vesta	1807	519	322
4	Hygeia	1849	450	279
5	Euphrosyne	1854	370	229
6	Interamnia	1910	349	217
7	Davida	1903	322	200
8	Cybele	1861	308	192
9	Europa	1858	288	179
10	Patienta	1899	275	171

Asteroids, sometimes known as "minor planets," are fragments of rock orbiting between Mars and Jupiter. There are perhaps 45,000 of them, but fewer than 10 percent have been named. The first (and largest) to be discovered was Ceres.

TOP 10

LONGEST YEARS IN THE SOLAR SYSTEM

	Body	Length of year* years	days
1	Pluto	247	256
2	Neptune	164	298
3	Uranus	84	4
4	Saturn	29	168
5	Jupiter	11	314
6	Mars		687
7	Earth		365
8	Venus		225
9	Mercury		88
10	Sun		0

* Period of orbit round Sun, in Earth years/days

TOP 10

BODIES IN THE SOLAR SYSTEM WITH THE GREATEST ESCAPE VELOCITY*

	Body	Escape velocity (mi/s)
1	Sun	383.68
2	Jupiter	37.42
3	Saturn	20.04
4	Neptune	14.85
5	Uranus	13.98
6	Earth	6.95
7	Venus	6.44
8	Mars	3.13
9	Mercury	2.64
10	Pluto	0.73

* Excluding satellites. Escape velocity is the speed a rocket has to attain to overcome the gravitational pull of the body it is leaving.

TOP 10

BODIES IN THE SOLAR SYSTEM WITH THE GREATEST SURFACE GRAVITY*

	Body	Surface gravity	Weight#		Body	Surface gravity	Weight#
1	Sun	27.90	4,000	6	Earth	1.00	143
2	Jupiter	2.64	378	7	Venus	0.90	129
3	Neptune	1.20	172	8=	Mars	0.38	55
4	Uranus	1.17	168	=	Mercury	0.38	55
5	Saturn	1.16	166	10	Pluto	0.06	9

* Excluding satellites
\# Of a 143 lb adult on the body's surface

TOP 10

MOST MASSIVE BODIES IN THE SOLAR SYSTEM

	Name	Mass*		Name	Mass*
1	Sun	332,800,000	6	Earth	1.000#
2	Jupiter	317.828	7	Venus	0.815
3	Saturn	95.161	8	Mars	0.10745
4	Neptune	17.148	9	Mercury	0.05527
5	Uranus	14.536	10	Pluto	0.0022

* Compared with Earth = 1; excluding satellites
\#' The mass of Earth is approximately 81,020,000,000,000,000,000 tons

SPACE FIRSTS

FIRST UNMANNED MOON LANDINGS

	Name	Country	Date (launch/impact)
1	*Lunik 2*	USSR	Sep 12/14, 1959
2	*Ranger 4**	US	Apr 23/26, 1962
3	*Ranger 6*	US	Jan 30/Feb 2, 1964
4	*Ranger 7*	US	Jul 28/31, 1964
5	*Ranger 8*	US	Feb 17/20, 1965
6	*Ranger 9*	US	Mar 21/24, 1965
7	*Luna 5**	USSR	May 9/12, 1965
8	*Luna 7**	USSR	Oct 4/8, 1965
9	*Luna 8**	USSR	Dec 3/7, 1965
10	*Luna 9*	USSR	Jan 31/Feb 3, 1966

* *Crash landing*

THE 10 FIRST PLANETARY PROBES

(Country/planet/arrival date)

❶ *Venera 4* (USSR, Venus, Oct 18, 1967) ❷ *Venera 5* (USSR, Venus, May 16, 1969) ❸ *Venera 6* (USSR, Venus, May 17, 1969) ❹ *Venera 7* (USSR, Venus, Dec 15, 1970) ❺ *Mariner 9* (US, Mars, Nov 13, 1971) ❻ *Mars 2* (USSR, Mars, Nov 27, 1971) ❼ *Mars 3* (USSR, Mars, Dec 2, 1971) ❽ *Venera 8* (USSR, Venus, Jul 22, 1972) ❾ *Venera 9* (USSR, Venus, Oct 22, 1975) ❿ *Venera 10* (USSR, Venus, Oct 25, 1975)

MARS SPACE PROBE

FIRST COUNTRIES TO HAVE ASTRONAUTS OR COSMONAUTS IN SPACE

	Country/name	Date*
1	USSR, Yuri Alekseyiviech Gagarin	Apr 12, 1961
2	US, John Herschell Glenn	Feb 20, 1962
3	Czechoslovakia, Vladimir Remek	Mar 2, 1978
4	Poland, Miroslaw Hermaszewski	Jun 27, 1978
5	East Germany, Sigmund Jahn	Aug 26, 1978
6	Bulgaria, Georgi I. Ivanov	Apr 10, 1979
7	Hungary, Bertalan Farkas	May 26, 1980
8	Vietnam, Pham Tuan	Jul 23, 1980
9	Cuba, Arnaldo T. Mendez	Sep 18, 1980
10	Mongolia, Jugderdemidiyn Gurragcha	Mar 22, 1981

* *Of first space entry of a national of that country*

Among early flights, neither Alan Shepard (May 5, 1961: *Freedom 7*) nor Gus Grissom (July 21, 1961: *Liberty-Bell 7*) actually entered space. John Glenn was the first American to orbit the Earth.

FIRST MOONWALKERS

	Name/spacecraft	Mission dates
1	Neil A. Armstrong (*Apollo 11*)	Jul 16–24, 1969
2	Edwin E. ("Buzz") Aldrin (*Apollo 11*)	Jul 16–24, 1969
3	Charles Conrad, Jr. (*Apollo 12*)	Nov 14–24, 1969
4	Alan L. Bean (*Apollo 12*)	Nov 14–24, 1969
5	Alan B. Shepard (*Apollo 14*)	Jan 31–Feb 9, 1971
6	Edgar D. Mitchell (*Apollo 14*)	Jan 31–Feb 9, 1971
7	David R. Scott (*Apollo 15*)	Jul 26–Aug 7, 1971
8	James B. Irwin (*Apollo 15*)	Jul 26–Aug 7, 1971
9	John W. Young (*Apollo 16*)	Apr 16–27, 1972
10	Charles M. Duke (*Apollo 16*)	Apr 16–27, 1972

FIRST BODIES TO HAVE BEEN VISITED BY SPACECRAFT*

	Body	Spacecraft/country	Year
1	Moon	*Pioneer 4* (US)	1959
2	Venus	*Mariner 2* (US)	1962
3	Mars	*Mariner 4* (US)	1965
4	Sun	*Pioneer 7* (US)	1966
5	Jupiter	*Pioneer 10* (US)	1973
6	Mercury	*Mariner 10* (US)	1974
7	Saturn	*Pioneer 11* (US)	1979
8	Comet Giacobini-Zinner	*International Sun-Earth Explorer 3* (International Cometary Explorer, US/Europe)	1985
9	Uranus	*Voyager 2* (US)	1986
10	Halley's Comet	*Giotto* (Europe)	1986

* *Spacecraft did not land*

THE 10 FIRST ANIMALS IN SPACE
(Animal/country/date)

❶ Laika (dog, USSR, November 3, 1957)
❷= Laska and Benjy (mice, US, December 13, 1958) ❹= Able (female rhesus monkey) and Baker (female squirrel monkey, US, May 28, 1959) ❻= Otvazhnaya (female Samoyed husky) and an unnamed rabbit, (USSR, July 2, 1959) ❽ Sam (male rhesus monkey, US, December 4, 1959) ❾ Miss Sam (female rhesus monkey, US, January 21, 1960) ❿= Belka and Strelka (female Samoyed huskies, USSR, August 19, 1960)

FIRST DOG IN SPACE
Launched in Sputnik II, *Laika, a female Samoyed, became the first animal in Space. She died when her oxygen supply was exhausted, and her capsule was incinerated on reentry to the Earth's atmosphere.*

THE 10

FIRST PEOPLE TO ORBIT THE EARTH

	Name	Age	Orbits	Duration hr:min	Spacecraft/ country of origin	Date
1	Fl. Major Yuri Alekseyivich Gagarin	27	1	1:48	*Vostok I* USSR	Apr 12, 1961
2	Major Gherman Stepanovich Titov	25	17	25:18	*Vostok II* USSR	Aug 6–7, 1961
3	Lt. Col. John Herschel Glenn	40	3	4:56	*Friendship 7* US	Feb 20, 1962
4	Lt. Col. Malcolm Scott Carpenter	37	3	4:56	*Aurora 7* US	May 24, 1962
5	Major Andrian Grigoryevich Nikolayev	32	64	94:22	*Vostok III* USSR	Aug 11–15, 1962
6	Col. Pavel Romanovich Popovich	31	48	70:57	*Vostok IV* USSR	Aug 12–15, 1962
7	Cdr. Walter Marty Schirra	39	6	9:13	*Sigma 7* US	Oct 3, 1962
8	Major Leroy Gordon Cooper	36	22	34:19	*Faith 7* US	May 15–16, 1963
9	Lt. Col. Valeri Fyodorovich Bykovsky	28	81	119:6	*Vostok V* USSR	Jun 14–19, 1963
10	Jr. Lt. Valentina VladimirovnaTereshkova	26	48	70:50	*Vostok VI* USSR	Jun 16–19, 1963

THE 10

FIRST WOMEN IN SPACE

	Name/country/ spacecraft/mission	Date
1	Valentina Vladimirovna Tereshkova, USSR, *Vostok 6*	Jun 16–19, 1963

Tereshkova (b. Mar 6, 1937) was the first and, at 26, the youngest woman in space.

2	Svetlana Savitskaya, USSR, *Soyuz T7*	Aug 19, 1982

On Jul 25, 1984, Savitskaya (b. Aug 4, 1948) also walked in space (from Soyuz T12).

3	Sally K. Ride, US, *STS-7*	Jun 18–24, 1983

Ride (b. May 26, 1951) was the first American woman in space.

4	Judith A. Resnik, US, *STS-41-D*	Aug 30–Sep 5, 1984

Resnik (b. Apr 5, 1949) was later killed in the STS-51-L Challenger *disaster.*

5	Kathryn D. Sullivan, US, *STS-41-G*	Oct 5–13, 1984

Sullivan (b. Oct 3, 1951) was the first American woman to walk in space.

6	Anna L. Fisher, US, *STS-51-A*	Nov 8–16, 1984

Fisher (b. Aug 24, 1949) was the first American mother in space.

7	Margaret Rhea Seddon, US, *STS-51-D*	Apr 12–19, 1985

Seddon (b. Nov 8, 1947) flew again in STS-40 *(Jun 5–14, 1991) and* STS-58 *(Oct 18–Nov 1, 1993).*

8	Shannon W. Lucid, US, *STS-51-G*	Jun 17–24, 1985

Lucid (b. Jan 14, 1943) also flew in STS-34 (Oct 18–23, 1989), STS-43 (Aug 2–11, 1991), and STS-58 (Oct 18–Nov 1, 1993). From STS-76 she transferred to the Russian Mir space station, then returned to Earth with STS-79 (Mar 22–Sep 26, 1996).

9	Bonnie J. Dunbar, US, *STS-61-A*	Oct 30–Nov 6, 1985

Dunbar (b. Mar 3, 1949) also flew in STS-32 (Jan 9–20, 1990), STS-50 (Jun 25– Jul 9, 1992), and STS-71 (Jun 27–Jul 7, 1995).

10	Mary L. Cleave, US, *STS-61-B*	Nov 26–Dec 3, 1985

Cleave (b. Feb 5, 1947) also flew in STS-30 (May 4–8, 1989).

ASTRONAUTS & COSMONAUTS

TOP 10

MOST EXPERIENCED SPACEMEN*

	Astronaut	Missions	Duration of missions			
			day	hr	min	sec
1	Valeri V. Polyakov	2	678	16	33	18
2	Anatoli Y. Solovyov	5	601	15	01	55
3	Musa K. Manarov	2	541	00	29	38
4	Alexander S. Viktorenko	4	489	01	35	17
5	Sergei K. Krikalyov	3#	471	14	18	39
6	Yuri V. Romanenko	3	430	18	21	30
7	Alexander A. Volkov	3	391	11	52	14
8	Vladimir G. Titov	5#	387	00	51	03
9	Vasily V. Tsibliev	2	381	15	53	02
10	Yuri V. Usachyov	2	375	19	34	36

* *Through January 1, 1998*

Including flights aboard US Space Shuttles

All the missions listed were undertaken by the USSR (and, recently, Russia). The new record-holder, Polyakov, gained 241 days' experience as a USSR *Mir* space station astronaut in 1988, and spent his second mission – and the longest-ever residence in space – at *Mir* from January 8, 1994, until March 26, 1995.

SHANNON W. LUCID
The US's 6th woman in space, and the most experienced, Shannon Lucid holds the record for time spent in space by a woman. In 1996 she traveled 75.2 million miles/121 million km during 188 days in orbit.

TOP 10

LONGEST SPACEWALKS*

	Astronaut	Spacecraft	EVA date	EVA# hr:min
1 =	Thomas D. Akers	STS-49	May 13, 1992	8:30
=	Richard J. Hieb	STS-49	May 13, 1992	8:30
=	Pierre J. Thuot	STS-49	May 13, 1992	8:30
4 =	Jeffrey A. Hoffman	STS-61	Dec 4, 1993	7:54
=	F. Story Musgrave	STS-61	Dec 4, 1993	7:54
6 =	Thomas D. Akers	STS-49	May 14, 1992	7:47
=	Kathryn C. Thornton	STS-49	May 14, 1992	7:47
8 =	Takao Doi	STS-87	Nov 24, 1997	7:43
=	Winston E. Scott	STS-87	Nov 24, 1997	7:43
10 =	Gregory J. Harbaugh	STS-82	Feb 15, 1997	7:27
=	Joseph R. Tanner	STS-82	Feb 15, 1997	7:27

* *Through January 1, 1998*

Extra Vehicular Activity

This Top 10 (which excludes the EVAs of Apollo astronauts on the lunar surface) consists entirely of spacewalks conducted by US astronauts during recent Space Shuttle missions.

TOP 10

YOUNGEST US ASTRONAUTS*

	Astronaut	First flight	Age#
1	Janice E. Voss	Jun 21, 1993	27
2	Kenneth D. Bowersox	Jun 25, 1984	28
3	Sally K. Ride	Jun 18, 1983	32
4	Tamara E. Jernigan	Jun 5, 1991	32
5	Eugene A. Cernan	Jun 3, 1966	32
6	Koichi Wakata	Jan 11, 1996	32
7	Steven A. Hawley	Aug 30, 1984	32
8	Mary E. Weber	Jul 13, 1995	32
9	Kathryn D. Sullivan	Oct 5, 1984	33
10	Ronald E. McNair†	Feb 3, 1984	33

* *Through January 1, 1998*

Those of apparently identical age have been ranked according to their precise age in days at the time of their first flight.

† *Killed in* Challenger *disaster, January 1986*

TOP 10

OLDEST US ASTRONAUTS*

	Astronaut	Last flight	Age#
1	F. Story Musgrave	Dec 7, 1996	61
2	Vance D. Brand	Dec 11, 1990	59
3	Karl G. Henize	Aug 6, 1985	58
4	Roger K. Crouch	Jul 17, 1997	56
5	William E. Thornton	May 6, 1985	56
6	Don L. Lind	May 6, 1985	54
7	Henry W. Hartsfield	Nov 6, 1988	54
8	John E. Blaha	Dec 7, 1996	54
9	William G. Gregory	Mar 18, 1995	54
10	Robert A. Parker	Dec 11, 1990	53

* *Including payload specialists, etc., January 1, 1998*

Those of apparently identical age have been ranked according to their precise age in days at the time of their last flight.

T O P 1 0

LONGEST SPACE SHUTTLE FLIGHTS*

	Flight	Dates	Duration of flights		
			hr	min	sec
1	STS-80 *Columbia*	Nov 19–Dec 7, 1996	423	53	18
2	STS-78 *Columbia*	Jun 20–Jul 7, 1996	405	48	30
3	STS-67 *Endeavour*	Mar 2–18, 1995	399	9	46
4	STS-73 *Columbia*	Oct 20–Nov 5, 1995	381	53	16
5	STS-75 *Columbia*	Feb 22–Mar 9, 1996	377	41	25
6	STS-94 *Columbia*	Jul 1–17, 1997	376	46	1
7	STS-87 *Atlantis*	Sep 25–Oct 6, 1997	376	35	1
8	STS-65 *Columbia*	Jul 8–23, 1994	353	55	0
9	STS-58 *Columbia*	Oct 18–Nov 1, 1993	336	12	32
10	STS-62 *Columbia*	Mar 9–18, 1994	335	16	41

* Through January 1, 1998

The acronym STS (Space Transportation System) has been used throughout the Shuttle program. The first nine flights were simply numbered STS-1 (April 12-14, 1981) to STS-9 (November 28–December 8, 1983). Thereafter a more complex system was employed until the ill-fated *Challenger* mission of January 28, 1986, which was designated STS-S1-L. Subsequent launches have reverted to the system of STS plus a number.

SPACE SHUTTLE
NASA's first space shuttle lifted off on April 12, 1981. The launch system consists of the orbiter, with two solid rocket boosters, and a gigantic external fuel tank weighing 1,667,667 lb/756,441 kg when full. The boosters parachute back to Earth and are reused, but the tank disintegrates in the atmosphere.

T O P 1 0

MOST EXPERIENCED SPACEWOMEN*

	Astronaut#	Missions	Duration of missions			
			day	hr	min	sec
1	Shannon W. Lucid	5	223	2	52	26
2	Yelena V. Kondakova	2	178	10	41	31
3	Tamara E. Jernigan	4	53	6	12	39
4	Marsha S. Ivins	4	43	0	27	43
5	Bonnie J. Dunbar	4	41	12	37	50
6	Kathryn C. Thornton	4	40	15	15	18
7	Janice E. Voss	4	37	21	10	18
8	Susan J. Helms	3	33	20	16	31
9	Margaret Rhea Seddon	3	30	2	22	15
10	Ellen S. Baker	3	28	14	31	42

* Through January 1, 1998
 # All US except No. 2 (Russian)

Already a veteran of four missions, Shannon Lucid became America's most experienced astronaut and the world's most experienced female astronaut in 1996. She took off in US Space Shuttle STS-76 *Atlantis* on March 22, and transferred to the Russian *Mir* space station, returning on board STS-79 *Atlantis* on September 26, after traveling 75,200,000 miles/121,000,000 km.

T O P 1 0

COUNTRIES WITH THE MOST SPACEFLIGHT EXPERIENCE*

	Country	No of astronauts	Total duration of missions			
			day	hr	min	sec
1	USSR/Russia#	85	13,094	2	7	17
2	US	234	5,768	3	44	1
3	Germany	9	298	11	30	13
4	France	7	137	20	8	27
5	Kazakhstan	2	133	21	6	15
6	Canada	6	73	3	0	34
7	Japan	5	55	4	54	50
8	Italy	3	39	10	35	47
9	Switzerland	1	34	12	53	58
10	Ukraine	1	15	16	34	4

* Through January 1, 1998
 # Russia became a separate independent state on December 25, 1991

The USSR, and now Russia, has clocked up its considerable lead on the rest of the world (claiming 66 percent of the total time spent by humans in space) largely through the long-duration stays of its cosmonauts on board the *Mir* space station, which has been continually occupied since 1986.

WORLD WEATHER

TOP 10
WETTEST CITIES IN THE US

	City	Total rainfall mm	in
1	Quillayute, WA	2,672	105.18
2	Astoria, OR	1,687	66.40
3	Tallahassee, FL	1,669	65.71
4	Mobile, AL	1,625	63.96
5	Pensacola, FL	1,581	62.25
6	New Orleans, LA	1,572	61.88
7	Baton Rouge, LA	1,547	60.89
8	West Palm Beach, FL	1,543	60.75
9	Meridian, MS	1,440	56.71
10	Tupelo, MS	1,419	55.87

Source: National Climatic Data Center

SNAP FACTS

- Most rainy days in a year: Mt. Waialeale, Kauai, Hawaii, up to 350 days per annum.

- Most intense rainfall: 1.5 in/38.1 mm in one minute, Barst, Guadeloupe, November 26, 1970.

TOP 10 HOTTEST CITIES IN THE US
(Mean temperature)

❶ Key West, FL (77.8°F/25.4°C) ❷ Miami, FL (75.9°F/24.2°C) ❸ West Palm Beach, FL (74.7°F/23.7°C) ❹ Fort Myers, FL (74.4°F/23.3°C) ❺ Yuma, AZ (74.2°F/23.3°C) ❻ Brownsville, TX (73.8°F/23.1°C) ❼= Tampa, FL (72.4°F/22.2°C), Vero Beach, FL (72.4°F/22.2°C) ❾ Corpus Christi, TX (71.6°F/22.3°C) ❿ Daytona Beach, FL (70.4°F/21.3°C)
Source: National Climatic Data Center

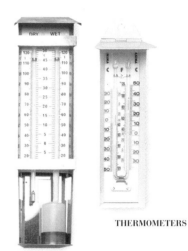
THERMOMETERS

TOP 10
LOWEST TEMPERATURES RECORDED IN THE US

	Weather station/state*	Date	°C	°F
1	Prospect Creek, Alaska	January 23, 1971	-62.2	-80
2	Rogers Pass, Montana	January 20, 1954	-56.7	-70
3	Peter's Sink, Utah	February 1, 1985	-56.1	-69
4	Riverside Ranger Station, Wyoming	February 9, 1933	-54.4	-66
5	Maybell, Colorado	February 1, 1985	-51.7	-61
6 =	Island Park Dam, Idaho	January 18, 1943	-51.1	-60
=	Parshall, North Dakota	February 15, 1936	-51.1	-60
=	Tower, Minnesota	February 2, 1996	-51.1	-60
9	McIntosh, South Dakota	February 17, 1936	-50.0	-58
10=	Seneca, Oregon	February 10, 1933	-47.8	-54
=	Danbury, Wisconsin	January 24, 1922	-47.8	-54

* Extreme low for each state   Source: National Climatic Data Center

WEATHER DOME

TOP 10
HIGHEST TEMPERATURES RECORDED IN THE US

	Weather station/state*	Date	°C	°F
1	Greenland Ranch, California	July 10, 1913	56.7	134
2	Lake Havasu City, Arizona	June 29, 1994	53.3	128
3	Laughlin, Nevada	June 29, 1994	51.7	125
4	Waste Isolation Pilot Plant, New Mexico	June 27, 1994	50.0	122
5=	Alton, Kansas	July 24, 1936	49.5	121
=	Steele, North Dakota	July 6, 1936	49.4	121
7=	Ozark, Arkansas	August 10, 1936	48.9	120
=	Tipton, Oklahoma	June 27, 1994	48.9	120
=	Gannvalley, South Dakota	July 5, 1936	48.9	120
=	Seymour, Texas	August 12, 1936	48.9	120

* Extreme high for each state   Source: National Climatic Data Center

BAROMETER

TOP 10 DRIEST CITIES IN THE US
(Mean annual precipitation)
❶ Yuma, AZ (3.17in/80.52mm) ❷ Las Vegas, NV (4.13in/104.9mm) ❸ Bishop, CA (5.37in/136.4mm) ❹ Bakersfield, CA (5.72in/ 145.3mm) ❺ Reno, NV (7.53in/191.3mm) ❻ Alamosa, CO (7.57in/192.3mm) ❼ Phoenix, AZ (7.66in/194.6mm) ❽ Yakima, WA (7.97in/202.4mm) ❾ Winslow, AZ (8.04in/204.2mm) ❿ Winnemucca, NV (8.23in/209.0mm)
Source: National Climatic Data Center

TOP 10 COLDEST CITIES IN THE US
(Mean temperature)
❶ International Falls, MN (36.8°F/2.67°C) ❷ Duluth, MN (38.5°F/3.61°C) ❸ Caribou, ME (38.8°F/3.78°C) ❹ Marquette, MI (39.1°F/3.94°C) ❺ Sault St. Marie, MI (39.7°F/4.28°C) ❻ Fargo, ND (41.00°F/5.00°C) ❼ Alamosa, CO (41.1°F/5.05°C) ❽= Saint Cloud, MN (41.5°F/5.28°C), Williston, MD (41.5°F/5.28°C) ❿ Bismark, ND (41.6°F/5.33°C)
Source: National Climatic Data Center

T O P   1 0
DRIEST INHABITED PLACES IN THE WORLD

	Location	Average annual rainfall	
		mm	in
1	Aswan, Egypt	0.5	0.02
2	Luxor, Egypt	0.7	0.03
3	Arica, Chile	1.1	0.04
4	Ica, Peru	2.3	0.09
5	Antofagasta, Chile	4.9	0.19
6	Minya el Qamn, Egypt	5.1	0.20
7	Asyût, Egypt	5.2	0.20
8	Callao, Peru	12.0	0.47
9	Trujillo, Peru	14.0	0.54
10	Fayyum, Egypt	19.0	0.75

The total annual rainfall of these 10 driest inhabited places, as recorded over extensive periods, is just 2.5 inches/64.8 mm.

WEATHER VANE

T O P   1 0
HOTTEST INHABITED PLACES IN THE WORLD

	Location	Average temperature	
		°C	°F
1	Dijbouti, Dijbouti	30.0	86.0
2 =	Timbuktu, Mali	29.3	84.7
=	Tirunelevi, India	29.3	84.7
=	Tuticorin, India	29.3	84.7
5 =	Nellore, India	29.2	84.6
=	Santa Marta, Colombia	29.2	84.6
7 =	Aden, South Yemen	28.9	84.0
=	Madurai, India	28.9	84.0
=	Niamey, Niger	28.9	84.0
10 =	Hudaydah, North Yemen	28.8	83.8
=	Ouagadougou, Burkina Faso	28.8	83.8
=	Thanjavur, India	28.8	83.8
=	Tiruchirapalli, India	28.8	83.8

T O P   1 0
WETTEST INHABITED PLACES IN THE WORLD

	Location	Average annual rainfall	
		mm	in
1	Buenaventura, Colombia	6,743	265.47
2	Monrovia, Liberia	5,131	202.01
3	Pago Pago, American Samoa	4,990	196.46
4	Moulmein, Myanmar	4,852	191.02
5	Lae, Papua New Guinea	4,645	182.87
6	Baguio, Luzon Island, Philippines	4,573	180.04
7	Sylhet, Bangladesh	4,457	175.47
8	Conakry, Guinea	4,341	170.91
9=	Padang, Sumatra Island, Indonesia	4,225	166.34
=	Bogor, Java, Indonesia	4,225	166.34

The total annual rainfall of the Top 10 locations is equivalent to more than 26 adults, each measuring 6 ft/1.83 m, standing on top of each other.

SNAP FACTS

- Most rainfall in 24 hours: Cilaos, La Réunion, 73.62 in/1,870 mm, March 15–16, 1952.

- Greatest rainfall in a year: Cherrapunji, Assam, 1,041.8 in/26,461 mm, August 1, 1860 to July 31, 1861.

RIVERS & LAKES

LAKE BAIKAL
Four Empire State Buildings stacked on top of one another still would not quite measure up to the depth of Lake Baikal at its deepest point. Because of its depth, Lake Baikal contains more water than any other freshwater lake, despite its small surface area.

T O P 1 0

DEEPEST FRESHWATER LAKES IN THE WORLD

	Lake/location	Greatest depth m	ft
1	Baikal, Russia	1,637	5,371
2	Tanganyika, Burundi/Tanzania/ Dem. Rep. of Congo/ Zambia	1,471	4,825
3	Malawi, Malawi/ Mozambique/Tanzania	706	2,316
4	Great Slave, Canada	614	2,015
5	Matana, Celebes, Indonesia	590	1,936
6	Crater, Oregon	589	1,932
7	Toba, Sumatra, Indonesia	529	1,736
8	Hornindals, Norway	514	1,686
9	Sarez, Tajikistan	505	1,657
10	Tahoe, California/ Nevada	501	1,645

T O P 1 0

LONGEST RIVERS IN THE WORLD

	River/location	Length km	miles
1	Nile, Tanzania/Uganda/ Sudan/Egypt	6,670	4,145
2	Amazon, Peru/Brazil	6,448	4,007
3	Yangtze–Kiang, China	6,300	3,915
4	Mississippi–Missouri– Red Rock, US	5,971	3,710
5	Yenisey–Angara–Selenga, Mongolia/Russia	5,540	3,442
6	Huang Ho (Yellow River), China	5,464	3,395
7	Ob–Irtysh, Mongolia/ Kazakhstan/Russia	5,410	3,362
8	Congo, Angola/Dem. Rep. of Congo	4,700	2,920
9	Lena–Kirenga, Russia	4,400	2,734
10	Mekong, Tibet/China/ Myanmar/Laos/ Cambodia/Vietnam	4,350	2,703

T O P 1 0

FRESHWATER LAKES WITH THE GREATEST VOLUME OF WATER

	Lake	Location	Volume km³	miles³
1	Baikal	Russia	22,995	5,517
2	Tanganyika	Burundi/Tanzania/ Dem. Rep. of Congo/ Zambia	18,304	4,391
3	Superior	Canada/US	12,174	2,921
4	Nyasa (Malawi)	Malawi/Mozambique/ Tanzania	6,140	1,473
5	Michigan	US	4,874	1,169
6	Huron	Canada/US	3,575	858
7	Victoria	Kenya/Tanzania/Uganda	2,518	604
8	Great Bear	Canada	2,258	542
9	Great Slave	Canada	1,771	425
10	Ontario	Canada/US	1,539	369

T O P 1 0

LONGEST GLACIERS IN THE WORLD

	Name	Location	Length km	mi
1	Lambert-Fisher	Antarctica	515	320
2	Novaya Zemlya	Russia	418	260
3	Arctic Institute	Antarctica	362	225
4	Nimrod-Lennox-King	Antarctica	290	180
5	Denman	Antarctica	241	150
6=	Beardmore	Antarctica	225	140
=	Recovery	Antarctica	225	140
8	Petermanns	Greenland	200	124
9	Unnamed	Antarctica	193	120
10	Slessor	Antarctica	185	115

Although the longest glacier in the world, the Lambert-Fisher Glacier was discovered only as recently as 1956; it is as much as 2.2 miles/3.5 km deep and 40 miles/64 km wide. The Hubbard Glacier, Alaska, which measures 91 miles/146 km, is the longest in North America, while in Europe the longest glacier is the Aletsch Glacier, Switzerland, which measures 22 miles/35 km.

T O P 1 0

GREATEST* WATERFALLS IN THE WORLD

	Waterfall	Location	Average flow (yd³/sec)
1	Boyoma (Stanley)	Dem. Rep. of Congo	22,235
2	Khône	Laos	15,041
3	Niagara (Horseshoe)	Canada	7,377
4	Grande	Uruguay	5,886
5	Paulo Afonso	Brazil	3,662
6	Iguaçu	Argentina/Brazil	2,224
7	Maribondo	Brazil	1,962
8	Churchill (Grand)	Canada	1,818
9	Kabalega (Murchison)	Uganda	1,570
10	Victoria	Zimbabwe	1,426

* Based on volume of water

With an average flow rate of 17,000 yd³/sec, and a peak of 65,400 yd³/sec, the Guaíra, between Brazil and Paraguay, once occupied second place in this list, but following the completion of the Itaipú dam in 1982, it is now "lost." At 6.7 miles/10.8 km, the Khône Falls are the widest in the world.

T O P 1 0

RIVERS PRODUCING THE MOST SEDIMENT

	River	Sediment discharged (tons per annum)
1	Yellow	2,094,000,000
2	Ganges	1,598,000,000
3	Brahmaputra	799,000,000
4	Yangtze	551,000,000
5	Indus	480,000,000
6	Amazon	397,000,000
7	Mississippi–Missouri	342,000,000
8	Irrawaddy	331,000,000
9	Mekong	187,000,000
10	Colorado	149,000,000

T O P 1 0

HIGHEST WATERFALLS IN THE WORLD

	Waterfall	Location	Total drop m	ft
1	Angel	Venezuela	979	3,212
2	Tugela	South Africa	948	3,110
3	Utigård	Nesdale, Norway	800	2,625
4	Mongefossen	Mongebekk, Norway	774	2,540
5	Yosemite	California	739	2,425
6	Østre Mardøla Foss	Eikisdal, Norway	657	2,154
7	Tyssestrengane	Hardanger, Norway	646	2,120
8	Cuquenán	Venezuela	610	2,000
9	Sutherland	South Island, New Zealand	580	1,904
10	Kjellfossen	Gudvangen, Norway	561	1,841

T O P 1 0

GREATEST RIVERS IN THE WORLD*

	River	Outflow/sea	Average flow(yd³/sec)
1	Amazon	Brazil/South Atlantic	229,000
2	Congo	Angola–Dem. Rep. of Congo/South Atlantic	51,000
3	Negro	Brazil/South Atlantic	45,800
4	Yangtze–Kiang	China/Yellow Sea	42,100
5	Orinoco	Venezuela/South Atlantic	32,900
6	Plata–Paraná–Grande	Uruguay/South Atlantic	29,900
7	Madeira–Mamoré–Grande	Brazil/South Atlantic	28,500
8	Brahmaputra	Bangladesh/Bay of Bengal	25,000
9	Yenisey–Angara–Selenga	Russia/Kara Sea	23,000
10	Lena–Kirenga	Russia/Arctic Ocean	20,900

* Based on rate of discharge at mouth

THE AMAZON RIVER
The output of water from the Amazon River into the Atlantic Ocean is so great that if it drained Lake Baikal, the deepest freshwater lake in the world would be empty in 1¹/₂ days.

20 ISLANDS & SEAS

TOP 10

MOST DENSELY POPULATED ISLAND COUNTRIES OF THE WORLD

	Country	Area sq mi	Population (1997)	Pop. per sq mi
1	Malta	122	371,000	3,041
2	Maldives	115	273,000	2,374
3	Bahrain	268	582,000	2,172
4	Barbados	166	262,000	1,578
5	Mauritius	720	1,141,000	1,545
6	Tuvalu	10	11,000	1,100
7	Japan	143,939	125,638,000	872
8	Marshall Islands	70	61,000	871
9	Comoros	863	652,000	756
10	Sri Lanka	25,332	18,273,000	721

Source: United Nations

TOP 10

LARGEST ISLANDS IN EUROPE

	Island	Location	Approx. area sq km	sq miles
1	Great Britain	North Atlantic	218,041	84,186
2	Iceland	North Atlantic	103,000	39,769
3	Ireland	North Atlantic	83,766	32,342
4	West Spitsbergen (Vestspitzbergen)	Arctic Ocean	39,368	15,200
5	Sicily	Mediterranean Sea	25,400	9,807
6	Sardinia	Mediterranean Sea	23,800	9,189
7	North East Land	Barents Sea	15,000	5,792
8	Cyprus	Mediterranean Sea	9,251	3,572
9	Corsica	Mediterranean Sea	8,720	3,367
10	Crete	Mediterranean Sea	8,260	3,189

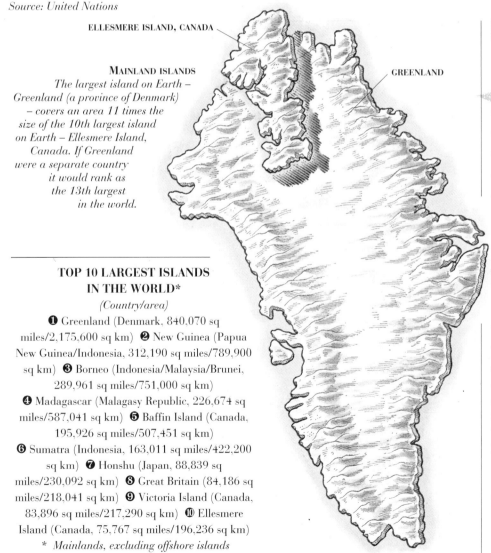

ELLESMERE ISLAND, CANADA

GREENLAND

MAINLAND ISLANDS
The largest island on Earth – Greenland (a province of Denmark) – covers an area 11 times the size of the 10th largest island on Earth – Ellesmere Island, Canada. If Greenland were a separate country it would rank as the 13th largest in the world.

TOP 10 LARGEST ISLANDS IN THE WORLD*
(Country/area)

❶ Greenland (Denmark, 840,070 sq miles/2,175,600 sq km) ❷ New Guinea (Papua New Guinea/Indonesia, 312,190 sq miles/789,900 sq km) ❸ Borneo (Indonesia/Malaysia/Brunei, 289,961 sq miles/751,000 sq km) ❹ Madagascar (Malagasy Republic, 226,674 sq miles/587,041 sq km) ❺ Baffin Island (Canada, 195,926 sq miles/507,451 sq km) ❻ Sumatra (Indonesia, 163,011 sq miles/422,200 sq km) ❼ Honshu (Japan, 88,839 sq miles/230,092 sq km) ❽ Great Britain (84,186 sq miles/218,041 sq km) ❾ Victoria Island (Canada, 83,896 sq miles/217,290 sq km) ❿ Ellesmere Island (Canada, 75,767 sq miles/196,236 sq km)
* Mainlands, excluding offshore islands

TOP 10

MOST HIGHLY POPULATED ISLAND COUNTRIES IN THE WORLD

	Country	Population (1997)
1	Indonesia	203,479,000
2	Japan	125,638,000
3	Philippines	70,724,000
4	Great Britain	57,138,000
5	Malaysia	21,018,000
6	Sri Lanka	18,273,000
7	Madagascar	15,845,000
8	Cuba	11,068,000
9	Dominican Republic	8,097,000
10	Haiti	7,395,000

There are 18 island countries in the world with populations of more than one million, of which these are the Top 10. Australia is regarded as a continental land mass, rather than an island, but if it were included, its population of 18,250,000 would put it in sixth place in the world.

Source: United Nations

TOP 10

LARGEST ISLAND COUNTRIES IN THE WORLD

	Country	Area sq km	sq miles
1	Indonesia	1,904,569	735,358
2	Madagascar	587,041	226,658
3	Papua New Guinea	462,840	178,704
4	Japan	372,801	143,939
5	Malaysia	329,758	127,320
6	Philippines	300,000	115,831
7	New Zealand	269,057	103,883*
8	Great Britain	218,041	84,186
9	Cuba	110,861	42,804
10	Iceland	103,000	39,769

* Total – South Island 58,093 sq mi/150,449 sq km, North Island 44,281 sq mi/114,678 sq km, others 1,362 sq mi/3,527 sq km

TOP 10

LARGEST ISLANDS IN THE US

	Island	Area sq km	sq miles
1	Hawaii, Hawaii	10,456	4,037
2	Kodiak, Alaska	9,510	3,672
3	Prince of Wales, Alaska	6,700	2,587
4	Chicagof, Alaska	5,400	2,085
5	Saint Lawrence, Alaska	4,430	1,710
6	Admiralty, Alaska	4,270	1,649
7	Nunivak, Alaska	4,210	1,625
8	Unimak, Alaska	4,160	1,606
9	Baranof, Alaska	4,140	1,598
10	Long Island, NY	3,630	1,396

Manhattan Island, New York, measures just 22 sq miles/57 sq km.

TOP 10

DEEPEST DEEP-SEA TRENCHES IN THE WORLD

	Trench/ocean	Deepest point m	ft
1	Marianas, Pacific	10,924	35,837
2	Tonga*, Pacific	10,800	35,430
3	Philippine, Pacific	10,497	34,436
4	Kermadec*, Pacific	10,047	32,960
5	Bonin, Pacific	9,994	32,786
6	New Britain, Pacific	9,940	32,609
7	Kuril, Pacific	9,750	31,985
8	Izu, Pacific	9,695	31,805
9	Puerto Rico, Atlantic	8,605	28,229
10	Yap, Pacific	8,527	27,973

* Some authorities consider these parts of the same feature

The eight deepest ocean trenches would be deep enough to submerge Mount Everest, which is 29,022 ft/8,846 m above sea level.

TOP 10

LARGEST OCEANS AND SEAS IN THE WORLD

	Island	Approx. area sq km	sq miles
1	Pacific Ocean	166,240,000	64,185,629
2	Atlantic Ocean	86,560,000	33,421,006
3	Indian Ocean	73,430,000	28,351,484
4	Arctic Ocean	13,230,000	5,108,132
5	South China Sea	2,974,600	1,148,499
6	Caribbean Sea	2,753,000	1,062,939
7	Mediterranean Sea	2,510,000	969,116
8	Bering Sea	2,261,000	872,977
9	Gulf of Mexico	1,542,985	595,749
10	Sea of Okhotsk	1,527,570	589,798

Geographers disagree with one another about whether certain bodies of water are regarded as seas in their own right or as parts of larger oceans – the Coral, Weddell, and Tasman Seas, for example, would be eligible for this list, but most authorities consider them to be part of the Pacific Ocean, whereas the Bering Sea is more commonly identified as an independent sea.

TOP 10

DEEPEST OCEANS AND SEAS IN THE WORLD

	Island	Greatest depth m	ft	Approx. depth m	ft
1	Pacific Ocean	10,924	35,837	4,028	13,215
2	Indian Ocean	7,455	24,460	3,963	13,002
3	Atlantic Ocean	9,219	30,246	3,926	12,880
4	Caribbean Sea	6,946	22,788	2,647	8,685
5	South China Sea	5,016	16,456	1,652	5,419
6	Bering Sea	4,773	15,659	1,547	5,075
7	Gulf of Mexico	3,787	12,425	1,486	4,874
8	Mediterranean Sea	4,632	15,197	1,429	4,688
9	Japan Sea	3,742	12,276	1,350	4,429
10	Arctic Ocean	5,625	18,456	1,205	3,953

The deepest point in the deepest ocean is the Marianas Trench in the Pacific at a depth of 35,837 ft/10,924 m according to a recent survey, although the slightly lesser depth of 35,814 ft/10,916 m was recorded on January 23, 1960 by Jacques Piccard and Donald Walsh in their 58-ft/17.7-m long bathyscaphe *Trieste 2* during the deepest ever ocean descent. Whichever is correct, it is close to 6.8 miles/11 km down, or almost 29 times the height of the Empire State Building.

ON TOP OF THE WORLD

TOP 10

COUNTRIES WITH THE HIGHEST ELEVATIONS IN THE WORLD

	Country/peak	Height* m	ft
1	Nepal#, Everest	8,846	29,022
2	Pakistan, K2	8,611	28,250
3	India, Kanchenjunga	8,598	28,208
4	Bhutan, Khula Kangri	7,554	24,784
5	Tajikistan, Mt. Garmo (formerly Kommunizma)	7,495	24,590
6	Afghanistan, Noshaq	7,499	24,581
7	Kyrgyzstan, Pik Pobedy	7,439	24,406
8	Kazakhstan, Khan Tengri	6,995	22,949
9	Argentina, Cerro Aconcagua	6,960	22,834
10	Chile, Ojos del Salado	6,885	22,588

* Based on the tallest peak in each country

Everest straddles Nepal and Tibet, which – now known as Xizang – is a province of China

NAMING THE HIGHEST
Originally named "Peak XV," the highest mountain was renamed Everest in 1865 after Sir George Everest, Surveyor General of India at the time.

TOP 10

LONGEST MOUNTAIN RANGES IN THE WORLD

	Range/location	Length km	miles
1	Andes, South America	7,242	4,500
2	Rocky Mountains, North America	6,035	3,750
3	Himalayas/Karakoram/ Hindu Kush, Asia	3,862	2,400
4	Great Dividing Range, Australia	3,621	2,250
5	Trans-Antarctic Mountains, Antarctica	3,541	2,200
6	Brazilian East Coast Range, Brazil	3,058	1,900
7	Sumatran/Javan Range, Sumatra, Java	2,897	1,800
8	Tien Shan, China	2,253	1,400
9	Eastern Ghats, India	2,092	1,300
10 =	Altai, Asia	2,012	1,250
=	Central New Guinean Range, Papua-New Guinea	2,012	1,250
=	Urals, Russia	2,012	1,250

TOP 10

HIGHEST MOUNTAINS IN AUSTRALIA

	Mountain	Height m	ft
1	Kosciusko	2,229	7,314
2	Townsend	2,209	7,249
3	Clarke	2,200	7,219
4	Twynham	2,195	7,203
5	Carruthers Peak	2,145	7,039
6	Sentinel	2,140	7,022
7	Northcote	2,131	6,992
8 =	Gungartan	2,068	6,786
=	Tate	2,068	6,786
10	Jagungal	2,062	6,766

TOP 10 HIGHEST MOUNTAINS IN THE WORLD
(Height)

❶ Everest, Nepal/Tibet (29,022 ft/8,846 m) ❷ K2, India/China (28,250 ft/8,611 m) ❸ Kanchenjunga, India/Nepal (28,208 ft/8,598 m) ❹ Lhotse, Nepal/Tibet (27,890 ft/8,501 m) ❺ Makalu I, Nepal/Tibet (27,790 ft/8,470 m) ❻ Dhaulagiri I, Nepal (26,810 ft/8,172 m) ❼ Manaslu I, Nepal (26,760 ft/8,156 m) ❽ Cho Oyu, Nepal (26,750 ft/8,153 m) ❾ Nanga Parbat, India (26,660 ft/8,126 m) ❿ Annapurna I, Nepal (26,504 ft/8,078 m)

TOP 10

STATES WITH THE HIGHEST ELEVATIONS IN THE US

	State/peak	Height m	ft
1	Alaska, Mount McKinley	6,194	20,320
2	California, Mount Whitney	4,418	14,494
3	Colorado, Mount Elbert	4,399	14,433
4	Washington, Mount Rainier	4,392	14,410
5	Wyoming, Gannett Peak	4,207	13,804
6	Hawaii, Mauna Kea	4,205	13,796
7	Utah, Kings Peak	4,123	13,528
8	New Mexico, Wheeler Peak	4,011	13,161
9	Nevada, Boundary Peak	4,005	13,140
10	Montana, Granite Peak	3,901	12,799

TOP 10

HIGHEST MOUNTAINS IN OCEANIA

	Mountain/location	Height m	ft
1	Jaya, Indonesia	5,030	16,503
2	Daam, Indonesia	4,920	16,142
3	Pilimsit, Indonesia	4,801	15,750
4	Trikora, Indonesia	4,749	15,580
5	Mandala, Indonesia	4,700	15,420
6	Wilhelm, Papua New Guinea	4,600	15,092
7	Wisnumurti, Indonesia	4,595	15,075
8	Yamin, Papua New Guinea	4,529	14,860
9	Kubor, Papua New Guinea	4,300	14,108
10	Herbert, Papua New Guinea	4,267	13,999

If the Hawaiian volcano Mauna Kea (13,796 ft/4,206 m) is measured from its undersea base, its total height is 33,484 ft/10,206 m.

TOP 10

HIGHEST MOUNTAINS IN EUROPE

	Mountain/location	Height* m	ft
1	Mont Blanc, France/Italy	4,807	15,771
2	Monte Rosa, Italy/Switzerland	4,634	15,203
3	Dom, Switzerland	4,545	14,911
4	Liskamm, Italy/Switzerland	4,527	14,853
5	Weisshorn, Switzerland	4,505	14,780
6	Täschorn, Switzerland	4,491	14,734
7	Matterhorn, Italy/Switzerland	4,477	14,688
8	La Dent Blanche, Switzerland	4,357	14,293
9	Nadelhorn, Switzerland	4,327	14,196
10	Le Grand Combin, Switzerland	4,314	14,153

* Height of principal peak; lower peaks of the same mountain are excluded

TOP 10

HIGHEST MOUNTAINS IN AFRICA

	Mountain/location	Height m	ft
1	Kibo (Kilimanjaro), Tanzania	5,895	19,340
2	Batian (Kenya), Kenya	5,199	17,058
3	Ngaliema, Uganda/ Dem. Rep. of Congo	5,109	16,763
4	Duwoni, Uganda	4,896	16,062
5	Baker, Uganda	4,843	15,889
6	Emin, Congo (Zaïre)	4,798	15,741
7	Gessi, Uganda	4,715	15,470
8	Sella, Uganda	4,627	15,179
9	Ras Dashen, Ethiopia	4,620	15,158
10	Wasuwameso, Dem. Rep. of Congo	4,581	15,030

TOP 10

HIGHEST MOUNTAINS IN SOUTH AMERICA

	Mountain/location	Height m	ft
1	Cerro Aconcagua, Argentina	6,960	22,834
2	Ojos del Salado, Argentina/Chile	6,885	22,588
3	Bonete, Argentina	6,873	22,550
4	Pissis, Argentina/Chile	6,780	22,244
5	Huascarán, Peru	6,768	22,205
6	Llullaillaco, Argentina/Chile	6,723	22,057
7	Libertador, Argentina	6,721	22,050
8	Mercadario, Argentina/Chile	6,670	21,884
9	Yerupajá, Peru	6,634	21,765
10	Tres Cruces, Argentina/Chile	6,620	21,720

TOP 10

HIGHEST MOUNTAINS IN NORTH AMERICA

	Mountain/location	Height m	ft
1	McKinley (Denali), US	6,194	20,320
2	Logan, Canada	6,050	19,850
3	Citlaltépetl (Orizaba), Mexico	5,700	18,700
4	St. Elias, US/Canada	5,489	18,008
5	Popocatépetl, Mexico	5,452	17,887
6	Foraker, US	5,304	17,400
7	Ixtaccíhuatl, Mexico	5,286	17,343
8	Lucania, Canada	5,226	17,147
9	King, Canada	5,173	16,971
10	Steele, Canada	5,073	16,644

THE FACE OF THE EARTH

TOP 10
LONGEST CAVES IN THE WORLD

	Cave	Location	Total known length m	ft
1	Mammoth Cave system	Kentucky	560,000	1,837,270
2	Optimisticeskaja	Ukraine	178,000	583,989
3	Hölloch	Switzerland	137,000	449,475
4	Jewel Cave	South Dakota	127,000	416,667
5	Siebenhengsteholensystem	Switzerland	110,000	360,892
6	Ozernaya	Ukraine	107,300	352,034
7	Réseau de la Coume d'Hyouernede	France	90,500	296,916
8	Sistema de Ojo Guarena	Spain	89,100	292,323
9	Wind Cave	South Dakota	88,500	290,354
10	Fisher Ridge Cave system	Kentucky	83,000	273,950

TOP 10
DEEPEST CAVES IN THE WORLD

	Cave	Location	Depth m	ft
1	Réseau Jean Bernard	France	1,602	5,256
2	Lampreschtsofen	Austria	1,535	5,036
3	Gouffre Mirolda	France	1,520	4,987
4	Shakta Pantjukhina	Georgia	1,508	4,947
5	Sistema Huautla	Mexico	1,475	4,839
6	Sistema del Trave	Spain	1,444	4,737
7	Boj Bulok	Ukbekistan	1,415	4,642
8	Illaminako Ateak	Spain	1,408	4,619
9	Lukina Jama	Croatia	1,392	4,567
10	Sistema Cheve	Mexico	1,386	4,547

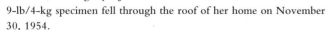

- The word "meteorite" was first used in 1834.
- No record exists of any human being killed by a meteorite, but Ann Hodges of Sylacauga, Alabama, was slightly injured when a 9-lb/4-kg specimen fell through the roof of her home on November 30, 1954.
- The largest known meteorite is that at Hoba West Grootfontein, South Africa. Discovered in 1920, its estimated weight is 53.54 tons.

TOP 10
LARGEST METEORITE CRATERS IN THE WORLD

	Crater/location	Diameter km	miles
1=	Sudbury, Ontario, Canada	140	87
=	Vredefort, South Africa	140	87
3=	Manicouagan, Quebec, Canada	100	62
=	Popigai, Russia	100	62
5	Puchezh-Katunki, Russia	80	50
6	Kara, Russia	60	37
7	Siljan, Sweden	52	32
8	Charlevoix, Quebec, Canada	46	29
9	Araguainha Dome, Brazil	40	25
10	Carswell, Saskatchewan, Canada	37	23

Unlike on the solar system's other planets and moons, many astroblemes (collision sites) on Earth have been weathered over time and obscured, and one of the ongoing debates in geology is thus whether or not certain craterlike structures are of meteoric origin or the remnants of long extinct volcanoes. The Vredefort Ring, for example, long thought to be meteoric, was declared in 1963 to be volcanic, but has since been claimed as a definite meteor crater, as are all the giant meteorite craters in the Top 10 that are listed as such (along with 106 others) by the International Union of Geological Sciences Commission on Comparative Planetology.

TOP 10
COUNTRIES WITH THE LOWEST ELEVATIONS IN THE WORLD

	Country	Highest point	Height m	ft
1	Maldives	Unnamed	3	10
2=	Marshall Islands	Unnamed	6	20
=	Tuvalu	Unnamed	6	20
4	Gambia	Unnamed	43	141
5	Bahamas	Mount Alvernia	63	206
6	Nauru	Unnamed	68	225
7	Quatar	Dukhan Heights	73	240
8	Kiribati	Banaba	81	270
9	Bahrain	Jabal al-Dukhan	134	440
10	Denmark	Yding Skovhøj	173	568

None of these 10 countries possesses a single elevation taller than a medium-sized skyscraper. Compared with these, even the Netherlands' 1,050 ft/321 m Vaalserberg hill makes the country's appellation as one of the "Low Countries" sound somewhat unfair.

DEAD LOW
The shore of the Dead Sea is the lowest point on the world's surface. It takes its name from the scarcity of plants and animals in it that results from its high salt content.

T O P 1 0

DEEPEST DEPRESSIONS IN THE WORLD

	Depression/location	Maximum depth below sea level m	ft
1	Dead Sea, Israel/Jordan	400	1,312
2	Turfan Depression, China	154	505
3	Qattâra Depression, Egypt	133	436
4	Poluostrov Mangyshlak, Kazakhstan	132	433
5	Danakil Depression, Ethiopia	117	383
6	Death Valley, US	86	282
7	Salton Sink, US	72	235
8	Zapadny Chink Ustyurta, Kazakhstan	70	230
9	Prikaspiyskaya Nizmennost, Kazakhstan/Russia	67	220
10	Ozera Sarykamysh, Turkmenistan/Uzbekistan	45	148

The shore of the Dead Sea, Israel/Jordan, is the lowest exposed ground below sea level. However, its bed, at 2,388 ft/728 m below sea level, is only half as deep as that of Lake Baikal, Russia, which is 4,872 ft/ 1,485 m below sea level.

T O P 1 0

LARGEST DESERTS IN THE WORLD

	Desert	Location	Approx. area sq km	sq miles
1	Sahara	North Africa	9,000,000	3,500,000
2	Australian	Australia	3,800,000	1,470,000
3	Arabian	Southwest Asia	1,300,000	502,000
4	Gobi	Central Asia	1,040,000	401,500
5	Kalahari	Southern Africa	520,000	201,000
6	Turkestan	Central Asia	450,000	174,000
7	Takla Makan	China	327,000	125,000
8 =	Namib	Southwest Africa	310,000	120,000
=	Sonoran	US/Mexico	310,000	120,000
10 =	Somali	Somalia	260,000	100,000
=	Thar	India/Pakistan	260,000	100,000

UNDERGROUND WORLD

According to tradition, the world's greatest cave system, the Mammoth Cave, Kentucky, was discovered in 1799 when a hunter who was pursuing a bear stumbled upon what is now called the "Historic Entrance" to the cave. Further exploration showed it to be part of a complex network with numerous underground streams containing rare fish and other animals. During the War of 1812, the caverns provided a valuable source of saltpeter, an ingredient of gunpowder. After the war they became a major tourist attraction. Mammoth Cave National Park was established in 1941. In 1972 a connection was discovered between the Mammoth and Flint Ridge caves.

YEARS AGO • 200 • YEARS AGO • YEARS AGO

This Top 10 presents the approximate areas and ranking of the world's great deserts. These are often broken down into smaller desert regions – the Australian Desert into the Gibson, Simpson, and Great Sandy Desert, for example. Of the total land surface of the Earth, as much as one quarter may be considered "desert," or land where more water is lost through evaporation than is acquired through precipitation. However, deserts may range from the extremely arid and barren sandy desert, through arid, to semiarid. Nearly every desert exhibits features that encompass all of these degrees of aridity without a precise line of demarcation between them.

OUT OF THIS WORLD

TOP 10
PRINCIPAL COMPONENTS OF AIR

	Component	Volume percent
1	Nitrogen	78.110
2	Oxygen	20.953
3	Argon	0.934
4	Carbon dioxide	0.01–0.10
5	Neon	0.001818
6	Helium	0.000524
7	Methane	0.0002
8	Krypton	0.000114
9=	Hydrogen	0.00005
=	Nitrous oxide	0.00005

Dry air at sea level consists of these 10 basic components plus one further component: xenon (0.0000087 percent). In addition to these, water vapor, ozone, and various pollutants, such as carbon monoxide from motor vehicle exhausts, are present in the air in variable amounts.

TOP 10
ELEMENTS WITH THE LOWEST MELTING POINTS*

	Element	Melting point °F
1	Mercury	-38.0
2	Francium	80.6#
3	Cesium	83.1
4	Gallium	85.6
5	Rubidium	102.0
6	Phosphorus	111.4
7	Potassium	145.9
8	Sodium	208.4
9	Sulfur	235.0
10	Iodine	236.3

* Solids only

Approximate

Among other familiar elements that melt at relatively low temperatures are tin (449.6°F) and lead (621.5°F).

THE 10 DEGREES OF HARDNESS*
❶ Talc ❷ Gypsum
❸ Calcite ❹ Fluorite ❺ Apatite
❻ Orthoclase ❼ Quartz ❽ Topaz
❾ Corundum ❿ Diamond
* According to Mohs Scale in which No. 1 is the softest mineral and No. 10 the hardest

TOP 10
HEAVIEST ELEMENTS

	Element	Year discovered	Density*
1	Osmium	1804	22.59
2	Iridium	1804	22.56
3	Platinum	1748	21.45
4	Rhenium	1925	21.01
5	Neptunium	1940	20.47
6	Plutonium	1940	20.26
7	Gold	Prehistoric	19.29
8	Tungsten	1783	19.26
9	Uranium	1789	19.05
10	Tantalum	1802	16.67

* Grams per cm³ at 20°C

The two heaviest elements were discovered by the British chemist Smithson Tennant (1761–1815), who was also the first to prove that diamonds are made of carbon. A cubic foot (0.028317 m³) of osmium weighs 1,410 lb/640 kg — equivalent to 10 people each weighing 141 lb/64 kg.

TOP 10
LIGHTEST ELEMENTS*

	Element	Year discovered	Density#
1	Lithium	1817	0.533
2	Potassium	1807	0.859
3	Sodium	1807	0.969
4	Calcium	1808	1.526
5	Rubidium	1861	1.534
6	Magnesium	1808	1.737
7	Phosphorus	1669	1.825
8	Beryllium	1798	1.846
9	Cesium	1860	1.896
10	Sulfur	Prehistoric	2.070

* Solids only

Grams per cm³ at 20°C

Osmium, the heaviest known element, is more than 42 times heavier than lithium, the lightest element.

TOP 10
ELEMENTS WITH THE HIGHEST MELTING POINTS

	Element	Melting point °F
1	Carbon	6,605
2	Tungsten	6,170
3	Rhenium	5,756
4	Osmium	5,513
5	Tantalum	5,425
6	Molybdenum	4,743
7	Niobium	4,474
8	Iridium	4,370
9	Ruthenium	4,190
10	Hafnium	4,041

Other elements that melt at high temperatures include chromium (3,375°F), iron (2,795°F), and gold (1,947°F). The surface of the Sun attains 9,626°F.

TOP 10

ELEMENTS MOST COMMON IN THE SUN

	Element	Parts per 1,000,000
1	Hydrogen	745,000
2	Helium	237,000
3	Oxygen	8,990
4	Carbon	3,900
5	Iron	1,321
6	Neon	1,200
7	Nitrogen	870
8	Silicon	830
9	Magnesium	720
10	Sulfur	380

Helium was discovered in the Sun before it was detected on Earth, its name deriving from *helios*, the Greek word for Sun. More than 70 elements have been detected in the Sun, the most common of which correspond closely to those found in the universe as a whole, but with some variations in their ratios, including a greater proportion of the principal element, hydrogen.

TOP 10

ELEMENTS MOST COMMON IN THE EARTH'S CRUST

	Element	Percent*
1	Oxygen	45.6
2	Silicon	27.3
3	Aluminum	8.4
4	Iron	6.2
5	Calcium	4.7
6	Magnesium	2.8
7	Sodium	2.3
8	Potassium	1.8
9	Hydrogen	1.5
10	Titanium	0.6

* *Totals more than 100% due to rounding*

This is based on the average percentages of the elements in igneous rock. At an atomic level, out of every million atoms, some 205,000 are silicon, 62,600 aluminum, and 29,000 hydrogen.

TOP 10

ELEMENTS MOST COMMON IN THE MOON

	Element	Percent
1	Oxygen	40.0
2	Silicon	19.2
3	Iron	14.3
4	Calcium	8.0
5	Titanium	5.9
6	Aluminum	5.6
7	Magnesium	4.5
8	Sodium	0.33
9	Potassium	0.14
10	Chromium	0.002

This list is based on the analysis of the 45.8 lb/20.77 kg of rock samples brought back to Earth by the crew of the 1969 *Apollo 11* lunar mission.

TOP 10

ELEMENTS MOST COMMON IN SEAWATER

	Element	Tons per mile^3
1	Oxygen*	4,340,810,000
2	Hydrogen*	546,020,000
3	Chlorine	100,640,000
4	Sodium	58,270,000
5	Magnesium	6,720,000
6	Sulfur	4,700,000
7	Calcium	2,140,000
8	Potassium	2,110,000
9	Bromine	340,000
10	Carbon	140,000

* *Combined as water*

A typical cubic mile of seawater is a treasury of often valuable elements, but sodium and chlorine (combined as sodium chloride, or common salt) are the only two that are extracted in substantial quantities. The costs of extracting such elements as gold (approximately fourteen pounds of which are found in the average mile^3 of seawater) would be far too high.

TOP 10

MOST VALUABLE TRADED METALLIC ELEMENTS

	Element*	Price per lb ($)
1	Rhodium	7,729
2	Osmium	5,833
3	Platinum	5,571
4	Iridium	4,938
5	Scandium	4,536
6	Gold	4,291
7	Palladium	3,441
8	Ruthenium	554
9	Rhenium	499
10	Germanium	454

* *Based on 10–100 kg quantities of minimum 99.9% purity; excluding radioactive elements, isotopes, and rare earth elements traded in minute quantities*

The prices of traded metals vary enormously according to their rarity, changes in industrial uses, fashion, and popularity as investments.

Source: London Metal Bulletin *March 9, 1998/Lipmann Walton & Co.*

TOP 10

ELEMENTS MOST COMMON IN THE UNIVERSE

	Element	Parts per 1,000,000
1	Hydrogen	739,000
2	Helium	240,000
3	Oxygen	10,700
4	Carbon	4,600
5	Neon	1,340
6	Iron	1,090
7	Nitrogen	970
8	Silicon	650
9	Magnesium	580
10	Sulfur	440

LIFE ON EARTH

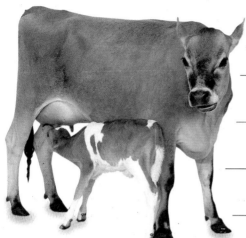

TOP 10

LARGEST DINOSAURS EVER DISCOVERED

Name/length/estimated weight

1 *Seismosaurus,*
98–119 ft/30–36 m
50–80 tons

A skeleton of this colossal plant eater was excavated in 1985 near Albuquerque, New Mexico, by US paleontologist David Gillette.

2 *Supersaurus,*
80–100 ft/24–30 m
50 tons

The remains of Supersaurus *were found in Colorado in 1972.*

3 *Antarctosaurus,*
60–98 ft/18–30 m
40–50 tons

Named Antarctosaurus *("southern lizard") by Friedrich von Huene in 1929, this creature's thigh bone alone measures 7 ft 6 in/2.3 m.*

4 *Barosaurus,*
75–90 ft/23–27.5 m
weight uncertain

Barosaurus *("heavy lizard," so named by US paleontologist Othniel C. Marsh in 1890.*

5 *Mamenchisaurus,*
89 ft/27 m
weight uncertain

An almost complete skeleton discovered in 1972 showed it had the longest neck of any known animal, perhaps up to 49 ft/15 m.

Name/length/estimated weight

6 *Diplodocus,*
75–89 ft/23–27 m
12 tons

Diplodocus *was probably one of the stupidest dinosaurs, having the smallest brain in relation to its body size.*

7 *Ultrasauros,*
Over 82 ft/25 m
50 tons

Ultrasauros *was discovered by US paleontologist James A. Jensen in Colorado in 1979.*

8 *Brachiosaurus,*
82 ft/25 m
50 tons

Some paleontologists have put the weight of Brachiosaurus *as high as 190 tons.*

9 *Pelorosaurus,*
80 ft/24 m
weight uncertain

The first fragments of Pelorosaurus *("monstrous lizard") were found in Sussex and named by British doctor and geologist Gideon Algernon Mantell as early as 1850.*

10 *Apatosaurus,*
66–70 ft/20–21 m
20–30 tons

Aptosaurus *(meaning "deceptive lizard") is better known by its former name of* Brontosaurus *("thunder reptile"). Its bones were discovered in Colorado in 1879.*

THE 10

FIRST DINOSAURS TO BE NAMED

	Name/meaning/named by	Year
1	*Megalosaurus*, great lizard, William Buckland	1824
2	*Iguanodon*, iguana tooth, Gideon Mantell	1825
3	*Hyleosaurus*, woodland lizard, Gideon Mantell	1832
4	*Macrodontophion*, large tooth snake, A. Zborzewski	1834
5 =	*Thecodontosaurus*, socket-toothed lizard, Samuel Stutchbury and H. Riley	1836
=	*Paleosaurus*, ancient lizard, Samuel Stutchbury and H. Riley	1836
7	*Plateosaurus*, flat lizard, Hermann von Meyer	1837
8 =	*Cladeiodon*, branch tooth, Richard Owen	1841
=	*Cetiosaurus*, whale lizard, Richard Owen	1841
10	*Pelorosaurus*, monstrous lizard, Gideon Mantell	1850

THE FINAL DATES THAT 10 ANIMALS WERE LAST SEEN ALIVE

Animal	Date
1 Aurochs	1627

This giant wild ox, once described by Julius Caesar, was last recorded in central Europe after the advance of agriculture forced it to retreat from its former territory, which once stretched to the west as far as Britian. It was extensively hunted, and the last few specimens died in the Jaktorow Forest in Poland.

Animal	Date
2 Aepyornis	1649

Also known as the "Elephant bird," the 10-ft/3-m wingless bird was a native of Madagascar.

Animal	Date
3 Dodo	1681

Discovered by European travelers in 1507, specimens of this curious bird were extensively collected – its lack of flight and tameness making it extremely vulnerable to capture – its name comes from the Portuguese for "stupid." The last dodo seen alive was on the island of Mauritius in 1681.

Animal	Date
4 Steller's sea cow	1768

This large marine mammal, named after its 1741 discoverer, German naturalist Georg Wilhelm Steller, and one of the creatures that gave rise to the legend of the mermaid, was rapidly hunted to extinction.

Animal	Date
5 Great auk	1844

The last example in Britain of a breeding Pinguinus impennis – a flightless North Atlantic seabird – was seen nesting in the Orkneys in 1812. The last surviving pair in the world was killed on June 4, 1844, on Eldey Island on behalf of an Icelandic collector. There are possibly as many as 80 specimens in natural history collections around the world.

Animal	Date
6 Tarpan	1851

The Tarpan, a European wild horse, was last seen in Ukraine. Another wild horse thought extinct, Przewalski's horse, has been rediscovered in Mongolia and new captive-bred stock has been reintroduced into its former territory around the fringes of the Gobi Desert.

Animal	Date
7 Quagga	1883

This zebralike creature, found in South Africa and first recorded in 1685, was hunted to such an extent that by 1870 the last wild specimen was killed. The last example, a female in Amsterdam Zoo, died on August 12, 1883.

Animal	Date
8 Pilori muskrat	1902

The species became extinct following the May 8, 1902, eruption of Mont Pelée, Martinique, which destroyed its habitat.

AS DEAD AS A DODO
The dodo, a flightless member of the dove family, was discovered in 1507, and specimens were taken to Europe, where its ungainly appearance was greeted with astonishment. Within 100 years, entirely as a result of human activity in hunting them down, the dodo had disappeared, its name becoming a symbol for "extinct," as in "dead as a dodo."

Animal	Date
9 Passenger pigeon	1914

The last moment of this creature can be stated very precisely. At 1:00 pm on Tuesday, September 1, 1914, at Cincinnati Zoo, the very last specimen, a 29-year-old bird named Martha, expired. Once there had been vast flocks of passenger pigeons, with estimated totals of five to nine billion in the 19th century, but as they were remorselessly killed for food and to protect crops in the US, and since the bird laid just one egg each season, its decline was inevitable. The last one in the wild was shot on March 24, 1900.

Animal	Date
10 Heath hen	1932

The prairie chicken known as the Heath hen (Tympanuchus cupido cupido) was extensively hunted until only a few specimens survived, all on the island of Martha's Vineyard, Massachusetts. Many were killed in a forest fire in 1916, and a virus decimated the survivors, the last of them dying on March 11, 1932.

DINOSAUR DISCOVERERS

	Name/country	Period	Dinosaurs named*
1	Friedrich von Huene (Germany)	1902–61	45
2	Othniel C. Marsh (US)	1870–94	36
3	Harry G. Seeley (UK)	1869–98	29
4	Dong Zhiming (China)	1973–93	24
5	José F. Bonaparte (Argentina)	1969–95	20
6 =	Edward Drinker Cope (US)	1866–92	18
=	Richard Owen (UK)	1841–84	18
8 =	Henry F. Osborn (US)	1902–24	17
=	Yang Zhong-Jian ("C.C. Young") (China)	1937–82	17
10	Barnum Brown (US)	1873–1963	14

* Including joint namings

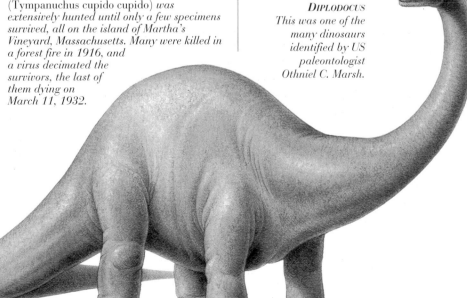

DIPLODOCUS
This was one of the many dinosaurs identified by US paleontologist Othniel C. Marsh.

ENDANGERED ANIMALS

THE 10

MOST ENDANGERED SPIDERS

	Spider	Country
1	Kauai cave wolf spider	US
2	Doloff cave spider	US
3	Empire cave pseudoscorpion	US
4	Glacier Bay wolf spider	US
5	Great raft spider	Europe
6	Kocevje subterranean spider (*Troglohyphantes gracilis*)	Slovenia
7	Kocevje subterranean spider (*Troglohyphantes similis*)	Slovenia
8	Kocevje subterranean spider (*Troglohyphantes spinipes*)	Slovenia
9	Lake Placid funnel wolf spider	US
10	Melones cave harvestman	US

Source: International Union for the Conservation of Nature

THE 10

COUNTRIES WITH THE MOST THREATENED BIRD SPECIES

	Country	Threatened bird species
1	Indonesia	104
2	Brazil	103
3	China	90
4	Philippines	86
5	India	73
6=	Colombia	64
=	Peru	64
8	Ecuador	53
9	US	50
10	Vietnam	47

Source: International Union for the Conservation of Nature

FRASER'S DOLPHIN
Discovered in 1956, this previously endangered member of the dolphin family has now increased in numbers.

THE 10

COUNTRIES WITH THE MOST THREATENED REPTILE AND AMPHIBIAN SPECIES

	Country	Total reptiles	Total amphibians
1	Australia	37	25
2	US	28	24
3	South Africa	19	9
4	Mexico	18	3
5=	Myanmar	20	0
=	Brazil	15	5
7=	Indonesia	19	0
=	Madagascar	17	2
=	India	16	3
10	Japan	8	10

Source: International Union for the Conservation of Nature

THE 10 MOST ENDANGERED BIG CATS*

❶ Amur leopard ❷ Anatolian leopard
❸ Asiatic cheetah ❹ Eastern puma
❺ Florida cougar ❻ North African leopard
❼ Siberian tiger ❽ South Arabian leopard
❾ South China tiger ❿ Sumatran tiger

* *Listed alphabetically, all 10 big cats are classed as being "critically endangered."*

Source: International Union for the Conservation of Nature

THE 10

COUNTRIES WITH THE MOST THREATENED INVERTEBRATE SPECIES

	Country	Threatened invertebrate species
1	US	594
2	Australia	281
3	South Africa	101
4	Portugal	67
5	France	61
6	Spain	57
7	Tanzania	46
8=	Dem. Rep. of Congo	45
=	Japan	45
10=	Austria	41
=	Italy	41

Source: International Union for the Conservation of Nature

THE 10

MOST ENDANGERED BIRDS IN THE US

1	Golden-cheeked warbler
2	Kirtland's warbler
3	Bachman's warbler
4	Black-capped vireo
5	Cerulean warbler
6	Colima warbler
7	Golden-winged warbler
8	Black swift
9	Baird's sparrow
10	Cassin's sparrow

Source: US Fish and Wildlife Service

Source: International Union for the Conservation of Nature

PUMA
The Eastern puma is one of the most endangered of all cat species.

THE 10
COUNTRIES WITH THE MOST THREATENED MAMMAL SPECIES

	Country	Threatened mammal species
1	Indonesia	128
2 =	China	75
=	India	75
4	Brazil	71
5	Mexico	64
6	Australia	58
7	Papua New Guinea	57
8	Philippines	49
9 =	Madagascar	46
=	Peru	46

Source: International Union for the Conservation of Nature

THE 10
COUNTRIES WITH THE MOST AFRICAN ELEPHANTS

	Country	Estimated no.
1	Tanzania	73,459 *
2	Dem. Rep. of Congo	65,974 #
3	Botswana	62,998 *
4	Gabon	61,794 †
5	Zimbabwe	56,297 *
6	Rep. of the Congo	32,563 #
7	Zambia	19,701 *
8	Kenya	13,834 *
9	South Africa	9,990 *
10	Cameroon	8,824 #

* Definite † Probable # Possible

There were once millions of African elephants, but the destruction of natural habitats and extensive poaching for ivory and hide have reduced the population. A survey in 1996 estimated the total population of African elephants at 286,234.

Source: International Union for the Conservation of Nature

THE 10
RAREST BIRDS IN THE WORLD

	Bird/country	Estimated no.*
1 =	Spix's macaw, Brazil	1
=	Cebu flower pecker, Philippines	1
3	Hawaiian crow, Hawaii	5
4	Black stilt, New Zealand	12
5	Echo parakeet, Mauritius	13
6	Imperial Amazon parrot, Dominica	15
7	Magpie robin, Seychelles	20
8	Kakapo, New Zealand	24
9	Pink pigeon, Mauritius	70
10	Mauritius kestrel	100

* Of breeding pairs reported since 1986

Several rare bird species are known from old records or from only one specimen, but must be assumed to be extinct in the absence of recent sightings or records of breeding pairs. With nowhere to seek refuge, rare birds come under the most pressure on islands like Mauritius, where the dodo notoriously met its fate in the seventeenth century.

AFRICAN ELEPHANT
Extensive programs have been established to rescue the African elephant from its threatened status.

PYGMY HOG
The smallest known pig, the pygmy hog is an increasingly rare inhabitant of the Himalayan foothills. It is estimated that only 150 remain.

THE 10
MOST THREATENED ANIMALS

	Class	Threatened animal species
1	Birds	1,107
2	Mammals	1,096
3	Gastropods (snails, etc.)	806
4	Actinopterygians (ray-finned fish)	715
5	Insects	537
6	Crustaceans	407
7	Reptiles	253
8	Amphibians	124
9	Bivalves (clams, etc.)	114
10	Elasmobranchii (sharks, etc.)	15

Source: International Union for the Conservation of Nature

THE 10
COUNTRIES WITH THE MOST ASIAN ELEPHANTS

	Country	Estimated no.
1	India	24,000 *
2	Myanmar	6,000
3	Indonesia	4,500
4	Laos	4,000
5	Sri Lanka	3,000
6 =	Thailand	2,000
=	Cambodia	2,000
8 =	Borneo	1,000
=	Malaysia	1,000
10	Vietnam	400

* Based on maximum estimates

Source: International Union for the Conservation of Nature

LAND ANIMALS

MAMMALS WITH THE LONGEST GESTATION PERIODS

	Mammal	Average gestation (days)
1	African elephant	660
2	Asiatic elephant	600
3	Baird's beaked whale	520
4	White rhinoceros	490
5	Walrus	480
6	Giraffe	460
7	Tapir	400
8	Arabian camel (dromedary)	390
9	Fin whale	370
10	Llama	360

MAMMALS WITH THE SHORTEST GESTATION PERIODS

	Mammal	Average gestation (days)
1	Short-nosed bandicoot	12
2	Opossum	13
3	Shrew	14
4	Golden hamster	16
5	Lemming	20
6	Mouse	21
7	Rat	22
8	Gerbil	24
9	Rabbit	30
10	Mole	38

The short-nosed bandicoot and the opossum are both marsupial mammals whose newborn young transfer to a pouch to complete their natal development. The babies of marsupials are minute when born: the opossum is smaller than a bee, and the ratio in size between the newborn kangaroo, at under 1 in/2.5 cm long, and the adult, is the greatest of all mammals.

SLOTHFUL SLOTH
One of nature's most somnolent creatures, even the name of the sloth has become a synonym for extreme laziness. The top speed of the three-toed sloth is 0.12 mph/0.2 km/hr.

SLEEPIEST ANIMALS

	Animal	Average hours of sleep		Animal	Average hours of sleep
1	Koala	22	6 =	Hamster	14
2	Sloth	20	=	Squirrel	14
3 =	Armadillo	19	8 =	Cat	13
=	Opossum	19	=	Pig	13
5	Lemur	16	10	Spiny anteater	12

This list excludes periods of hibernation, which can last up to several months among creatures such as the ground squirrel. At the other end of the scale comes the frantic shrew, which has to hunt and eat constantly or else perish: it literally has no time for sleep. Even some large mammals, such as elephants, cows, and horses, generally sleep for periods of less than four hours out of every 24.

MOST PROLIFIC WILD MAMMALS

	Animal	Average litter
1	Malagasy tenrec	25
2	Virginian opossum	22
3	Golden hamster	11
4	Ermine	10
5	Prairie vole	9
6	Coypu	8.5
7 =	European hedgehog	7
=	African hunting dog	7
9 =	Meadow vole	6.5
=	Wild boar	6.5

The prairie vole probably holds the record for most offspring produced in a season. It has up to 17 litters in rapid succession, bringing up to 150 young into the world.

FASTEST MAMMALS

	Mammal	Maximum recorded speed km/h	mph
1	Cheetah	105	65
2	Pronghorn antelope	89	55
3 =	Mongolian gazelle	80	50
=	Springbok	80	50
5 =	Grant's gazelle	76	47
=	Thomson's gazelle	76	47
7	Brown hare	72	45
8	Horse	69	43
9 =	Greyhound	68	42
=	Red deer	68	42

Although several animals on the list are capable of higher speeds, these figures are based on controlled measurements of average speeds over ¼ mile (0.4 km).

TOP 10

HEAVIEST TERRESTRIAL MAMMALS*

	Mammal	Length m	ft	Weight kg	lb
1	African elephant	7.3	24	7,000	14,432
2	White rhinoceros	4.2	14	3,600	7,937
3	Hippopotamus	4.0	13	2,500	5,512
4	Giraffe	5.8	19	1,600	2,527
5	American bison	3.9	13	1,000	2,205
6	Arabian camel (dromedary)	3.5	12	690	1,521
7	Polar bear	2.6	8.6	600	1,323
8	Moose	3.0	10	550	1,213
9	Siberian tiger	3.3	11	300	661
10	Gorilla	2.0	7	220	485

* *Excluding domesticated cattle and horses*

TOP 10

DEADLIEST SNAKES

	Snake	Lethal venom dose (mg)	Maximum venom yield (mg)	Potential deaths per bite	Mortality rate range (percent)
1	Black mamba	10.0	800	80	95–100
2	Common krait	1.0	50	50	77–93
3	Russell's viper	12.0	270	22	30–65
4	Taipan	3.0	400	130	25–50
5	Indian cobra	20.0	375	18	33
6	Cape cobra	15.0	150	10	25
7	Egyptian cobra	20.0	400	20	Not known
8	Multibanded krait	0.5	22	44	Not known
9	Tropical rattlesnake	7.0	105	15	15–25
10	King cobra	40.0	1,000	20	18

TOP 10

HEAVIEST PRIMATES

	Primate	Length* cm	in	Weight kg	lb
1	Gorilla	200	79	220	485
2	Man	177	70	77	170
3	Orangutan	137	54	75	165
4	Chimpanzee	92	36	50	110
5=	Baboon	100	39	45	99
=	Mandrill	95	37	45	99
7	Gelada baboon	75	30	25	55
8	Proboscis monkey	76	30	24	53
9	Hanuman langur	107	42	20	44
10	Siamung gibbon	90	35	13	29

* *Excluding tail*

The largest primates (including man) and all the apes are rooted in the Old World (Africa, Asia, and Europe): only one member of a New World species of monkeys (the Guatemalan howler at 36 in/91 cm; 20 lb/9 kg) is a close contender for the Top 10. The difference between the prosimians (primitive primates), great apes, lesser apes, and monkeys has more to do with shape than size, although the great apes mostly top the table anyway.

TOP 10

LARGEST CARNIVORES

	Animal	Length m	ft in	Weight kg	lb
1	Southern elephant seal	6.5	21 4	3,500	7,716
2	Walrus	3.8	12 6	1,200	2,646
3	Steller sea lion	3	9 8	1,100	2,425
4	Grizzly bear	3	9 8	780	1,720
5	Polar bear	2.6	8 6	600	1,543
6	Tiger	2.8	9 2	300	661
7	Lion	1.9	6 3	250	551
8	American black bear	1.8	6 0	227	500
9	Giant panda	1.5	5 0	160	353
10	Spectacled bear	1.8	6 0	140	309

Of the 273 mammal species in the order *Carnivora* (meat-eaters), many (including its largest representatives on land, the bears) are, in fact, omnivorous and around 40 specialize in eating fish or insects. All, however, share a common ancestry indicated by the butcher's-knife form of their canine teeth. Since the Top 10 would otherwise consist exclusively of seals and related marine carnivores, only the first three marine representatives have been included in the list to enable the terrestrial heavyweight division to make an appearance.

CHEETAH

MARINE ANIMALS

TOP 10

LARGEST SHARKS IN THE WORLD

Species	Maximum weight kg	lb
1 Whale shark	21,000	46,297
2 Basking shark	14,515	32,000
3 Great white shark	3,314	7,300
4 Greenland shark	1,020	2,250
5 Tiger shark	939	2,070
6 Great hammerhead shark	844	1,860
7 Six-gill shark	590	1,300
8 Gray nurse shark	556	1,225
9 Mako shark	544	1,200
10 Thresher shark	500	1,100

TOP 10

FISHING COUNTRIES IN THE WORLD

Country	Annual catch (tons)
1 China	19,365,303
2 Peru	9,315,192
3 Japan	8,959,720
4 Chile	6,655,739
5 US	6,547,001
6 Russia	4,917,824
7 India	4,665,048
8 Indonesia	4,009,878
9 Thailand	3,690,703
10 South Korea	2,809,766
World total	*111,793,657*
Total caught inland	*18,925,0320*

TOP 10

LARGEST TURTLES AND TORTOISES IN THE WORLD

Turtle/tortoise	Maximum weight kg	lb
1 Pacific leatherback turtle	865	1,908
2 Atlantic leatherback turtle	454	1,000
3 = Green sea turtle	408	900
= Aldabra giant tortoise	408	900
5 Loggerhead turtle	386	850
6 Galapagos giant or elephant tortoise	385	849
7 Alligator snapping turtle	183	403
8 Black sea turtle	126	278
9 Flatback turtle	84	185
10 Hawksbill turtle	68	150

Both the sizes and the longevity of turtles and tortoises remain hotly debated by zoologists, and although the weights on which this Top 10 are ranked are from corroborated sources, there are many claims of even larger specimens among the 265 species of *Chelonia* (turtles and tortoises). The largest are marine turtles. The Aldabra giant tortoises, found on an island in the Seychelles, are the largest land-dwellers – and probably the longest-lived land creatures of all, at more than 150 years. The alligator snapping turtle is the largest freshwater species. All living examples would be dwarfed in size by prehistoric monster turtles such as *Stupendemys geographicus*, which measured up to 10 ft/3 m in length and weighed over 4,497 lb/2,040 kg.

TOP 10

LARGEST MARINE MAMMALS IN THE WORLD

Mammal	Length m	ft	Weight (tons)
1 Blue whale	33.5	110.0	143.3
2 Fin whale	25.0	82.0	49.6
3 Right whale	17.5	57.4	44.1
4 Sperm whale	18.0	59.0	39.7
5 Gray whale	14.0	46.0	36.0
6 Humpback whale	15.0	49.2	29.2
7 Baird's whale	5.5	18.0	12.1
8 Southern elephant seal	6.5	21.3	4.0
9 Northern elephant seal	5.8	19.0	3.7
10 Pilot whale	6.4	21.0	3.2

Probably the largest animal that ever lived, the blue whale dwarfs even the other whales listed here, all but one of which far outweigh the biggest land animal, the elephant.

TOP 10 FASTEST FISH IN THE WORLD
(Maximum recorded speed)

❶ Sailfish (68 mph/110 km/h) ❷ Marlin (50 mph/80 km/h) ❸ Bluefin tuna (46 mph/74 km/h) ❹ Yellowfin tuna (44 mph/70 km/h) ❺ Blue shark (43 mph/69 km/h) ❻ Wahoo (41 mph/66 km/h) ❼= Bonefish, Swordfish (40 mph/64 km/h) ❾ Tarpon (35 mph/56 km/h) ❿ Tiger shark (33 mph/53 km/h)

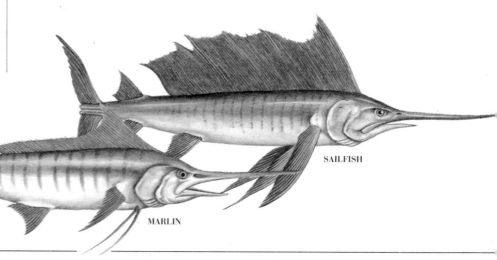

BLUEFIN TUNA

MARLIN

SAILFISH

TOP 10

LARGEST SPECIES OF SALTWATER FISH CAUGHT IN THE WORLD

	Species	Angler/location/date	Weight kg	g	lb	oz
1	Great white shark	Alfred Dean, Ceduna, South Australia, Apr 21, 1959	1,208	39	2,664	0
2	Tiger shark	Walter Maxwell, Cherry Grove, California, Jun 14, 1964	807	41	1,780	0
3	Greenland shark	Terje Nordtvedt, Trondheimsfjord, Norway, Oct 18, 1987	775	0	1,708	9
4	Black marlin	A. C. Glassell, Jr., Cabo Blanco, Peru, Aug 4, 1953	707	62	1,560	0
5	Bluefin tuna	Ken Fraser, Aulds Cove, Nova Scotia, Canada, Oct 26, 1979	678	59	1,496	0
6	Atlantic blue marlin	Paulo Amorim, Vitoria, Brazil, Feb 29, 1992	635	99	1,402	0
7	Pacific blue marlin	Jay W. de Beaubien, Kaaiwi Point, Kona, Hawaii, May 31, 1982	624	15	1,376	0
8	Swordfish	L. Marron, Iquique, Chile, May 7, 1953	536	16	1,182	0
9	Mako shark	Patrick Guillanton, Black River, Mauritius, Nov 16, 1988	505	76	1,115	0
10	Hammerhead shark	Allen Ogle, Sarasota, Florida, May 20, 1982	449	52	991	0

TOP 10

LARGEST SPECIES OF FRESHWATER FISH CAUGHT IN THE WORLD

	Species	Angler/location/date	Weight kg	g	lb	oz
1	White sturgeon	Joey Pallotta III, Benicia, California, Jul 9, 1983	212	28	468	0
2	Alligator gar	Bill Valverde, Rio Grande, Texas, Dec 2, 1951	126	55	279	0
3	Beluga sturgeon	Merete Lehne, Guryev, Kazakhstan, May 3, 1993	101	97	224	13
4	Nile perch	Andy Davison, Lake Victoria, Kenya, Sept 5, 1991	86	86	191	8
5	Blue catfish	George Lijewski, Cooper River, South Carolina, Mar 14, 1991	48	19	109	4
6	Chinook salmon	Les Anderson, Kenai River, Arkansas, May 17, 1985	44	11	97	4
7	Tigerfish	Raymond Houtmans, Zaire River, Kinshasa, Dem. Rep. of Congo, Jul 9, 1988	44	00	97	0
8	Flathead catfish	Mike Rogers, Lake Lewisville, Texas, Mar 28, 1982	41	39	91	4
9	Atlantic salmon	Henrik Henrikson, Tana River, Norway, 1928 (specific date unknown)	35	89	79	2
10	Carp	Leo van der Gugten, Lac de St. Cassien, France, May 21, 1987	34	33	75	11

Source: International Game Fish Association

IN THE CAN
Sardines, along with other species of herring and pilchard, are components of a world fishing industry that in the 1990s first topped 100 million tons a year.

TOP 10

SPECIES OF FISH MOST CAUGHT IN THE WORLD

	Species	Tons caught per annum
1	Anchoveta	13,113,986
2	Alaska pollock	4,738,416
3	Chilean jack mackerel	4,689,926
4	Silver carp	2,572,430
5	Atlantic herring	2,079,075
6	Grass carp	2,007,977
7	South American pilchard	1,976,913
8	Common carp	1,793,679
9	Chubb mackerel	1,661,731
10	Skipjack tuna	1,612,281

The Food and Agriculture Organization of the United Nations estimates the volume of the world's fishing catch to total almost 122000,000 tons a year, of which about 83,000,000 tons is reckoned to be destined for human consumption – equivalent to approximately 29 lb/13 kg a year for every inhabitant. The foremost species, anchoveta, are small anchovies used principally as bait to catch tuna. In recent years, the amount of carp – especially of farmed varieties in China – has increased markedly. Among broader groupings, 3,000,000 tons of shrimp and a similar tonnage of squid, cuttlefish, and octopus are caught annually.

FLYING ANIMALS

SMALLEST BATS IN THE WORLD

	Bat/habitat	Weight		Length	
		gm	oz	cm	in
1	Kitti's hognosed bat (*Craseonycteris thonglongyai*), Thailand	2.0	0.07	2.9	1.10
2	Proboscis bat (*Rhynchonycteris naso*), Central and South America	2.5	0.09	3.8	1.50
3=	Banana bat (*Pipistrellus nanus*), Central Africa	3.0	0.11	3.8	1.50
=	Smoky bat (*Furiptera horrens*), Central and South America	3.0	0.11	3.8	1.50
5=	Little yellow bat (*Rhogeessa mira*), Central America	3.5	0.12	4.0	1.57
=	Lesser bamboo bat (*Tylonycteris pachypus*), Southeast Asia	3.5	0.12	4.0	1.57
7	Disc-winged bat (*Thyroptera tricolor*), Central and South America	4.0	0.14	3.6	1.42
8	Lesser horseshoe bat (*Rhynolophus hipposideros*), Europe and Western Asia	5.0	0.18	3.7	1.46
9	California small brown bat (*Myotis californienses*), North America	5.0	0.18	4.3	1.69
10	Northern blossom bat (*Macroglossus minimus*), Southeast Asia to Australia	15.0	0.53	6.4	2.52

This list focuses on the smallest examples of 10 different bat families. The weights shown are typical, rather than extreme. The smallest of all weighs less than a ping-pong ball, and even the heaviest listed here weighs less than an empty aluminum soda can. Length is of head and body only, since tail lengths vary from zero (as in Kitti's hognosed bat and the Northern blossom bat) to long, as in the Proboscis bat and the Lesser horseshoe bat.

WINGED WONDER
The albatross is among the world's largest birds, with one of the most impressive wingspans. It is compared here with a seagull.

FASTEST BIRDS IN THE WORLD

	Bird	Maximum recorded speed	
		km/h	mph
1	Spine-tailed swift	171	106
2	Frigate bird	153	95
3	Spur-winged goose	142	88
4	Red-breasted merganser	129	80
5	White-rumped swift	124	77
6	Canvasback duck	116	72
7	Eider duck	113	70
8	Teal	109	68
9=	Mallard	105	65
=	Pintail	105	65

Until pilots cracked 190 mph/306 km/h in 1919, birds were the fastest creatures on the Earth: diving peregrine falcons approach 185 mph/298 km/h. However, most comparisons of the air speed of birds rule out diving or wind-assisted flight: most small birds on migration can manage a ground speed (speed relative to ground) of 60 mph/97 km/h to 70 mph/113 km/h. This list therefore picks out star performers among the medium- to large-sized birds that do not need help from wind or gravity to hit their top speed.

SWIFT BY NAME
and swift by nature, it holds the world record for avian speed.

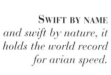

MOST COMMON NORTH AMERICAN BIRDS (1996–97)

	Bird	Percentage of feeders visited
1	Dark-eyed junco	83
2	House finch	70
3=	American goldfinch	69
=	Downy woodpecker	69
5	Blue jay	67
6	Mourning dove	65
7	Black-capped chickadee	60
8	House sparrow	59
9	Northern cardinal	56
10	European starling	52

Source: Project FeederWatch/Cornell Lab of Ornithology

FRUIT BAT
*Among the most
endangered of bats, fruit
bats – or flying foxes –
are also the largest bats,
with wingspans over
10 times that of the
smallest species.*

T O P 1 0

BIRDS WITH THE LARGEST WINGSPANS IN THE WORLD

	Bird	Maximum wingspan	
		m	ft
1	Marabou stork	4.0	13
2	Albatross	3.7	12
3	Trumpeter swan	3.4	11
4=	Mute swan	3.1	10
=	Whooper swan	3.1	10
=	Gray pelican	3.1	10
=	Californian condor	3.1	10
=	Black vulture	3.1	10
9=	Great bustard	2.7	9
=	Kori bustard	2.7	9

T O P 1 0

LARGEST BIRDS OF PREY IN THE WORLD*

	Bird	Length	
		cm	in
1	Californian condor	124	49
2=	Steller's sea eagle	114	45
=	Lammergeier	114	45
4	Bald eagle	109	43
5=	Andean condor	107	42
=	European black vulture	107	42
=	Ruppell's griffon	107	42
8	Griffon vulture	104	41
9	Wedge-tailed eagle	102	40
10	Lappet-faced vulture	100	39

* Diurnal only – hence excluding owls

The entrants in this Top 10 all measure
more than 39 in/1 m from beak to tail, but
birds of prey generally have smaller body
weights than those appearing in the list of
the 10 largest flighted birds. All of these
raptors, or aerial hunters, have remarkable
eyesight and can spot their victims from
great distances. However, even if they kill
animals heavier than themselves, they are
generally unable to fly with them: stories
of eagles carrying off lambs and small
children are usually fictitious.

T O P 1 0

LARGEST FLIGHTED BIRDS IN THE WORLD

	Bird	Weight		
		kg	lb	oz
1	Great bustard	20.9	46	1
2	Trumpeter swan	16.8	37	1
3	Mute swan	16.3	35	15
4=	Albatross	15.8	34	13
=	Whooper swan	15.8	34	13
6	Manchurian crane	14.9	32	14
7	Kori bustard	13.6	30	0
8	Gray pelican	13.0	28	11
9	Black vulture	12.5	27	8
10	Griffon vulture	12.0	26	7

Wing size does not necessarily correspond
to weight in flighted birds. The 13 ft/4 m
wingspan of the marabou stork beats all the
birds listed here, yet its body weight is
usually no heavier than any of these.

T O P 1 0

MOST COMMON BREEDING BIRDS IN THE US

1	Red-winged blackbird
2	House sparrow
3	Mourning dove
4	European starling
5	American robin
6	Horned lark
7	Common grackle
8	American crow
9	Western meadowlark
10	Brown-headed cowbird

This list, based on research carried out by
the Breeding Bird Survey of the US Fish
and Wildlife Service, ranks birds breeding
in the US, with the red-winged blackbird
(*Agelaius phoeniceus*) heading the list.

T O P 1 0

LARGEST FLIGHTLESS BIRDS IN THE WORLD

	Bird	Weight			Height	
		kg	lb	oz	cm	in
1	Ostrich	156.5	345	0	274.3	108.0
2	Emu	40.0	88	3	152.4	60.0
3	Cassowary	33.5	73	14	152.4	60.0
4	Rhea	25.0	55	2	137.1	54.0
5	Emperor penguin	29.4	64	13	114.0	45.0
6	Flightless cormorant	4.5	9	15	95.0	37.3
7	Flightless steamer	5.5	12	2	84.0	33.0
8	Kakapo	2.5	5	8	66.0	26.0
9	Kagu	5.0	11	0	59.9	23.6
10	Kiwi	3.5	7	12	55.9	22.0

LIVESTOCK

T O P 1 0

SHEEP COUNTRIES

	Country	Sheep (1997)
1	China	140,150,700
2	Australia	121,900,000
3	Iran	51,499,000
4	New Zealand	47,394,000
5	India	45,653,000
6	UK	41,530,000
7	Turkey	33,791,000
8	Pakistan	31,000,000
9	South Africa	29,016,000
10	Russia	25,800,000
	World total	*1,072,567,000*

This is one of the few world Top 10 lists in which the UK ranks considerably higher than the US, which has only 8,303,000 head of sheep in total. New Zealand's human population is outnumbered by its sheep by a factor of 13:1.

Source: Food and Agriculture Organization of the United Nations

T O P 1 0

TURKEY COUNTRIES

	Country	Turkeys (1997)
1	US	88,000,000
2	France	38,000,000
3	Italy	21,500,000
4	UK	12,408,000
5	Germany	6,800,000
6	Brazil	6,000,000
7	Canada	5,800,000
8	Portugal	5,400,000
9	Israel	4,000,000
10	Mexico	3,800,000
	World total	*232,427,000*

Some 82 percent of the world's turkeys are found in the Top 10 countries listed – with the largest number, appropriately, in North America, their place of origin. The name turkey was applied originally to guinea fowl, since they were brought to the West from Turkish territory; it was then confusingly applied to the birds from the New World. The name is equally misleading in French: in France they are known as *dinde* in the erroneous belief that they originally came from India.

Source: Food and Agriculture Organization of the United Nations

T O P 1 0

TYPES OF LIVESTOCK

	Animal	World total (1997)
1	Chickens	13,384,560,000
2	Cattle	1,323,962,000
3	Sheep	1,072,567,000
4	Pigs	938,944,200
5	Ducks	735,611,000
6	Goats	703,388,000
7	Rabbits	408,524,000
8	Turkeys	232,427,000
9	Buffaloes	153,078,300
10	Horses	62,129,770

The 19,007,794,670 animals accounted for by the Top 10 outnumber the world's human population by three to one. The world chicken population is more than double the human population, while the cattle population outnumbers the population of China. There are more pigs in the world than the population of India, and almost sufficient turkeys for every citizen of the US to have one each for Thanksgiving.

Source: Food and Agriculture Organization of the United Nations

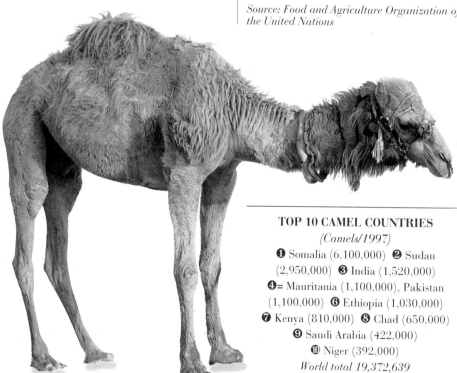

TOP 10 CAMEL COUNTRIES
(Camels/1997)
❶ Somalia (6,100,000) ❷ Sudan (2,950,000) ❸ India (1,520,000)
❹= Mauritania (1,100,000), Pakistan (1,100,000) ❻ Ethiopia (1,030,000)
❼ Kenya (810,000) ❽ Chad (650,000)
❾ Saudi Arabia (422,000)
❿ Niger (392,000)
World total 19,372,639

T O P 1 0

MILK-PRODUCING COUNTRIES

	Country	US gallons (1997) *
1	US	18,228,546,560
2	India	8,848,560,000
3	Russia	8,720,320,000
4	Germany	7,373,800,000
5	France	6,406,870,400
6	Brazil	4,898,768,000
7	Ukraine	3,924,144,000
8	UK	3,798,032,784
9	Poland	2,923,872,000
10	Netherlands	2,869,498,240
	World total	*120,855,400,653*

* *Fresh cow milk*

Source: Food and Agriculture Organization of the United Nations

TOP 10 GOAT COUNTRIES
(Goats/1997)

❶ China (170,993,000) ❷ India (120,600,000) ❸ Pakistan (47,000,000) ❹ Bangladesh (34,478,000) ❺ Iran (26,000,000) ❻ Nigeria (24,500,000) ❼ Sudan (16,900,000) ❽ Ethiopia (16,850,000) ❾ Indonesia (14,400,000) ❿ Somalia (12,500,000)
World total 703,388,000

TOP 10
HORSE COUNTRIES

	Country	Horses (1997)
1	China	10,200,800
2	Brazil	6,394,140
3	Mexico	6,250,000
4	US	6,150,000
5	Argentina	3,300,000
6	Ethiopia	2,750,000
7	Colombia	2,450,452
8	Mongolia	2,400,000
9	Russia	2,300,000
10	Kazakhstan	1,700,000
	World total	*62,129,770*

Mongolia makes an appearance in few Top 10 lists, but here it scores doubly as it is also the only country in the world where the horse population is greater than its human population (2,363,000).

Source: Food and Agriculture Organization of the United Nations

TOP 10
EGG-PRODUCING COUNTRIES

	Country	Hen egg production (1997) (eggs)*
1	China	278,564,356,980
2	US	77,746,890,000
3	Japan	43,198,272,000
4	Russia	29,115,502,000
5	India	27,032,252,000
6	Brazil	23,588,223,100
7	Mexico	21,499,140,000
8	France	16,449,342,000
9	Germany	14,171,766,440
10	Spain	11,599,536,000
	World	*775,452,647,320*

* *Based on 1 egg = 60 gm*

The world annual total hen egg production would be sufficient for everyone on the planet to eat an egg every three days.

Source: Food and Agriculture Organization of the United Nations

TOP 10
CHICKEN COUNTRIES

	Country	Chickens (1997)
1	China	3,010,535,000
2	US	1,553,000,000
3	Indonesia	1,103,310,000
4	Brazil	970,000,000
5	India	570,000,000
6	Russia	415,000,000
7	Mexico	393,000,000
8	Japan	309,000,000
9	France	221,000,000
10	Iran	202,140,000
	World total	*13,384,560,000*

Source: Food and Agriculture Organization of the United Nations

TOP 10 PIG COUNTRIES
(Pigs/1997)

❶ China (467,828,400) ❷ US (56,171,000) ❸ Brazil (36,900,000) ❹ Germany (24,144,610) ❺ Russia (22,631,000) ❻ Spain (18,155,000) ❼ Poland (18,152,000) ❽ Vietnam (17,500,000) ❾ India (15,419,000) ❿ Mexico (15,020,000)
World total 938,944,200

TOP 10
CATTLE COUNTRIES

	Country	Cattle (1997)
1	India	196,702,000
2	Brazil	163,000,000
3	China	116,560,100
4	US	101,209,000
5	Argentina	51,696,000
6	Russia	39,696,000
7	Ethiopia	29,900,000
8	Mexico	26,900,000
9	Colombia	26,346,000
10	Australia	26,250,000
	World total	*1,277,793,000*

Source: Food and Agriculture Organization of the United Nations

CATS, DOGS & OTHER PETS

THE 10

LATEST WINNERS OF THE BEST IN SHOW AT THE WESTMINSTER KENNEL CLUB DOG SHOW

Year	Breed	Champion
1998	Norwich Terrier	Fairewood Frolic
1997	Standard Schnauzer	Parsifal Di Casa Netzer
1996	Clumber Spaniel	Clussexx Country Sunrise
1995	Scottish Terrier	Gaelforce Post Script
1994	Norwich Terrier	Chidley Willum The Conqueror
1993	English Springer Spaniel	Salilyn's Condor
1992	Wire Fox Terrier	Registry's Lonesome Dove
1991	Standard Poodle	Whisperwind On Carousel
1990	Pekingese	Wendessa Crown Prince
1989	Doberman Pinscher	Royal Tudor's Wild As The Wind

Source: Westminster Kennel Club

TOP 10

MOVIES STARRING DOGS

	Film	Year
1	*101 Dalmatians*	1996
2	*One Hundred and One Dalmatians**	1961
3	*Lady and the Tramp**	1955
4	*Oliver and Company*	1988
5	*Turner and Hooch*	1989
6	*The Fox and the Hound**	1981
7	*Beethoven*	1992
8	*Homeward Bound II: Lost in San Francisco*	1996
9	*Beethoven's 2nd*	1993
10	*K-9*	1991

* *Animated*

Man's best friend has been stealing scenes since the earliest years of movie-making, with the 1905 low-budget *Rescued by Rover* outstanding as one of the most successful productions of the pioneer period. Since the 1950s, dogs – both real and animated – have been a consistently popular mainstay of the Disney Studios, who were responsible for several movies in this Top 10, which includes only movies in which a dog or dogs is the principal star.

101 DALMATIONS

LIZARD

TOP 10

CAT NAMES IN THE US

1	Puss/Pussy	6	Ginger
2	Tiger	7	Sooty
3	Smokey/Smokie	8	Sam
4	Misty	9	Kitty
5	Fluff/Fluffy	10	Max

Source: National Pet Register

TOP 10

TRICKS PERFORMED BY DOGS IN THE US

	Trick	Percentage of dogs performing
1	Sit	21.0
2	Shake paw	15.0
3	Roll over	11.4
4	"Speak"	10.6
5 =	Lie down	7.4
=	Stand on hind legs	7.4
7	Beg	7.2
8	Dance	6.1
9	"Sing"	3.0
10	Fetch newspaper	1.7

A survey conducted in the US by the Pet Food Institute and Frosty Paws, a pet food trade organization, concluded that 25,300,500 out of the more than 40,000,000 dogs in the country performed at least one trick. The survey ranked them by the numbers doing each. Extrapolating from these results, it was claimed that 5,313,105 dogs sit, 3,795,075 shake paw, and so on. Only 1.5 percent (379,508 dogs) "say prayers," and hence are not included.

TOP 10

PETS IN THE US

	Pet	Estimated no.
1	Cats	66,150,000
2	Dogs	58,200,000
3	Small animal pets*	12,740,000
4	Parakeets	11,000,000
5	Freshwater fish	10,800,000#
6	Reptiles	7,540,000
7	Finches	7,350,000
8	Cockatiels	6,320,000
9	Canaries	2,580,000
10	Parrots	1,550,000

* *Includes small rodents – rabbits, ferrets, hamsters, guinea pigs, and gerbils*

\# *Number of households owning, rather than individual specimens*

Source: Pet Industry Joint Advisory Council

TOP 10

DOG BREEDS IN THE US

	Breed	No. registered by American Kennel Club, Inc. (1997)
1	Labrador Retriever	158,366
2	Rottweiler	75,489
3	German Shepherd	75,177
4	Golden Retriever	70,158
5	Poodle	54,773
6	Beagle	54,470
7	Dachshund	51,904
8	Cocker Spaniel	41,439
9	Yorkshire Terrier	41,283
10	Pomeranian	39,357

The Labrador Retriever tops the list for the seventh consecutive year, its numbers up from 149,505 in 1996. This breed is also No. 1 in the UK.

Source: The American Kennel Club

THE 10

MOST INTELLIGENT DOG BREEDS

1	Border Collie
2	Poodle
3	German Shepherd
4	Golden Retriever
5	Doberman Pinscher
6	Shetland Sheepdog
7	Labrador Retriever
8	Papillon
9	Rottweiler
10	Australian Cattle Dog

American psychology professor and pet trainer Stanley Coren devised a ranking of 133 breeds of dogs after studying their responses to a range of IQ tests as well as the opinions of judges in dog obedience tests. Dog owners who have criticized the results (mostly those whose own pets scored badly) point out that dogs are bred for specialized abilities, such as speed or ferocity, and that the level of obedience to their human masters is only one feature of their "intelligence."

Source: Stanley Coren, The Intelligence of Dogs (Scribner, 1994)

THE 10

LEAST INTELLIGENT DOG BREEDS

1	Afghan Hound
2	Basenji
3	Bulldog
4	Chow Chow
5	Borzoi
6	Bloodhound
7	Pekinese
8 =	Beagle
=	Mastiff
10	Bassett Hound

Source: Stanley Coren, The Intelligence of Dogs (Scribner, 1994)

TOP 10

DOG NAMES IN THE US

1	Jessy/Jessie/Jess
2	Max
3	Jack
4	Sam
5	Sasha
6	Ben
7	Toby
8	Chloe
9	Bonny/Bonnie
10	Rocky

Source: National Pet Register

TOP 10

CAT BREEDS IN THE US

	Breed	No. registered*
1	Persian	39,119
2	Maine coon	4,819
3	Siamese	2,657
4	Abyssinian	2,308
5	Exotic	2,037
6	Oriental	1,337
7	Scottish fold	1,202
8	American shorthair	1,072
9	Birman	1,007
10	Burmese	939

* *Year ending December 31, 1997*

Of the 36 different breeds of cats listed with the Cat Fancier's Association, these were the Top 10 registered in 1997 out of a total of 65,183 (a decrease from 68,948 the previous year).

Source: Cat Fancier's Association

PLANTS & FOOD CROPS

T O P   1 0

POTATO-PRODUCING COUNTRIES

	Country	Production 1997 (tons)
1	China	52,947,903
2	Russia	44,092,452
3	Poland	30,001,607
4	US	23,699,693
5	Ukraine	20,943,915
6	India	20,392,759
7	Germany	13,710,548
8	Belarus	12,676,580
9	Netherlands	8,907,778
10	UK	7,957,585
	World	333,449,943

Dividing a country's population by the weight of potatoes grown will not reveal who eats the most, since a great deal of the world's potato harvest is used in the manufacture of alcohol and other products. Nonetheless, large populations of the world depend on potatoes for their nutrition.

Source: Food and Agriculture Organization of the United Nations

T O P   1 0

COTTON-PRODUCING COUNTRIES

	Country	Production 1997 (tons)
1	China	4,519,476
2	US	4,418,064
3	India	2,998,287
4	Pakistan	1,943,375
5	Uzbekistan	1,164,041
6	Turkey	832,245
7	Australia	634,931
8	Mexico	417,776
9	Greece	388,014
10	Argentina	352,740
	World	21,561,375

Source: Food and Agriculture Organization of the United Nations

TOP 10 FRUIT CROPS IN THE WORLD
(Production 1997 in tons)

❶ Oranges (66,432,037) ❷ Bananas (63,838,607) ❸ Grapes (63,073,360) ❹ Apples (60,281,173)
❺ Watermelons (51,231,770) ❻ Coconuts (50,713,144) ❼ Plantains (32,651,464) ❽ Mangoes (24,211,562) ❾ Tangerines, clementines, satsumas (17,136,752) ❿ Pears (14,406,393)

T O P   1 0

VEGETABLE CROPS

	Crop	Production 1997 (tons)		Crop	Production 1997 (tons)
1	Sugarcane	1,340,348,824	6	Sugar beets	302,117,626
2	Wheat	664,124,927	7	Cassava	183,495,811
3	Corn	639,340,670	8	Barley	168,182,503
4	Rice	630,237,342	9	Soybeans	156,007,584
5	Potatoes	333,449,943	10	Sweet potatoes	148,644,806

Source: Food and Agriculture Organization of the United Nations

T O P   1 0

APPLE-PRODUCING COUNTRIES

	Country	Production 1997 (tons)		Country	Production 1997 (tons)
1	China	8,828,940	7	Poland	2,094,391
2	US	5,211,728	8	Italy	1,600,088
3	Turkey	2,314,854	9	Germany	1,543,236
4 =	Iran	2,204,623	10 =	Argentina	1,322,774
=	Russia	2,204,623	=	India	1,322,774
6	France	2,114,233		World	60,281,173

Source: Food and Agriculture Organization of the United Nations

TOP 10

RICE-PRODUCING COUNTRIES

	Country	Production 1997 (tons)
1	China	217,123,692
2	India	133,944,052
3	Indonesia	56,217,877
4	Bangladesh	30,757,792
5	Vietnam	29,097,381
6	Thailand	23,920,155
7	Myanmar	23,369,000
8	Japan	14,330,047
9	Philippines	12,862,871
10	Brazil	10,522,994
	US	*8,969,176*
	World	*630,237,342*

World production of rice has risen dramatically during this century. It remains the staple diet for a huge proportion of the global population, especially in Asian countries. Relatively small quantities are grown elsewhere.

Source: Food and Agriculture Organization of the United Nations

TOP 10

MOST FORESTED COUNTRIES

	Country	Percent forest cover
1	Surinam	92
2	Papua New Guinea	91
3	Solomon Islands	85
4	French Guiana	81
5	Guyana	77
6	Gabon	74
7	Finland	69
8 =	Bhutan	66
=	Japan	66
10	North Korea	65

Source: Food and Agriculture Organization of the United Nations

FLOWER POWER
Sunflowers come from North and Central America, but the plant has been successfully introduced into many other parts of the world.

TOP 10

TALLEST TREES IN THE US

(The tallest-known example of each of the 10 tallest species)

	Tree	Location	Height m	ft
1	Coast Douglas fir	Coos County, Oregon	100.3	329
2	Coast redwood	Prairie Creek Redwoods State Park, California	95.4	313
3	General Sherman giant sequoia	Sequoia National Park, California	83.8	275
4	Noble fir	Mount St. Helens National Monument, Washington	82.9	272
5	Grand fir	Redwood National Park, California	78.3	257
6	Western hemlock	Olympic National Park, Washington	73.5	241
7	Sugar pine	Dorrington, California	70.7	232
8	Ponderosa pine	Plumas National Forest, California	68.0	223
9	Port-Orford cedar	Siskiyou National Forest, Oregon	66.8	219
10	Pacific silver fir	Forks, Washington	66.1	217

A coast redwood, which formerly topped this list, fell during 1992. The General Sherman giant sequoia is thought to be the planet's most colossal living thing, weighing about 1,500 tons, which is equivalent to the weight of nine blue whales or 360 elephants.

Source: American Forests

TOP 10 SUNFLOWER SEED-PRODUCING COUNTRIES
(Production 1997 in tons)

❶ Argentina (5,534,705) ❷ Ukraine (3,086,472) ❸ Russia (3,031,356) ❹ France (2,417,369)
❺ US (1,796,767) ❻ India (1,653,467) ❼ China (1,488,120) ❽ Romania (1,333,037)
❾ Spain (992,080) ❿ Hungary (870,826)

THE HUMAN WORLD

TOP 10

LARGEST HUMAN ORGANS

	Organ		Average weight g	oz
1	Liver		1,560	55.0
2	Brain	male	1,408	49.7
		female	1,263	44.6
3	Lungs	right	580	20.5
		left	510	18.0
		total	1,090	38.5
4	Heart	male	315	11.1
		female	265	9.3
5	Kidneys	left	150	5.3
		right	140	4.9
		total	290	10.2
6	Spleen		170	6.0
7	Pancreas		98	3.5
8	Thyroid		35	1.2
9	Prostate	male only	20	0.7
10	Adrenals	left	6	0.2
		right	6	0.2
		total	12	0.4

If the skin is considered an organ (as it is by some definitions), it would head the Top 10, since it can constitute 384 oz/10,886 g in a person weighing 150 lb/68 kg.

THE 10

MOST COMMON HOSPITAL ER CASES IN THE US

	Reason	No. of visits 1996 (in 1,000s)
1	Contusion with intact skin surface	4,913
2	Open wound, excluding head	4,655
3	Acute upper respiratory infections, excluding pharyngitis	3,706
4	Otitis media and eustachian tube disorders	2,701
5	Open wound of head	2,585
6	Chest pain	2,480
7	Abdominal pain	2,464
8	Fractures, excluding lower limb	2,444
9	Sprains and strains of back	2,274
10	Asthma	1,935

Source: Center for Disease Control/National Center for Health Statistics

TOP 10

MOST COMMON REASONS FOR VISITS TO A PHYSICIAN IN THE US

	Reason	No. of visits 1996 (in 1,000s)
1	General medical examination	50,669
2	Progress visit, not otherwise specified	28,804
3	Routine prenatal examination	23,948
4	Cough	22,800
5	Postoperative visit	18,683
6	Symptoms referable to throat	17,967
7	Well baby examination	15,236
8	Skin rash	11,997
9	Stomach pain, cramps, and spasms	11,721
10	Back symptoms	11,438
	Total	734,493,000

Source: National Ambulatory Medical Care Survey/Center for Disease Control/National Center for Health Statistics

THE HUMAN BODY & HEALTH

THE 10
COUNTRIES THAT SPEND THE MOST ON HEALTH CARE

	Country	Total spending as a percentage of GDP *
1	US	14.3
2	Argentina	10.6
3	Croatia	10.1
4	Czech Republic	9.9
5	Canada	9.8
6 =	Austria	9.7
=	France	9.7
8	Switzerland	9.6
9	Germany	9.5
10	Netherlands	8.8

* *Gross Domestic Product*

Source: World Bank, World Development Indicators 1997

THE 10
COUNTRIES THAT SPEND THE LEAST ON HEALTH CARE

	Country	Public spending as a percentage of GDP
1	Georgia	0.3
2 =	Gabon	0.5
=	Myanmar	0.5
4 =	Cambodia	0.7
=	India	0.7
=	Indonesia	0.7
7 =	Laos	0.8
=	Pakistan	0.8
9 =	Burundi	0.9
=	Guatemala	0.9
=	Guinea	0.9
	US	14.3

Source: World Bank, World Development Indicators 1997

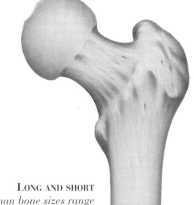

LONG AND SHORT
Human bone sizes range from the longest – the femur – at 19.88 in/ 50.50 cm, about 28 percent of a person's height, to the minute stapes or stirrup bone in the ear, which averages 0.12 in/3.0 mm.

TOP 10
MOST COMMON ELEMENTS IN THE HUMAN BODY

	Element	gm*
1	Oxygen	45,500
2	Carbon	12,600
3	Hydrogen	7,000
4	Nitrogen	2,100
5	Calcium	1,050
6	Phosphorus	700
7	Sulfur	175
8	Potassium	140
9 =	Chlorine	105
=	Sodium	105

* *Average in 155 lb person*

TOP 10
MOST COMMON ALLERGENS
(Substances that cause allergies)

Food allergen		Environmental allergen
Nuts	1	Dust mite
Shellfish/seafood	2	Grass pollens
Milk	3	Tree pollens
Wheat	4	Cats
Eggs	5	Dogs
Fresh fruit (apples, oranges, strawberries, etc.)	6	Horses
Fresh vegetables (potatoes, cucumbers, etc.)	7	Molds (*Aspergillus fumigatus*, etc.)
Cheese	8	Birch pollen
Yeast	9	Weed pollen
Soy protein	10	Wasp/bee venom

TOP 10 LONGEST BONES IN THE HUMAN BODY *(Length)*
❶ Femur/thighbone – upper leg (19.88 in/50.50 cm) ❷ Tibia/shinbone – inner lower leg (16.94 in/43.03 cm) ❸ Fibula/outer lower leg (15.94 in/40.50 cm) ❹ Humerus/upper arm (14.35 in/36.46 cm) ❺ Ulna/inner lower arm (11.10 in/28.20 cm) ❻ Radius/outer lower arm (10.40 in/26.42 cm) ❼ 7th rib (9.45 in/24.00 cm) ❽ 8th rib (9.06 in/23.00 cm) ❾ Innominate bone/hipbone – half pelvis (7.28 in/18.50 cm) ❿ Sternum/breastbone (6.69 in/17.00 cm)

MATTERS OF LIFE & DEATH

THE 10

COUNTRIES WITH THE MOST CREMATIONS

	Country	Percentage of deaths	Cremations (1996)
1	China	35.20	2,830,000
2	Japan	98.70	938,777
3	US	21.31	492,434
4	UK	71.28	445,934
5	Germany	37.76	333,373
6	Czech Republic	75.93	85,650
7	Canada*	39.58	84,246
8	France	12.73	68,317
9	Australia	54.00	68,208
10	The Netherlands	47.26	65,014

* 1995

Cremation is least practiced in traditionally Roman Catholic countries, such as Spain (5.92 percent of deaths), Italy (3.27 percent of deaths), and the Republic of Ireland (3.92 percent of deaths).

Source: The Cremation Society

THE 10

MOST COMMON CAUSES OF DEATH IN THE WORLD

	Cause	Approximate deaths per annum
1	Ischemic heart disease	7,200,000
2	Cerebrovascular disease	4,600,000
3	Acute lower respiratory infection	3,905,000
4	Tuberculosis	3,000,000
5	Chronic obstructive pulmonary disease	2,888,000
6	Diarrhea, including dysentery	2,473,000
7	Malaria	1,500,000– 2,700,000
8	HIV/AIDS	1,500,000
9	Hepatitis B	1,156,000
10	Prematurity	1,150,000

If all the different forms of cancer were considered as one, then cancers would fall at No. 2 in the Top 10 with approximately 6,346,000 deaths caused annually.

Source: World Health Organization

THE 10

MOST COMMON CAUSES OF DEATH CAUSED BY INFECTIOUS AND PARASITIC DISEASES

	Cause	Approximate deaths per annum
1	Acute lower respiratory infection	3,905,000
2	Tuberculosis	3,000,000
3	Diarrhea (including dysentery)	2,473,000
4	Malaria	1,500,000– 2,700,000
5	HIV/AIDS	1,500,000
6	Hepatitis B	1,156,000
7	Measles	1,010,000
8	Whooping cough (pertussis)	355,000
9	Neonatal tetanus	310,000
10	Trypanosomiasis (sleeping sickness)	150,000

Infectious and parasitic diseases account for approximately 17,000,000 of the 52,000,000 annual deaths worldwide.

Source: World Health Organization

THE 10

MOST SUICIDAL COUNTRIES IN THE WORLD

	Country	Suicides per 100,000 population
1	Lithuania	45.8
2	Russia	41.8
3	Estonia	41.0
4	Latvia	40.7
5	Hungary	32.9
6	Slovenia	28.4
7	Belarus	27.9
8	Finland	27.3
9	Kazakhstan	23.8
10	Croatia	22.8
	US	*12.0*

Source: United Nations

THE 10

COUNTRIES WITH THE HIGHEST DEATH RATE

	Country	Death rate per 1,000
1	Sierra Leone	25.1
2	Afghanistan	21.8
3	Guinea Bissau	21.3
4	Guinea	20.3
5=	Angola	19.2
=	Uganda	19.2
7	Niger	18.9
8	Gambia	18.8
9=	Mozambique	18.5
=	Somalia	18.5
	US	*8.8*

Source: United Nations

THE 10

COUNTRIES WITH THE MOST DEATHS FROM LUNG CANCER

	Country	Death rate per 100,000 population
1	Hungary	73.8
2	UK	66.8
3	Belgium	64.5
4	US	57.7
5	Czech Republic	56.2
6	Netherlands	55.7
7	Italy	54.1
8	Canada	51.8
9	Greece	49.8
10	Poland	49.3

Source: United Nations

THE 10
COUNTRIES WITH THE MOST CASES OF AIDS

	Country	Number of cases
1	US	40,051
2	Tanzania	28,341
3	Thailand	17,949
4	Zimbabwe	13,356
5	Brazil	9,695
6	Kenya	8,232
7	Côte d'Ivoire	6,727
8	Spain	6,227
9	Italy	5,476
10	Malawi	5,261

Two points should be considered with respect to these figures. First, they refer to total numbers of cases, so countries with larger populations are likely to have more cases. Second, the accuracy of reporting of cases of such a sensitive disease varies markedly among countries – this may be due to failure to diagnose, or reluctance to report cases for social, cultural, or religious reasons. On the basis of the data that exists, 22,600,000 people in the world are now living with the HIV infection or AIDS. In 1996 alone, 3,100,000 new HIV infections were reported, and an estimated 1,500,000 people died.

Source: World Health Organization

THE 10
MOST COMMON CAUSES OF DEATH IN THE US

	Cause	No. of deaths (1996)
1	Diseases of the heart	733,834
2	Cancer	544,278
3	Cerebrovascular diseases	160,431
4	Chronic obstructive pulmonary diseases and allied conditions	106,146
5	Accidents and adverse effects	93,874
6	Pneumonia and influenza	82,579
7	Diabetes	61,559
8	Human Immune deficiency Virus infection	32,655
9	Suicide	30,862
10	Chronic liver disease and cirrhosis	25,135

Preliminary figures are for 1996 based on a total number of 2,322,421 deaths estimated in the US for that year. "Accidents and adverse effects" include 43,449 deaths resulting from motor vehicle accidents. The category "Homicide and legal intervention" remains 11th with 20,738 deaths.

Source: US National Center for Health Statistics

TOP 10
COUNTRIES WITH THE LOWEST DEATH RATE

	Country	Death rate per 1,000
1	Qatar	1.6
2	Kuwait	2.1
3	United Arab Emirates	2.7
4	Andorra	2.8
5	Belize	3.2
6	Brunei	3.7
7	Marshall Islands	3.9
8	Bahrain	4.0
9	Costa Rica	4.2
10	Tonga	4.2
	US	8.8

Although it is not an independent country, the lowest death rate in the world is recorded by the island of St. Helena, at 0.6 per 1,000 population per year.

Source: United Nations

THE 10
MOST COMMON CAUSES OF ILLNESS IN THE WORLD

	Cause	New cases annually
1	Diarrhea (including dysentery)	4,002,000,000
2	Malaria	300,000,000– 500,000,000
3	Acute lower respiratory infections	394,000,000
4	Trichomoniasis	170,000,000
5	Occupational diseases	160,000,000
6	Occupational injuries	125,000,000
7	Mood (affective) disorders	122,865,000
8	Chlamydial infections	89,000,000
9	Alcohol dependence	75,000,000
10	Gonococcal (bacterial) infections	62,000,000

Source: World Health Organization

BANDAGE PIONEER

In 1899 the US pharmaceutical company Johnson & Johnson introduced a new product that we now take for granted. Back in 1876, one of the company's founders, Robert Wood Johnson, had heard an address by English surgeon James Lister on the subject of the prevention of infection in wounds and during surgical operations. Ten years later, in partnership with his brothers James Wood and Edward Mead Johnson, he introduced the first ready-made sterile dressings to replace the often contaminated and hence dangerous cotton bandages then in use. In 1899, the company launched the zinc oxide adhesive bandage. First used by surgeons, in 1921 these were marketed to the general public under the brand name Band-Aid®, and the disposable bandage revolution was born.

100 YEARS AGO · YEARS AGO · YEARS AGO

CHARITIES

TOP 10
RELIGIOUS FOUNDATIONS IN THE US

	Foundation	Amount given away ($)
1	Lilly Endowment	12,310,417
2	Pew Charitable Trusts	7,795,500
3	Dan Murphy Foundation	7,008,500
4	Koch Foundation	6,205,195
5	Callaway Foundation	4,311,605
6	Harry and Jeanette Weinberg Foundation	3,798,500
7	Maclellan Foundation	3,187,929
8	Samuel Bronfman Foundation	2,856,595
9	Lutheran Brotherhood Foundation	2,414,020
10	Revlon Group Foundation	2,412,590

Source: The Foundation Center

SONG FOR DIANA, PRINCESS OF WALES
Elton John's recorded tribute to Diana, "Candle in the Wind 1997," became the best-selling single ever in the UK. Only five weeks after its release on September 13, 1997, 31.8 million copies had been sold. All royalties from the single are donated to Diana's favorite charities.

CHARITIES ASSOCIATED WITH DIANA, PRINCESS OF WALES
(Voluntary income in £s)

❶ Barnados (47,300,000) ❷ Help the Aged (43,178,000) ❸ Red Cross (38,446,000) ❹ Leprosy Mission (6,811,000) ❺ Parkinson's Disease Society (4,173,000) ❻ Malcolm Sargent Cancer Fund for Children (2,006,000) ❼ Centrepoint (1,647,000) ❽ Relate (1,274,000) ❾ British Lung Foundation (1,231,000) ❿ British Deaf Association (1,196,000)

TOP 10
CHARITIES IN THE US

	Organization	Total revenue ($)
1	YMCA of the USA	2,473,023,000
2	Catholic Charities USA	2,103,548,164
3	American Red Cross	1,813,928,000
4	Salvation Army	1,563,105,907
5	Goodwill Industries International	1,200,000,000
6	Shriners Hospitals for Children	1,047,590,000
7	Boy Scouts of America	553,471,000
8	YWCA of the USA	510,829,407
9	American Cancer Society, Inc.	510,632,000
10	Planned Parenthood Federation of America	504,000,000

Source: NonProfit Times

TOP 10
CHARITIES WITH PUBLIC SUPPORT IN THE US

	Organization	Revenue ($)		Organization	Revenue ($)
1	Salvation Army	815,916,460	6	YMCA of the USA	340,337,000
2	American Red Cross	471,929,000	7	Catholic Charities	335,587,140
3	American Cancer Society	426,695,000	8	Habitat For Humanity	325,000,000
4	United Jewish Appeal	359,488,000	9	American Heart Association	273,989,000
5	Second Harvest	351,376,162	10	World Vision	251,903,000

Source: NonProfit Times

GREENPEACE INTERNATIONAL
Conceived in 1971 in Vancouver, Canada, by 12 people, Greenpeace now has 43 offices in 30 countries around the world. Dedicated to protecting the environment by highlighting its abuse, Greenpeace is funded by contributions from 5 million supporters in 158 countries.

TOP 10
HUMAN SERVICES CHARITIES IN THE US

	Organization	Total revenue ($)		Organization	Total revenue ($)
1	The National Council of YMCAs	2,473,023,000	6	Boy Scouts of America	553,471,000
2	Catholic Charities USA	2,103,548,164	7	YWCA of the USA	510,829,407
3	American Red Cross	1,813,928,000	8	Planned Parenthood Federation of America	504,000,000
4	Salvation Army	1,563,105,907	9	Girl Scouts of the USA	492,302,000
5	Goodwill Industries International	1,200,000,000	10	Boys and Girls Club of America	437,764,871

Source: NonProfit Times

TOP 10

ENVIRONMENT AND ANIMAL FOUNDATIONS IN THE US

	Foundation	Amount ($)
1	Ford Foundation	16,957,088
2	Pew Charitable Trusts	16,832,400
3	John D. and Catherine T. MacArthur Foundation	16,744,988
4	Robert W. Woodruff Foundation	16,095,000
5	Andrew W. Mellon Foundation	12,265,000
6	W. Alton Jones Foundation	9,812,685
7	Charles Stewart Mott Foundation	7,233,553
8	Joyce Foundation	6,053,453
9	Kresge Foundation	5,950,000
10	Freeman Foundation	5,873,550

Source: The Foundation Center

TOP 10

HEALTH CHARITIES IN THE US (1996)

	Organization	Annual revenue ($)
1	Shriners Hospitals for Children	1,047,590,000
2	American Cancer Society, Inc.	510,632,000
3	National Easter Seal Society	429,419,000
4	American Heart Association	345,230,000
5	ALSAC-St. Jude's Children's Research Hospital	303,857,816
6	City of Hope	247,081,147
7	American Lung Association	154,512,000
8	March of Dimes	153,082,000
9	American Diabetes Association	108,262,265
10	Muscular Dystrophy Association	107,690,417

Source: NonProfit Times

TOP TEN FOUNDATIONS BY TOTAL GIVEN AWAY
(Total given away in $)

❶ The Ford Foundation (332,412,106) ❷ W. K. Kellogg Foundation (255,259,633) ❸ Robert W. Woodruff Foundation, Inc. (253,271,554) ❹ The Robert Wood Johnson Foundation (229,275,359) ❺ The Pew Charitable Trusts (175,059,312) ❻ Lilly Endowment, Inc. (168,322,607) ❼ John D. and Catherine T. MacArthur Foundation (137,291,138) ❽ The Andrew W. Mellon Foundation (113,698,038) ❾ The David and Lucile Packard Foundation (102,778,997) ❿ The Annenberg Foundation (97,190,186)
Source: The Foundation Center

TOP 10

EDUCATION & CULTURE CHARITIES (1996)

	Organization	Total revenue ($)
1	Smithsonian Institution	337,395,401
2	The Metropolitan Museum of Art	233,455,812
3	Art Institute of Chicago	165,132,239
4	Metropolitan Opera Association, Inc.	149,159,400
5	Museum of Fine Arts, Boston	114,895,189
6	Colonial Williamsburg Foundation	111,087,367
7	J. F. Kennedy Center for the Performing Arts	110,383,000
8	National Gallery of Art	109,856,349
9	American Museum of Natural History	108,269,574
10	The College Fund/UNCF	100,535,763

Source: NonProfit Times

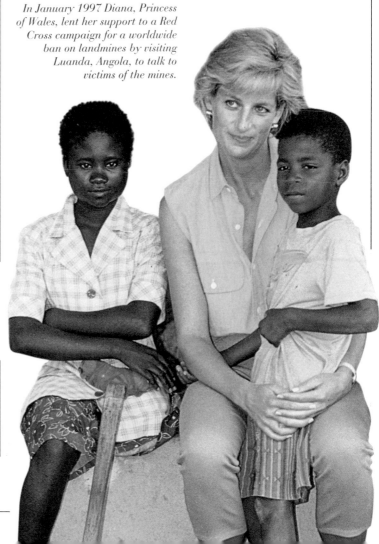

SUPPORT FOR LANDMINE BAN
In January 1997 Diana, Princess of Wales, lent her support to a Red Cross campaign for a worldwide ban on landmines by visiting Luanda, Angola, to talk to victims of the mines.

FOR BETTER OR FOR WORSE

COUNTRIES WITH THE LOWEST DIVORCE RATES

Country	Divorce rate per 1,000	Country	Divorce rate per 1,000
1 Vatican City	0.00	**=** Turkey	0.46
2 Guatemala	0.15	**7** Italy	0.48
3 Macedonia	0.27	**8=** Iran	0.50
4 Mexico	0.35	**=** Libya	0.50
5= Chile	0.46	**10** El Salvador	0.51

The UN data on divorce rates omit a number of large countries, and ones that we might expect to have a very low divorce rate, such as Ireland. The data are very difficult to collect, given the different laws relating to divorce in each country.

Source: United Nations

FIRST WEDDING ANNIVERSARY GIFTS

1	Cotton
2	Paper
3	Leather
4	Fruit and flowers
5	Wood
6	Sugar (or iron)
7	Wool (or copper)
8	Bronze (or electrical appliances)
9	Pottery (or willow)
10	Tin (or aluminum)

COUNTRIES WITH THE HIGHEST DIVORCE RATES

Country	Divorce rate per 1,000	Country	Divorce rate per 1,000
1 Maldives	10.75	**6** Belarus	4.26
2 Cuba	5.95	**7** Surinam	4.15
3 China	4.63	**8** Ukraine	4.00
4 Russia	4.60	**9** Estonia	3.74
5 US	4.57	**10** Latvia	3.20

Source: United Nations

TOP 10 US STATES WITH THE MOST MARRIAGES

(Marriages in 1996)

❶ California (219,039) ❷ Texas (179,693) ❸ New York (152,263) ❹ Florida (149,941) ❺ Nevada (141,228) ❻ Illinois (90,178) ❼ Ohio (82,844) ❽ Tennessee (82,064) ❾ Pennsylvania (70,173) ❿ Michigan (69,091)

Source: National Center for Health Statistics

TOP 10

MONTHS FOR MARRIAGES IN THE US

	Month	Marriages (1996)
1	June	242,000
2	May	241,000
3	August	239,000
4	July	235,000
5	October	231,000
6	September	225,000
7	December	184,000
8	April	172,000
9	November	171,000
10	February	155,000

Figures are estimates for 1996 from a US total of about 2,342,000 weddings, an increase of just 6,000 compared with the previous year. March was at No. 11 with 147,000, and January the least popular month with 100,000 marriages.

Source: National Center for Health Statistics

THE 10

COUNTRIES WITH THE LOWEST MARRIAGE RATE

	Country	Marriages per 1,000 per annum
1	Andorra	2.0
2	Malaysia	3.2
3	South Africa	3.3
4	St. Lucia	3.4
5=	Dominican Republic	3.6
=	Paraguay	3.6
7	Cape Verde	3.8
8=	Bulgaria	4.0
=	United Arab Emirates	4.0
10	El Salvador	4.2

THE 10

COUNTRIES WITH THE HIGHEST MARRIAGE RATE

	Country	Marriages per 1,000 per annum
1	Maldives	19.7
2	Cuba	17.7
3	Bermuda	14.2
4	Liechtenstein	12.9
5	Seychelles	11.9
6	Barbados	11.2
7	Bangladesh	10.9
8	Tajikistan	9.6
9	Mauritius	9.5
10	Bahamas	9.3
	US	*9.1*

TOP 10

GROUNDS FOR DIVORCE MOST ON THE US STATES STATUTE BOOKS

1	Irretrievable breakdown		7	Addiction
2	Separation		8	Felony
3	Desertion/abandonment		9=	Incompatability of temperament
4	Adultery		=	Imprisonment
5	Cruelty		=	Impotence
6	Insanity			

WHAT'S IN A NAME?

TOP 10

GIRLS' AND BOYS' NAMES IN THE US*

Girls		Boys
Sarah	1	Michael
Emily	2	Matthew
Kaitlyn	3	Nicholas
Brianna	4	Jacob
Ashley	5	Christopher
Jessica	6	Austin
Taylor	7	Joshua
Megan	8	Zachary
Hannah	9	Andrew
Samantha	10	Brandon

* Based on sample of new Social Security registrations from January–August 1997.

Source: BabyCenter, Inc.

TOP 10

MOST COMMON SURNAMES IN THE MANHATTAN TELEPHONE DIRECTORY

1	Smith/Smyth/Smythe
2	Lee/Lea/Leigh/Ley/Li
3	Brown/Browne
4	Cohen/Coan/Coen/Cohn/Cone/Kohn
5	Johnson/Johnston/Johnsen
6	Rodriguez
7	Miller
8	Williams
9	Jones
10	Davis/Davies

TOP 10

MOST COMMON SURNAMES IN THE UK

1	Smith	6	Davies/Davis
2	Jones	7	Evans
3	Williams	8	Thomas
4	Brown	9	Roberts
5	Taylor	10	Johnson

TOP 10

MOST COMMON FEMALE FIRST NAMES IN THE US

	Name	Percentage of all first names
1	Mary	2.629
2	Patricia	1.073
3	Linda	1.035
4	Barbara	0.980
5	Elizabeth	0.937
6	Jennifer	0.932
7	Maria	0.828
8	Susan	0.794
9	Margaret	0.768
10	Dorothy	0.727

The Top 10 female names according to the latest (1990) US Census account for 10.703 percent of all names. This list includes females of all age groups.

Source: US Bureau of the Census

THEN & NOW

TOP 10 BOYS' NAMES IN ENGLAND AND WALES

1987		1997
Daniel	1	Jack
Christopher	2	James
Michael	3	Thomas
James	4	Daniel
Matthew	5	Joshua
Andrew	6	Matthew
Adam	7	Samuel
Thomas	8	Joseph
David	9	Ryan
Richard	10	Jordan

TOP 10

MOST COMMON PATRONYMS IN THE US

	Name/origin	Percentage of all US names
1	Johnson ("son of John")	0.810
2	Williams ("son of William")	0.699
3	Jones ("son of John")	0.621
4	Davis ("son of Davie/David")	0.480
5	Wilson ("son of Will")	0.339
6 =	Anderson ("son of Andrew")	0.311
=	Thomas ("son of Thomas")	0.311
8	Jackson ("son of Jack")	0.310
9	Harris ("son of Harry")	0.275
10	Martin ("son of Martin")	0.273

Patronyms are names recalling a father or other ancestor. Up to one-third of all US surnames may be patronymic in origin. Four US Presidents have borne names within the Top 10, along with possessors of other, less common, patronyms, such as Jefferson.

THEN & NOW

TOP 10 GIRLS' NAMES IN ENGLAND AND WALES

1987		1997
Rebecca	1	Chloe
Sarah	2	Emily
Emma	3	Sophie
Laura	4	Jessica
Rachel	5	Megan
Samantha	6	Hannah
Charlotte	7	Rebecca
Kirsty	8	Lauren
Nicola	9	Charlotte
Amy	10	Georgia

- French composer Louis Julien (1812–60) had 36 first names.
- Ann Pepper, born in Derby, England, in 1882, was given 26 first names, one for each letter of the alphabet, in alphabetical order.
- O is the world's most common single-letter surname; it is especially common in Korea. However, Social Security records list individuals with one-letter names for the entire alphabet from A to Z.

TOP 10

GIRLS' AND BOYS' NAMES IN THE US 100 YEARS AGO

Girls		Boys
Mary	**1**	John
Ruth	**2**	William
Helen	**3**	Charles
Margaret	**4**	Robert
Elizabeth	**5**	Joseph
Dorothy	**6**	James
Catherine	**7**	George
Mildred	**8**	Samuel
Frances	**9**	Thomas
Alice/Marion	**10**	Arthur

TOP 10

MOST COMMON MALE FIRST NAMES IN THE US

	Name	Percentage of all first names
1	James	3.318
2	John	3.271
3	Robert	3.143
4	Michael	2.629
5	William	2.451
6	David	2.363
7	Richard	1.703
8	Charles	1.523
9	Joseph	1.404
10	Thomas	1.380

The Top 10 male names according to the latest (1990) US Census account for 23.185 percent of all names. It should be noted that this represents names of people of all age groups enumerated, and not the current popularity of first names.

Source: US Bureau of the Census

TOP 10

MOST COMMON SURNAMES IN THE US

	Name	Percentage of all names
1	Smith	1.006
2	Johnson	0.810
3	Williams	0.699
4=	Jones	0.621
=	Brown	0.621
6	Davis	0.480
7	Miller	0.424
8	Wilson	0.339
9	Moore	0.312
10=	Anderson	0.311
=	Taylor	0.311
=	Thomas	0.311

The Top 10 (or, in view of those in equal 10th place, 12) most common US surnames together make up over six percent of the entire US population. In other words, one American in every 16 bears one of these 12 surnames.

TOP 10

MOST COMMON INITIAL LETTERS OF SURNAMES IN THE US

	Surname initial	Percentage of surnames
1	S	9.8
2	B	7.0
3	M	6.5
4	K	6.4
5	D	5.9
6=	C	5.5
=	P	5.5
8	G	5.2
9	L	5.0
10	A	4.8

TOP 10

MOST COMMON DESCRIPTIVE SURNAMES IN THE US

	Name/origin	Percentage of all names
1	Brown (brown-haired)	0.621
2	White (light-skinned, or white-haired)	0.279
3	Young (youthful, or a younger brother)	0.193
4	Gray (gray-haired)	0.106
5	Long (tall)	0.092
6	Russell (red-haired)	0.085
7	Black (black-haired, or black-skinned)	0.063
8=	Little (small)	0.046
=	Reid (red-haired)	0.046
10	Curtis (courteous, or well-educated)	0.040

As many as one in 10 of all US surnames may be derived from a simple physical description that was once applied to an ancestor. The list is headed by the Browns.

TOP 10

MOST COMMON SURNAMES OF LATINO ORIGIN IN THE US

	Name/origin	Percentage of all names
1	Garcia	0.254
2	Martinez	0.234
3	Rodriguez	0.229
4	Hernandez	0.192
5	Lopez	0.187
6	Gonzalez	0.166
7	Perez	0.155
8	Sanchez	0.130
9	Rivera	0.113
10	Torres	0.108

ROYALTY & TITLES

THEN & NOW

TOP 10 BUSIEST MEMBERS OF THE BRITISH ROYAL FAMILY

1987 engagements*			1997 engagements*	
The Queen	432	1	498	The Princess Royal
The Princess Royal	367	2	487	The Queen
The Duke of Edinburgh	322	3	339	The Prince of Wales
The Prince of Wales	276	4	284	The Duke of Edinburgh
The Princess of Wales	180	5	168	The Duke of Kent
The Duchess of York	132	6	156	The Duke of York
The Duke of Kent	131	7	153	The Duke of Gloucester
Princess Margaret	129	8	136	Princess Margaret
The Duke of Gloucester	123	9	128	The Duchess of Gloucester
The Duchess of Gloucester	111	10	111	Princess Alexandra
Total	*2,203*		*2,460*	

* Domestic total, excluding engagements abroad

Source: Tim O'Donovan

TOP 10

BEST-PAID MEMBERS OF THE BRITISH ROYAL FAMILY

	Member	Annual payment (£)
1	The Queen	7,900,000
2	The Queen Mother	643,000
3	The Duke of Edinburgh	359,000
4	The Duke of York	249,000
5	The Duke of Kent	236,000
6	The Princess Royal	228,000
7	Princess Alexandra	225,000
8	Princess Margaret	219,000
9	The Duke of Gloucester	175,500
10	Prince Edward	96,000

The Civil List is not technically the Royal Family's "pay," but the allowance made by the Government for their staff and costs incurred in the course of performing their public duties. The amount of the Civil List was fixed for 10 years from January 1, 1991 and provides a total allocation of £10,417,000. Of that sum, £1,515,000 is refunded to the Treasury. The Prince of Wales receives nothing from the Civil List. His income derives largely from the Duchy of Cornwall.

THE 10

FIRST IN LINE TO THE BRITISH THRONE

	Title	Date of birth
1	The Prince of Wales then his elder son:	November 14, 1948
2	Prince William of Wales then his younger brother:	June 21, 1982
3	Prince Henry of Wales then his uncle:	September 15, 1984
4	The Duke of York then his elder daughter:	February 19, 1960
5	Princess Beatrice of York then her younger sister:	August 8, 1988
6	Princess Eugenie of York then her uncle:	March 23, 1990
7	Prince Edward then his sister:	March 10, 1964
8	The Princess Royal then her son:	August 15, 1950
9	Master Peter Mark Andrew Phillips then his sister:	November 15, 1977
10	Miss Zara Anne Elizabeth Phillips	May 15, 1981

The birth in 1988 of Princess Beatrice ousted David Albert Charles Armstrong-Jones, Viscount Linley (b. November 3, 1961), from the No. 10 position, while the birth in 1990 of her sister, Princess Eugenie, evicted Princess Margaret, Countess of Snowdon (Princess Margaret Rose, b. August 21, 1930) from the Top 10.

TOP 10

LONGEST-REIGNING MONARCHS IN THE WORLD

	Monarch	Country	Reign	Age at accession	Years reigned
1	Louis XIV	France	1643–1715	5	72
2	John II	Liechtenstein	1858–1929	18	71
3	Franz-Josef	Austria–Hungary	1848–1916	18	67
4	Victoria	Great Britain	1837–1901	18	63
5	Hirohito	Japan	1926–89	25	62
6	Kangxi	China	1662–1722	8	61
7	Qianlong	China	1736–96	25	60
8	George III	Great Britain	1760–1820	22	59
9	Louis XV	France	1715–74	5	59
10	Pedro II	Brazil	1831–89	6	58

Some authorities claim a 73-year reign for Alfonso I of Portugal, but he did not assume the title of king until July 25, 1139. He thus ruled as king for 46 years until his death on December 6, 1185.

THE 10 — LATEST BRITISH MONARCHS TO DIE VIOLENTLY

	Monarch/cause*	Date
1	William III, riding accident	Mar 8, 1702
2	Charles I, beheaded	Jan 30, 1649
3	Jane, beheaded	Feb 12, 1554
4	Richard III, killed in battle	Aug 22, 1485
5	Edward V, murdered	1483 #
6	Henry VI, murdered	May 21, 1471
7	Edward II, murdered	Sep 21, 1327
8	Richard I, arrow wound	Apr 6, 1199
9	William II, arrow wound	Aug 2, 1100
10	William I, riding accident	Sep 9, 1087

Includes illnesses resulting from injuries

 # Precise date unknown

THE 10 — SHORTEST-REIGNING BRITISH MONARCHS

	Monarch	Reign	Duration
1	Jane	1553	9 days
2	Edward V	1483	75 days
3	Edward VIII	1936	325 days
4	Richard III	1483–85	2 years
5	James II	1685–88	3 years
6	Mary I	1553–58	5 years
7	Mary II	1689–94	5 years
8	Edward VI	1547–53	6 years
9	William IV	1830–37	7 years
10	Edward VII	1901–10	9 years

Queen Jane, Lady Jane Grey, ruled from July 10 to 19, 1553, before being sent to the Tower of London, where she was executed the following year. Edward V was one of the "Princes in the Tower," allegedly murdered on the orders of their uncle, Richard III. Edward VIII abdicated on December 11, 1936, before his coronation.

QUEEN VICTORIA

TOP 10 LONGEST-LIVED BRITISH MONARCHS
(Age at death)

❶ Victoria (81) ❷ George III (81)
❸ Edward VIII (77) ❹ George II (76)
❺ William IV (71) ❻ George V (70)
❼ Elizabeth I (69) ❽ Edward VII (68)
❾ Edward I (68) ❿ James II (67)

TOP 10 — LONGEST-REIGNING LIVING MONARCHS IN THE WORLD*

	Monarch/country	Date of birth	Accession
1	Bhumibol Adulyadej, Thailand	Dec 5, 1927	Jun 9, 1946
2	Prince Rainier III, Monaco	May 31, 1923	May 9, 1949
3	Elizabeth II, UK	Apr 21, 1926	Feb 6, 1952
4	Hussein, Jordan	Nov 14, 1935	Aug 11, 1952
5	Hassan II, Morocco	Jul 9, 1929	Feb 26, 1961
6	Isa bin Sulman al-Khalifa, Bahrain	Jul 3, 1933	Nov 2, 1961
7	Malietoa Tanumafili II, Western Samoa	Jan 4, 1913	Jan 1, 1962
8	Grand Duke Jean, Luxembourg	Jan 5, 1921	Nov 12, 1964
9	Taufa'ahau Tupou IV, Tonga	Jul 4, 1918	Dec 16, 1965
10	Qaboos Bin-Said, Oman	Nov 18, 1942	Jul 23, 1970

Including hereditary rulers of principalities, dukedoms, etc.

THE 10 — LONGEST-REIGNING BRITISH MONARCHS

	Monarch	Reign	Age at accession	Age at death	Years reigned
1	Victoria	1837–1901	18	81	63
2	George III	1760–1820	22	81	59
3	Henry III	1216–72	9	64	56
4	Edward III	1327–77	14	64	50
5	Elizabeth II	1952–	25	–	46
6	Elizabeth I	1558–1603	25	69	44
7	Henry VI	1422–61	8 months	49	38
8	Henry VIII	1509–47	17	55	37
9	Charles II	1649–85	19	54	36
10	Henry I	1100–35	31–32*	66–67*	35

Henry I's birthdate is unknown, so his age at accession and death are uncertain

This list excludes monarchs before 1066, so omits such rulers as Ethelred II who reigned for 37 years. Queen Elizabeth II overtook her namesake Queen Elizabeth I in June 1996. If she is still on the throne on September 11, 2015, she will have passed Queen Victoria.

US PRESIDENTS

THE 10
LONGEST-SERVING US PRESIDENTS

	President	Period in office years	days
1	Franklin D. Roosevelt	12	39 *
2 =	Grover Cleveland	8#	
=	Dwight D. Eisenhower	8#	
=	Ulysses S. Grant	8#	
=	Andrew Jackson	8#	
=	Thomas Jefferson	8#	
=	James Madison	8#	
=	James Monroe	8#	
=	Ronald Reagan	8#	
=	Woodrow Wilson	8#	

* *Died in office*

Two four-year terms – now the maximum any US President may remain in office

THE 10
FIRST PRESIDENTS OF THE US

	President/dates	Period of office
1	George Washington (1732–99)	1789–97
2	John Adams (1735–1826)	1797–1801
3	Thomas Jefferson (1743–1826)	1801–09
4	James Madison (1751–1836)	1809–17
5	James Monroe (1758–1831)	1817–25
6	John Quincy Adams (1767–1848)	1825–29
7	Andrew Jackson (1767–1845)	1829–37
8	Martin Van Buren (1782–1862)	1837–41
9	William H. Harrison (1773–1841)	1841
10	John Tyler (1790–1862)	1841–45

THE 10
SHORTEST-SERVING US PRESIDENTS

	President	Period in office years	days
1	William H. Harrison		31*
2	James A. Garfield		199*
3	Zachary Taylor	1	127*
4	Warren G. Harding	2	151*
5	Gerald Ford	2	166
6	Millard Fillmore	2	238
7	John F. Kennedy	2	304*
8	Chester A. Arthur	3	165
9	Andrew Johnson	3	323
10	John Tyler	3	332

* *Died in office*

TOP 10
LONGEST-LIVED US PRESIDENTS

	President	Age at death years	months
1	John Adams	90	8
2	Herbert Hoover	90	2
3	Harry S. Truman	88	7
4	James Madison	85	3
5	Thomas Jefferson	83	2
6	Richard Nixon	81	3
7	John Quincy Adams	80	7
8	Martin Van Buren	79	7
9	Dwight D. Eisenhower	78	5
10	Andrew Jackson	78	2

TOP 10 YOUNGEST US PRESIDENTS
(Age on taking office)

❶ Theodore Roosevelt (42 yrs/322 days) ❷ John F. Kennedy (43 yrs/236 days) ❸ Bill Clinton (46 yrs/154 days) ❹ Ulysses S. Grant (46 yrs/236 days) ❺ Grover Cleveland (47 yrs/352 days) ❻ Franklin Pierce (48 yrs/101 days) ❼ James A. Garfield (49 yrs/105 days) ❽ James K. Polk (49 yrs/122 days) ❾ Millard Fillmore (50 yrs/184 days) ❿ John Tyler (51 yrs/8 days)

JOHN F. KENNEDY
His dramatic assassination ended the short period in office of America's second-youngest president.

THE 10
LEAST POPULAR US PRESIDENTS

	President	Survey date	Disapproval rating (%)
1	Richard Nixon	Aug 2, 1974	66
2	Harry S. Truman	Jan, 1952	62
3	George Bush	Jul 31, 1992	60
4	Jimmy Carter	Jun 29, 1979	59
5	Ronald Reagan	Jan 28, 1983	56
6	Bill Clinton	Sep 6–7, 1994	54
7	Lyndon B. Johnson	Mar 10, Aug 7, 1968	52
8=	Franklin D. Roosevelt	Nov, 1938	46
=	Gerald Ford	Apr 18, Nov 21, Dec 12, 1975	46
10	Dwight D. Eisenhower	Mar 27, 1958	36

Source: The Gallup Organization

TOP 10
US PRESIDENTS WITH THE GREATEST PERCENTAGE OF POPULAR VOTE

	President	Year	Winner's total	Loser's total	Winner's percentage
1	T. Roosevelt	1904	7,628,834	5,084,491	60.01
2	Reagan	1984	54,281,858	37,457,215	59.17
3	Hoover	1928	21,392,190	15,016,443	58.76
4	Van Buren	1836	762,678	548,007	58.19
5	Buchanan	1856	1,927,995	1,391,555	58.08
6	F.D. Roosevelt	1932	22,821,857	16,646,622	57.82
7	Eisenhower	1956	35,585,316	26,031,322	57.75
8	Jackson	1832	687,502	530,189	56.46
9	Jackson	1828	647,231	509,097	55.97
10	Grant	1872	3,597,070	2,834,079	55.93

Source: World Almanac and Book of Facts

TOP 10
SHORTEST US PRESIDENTS

	President	Height m	ft	in
1	James Madison	1.63	5	4
2=	Benjamin Harrison	1.68	5	6
=	Martin Van Buren	1.68	5	6
4=	John Adams	1.70	5	7
=	John Quincy Adams	1.70	5	7
=	William McKinley	1.70	5	7
7=	William H. Harrison	1.73	5	8
=	James K. Polk	1.73	5	8
=	Zachary Taylor	1.73	5	8
10=	Ulysses S. Grant	1.74	5	8½
=	Rutherford B. Hayes	1.74	5	8½

TOP 10
TALLEST US PRESIDENTS

	President	Height m	ft	in
1	Abraham Lincoln	1.93	6	4
2	Lyndon B. Johnson	1.91	6	3
3=	Bill Clinton	1.89	6	2½
=	Thomas Jefferson	1.89	6	2½
5=	Chester A. Arthur	1.88	6	2
=	George Bush	1.88	6	2
=	Franklin D. Roosevelt	1.88	6	2
=	George Washington	1.88	6	2
9=	Andrew Jackson	1.85	6	1
=	Ronald Reagan	1.85	6	1

THE 10
MOST POPULAR US PRESIDENTS

	President	Survey date	Approval rating %
1	George Bush	Feb 28, 1991	89
2	Harry S. Truman	May/Jun, 1945	87
3	Franklin D. Roosevelt	Jan, 1942	84
4	John F. Kennedy	Apr 28, 1961	83
5	Dwight D. Eisenhower	Dec 14, 1956	79
6	Lyndon B. Johnson	Dec 5, 1963	78
7	Jimmy Carter	Mar 18, 1977	75
8	Gerald Ford	Aug 16, 1974	71
9	Bill Clinton	Jan 30– Feb 1, 1998	69
10	Ronald Reagan	May 8, 1981; May 16, 1986	68

The Gallup Organization began surveying ratings of US Presidents in October 1938.

Source: The Gallup Organization

TOP 10
OLDEST US PRESIDENTS

	President	Age on taking office years	days		President	Age on taking office years	days
1	Ronald Reagan	69	349	6	Dwight D. Eisenhower	62	98
2	William H. Harrison	68	23	7	Andrew Jackson	61	354
3	James Buchanan	65	315	8	John Adams	61	125
4	George Bush	64	223	9	Gerald Ford	61	26
5	Zachary Taylor	64	100	10	Harry Truman	60	339

HUMAN ACHIEVEMENTS

FIRST EXPLORERS TO LAND IN THE AMERICAS

	Explorer	Nationality	Place explored	Year
1	Christopher Columbus	Italian	West Indies	1492
2	John Cabot	Italian/English	Nova Scotia/Newfoundland	1497
3	Alonso de Hojeda	Spanish	Brazil	1499
4	Vicente Yañez Pinzón	Spanish	Amazon	1500
5	Pedro Alvarez Cabral	Portuguese	Brazil	1500
6	Gaspar Corte Real	Portuguese	Labrador	1500
7	Rodrigo de Bastidas	Spanish	Central America	1501
8	Vasco Nuñez de Balboa	Spanish	Panama	1513
9	Juan Ponce de León	Spanish	Florida	1513
10	Juan Díaz de Solís	Spanish	Río de la Plata	1515

After his voyage of 1492, Columbus made three subsequent journeys to the West Indies and South America. Other expeditions landing on the same West Indian islands have not been included.

THE 10 FIRST MOUNTAINEERS TO CLIMB EVEREST

❶ Edmund Hillary, (New Zealander, May 29, 1953) ❷ Tenzing Norgay, (Nepalese, May 29, 1953) ❸ Jürg Marmet, (Swiss, May 23, 1956) ❹ Ernst Schmied, (Swiss, May 23, 1956) ❺ Hans-Rudolf von Gunten, (Swiss, May 24, 1956) ❻ Adolf Reist, (Swiss, May 24, 1956) ❼ Wang Fu-chou, (Chinese, May 25, 1960) ❽ Chu Ying-hua, (Chinese, May 25, 1960) ❾ Konbu, (Tibetan, May 25, 1960) ❿= Nawang Gombu, (Indian, May 1, 1963), James Whittaker, (American, May 1, 1963)

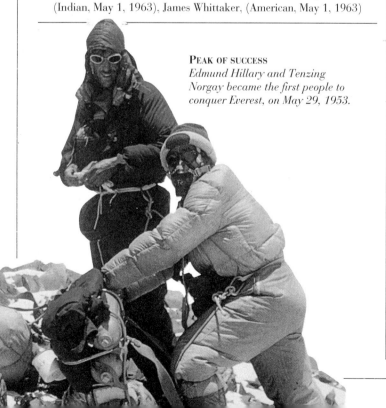

PEAK OF SUCCESS
Edmund Hillary and Tenzing Norgay became the first people to conquer Everest, on May 29, 1953.

FIRST PEOPLE TO GO OVER NIAGARA FALLS AND SURVIVE

	Name	Method	Date
1	Annie Edison Taylor	Barrel	Oct 24, 1901
2	Bobby Leach	Steel barrel	Jul 25, 1911
3	Jean Lussier	Rubber ball fitted with oxygen cylinders	Jul 4, 1928
4	William Fitzgerald (aka Nathan Boya)	Rubber ball	Jul 15, 1961
5	Karel Soucek	Barrel	Jul 3, 1984
6	Steven Trotter	Barrel	Aug 18, 1985
7	Dave Mundy	Barrel	Oct 5, 1985
8=	Peter de Bernardi	Metal container	Sep 28, 1989
=	Jeffrey Petkovich	Metal container	Sep 28, 1989
10	Dave Mundy	Diving bell	Sep 26, 1993

Captain Matthew Webb, the first person to swim the English Channel, was killed on July 24, 1883 attempting to swim the rapids beneath Niagara Falls. Many people have lost their lives attempting to go over the mighty Falls. They include, in 1901, Maud Willard, who was killed when her dog, which she had cajoled into performing the feat with her, retaliated by pressing its nose against the air vent in the barrel, thus suffocating its owner.

Source: Niagara Falls Museum

FIRST CROSS-CHANNEL SWIMMERS

	Swimmer/nationality	Time hr:min	Date
1	Matthew Webb, British	21:45	Aug 24–25, 1875
2	Thomas Burgess, British	22:35	Sep 5–6, 1911
3	Henry Sullivan, American	26:50	Aug 5–6, 1923
4	Enrico Tiraboschi, Italian	16:33	Aug 12, 1923
5	Charles Toth, American	16:58	Sep 8–9, 1923
6	Gertrude Ederle, American	14:39	Aug 6, 1926
7	Millie Corson, American	15:29	Aug 27–28, 1926
8	Arnst Wierkotter, German	12:40	Aug 30, 1926
9	Edward Temme, British	14:29	Aug 5, 1927
10	Mercedes Gleitze, British	15:15	Oct 7, 1927

The first three crossings were from England to France, while the rest were from France to England. Gertrude Ederle was the first woman to swim the Channel, but it was not until September 11, 1951 that American swimmer Florence Chadwick became the first woman to swim from England to France.

THE 10
FIRST PEOPLE TO REACH THE NORTH POLE

Name/nationality	Date
1= Robert Edwin Peary, American	Apr 6, 1909
= Matthew Alexander Henson, American	Apr 6, 1909
= Ooqueah, Eskimo	Apr 6, 1909
= Ootah, Eskimo	Apr 6, 1909
= Egingwah, Eskimo	Apr 6, 1909
= Seegloo, Eskimo	Apr 6, 1909

THE 10
FIRST PEOPLE TO REACH THE SOUTH POLE

Name/nationality	Date
1= Roald Amundsen*, Norwegian	Dec 14, 1911
= Olav Olavsen Bjaaland, Norwegian	Dec 14, 1911
= Helmer Julius Hanssen, Norwegian	Dec 14, 1911
= Helge Sverre Hassel, Norwegian	Dec 14, 1911
= Oscar Wisting, Norwegian	Dec 14, 1911
6= Robert Falcon Scott*, British	Jan 17, 1912
= Henry Robertson Bowers, British	Jan 17, 1912
= Edgar Evans, British	Jan 17, 1912
= Lawrence Edward Grace Oates, British	Jan 17, 1912
= Edward Adrian Wilson, British	Jan 17, 1912

* *Expedition leader*

Scott's British Antarctic Expedition was organized with its avowed goal "to reach the South Pole and to secure for the British Empire the honour of this achievement." Meanwhile, Amundsen also set out for the Pole. When Scott eventually reached his goal, he discovered that the Norwegians had beaten him by 33 days. Scott's entire team died on the return journey.

Name/nationality	Date
7= Pavel Afanaseyevich Geordiyenko, Soviet	Apr 23, 1948
= Mikhail Yemel'yenovich Ostrekin, Soviet	Apr 23, 1948
= Pavel Kononovich Sen'ko, Soviet	Apr 23, 1948
= Mikhail Mikhaylovich Somov, Soviet	Apr 23, 194

TOP 10
CELEBRITIES ON *PEOPLE* MAGAZINE COVERS

Celebrity	Covers
1 Princess Diana	53
2 = Duchess of York (Sarah Ferguson)	14
= Elizabeth Taylor	14
4 = Michael Jackson	13
= Jacqueline Kennedy Onassis	13
6 Cher	10
7 John Travolta	8
8 = Farrah Fawcett	7
= Olivia Newton-John	7
10= Jane Fonda	6
= John Ritter	6

Source: People *magazine*

THE 10
FIRST *TIME* MAGAZINE "MEN OF THE YEAR"

Recipient	Year		Recipient	Year
1 Charles Lindbergh (1902–74), US aviator	1927		6 Franklin D. Roosevelt (1882–1945), US President	1932
2 Walter P. Chrysler (1875–1940), US businessman	1928		7 Hugh S. Johnson (1882–1942), US soldier	1933
3 Owen D. Young (1874–1962), US lawyer	1929		8 Franklin D. Roosevelt, US President	1934
4 Mohandas K. Gandhi (1869–1948), Indian politician	1930		9 Haile Salassie (1891–1975), Emperor of Ethiopia	1935
5 Pierre Laval (1883–1945), French President	1931		10 Wallis Simpson (1896–1986), Duchess of Windsor	1936

THE 10
LATEST *TIME* MAGAZINE "MEN OF THE YEAR"

Recipient	Year
1 Dr. Andrew S. Grove (1936–), CEO of Intel (microchip mfg.)	1997
2 Dr. David Ho (1952–), AIDS researcher	1996
3 Newt Gingrich (1943–), US politician	1995
4 Pope John Paul II (1920–)	1994
5 Yasir Arafat (1929–), F.W. de Klerk (1936–), Nelson Mandela (1918–), Yitzhak Rabin (1922–95), "Peacemakers"	1993
6 Bill Clinton (1946–), US President	1992
7 George Bush (1924–), US President	1991
8 Ted Turner (1938–), US businessman	1990
9 Mikhail Gorbachev (1931–), Soviet leader	1989
10 "Endangered Earth"	1988

Time magazine's "Man of the Year" may be one man, a group of men (such as 15 US scientists in 1960), a couple (General and Madame Chiang Kai-shek in 1937), a woman (as, in 1952, Queen Elizabeth II), a group of women (12 were listed in 1975), a machine (in 1982 a computer), or even (as in 1988) "Endangered Earth."

Source: Time *magazine*

60 NOBEL PRIZE WINNERS

NOBEL PRIZE-WINNING COUNTRIES*

	Country	Phy	Che	Ph/Med	Lit	Pce	Eco	Total
1	US	65	42	75	10	18	25	235
2	UK	21	24	24	8	11	7	95
3	Germany	19	27	15	6	4	1	72
4	France	12	7	7	12	9	1	48
5	Sweden	4	4	7	7	5	2	29
6	Switzerland	2	5	6	2	3	–	18
7	USSR	7	1	2	3	2	1	16
8	Italy	3	1	3	6	1	–	14
9	Netherlands	6	3	2	–	1	1	13
10	Denmark	3	–	5	3	1	–	12

Phy – Physics; Che – Chemistry; Ph/Med – Physiology or Medicine; Lit – Literature; Pce – Peace; Eco – Economic Sciences. Germany includes the united country before 1948, West Germany to 1990, and the united country since 1990.

* In addition, institutions, such as the Red Cross, have been awarded 16 Nobel Peace Prizes

LATEST WOMEN TO WIN A NOBEL PRIZE

	Winner	Country	Prize	Year
1	Jody Williams*	US	Peace	1997
2	Christiane Nüsslein-Volhard#	Germany	Phys/Med	1995
3	Toni Morrison	US	Literature	1993
4	Rigoberta Menchu	Guatemala	Peace	1992
5 =	Nadine Gordimer	South Africa	Literature	1991
=	Aung San Suu Kyi	Myanmar	Peace	1991
7	Gertrude B. Ellinson†	US	Phys/Med	1988
8	Rita Levi-Montalcini★	Italy	Phys/Med	1986
9	Barbara McClintock	US	Phys/Med	1983
10	Mother Teresa	Macedonia	Peace	1979

* Shared with International Campaign to Ban Landmines

 # Shared with Eric F. Wieschaus and Edward B. Lewis

† Shared with Sir James Black and George H. Hitchings

★ Shared with Stanley Cohen

- The youngest-ever Nobel prizewinner was Australian-born Lawrence Bragg, who won the Physics Prize jointly with his father in 1915, at the age of 25.
- Rudyard Kipling was 41 when he won the Literature Prize in 1907.
- Linus Pauling uniquely won in two completely different categories at completely different times: the Chemistry Prize in 1954 and the Peace Prize in 1962.
- Joint Peace Prize winner Mairead Corrigan was 32 at the time of receiving her 1976 award.

SNAP FACTS

LATEST WINNERS OF THE NOBEL PEACE PRIZE

Prize year	Winner	Country
1997 =	International Campaign to Ban Landmines	
=	Jody Williams (1950–)	US
1996 =	Carlos Filipe Ximenes Belo (1948–)	East Timor
=	José Ramos-Horta (1949–)	East Timor
1995	Joseph Rotblat (1908–)	UK
1994 =	Yasir Arafat (1929–)	Palestine
=	Shimon Peres (1923–)	Israel
=	Itzhak Rabin (1922–95)	Israel
1993 =	Nelson Rolihlahla Mandela (1918–)	South Africa
=	Frederik Willem de Klerk (1936–)	South Africa

LATEST WINNERS OF THE NOBEL PRIZE FOR ECONOMIC SCIENCES

Prize year	Winner	Country
1997 =	Professor Robert C. Merton (1944–)	US
=	Professor Myron S. Scholes (1941–)	US
1996 =	James A. Mirrlees (1936–)	UK
=	Professor William Vickrey (1914–)	Canada
1995	Robert E. Lucas (1937–)	US
1994 =	John C. Harsanyi (1920–)	Hungary/ US
=	Reinhard Selten (1930–)	Germany
=	John F. Nash (1928–)	US
1993 =	Robert W. Fogel (1926–)	US
=	Douglas C. North (1920–)	US

The Nobel Prize for Economic Sciences was first awarded in 1969. It is presented by the Royal Swedish Academy of Sciences.

THE 10

LATEST WINNERS OF THE NOBEL PRIZE FOR PHYSIOLOGY OR MEDICINE

Prize year	Winner	Country
1997	Stanley B. Prusiner (1942–)	US
1996	= Peter C. Doherty (1940–)	Australia
	= Rolf M. Zinkernagel (1944–)	Switzerland
1995	= Christiane Nüsslein-Volhard (1942–)	Germany
	= Eric F. Wieschaus (1947–)	US
	= Edward B. Lewis (1918–)	US
1994	= Alfred G. Gilman (1941–)	US
	= Martin Rodbell (1925–)	US
1993	= Richard J. Roberts (1943–)	US
	= Phillip A. Sharp (1944–)	US

THE 10

LATEST WINNERS OF THE NOBEL PRIZE FOR CHEMISTRY

Prize year	Winner	Country
1997	= Paul D. Boyer (1918–)	US
	= John E. Walker (1941–)	UK
	= Jens C. Skou (1918–)	Denmark
1996	= Sir Harold W. Kroto (1939–)	UK
	= Richard E. Smalley (1943–)	US
1995	= Paul Crutze (1933–)	Netherlands
	= Mario Molina (1943–)	Mexico
	= Frank Sherwood Rowland (1927–)	US
1994	= George A. Olah (1927–)	Hungary/ US
1993	= Michael Smith (1932–)	UK/ Canada
	= Kary Banks Mullis (1944–)	US

THE 10

LATEST WINNERS OF THE NOBEL PRIZE FOR PHYSICS

Prize year	Winner	Country
1997	= Steven Chu (1948–)	US
	= William D. Phillips (1948–)	US
	= Professor Claude Cohen-Tannoudji (1933–)	France
1996	= David M. Lee (1931–)	US
	= Douglas D. Osheroff (1945–)	US
	= Robert C. Richardson (1937–)	US
1995	= Martin L. Perl (1927–)	US
	= Frederick Reines (1918–)	US
1994	= Bertram Neville Brockhouse (1918-)	Canada
	= Clifford G. Shull (1915–)	US

THE 10

LATEST WINNERS OF THE NOBEL PRIZE FOR LITERATURE

Prize year	Winner	Country
1997	Dario Fo (1926–)	Italy
1996	Wislawa Szymborska (1923–)	Poland
1995	Seamus Heaney (1939–)	Ireland
1994	Kenzaburo Oe (1935–)	Japan
1993	Toni Morrison (1931–)	US
1992	Derek Walcott (1930–)	Saint Lucia
1991	Nadine Gordimer (1923–)	South Africa
1990	Octavio Paz (1914–98)	Mexico
1989	Camilo José Cela (1916–)	Spain
1988	Naguib Mahfouz (1911–)	Egypt

THE 10

FIRST WOMEN TO WIN A NOBEL PRIZE

	Winner	Country	Prize	Year
1	Marie Curie* (1867–1934)	Poland	Physics	1903
2	Bertha von Suttner (1843–1914)	Austria	Peace	1905
3	Selma Lagerlöf (1858–1940)	Sweden	Literature	1909
4	Marie Curie (1867–1934)	Poland	Chemistry	1911
5	Grazia Deledda (1875–1936)	Italy	Literature	1926#
6	Sigrid Undset (1882–1949)	Norway	Literature	1928
7	Jane Addams† (1860–1935)	US	Peace	1931
8	Irène Joliot-Curie★ (1897–1956)	France	Chemistry	1935
9	Pearl Buck (1892–1973)	US	Literature	1938
10	Gabriela Mistral (1899–1957)	Chile	Literature	1945

* *Shared half with husband Pierre Curie; other half to Henri Becquerel*

\# *Awarded 1927*

† *Shared with Nicholas Murray Butler*

★ *Shared with husband Frédéric Joliot-Curie*

THE GOOD & THE BAD

THE 10

COUNTRIES WITH THE HIGHEST CRIME RATES

	Country	Reported crime rate per 100,000 population
1	Surinam	17,819
2	St. Kitts and Nevis	15,468
3	Gibraltar	14,970
4	New Zealand	14,496
5	Sweden	13,750
	US	*5,278*

	Country	Reported crime rate per 100,000 population
6	Canada	13,297
7	US Virgin Islands	10,441
8	Denmark	10,399
9	The Netherlands	10,181
10	Guam	10,080

THE 10

COUNTRIES WITH THE LOWEST CRIME RATES

	Country	Reported crime rate per 100,000 population
1	Togo	11.0
2	Nepal	13.0
3	Guinea	18.4
4=	Dem. Rep. of Congo	32.0
=	Niger	32.0
6	Mali	33.0
7	Burkina Faso	41.0
8	Bangladesh	64.0
9	Côte d'Ivoire	67.0
10	Burundi	84.0

There are just 13 countries in the world with reported crime rates of fewer than 100 per 100,000 inhabitants.

TOP 10 COUNTRIES WITH THE MOST BURGLARIES
(No. of burglaries in 1996)

❶ US (2,501,524) ❷ UK (651,444) ❸ Poland (305,703)
❹ Australia (269,554) ❺ Russia (268,000) ❻ Canada (242,132)
❼ France (236,272) ❽ Italy (230,258) ❾ Japan (223,590)
❿ Germany (195,801)

BRASS KNUCKLES

T H E   1 0

FBI "MOST WANTED" FUGITIVES, 1998

1 Ramon Eduardo Arellano-Felix
(b. August 31, 1964)

Drug smuggling.

2 Harry Joseph Bowman
(b. July 17, 1949)

Violent racketeering, murder, bombing, drug trafficking.

3 Lamen Khalifa Fhimah
(b. April 4, 1956)

Blowing up PanAm flight over Lockerbie, 1988. Up to $4,000,000 reward.

4 Victor Manuel Gerena
(b. June 24, 1958)

Bank robbery and armed robbery in 1983.

5 Glen Stewart Godwin
(b. June 26, 1958)

Escape from Folsom State Prison (June 30,1987), where he was serving 25 years for murder.

6 Abdel Basset Ali Al-Megrahi
(b. April 1, 1952)

Blowing up PanAm flight over Lockerbie, 1988. Up to $4,000,000 reward.

7 Eric Robert Rudolph
(b. September 19, 1966)

Bombing a clinic in Birmingham, Alabama, on January 29, 1998.

8 Augustin Vasquez-Mendoza
(b. October 1, 1969)

Murder of Drug Enforcement Administration Special Agent. Total reward of $100,000.

9 Arthur Lee Washington, Jr.
(b. November 30, 1949)

Attempted murder of a state trooper.

10 Donald Eugene Webb (b. July 14, 1931)

Murder in 1980 of police chief.

Since its inception on March 14, 1950 by FBI Director J. Edgar Hoover, the FBI's "10 Most Wanted Fugitives" Program has been used to publicize a wide variety of fugitives sought for many different crimes. When a fugitive is taken off the list, another who fulfills the criteria may be subsequently added. The list is not ranked in any special order (here, it is arranged alphabetically). The criteria used for selections are that the individual must have a lengthy record of committing serious crimes and/or be considered a particularly dangerous menace to society, and it must be believed that the nationwide publicity afforded by the program can be of assistance in apprehending the fugitive.

ARREST

CARS MOST STOLEN IN THE US, 1996

Car	Stolen
1 Chrysler Jeep Grand Cherokee	1,978
2 Honda Accord	1,629
3 Toyota Camry	1,447
4 Ford Explorer	1,427
5 Toyota Corolla	1,136
6 Ford Taurus	1,031
7 Chevrolet Cavalier	1,001
8 Chrysler Dodge Neon	925
9 Nissan Sentra/200SX	894
10 Nissan Maxima	893

Source: Department of Transportation – National Highway Traffic Safety Administration

MOST COMMON REASONS FOR ARREST IN THE US

	Offense	Rate*	Arrests (1996)
1	Drug abuse violations	594.3	1,128,647
2	Larceny-theft	577.3	1,096,488
3	Driving under the influence	533.9	1,013,932
4	Disorderly conduct	330.1	626,918
5	Drunkenness	275.3	522,869
6	Liquor laws	258.6	491,176
7	Aggravated assault	204.1	387,571
8	Fraud	171.0	324,776
9	Burglary	139.1	264,193
10	Vandalism	123.3	234,215
	Total (including others not in Top 10)	5,838.2	11,088,352

* Per 100,000 inhabitants

COUNTRIES WITH THE MOST CAR THEFTS

	Country	Car thefts (1996)
1	US	1,395,192
2	Japan	687,960
3	UK	536,065
4	France	344,860
5	Italy	317,897
6	Germany	225,787
7	Canada	178,850
8	Australia	122,931
9	Russia	113,916*
10	Switzerland	83,782

* 1995 figure (latest available)

POLICE & PRISONS

TOP 10

COUNTRIES WITH THE MOST PRISONERS

	Country	Prisoners*
1	US	1,630,940
2	Russia	1,051,515
3	Germany	71,047
4	Poland	57,320
5	England and Wales	55,537
6	France	54,014
7	Italy	48,747
8	Spain	42,105
9	Japan	40,389
10	Canada	33,785

* In latest year for which figures are available

If reranked according to the incarceration rate per 1,000, Russia takes the lead, with 7.1, and the US a close second on 6.2 per 1,000. The rate among the other countries is scarcely more than one per 1,000.

TOP 10

LARGEST PRISONS IN THE UK

	Prison	Inmates
1	Walton, Liverpool	1,467
2	Wormwood Scrubs, London	1,360
3	Barlinnie, Glasgow	1,150
4	Armley, Leeds	1,148
5	Doncaster	1,042
6	Winson Green, Birmingham	1,023
7	Strangeways, Manchester	999
8	Holme House, Cleveland	945
9	Pentonville, London	920
10	Durham	916

THE CITY'S FINEST
New York's police force is by far the largest of any US city.

TOP 10

COUNTRIES WITH THE MOST POLICE OFFICERS

	Country	Population per police officer
1	Angola	14*
2	Kuwait	80
3	Nicaragua	90*
4	Brunei	100
5=	Nauru	110
=	Cape Verde	110
7=	Antigua and Barbuda	120
=	Mongolia	120
=	Seychelles	120
10=	Iraq	140
=	United Arab Emirates	140
	US	*318*

* Including civilian militia

Police personnel figures generally include only full-time paid officials and exclude clerical and volunteer staff. However, there are variations around the world in the way in which these categories are defined.

TOP 10

LARGEST PRISONS IN THE US

	Prison	Capacity
1	Mississippi State Penitentiary, Parchman, Mississippi	5,369
2	Louisana State Penitentiary, Angola, Louisiana	5,108
3	Coffield Unit, Tennessee Colony, Texas	4,032
4	Men's Colony, San Luis Obispo, California	3,859
5	Federal Correctional Institution, Fort Dix, New Jersey	3,683
6	Beto Unit, Tennessee Colony, Texas	3,364
7	California State Prison, San Quentin, California	3,286
8	Clements Unit, Amarillo, Texas	3,198
9	Eastern Correctional Institution, Westover, Maryland	3,180
10	Michael Unit, Tennessee Colony, Texas	3,114

Source: American Correctional Association

TOP 10

LARGEST FEDERAL CORRECTIONAL INSTITUTIONS IN THE US

	Institutions	Location	Rated capacity
1	Federal Correctional Institution	Fort Dix, New Jersey	3,683
2=	Federal Correctional Institution	Beaumont, Texas	1,536
=	Federal Correctional Institution (Medium Security)	Coleman, Florida	1,536
=	Federal Correctional Institution	Elkton, Ohio	1,536
=	Federal Correctional Institution	Forrest City, Arkansas	1,536
=	Federal Correctional Institution	Yazoo City, Mississippi	1,536
7	US Penitentiary	Atlanta, Georgia	1,429
8	Federal Detention Center	Miami, Florida	1,259
9	US Penitentiary	Leavenworth, Kansas	1,197
10	Federal Correctional Institution	Beckley, West Virginia	1,152

Source: Bureau of Federal Prisons

TOP 10

COUNTRIES WITH THE FEWEST POLICE OFFICERS

	Country	Population per police officer
1	Maldives	35,710
2	Canada	8,640
3	Rwanda	4,650
4	Côte d'Ivoire	4,640
5	The Gambia	3,310
6	Benin	3,250
7	Madagascar	2,900
8	Central African Republic	2,740
9	Bangladesh	2,560
10	Niger	2,350*

* *Including paramilitary forces*

The saying "there's never a cop around when you need one" is nowhere truer than in the countries appearing in this list, where the police are remarkably thin on the ground. There are various possible and contradictory explanations for these ratios: countries may be so law-abiding that there is simply no need for large numbers of police officers, or a force may be so underfunded and inefficient as to be virtually irrelevant.

TOP 10

US CITIES WITH THE MOST POLICE OFFICERS

	City	Officers
1	New York	37,090
2	Los Angeles	9,148
3	Philadelphia	6,455
4	Houston	5,252
5	Detroit	3,917
6	Washington	3,611
7	Baltimore	3,081
8	Dallas	2,822
9	Phoenix	2,255
10	Boston	2,218

Source: FBI Uniform Crime Reports

TOP 10

MOST REPORTED INCIDENTS OF POLICE USE OF FORCE IN THE US

	Force	Rate per 1,000 sworn officers
1	Handcuff/leg restraint	490.4
2	Bodily force (arm, foot, leg)	272.2
3	Come-alongs*	226.8
4	Unholstering weapon	129.9
5	Swarm#	126.7
6	Twist locks/wrist locks	80.9
7	Firm grip	57.7
8	Chemical agents (mace or cap-stun)	36.2
9	Batons	36.0
10	Flashlights	21.7

* *Use of restraint rather than handcuffs.*

\# *Swarming is when several officers surround, immobilize, and handcuff a suspect.*

TOP 10

US STATES WITH THE HIGHEST RATE OF PRISON INCARCERATION

	State	Rate*
1	District of Columbia	1,373
2	Texas	677
3	Louisiana	651
4	Oklahoma	599
5	South Carolina	542
6=	Nevada	505
=	Mississippi	505
8	Alabama	499
9	Arizona	484
10	Georgia	476

* *Of sentenced prisoners in state and federal institutions per 100,000 resident population, as of June 30, 1997*

Source: US Department of Justice

TOP 10

US STATES WITH THE MOST PRISON INMATES*

	State	Inmates
1	California	153,010
2	Texas	136,599
3	New York	69,530
4	Florida	64,713
5	Ohio	47,248
6	Michigan	43,784
7	Illinois	40,425
8	Georgia	36,329
9	Pennsylvania	34,703
10	North Carolina	32,334

* *As of June 30, 1997*

Source: Department of Justice

• The first police force was established in Paris in 1667 • Police dogs were first introduced in Scotland in 1816 • The Texas Rangers, established in 1835, were the first US state police force • In 1893 in Detroit, Marie Owen became the first policewoman • In 1899 in Akron, Ohio, an electric-powered vehicle was the first police car

SNAP FACTS

MURDER FILE

MOST COMMON MURDER WEAPONS AND METHODS IN THE US

	Weapon/method	Victims (1996)
1	Handguns	8,594
2	Knives or cutting instruments	2,142
3	"Personal weapons" (hands, feet, fists, etc.)	939
4	Firearms (type not stated)	911
5	Blunt objects (hammers, clubs, etc.)	733
6	Shotguns	673
7	Rifles	546
8	Strangulation	243
9	Fire	151
10	Asphyxiation	92

In 1996 "other weapons or weapons not stated" were used in 726 murders. Relatively rare methods included narcotics (32 cases), drowning (24), explosives (14), and poison (8). Total murders amounted to 15,848, as compared with 20,232 the previous year. The proportion involving guns has actually gone down this century – for example, 72 percent in 1920 as against 68 percent in 1996.

WORST METROPOLITAN AREAS FOR VIOLENT CRIME*

	Metropolitan area	Violent crimes per 1,000 people (1995)
1	Miami-Dade, FL	18.9
2=	Los Angeles-Long Beach, CA	14.2
=	Gainesville, GA	14.2
4=	New York, NY	13.9
=	Baton Rouge, LA	13.9
6	Baltimore, MD	13.4
7=	New Orleans, LA	13.3
=	Lawton, OK	13.3
9	Sioux City, IA	12.7
10	Memphis, TN	12.5

Murder, rape, aggravated assault, and robbery

THE 10 WORST CITIES IN THE US FOR MURDER

	1986			1996	
	City	Murders		Murders	City
1	New York	1,582	1	983	New York
2	Los Angeles	834	2	789	Chicago
3	Chicago	744	3	709	Los Angeles
4	Detroit	648	4	428	Detroit
5	Houston	408	5	414	Philadelphia
6	Dallas	347	6	397	Washington
7	Philadelphia	343	7	351	New Orleans
8	Baltimore	240	8	328	Baltimore
9	New Orleans	197	9	261	Houston
10	Washington	194	10	217	Dallas

Source: FBI Uniform Crime Reports

COUNTRIES WITH THE LOWEST MURDER RATES

	Country	Murders p.a. per 100,000 population
1 =	Argentina	0.1
=	Brunei	0.1
3 =	Burkina Faso	0.2
=	Niger	0.2
5 =	Guinea	0.5
=	Guinea-Bissau	0.5
=	Iran	0.5
8 =	Finland	0.6
=	Saudi Arabia	0.6
10 =	Cameroon	0.7
=	Ireland	0.7
=	Mongolia	0.7

WORST STATES FOR MURDER IN THE US

	State	Firearms used	Total murders
1	California	2,061	2,916
2	Texas	962	1,476
3	Illinois*	585	765
4	Louisiana	547	704
5	Michigan	480	695
6	Pennsylvania	493	665
7	North Carolina	397	615
8	Georgia	445	610
9	Maryland	424	578
10	Virginia	322	490

Provisional figures

Of the 9,514 murders committed in the Top 10 states in 1996, firearms were used in 7,616, or 80 percent of the cases.

• The worst murderess and most prolific poisoner of modern times was Susannah Olah, a Hungarian nurse who killed as many as 100 people in the 1920s. Captured in 1929, she committed suicide.

• The worst serial killer of the 20th century is believed to be Pedro Alonzo (or Armando) López, who killed more than 300 girls in Colombia, Ecuador, and Peru. Captured in 1980, he was sentenced to life imprisonment.

SNAP FACTS

THE 10
YEARS WITH THE FEWEST MURDERS IN THE US*

	Year	No. of victims
1	1920	5,815
2	1944	6,675
3	1943	6,823
4	1921	7,090
5	1922	7,381
6	1955	7,418
7	1951	7,495
8	1945	7,547
9	1923	7,557
10	1956	7,629

* Since 1920

There were fewer than 300 murders a year in the US in the first five years of the 20th century. The inexorable rise that followed was not a steady progression, however: figures of more than 10,000 a year were recorded from 1930–36, totals that were not exceeded again until 1965.

THE 10
COUNTRIES WITH THE HIGHEST MURDER RATES

	Country	Murders p.a. per 100,000 population
1	Swaziland	87.8
2	Bahamas	52.6
3	Monaco	36.0
4	Philippines	30.1
5	Guatemala	27.4
6	Jamaica	20.9
7	Russia	19.9*
8	Botswana	19.5
9	Zimbabwe	17.9
10	Netherlands	14.8
	US	8.4

* Includes attempted murder

TOP 10
REASONS FOR MURDER IN THE US

	Reason	Murders (1996)
1	Arguments	4,383
2	Robbery	1,493
3	Juvenile gang killings	855
4	Narcotic drug laws	819
5	Arguments over money or property	327
6	Brawl due to influence of alcohol	253
7	Romantic triangle	187
8	Brawl due to influence of narcotics	161
9	Burglary	117
10	Arson	95

A total of 15,848 murders was reported in 1996, including 2,208 without a specified reason and 4,582 that were unknown.

Source: FBI Uniform Crime Reports

TOP 10
RELATIONSHIPS OF MURDER VICTIMS TO PRINCIPAL SUSPECTS IN THE US

	Relationship	Victims (1996)
1	Acquaintance	4,797
2	Stranger	2,321
3	Wife	679
4	Friend	478
5	Girlfriend	424
6	Son	261
7	Daughter	207
8	Husband	206
9	Boyfriend	163
10	Neighbor	162

These offenses – which remain in similar order from year to year – accounted for 9,698, or over 60 percent of the 15,848 murders committed in the US in 1996.

THE 10
WORST YEARS FOR GUN MURDERS IN THE US

	Year	Victims		Year	Victims
1	1993	16,136	6	1990	13,035
2	1994	15,546	7	1981	12,523
3	1992	15,489	8	1974	12,474
4	1991	14,373	9	1975	12,061
5	1980	13,650	10	1989	11,832

BIRTH OF A GANGSTER

The mobster Al Capone, whose name became virtually synonymous with crime in the US in the 1920s, was born in Brooklyn on January 17, 1899. He gained a reputation as a thug, and acquired the nickname "Scarface." He moved to Chicago where he is known to have killed his rival Jim Colosimo, as well as many others, as battles were fought between gangs for control of the city, with Capone emerging as eventual victor. Capone literally got away with murder on numerous occasions, and organized such gangland killings as the legendary St. Valentine's Day Massacre of February 14, 1929. He was finally jailed in 1931 – but for income tax evasion rather than murder or the many other crimes of which he was guilty. Released in 1939, Al Capone died insane in 1947.

100 YEARS AGO

CAPITAL PUNISHMENT

THE 10

US STATES WITH THE MOST WOMEN ON DEATH ROW

	State	No. under death sentence*
1	California	8
2 =	Florida	6
=	Texas	6
4 =	Alabama	4
=	Illinois	4
=	Oklahoma	4
=	Pennsylvania	4
8	North Carolina	3
9 =	Mississippi	2
=	Missouri	2

* As of December 31, 1996, when a total of 48 women were on death row

Source: U.S. Department of Justice

THE 10

STATES WITH THE MOST EXECUTIONS 1977–97

	State	Executions		State	Executions
1	Texas	144	6	Georgia	22
2	Virginia	46	7 =	Alabama	16
3	Florida	39	=	Arkansas	16
4	Missouri	29	9	South Carolina	13
5	Louisiana	24	10	Illinois	10

Source: U.S. Department of Justice

SING SING'S FIRST FEMALE ELECTROCUTION VICTIM

On March 20, 1899, the famous electric chair at Sing Sing Prison, Ossining, New York, claimed its 26th victim when 44-year-old Martha M. Place of Brooklyn, New York, was executed. The first female to be electrocuted, she had been convicted of the murder on February 7, 1898, of her stepdaughter Ida. It was not until January 12, 1928, that the second female victim, Ruth Snyder, was electrocuted. On June 19, 1953, Ethel Rosenberg, who had been found guilty of spying for the Soviet Union, became the 8th and last woman to be electrocuted at Sing Sing. Her husband, Julius, had been electrocuted in the same chair on the same day.

THE 10

NAZI WAR CRIMINALS HANGED AT NUREMBERG

1	Joachim von Ribbentrop
2	Field Marshal Wilhelm von Keitel
3	General Ernst Kaltenbrunner
4	Reichminister Alfred Rosenburg
5	Reichminister Hans Frank
6	Reichminister Wilhelm Frick
7	Gauleiter Julius Streicher
8	Reichminister Fritz Sauckel
9	Colonel-General Alfred Jodl
10	Gauleiter Artur von Seyss-Inquart

Following the International Military Tribunal trials from November 20, 1945 to August 31, 1946, 12 Nazi war criminals were found guilty and sentenced to death. They included Martin Bormann, who had escaped and was tried in absentia, and Herman Goering, who committed suicide.

THE 10

LAST PEOPLE EXECUTED AT THE TOWER OF LONDON

	Name	Executed
1	Josef Jakobs	Aug 15, 1941

A German army sergeant who was caught when he parachuted into England wearing civilian clothes and carrying an identity card in the name of James Rymer. Following General Court Martial, he was shot at 7:15 a.m.– the only spy executed at the Tower during the course of World War II.

2	Y.L. Zender-Hurwitz	Apr 11, 1916

A spy of Peruvian descent charged with sending information to Germany about British troop movements.

3	Albert Meyer	Dec 2, 1915

Like Ries, Meyer was a German spy posing as a traveling salesman.

4	Irving Guy Ries	Oct 27, 1915

A German traveling salesman who was sentenced to death on spying charges.

5	Georg T. Breeckow	Oct 26, 1915

Posing as an American (Reginald Rowland) with a forged passport, he was caught when he sent a parcel containing secret messages, but addressed in German style, with country and town name preceding that of the street.

6	Fernando Buschman	Oct 19, 1915

Posing as a Dutch violinist, he spied while offering entertainment at Royal Navy bases.

7	Agusto Alfredo Roggen	Sep 17, 1915

A German who attempted to escape the death penalty by claiming to be Uruguayan. He was found guilty of spying on the tests of a new torpedo at Loch Lomond, then sending the information in invisible ink.

8	Ernst Waldemar Melin	Sep 10, 1915

A German spy who was shot after general court martial during World War I.

9	Haike Marinus Petrus Janssen	Jul 30, 1915

An accomplice of Roos who used the same methods. The two were tried together and executed the same day. Janssen was shot 10 minutes after Roos, at 6:10 a.m.

10	Wilhelm Johannes Roos	Jul 30, 1915

Roos was a Dutchman who sent coded messages to a firm in Holland detailing ship movements in British ports. Roos was the 3rd spy of World War I to be executed at the Tower of London. He was shot.

100 YEARS AGO

THE 10

YEARS WITH THE MOST EXECUTIONS IN THE US*

	Year	Executions
1	1935	199
2	1936	195
3	1938	190
4	1934	168
5=	1933	160
=	1939	160
7	1930	155
8=	1931	153
=	1947	153
10	1937	147

* All offenses, 1930 to 1997

The total number of executions in the US fell below three figures for the first time this century in 1952, when 82 prisoners were executed, and below double figures in 1965, with seven executions. Only one prisoner was executed in 1966, in 1977 (when Gary Gilmore became the first person for 10 years to receive the death penalty), and in 1981. There were no executions at all between 1968 and 1976, but double figures were recorded again in 1984 (21 executions) and in all subsequent years.

THE 10

FIRST COUNTRIES TO ABOLISH CAPITAL PUNISHMENT

	Country	Abolished
1	Russia	1826
2	Venezuela	1863
3	Portugal	1867
4=	Brazil	1882
=	Costa Rica	1882
6	Ecuador	1897
7	Panama	1903
8	Norway	1905
9	Uruguay	1907
10	Colombia	1910

Some countries abolished capital punishment in peacetime only, or for all crimes except treason, although several countries later reinstated the penalty. Some countries retained capital punishment on their statute books, but effectively abolished it: the last execution in Liechtenstein, for example, took place in 1795, and in Mexico in 1946.

THE 10

FIRST ELECTROCUTIONS AT SING SING PRISON, NEW YORK

	Name	Electrocuted
1	Harris A. Smiler	Jul 7, 1891
2	James Slocum	Jul 7, 1891
3	Joseph Wood	Jul 7, 1891
4	Schihick Judigo	Jul 7, 1891
5	Martin D. Loppy	Dec 7, 1891
6	Charles McElvaine	Feb 8, 1892
7	Jeremiah Cotte	Mar 28, 1892
8	Fred McGuire	Dec 19, 1892
9	James L. Hamilton	Apr 3, 1893
10	Carlyle Harris	May 8, 1893

The electric chair was installed in Sing Sing Prison, New York, in 1891. By the end of the 19th century, 29 inmates had been executed by this means.

THE 10

US STATES WITH THE MOST PRISONERS ON DEATH ROW

	State	Prisoners under death sentence*
1	California	454
2	Texas	438
3	Florida	373
4	Pennsylvania	203
5	Ohio	170
6=	Illinois	161
=	North Carolina	161
8	Alabama	151
9	Oklahoma	133
10	Arizona	121

* As of December 31, 1996

A total of 3,219 prisoners were under sentence of death, a 5 percent increase from year end 1995.

Source: U.S. Department of Justice

THE 10

FIRST EXECUTIONS BY LETHAL INJECTION IN THE US

	Name	Executed
1	Charles Brooks	Dec 7, 1982
2	James Autry	Mar 14, 1984
3	Ronald O'Bryan	Mar 31, 1984
4	Thomas Barefoot	Oct 30 1984
5	Doyle Skillern	Jan 16, 1985
6	Stephen Morin	Mar 13, 1985
7	Jesse De La Rosa	May 15, 1985
8	Charles Milton	Jun 25, 1985
9	Henry Porter	Jul 9, 1985
10	Charles Rumbaugh	Sep 11 1985

Although Oklahoma was the first State to legalize execution by lethal injection, it was not used there until 1990. All of the above were executed in Texas.

Source: Death Penalty Information Center

BATTLES & MEDALS

THE AMERICAN CIVIL WAR
There were more than 50,000 casualties in the Battle of Gettysburg, Pennsylvania, on July 1–3, 1863. Its site is now preserved as a National Battlefield. The action was the bloodiest of the Civil War, itself the second most devastating war in US history.

THE 10

WORST US CIVIL WAR BATTLES

	Battle/dates	Casualties*
1	Gettysburg, Jul 1–3, 1863	51,116
2	Battles of the Seven Days, Jun 25–Jul 1, 1862	36,463
3	Chickamauga, Sep 19–20, 1863	34,624
4	Chancellorsville/ Fredericksburg, May 1–4, 1863	29,609
5	Wilderness, 5–7 May 1862	25,416 #
6	Manassas/Chantilly, Aug 27–Sep 2, 1862	25,340
7	Stone's River, Dec 31, 1862–Jan 1, 1863	24,645
8	Shiloh, Apr 6–7, 1862	23,741
9	Antietam, Sep 17, 1862	22,726
10	Fredericksburg, Dec 13, 1862	17,962

* *Killed, missing, and wounded*
\# *Confederate totals estimated*

THE 10

FIRST NATIONAL BATTLEFIELDS IN THE US*

	National Battlefield	Battle	Established
1	Chickamauga and Chattanooga, Georgia/Tennessee	Sep 19–20, 1863	Aug 19, 1890
2	Antietam, Maryland	Sep 17, 1862	Aug 30, 1890
3	Shiloh, Tennessee	Apr 6–7, 1862	Dec 27, 1894
4	Gettysburg, Pennsylvania	Jul 1–3, 1863	Feb 11, 1895
5	Vicksburg, Mississippi	Jan 9–Jul 4, 1863	Feb 21, 1899
6	Big Hole, Montana	Aug 9, 1877	Jun 23, 1910
7	Guilford Courthouse, North Carolina	Mar 15, 1781	Mar 2, 1917
8	Kennesaw Mountain, Georgia	Jun 20–Jul 2, 1864	Apr 22, 1917
9	Moores Creek, North Carolina	Feb 27, 1776	Jun 2, 1926
10	Petersburg, Virginia	Jun 15, 1864–Apr 3, 1865	Jul 3, 1926

* *Dates include those for locations originally assigned other designations but later authorized as National Battlefields, National Battlefield Parks, and National Military Parks*

There are in all 24 National Battlefields, National Battlefield Parks, and National Military Parks, but just one National Battlefield Site: Brices Cross Roads, Mississippi. (The scene of a Civil War engagement on June 10, 1864, the Site was established on February 21, 1929.) The earliest battle to be so commemorated is Fort Necessity, Pennsylvania (July 3, 1754; National Battlefield established March 4, 1931), the opening hostility in the French and Indian War, in which the militia led by George Washington, then a 22-year-old Lt. Colonel, was defeated and captured.

TOP 10

US MEDAL OF HONOR CAMPAIGNS

	Campaign	Years	Medals awarded
1	Civil War	1861–65	1,520
2	World War II	1941–45	440
3	Indian Wars	1861–98	428
4	Vietnam War	1965–73	239
5	Korean War	1950–53	131
6	World War I	1917–18	124
7	Spanish-American War	1898	109
8	Philippines/Samoa	1899–1913	91
9	Boxer Rebellion	1900	59
10	Vera Cruz	1914	55

The Medal of Honor, the US's highest military award, was first issued by Congress in 1863.

Source: Congressional Medal of Honor Society

20TH-CENTURY WARS WITH THE MOST MILITARY FATALITIES*

	War/years	Approx. no. of fatalities
1	World War II (1939–45)	15,843,000
2	World War I (1914–18)	8,545,800
3	Korean War (1950–53)	1,893,100
4=	Sino-Japanese War (1937–41)	1,000,000
=	Biafra–Nigeria Civil War (1967–70)	1,000,000
6	Spanish Civil War (1936–39)	611,000
7	Vietnam War (1961–73)	546,000
8=	India–Pakistan War (1947)	200,000
=	Soviet invasion of Afghanistan (1979–89)	200,000
=	Iran–Iraq War (1980–88)	200,000

Battlefield deaths only

The statistics of warfare have always been an imperfect science. Not only are battle deaths seldom recorded accurately, but figures are often deliberately inflated by both sides in a conflict. For political reasons and to maintain morale, each is anxious to enhance reports of its military success and low casualty figures, so that often quite contradictory reports of the same battle may be issued. These figures thus represent military historians' "best guesses," and precise numbers may never actually be known.

BATTLES WITH THE MOST CASUALTIES

	Battle	War/date	Casualties*
1	Stalingrad	World War II, 1942–43	2,000,000
2	Somme River I	World War I, 1916	1,000,000
3	Po Valley	World War II, 1945	740,000
4	Moscow	World War II, 1941–42	700,000
5	Gallipoli	World War I, 1915–16	500,000
6	Artois-Loos	World War I, 1915	428,000
7	Berezina	War of 1812	400,000
8	38th Parallel	Korean War, 1951	320,000
9	Somme River II	World War I, 1918	300,000
10	Ypres I	World War I, 1914	250,000

* *Estimated total of military and civilian dead, wounded, and missing*

Total numbers of casualties in the Battle of Stalingrad are, at best, estimates, but it was undoubtedly one of the longest and almost certainly the bloodiest battles of all time. Fought between German and Soviet forces, it continued from August 19, 1942, to February 2, 1943, with huge losses, especially on the German side as the Sixth Army was decimated. Of almost 100,000 German troops captured, only about 5,000 were eventually repatriated.

YOUNGEST RECIPIENTS OF THE MEDAL OF HONOR DURING THE VIETNAM WAR

	Recipient	years	Age months	days
1	Private First Class Robert Burke	18	6	10
2	Private First Class Jimmy Phipps	18	6	26
3	Private First Class Gary Martini	18	7	–
4	Private First Class Melvin Newlin	18	9	7
5	Private First Class Daniel Bruce	18	9	12
6	Corporal Larry Smedley	18	9	17
7	Lance Corporal Miguel Keith	18	10	3
8	Lance Corporal Thomas Creek	18	10	6
9	Private First Class Milton Olive	18	11	15
10	Private First Class Dewayne Williams	19	–	–

Source: Congressional Medal of Honor Society

WAR WOUNDED
As well as innumerable civilians who were injured and killed, more than 30 million military fatalities have resulted from 20th-century conflicts.

THE WORLD WARS

THE 10
COUNTRIES SUFFERING THE GREATEST MILITARY LOSSES IN WORLD WAR II

	Country	No. killed
1	USSR	13,600,000*
2	Germany	3,300,000
3	China	1,324,516
4	Japan	1,140,429
5	British Empire# (UK 264,000)	357,116
6	Romania	350,000
7	Poland	320,000
8	Yugoslavia	305,000
9	US	292,131
10	Italy	279,800
	Total	*21,268,992*

* Total, of which 7,800,000 were battlefield deaths

\# Including Australia, Canada, India, New Zealand, etc.

THE 10
COUNTRIES SUFFERING THE GREATEST MERCHANT SHIPPING LOSSES IN WORLD WAR I

	Country	Vessels sunk No.	tonnage		Country	Vessels sunk No.	tonnage
1	UK	2,038	6,797,802	6	Greece	115	304,992
2	Italy	228	720,064	7	Denmark	126	205,002
3	France	213	651,583	8	Netherlands	74	194,483
4	US	93	372,892	9	Sweden	124	192,807
5	Germany	188	319,552	10	Spain	70	160,383

THE 10
COUNTRIES WITH THE MOST PRISONERS OF WAR CAPTURED, 1914–18

	Country	Prisoners		Country	Prisoners
1	Russian Empire	2,500,000	6	Turkey	250,000
2	Austria–Hungary	2,200,000	7	British Empire	191,652
3	Germany	1,152,800	8	Serbia	152,958
4	Italy	600,000	9	Romania	80,000
5	France	537,000	10	Belgium	34,659

TOP 10
US AIR ACES OF WORLD WAR II

	Pilot	Kills claimed
1	Maj. Richard I. Bong	40
2	Maj. Thomas B. McGuire	38
3	Cdr. David S. McCampbell	34
4 =	Col. Francis S. Gabreski	28
=	Lt. Col. Gregory Boyington	28
6 =	Maj. Robert S. Johnson	27
=	Col. Charles H. MacDonald	27
8 =	Maj. George E. Preddy	26
=	Maj. Joseph J. Foss	26
10	Lt. Robert M. Hanson	25

The definition of an "ace" varied from three to ten aircraft and was never officially approved, remaining an informal concept during both World Wars. The German equivalent was Oberkanone – which means "top gun."

THE 10
COUNTRIES SUFFERING THE GREATEST MERCHANT SHIPPING LOSSES IN WORLD WAR II

	Country	Vessels sunk No.	tonnage
1	UK	4,786	21,194,000
2	Japan	2,346	8,618,109
3	Germany	1,595	7,064,600
4	US	578	3,524,983
5	Norway	427	1,728,531
6	Netherlands	286	1,195,204
7	Italy	467	1,155,080
8	Greece	262	883,200
9	Panama	107	542,772
10	Sweden	204	481,864

FIGHTING FORCE
More Russian troops served in World War I than those of any other nation, with one in seven killed and one in five taken prisoner.

THE 10 COUNTRIES SUFFERING THE GREATEST MILITARY LOSSES IN WORLD WAR I
(No. killed)

❶ Germany (1,773,700) ❷ Russia (1,700,000) ❸ France (1,357,800) ❹ Austria–Hungary (1,200,000) ❺ British Empire (908,371) ❻ Italy (650,000) ❼ Romania (335,706) ❽ Turkey (325,000) ❾ US (116,516) ❿ Bulgaria (87,500)

TOP 10

US AIR ACES OF WORLD WAR I

	Pilot*	Kills claimed
1	Capt. Edward Vernon Rickenbacker	26
2	Capt. William C. Lambert	22
3=	Capt. August T. Iaccaci	18
=	2nd Lt. Frank Luke Jr.	18
5=	Capt. Frederick W. Gillet	17
=	Maj. Gervais Raoul Lufbery	17
7=	Capt. Howard A. Kuhlberg	16
=	Capt. Oren J. Rose	16
9	Capt. Clive W. Warman	15
10=	1st Lt. David Endicott Putnam	13
=	1st Lt. George Augustus Vaughan Jr.	13

* *Includes American pilots flying with RAF and French flying service*

The term "ace" was first used during World War I for a pilot who had brought down at least five enemy aircraft. The first-ever reference in print to an air "ace" appeared in an article in *The Times* (September 14, 1917), which described Raoul Lufbery as "the 'ace' of the American Lafayette Flying Squadron."

TOP 10 LARGEST ARMED FORCES OF WORLD WAR I
(Personnel)

❶ Russia (12,000,000) ❷ Germany (11,000,000) ❸ British Empire (8,904,467) ❹ France (8,410,000) ❺ Austria–Hungary (7,800,000) ❻ Italy (5,615,000) ❼ US (4,355,000) ❽ Turkey (2,850,000) ❾ Bulgaria (1,200,000) ❿ Japan (800,000)

WORLD WAR I CEMETERY

THE 10

SMALLEST ARMED FORCES OF WORLD WAR II

	Country	Personnel*
1	Costa Rica	400
2	Liberia	1,000
3=	El Salvador	3,000
=	Honduras	3,000
=	Nicaragua	3,000
6	Haiti	3,500
7	Dominican Republic	4,000
8	Guatemala	5,000
9=	Bolivia	8,000
=	Paraguay	8,000
=	Uruguay	8,000

* *Total at peak strength – of combatants*

THE 10

FIRST DECLARATIONS OF WAR IN WORLD WAR II

	Declaration	Date
1=	UK on Germany	Sep 3, 1939
=	Australia on Germany	Sep 3, 1939
=	New Zealand on Germany	Sep 3, 1939
=	France on Germany	Sep 3, 1939
5	South Africa on Germany	Sep 6, 1939
6	Canada on Germany	Sep 10, 1939
7	Italy on UK and France	Jun 10, 1940
8	France on Italy	Jun 11, 1940
9	UK on Finland, Hungary, Romania	Dec 6, 1941
10	Japan on US, UK, Australia, Canada, New Zealand, and South Africa	Dec 7, 1941

THE 10

LARGEST ARMED FORCES OF WORLD WAR II

	Country	Personnel*		Country	Personnel*
1	USSR	12,500,000	6	UK	4,683,000
2	US	12,364,000	7	Italy	4,500,000
3	Germany	10,000,000	8	China	3,800,000
4	Japan	6,095,000	9	India	2,150,000
5	France	5,700,000	10	Poland	1,000,000

* *Total at peak strength – of combatants*

MODERN MILITARY

NUCLEAR TEST EXPLOSION

THEN & NOW

TOP 10 COUNTRIES WITH THE HIGHEST MILITARY/CIVILIAN RATIO

Country	1987 Ratio*		1997 Ratio*	Country
North Korea	396	1	427	North Korea
Syria	362	2	301	Israel
United Arab Emirates	331	3	250	United Arab Emirates
Israel	317	4	231	Singapore
Jordan	291	5	221	Jordan
Iraq	269	6	209	Syria
Qatar	226	7	208	Qatar
Singapore	213	8	184	Bahrein
Taiwan	208	9	174	Taiwan
Vietnam	204	10	173	Iraq

* *Military personnel per 10,000 population*

THE 10

LARGEST ARMED FORCES IN THE WORLD

	Country	Estimated active forces Army	Navy	Air	Total
1	China	2,090,000	280,000	470,000	2,840,000
2	US	495,000	395,500	382,200	1,447,600 *
3	Russia	420,000	220,000	130,000	1,240,000 #
4	India	980,000	55,000	110,000	1,145,000
5	North Korea	923,000	47,000	85,000	1,055,000
6	South Korea	560,000	60,000	52,000	672,000
7	Turkey	525,000	51,000	63,000	639,000
8	Pakistan	520,000	22,000	45,000	587,000
9	Iran	350,000	18,000	30,000	518,000†
10	Vietnam	420,000	42,000	15,000	492,000

* *Includes 174,900 Marine Corps*

\# *Includes Strategic Deterrent Forces, Paramilitary, National Guard, etc.*

† *Includes 120,000 Revolutionary Guards*

In addition to the active forces listed here, many of the world's foremost countries have substantial reserves on standby; South Korea's have been estimated at about 4,500,000, Vietnam's at 3–4,000,000, and China's at 1,200,000.

TOP 10

DEFENSE COMPANIES IN THE WESTERN WORLD

	Company/country	Annual revenue ($)
1	Lockheed Martin, US	19,390,000,000
2	Boeing/McDonnell Douglas, US	17,900,000,000
3	Raytheon/Hughes/Texas Instruments, US	11,670,000,000
4	British Aerospace, UK	6,470,000,000
5	Northropp Grumman, US	5,700,000,000
6	Thomson, France	4,680,000,000
7	Aérospatiale/Dassault, France	4,150,000,000
8	GEC, UK	4,120,000,000
9	United Technologies, US	3,650,000,000
10	Lagardère Group, France	3,290,000,000

TOP 10

YEARS WITH THE MOST NUCLEAR EXPLOSIONS

	Year	Nuclear explosions US	USSR	UK	France	China	Total
1	1962	96	79	2	1	—	178
2	1958	77	34	5	—	—	116
3	1968	56	17	—	5	1	79
4	1966	48	18	—	7	3	76
5	1961	10	59	—	2	—	71
6	1969	46	19	—	—	2	67
7	1978	19	31	2	11	3	66
8=	1967	42	17	—	3	2	64
=	1970	39	16	—	8	1	64
10	1964	45	9	2	3	1	60

TOP 10
COUNTRIES WITH THE LARGEST DEFENSE BUDGETS (1997)

	Country	Budget ($)
1	US	259,400,000,000
2	Japan	43,300,000,000
3	UK	37,100,000,000
4	France	33,100,000,000
5	Russia	32,000,000,000
6	Germany	27,300,000,000
7	Italy	18,300,000,000
8	Saudi Arabia	17,900,000,000
9	South Korea	15,500,000,000
10	Taiwan	11,300,000,000

The so-called "peace dividend" – the savings made as a consequence of the end of the Cold War between the West and the former Soviet Union – means that both the numbers of personnel and the defense budgets of many countries have been cut.

TOP 10
ARMS IMPORTERS IN THE WORLD

	Country	Annual imports ($)
1	Saudi Arabia	9,050,000,000
2	Egypt	2,300,000,000
3	Japan	2,000,000,000
4	China	1,500,000,000
5	Taiwan	1,300,000,000
6	South Korea	1,100,000,000
7	Kuwait	1,036,000,000
8	Turkey	917,000,000
9	Israel	900,000,000
10=	Indonesia	700,000,000
=	Thailand	700,000,000
	US (imports from Europe only)	500,000,000

THE 10
SMALLEST ARMED FORCES IN THE WORLD*

	Country	Estimated total active forces		Country	Estimated total active forces
1	Antigua and Barbuda	200	6	The Bahamas	900
2	Seychelles	300	7=	Belize	1,100
3	Barbados	600	=	Cape Verde	1,100
4=	The Gambia	800	9=	Equatorial Guinea	1,300
=	Luxembourg	800	=	Mauritius	1,300

Excluding countries not declaring a defense budget

TOP 10
COUNTRIES WITH THE SMALLEST DEFENSE BUDGETS

	Country*	Budget ($)		Country*	Budget ($)
1	Equatorial Guinea	2,300,000	8	Sierra Leone	11,000,000
2	Antigua and Barbuda	3,200,000	9	Kyrgyzstan	13,000,000
3	Cape Verde	4,000,000	10=	Barbados	14,000,000
4	Guyana	7,000,000	=	Surinam	14,000,000
5	Guinea-Bissau	8,000,000			
6=	Belize	10,000,000			
=	Seychelles	10,000,000			

Includes only those countries that declare defense budgets

TOP 10
COUNTRIES WITH THE MOST CONSCRIPTED PERSONNEL

	Country	Conscripts		Country	Conscripts
1	China	1,275,000	6	Italy	163,000
2	Turkey	462,000	7	South Korea	159,000
3	Russia	381,000	8	France	156,950
4	Egypt	320,000	9	Poland	141,600
5	Iran	250,000	10	Israel	138,500

BELL JETRANGER
Expenditure on aircraft and other military equipment is a component of worldwide military budgets running into billions of dollars.

WORLD RELIGIONS

THEN & NOW

TOP 10 FASTEST-GROWING RELIGIOUS AFFILIATIONS IN THE US*

	Affiliation	Members 1970	1995	% growth
1	Sikh	1,000	190,000	18,900.0
2	Hindu	100,000	910,000	810.0
3	Muslim	800,000	5,100,000	537.5
4	Buddhist	200,000	780,000	290.0
5	Baha'i	138,000	300,000	117.4
6	Evangelical Christians	50,688,000	72,363,000	42.8
7	Orthodox	4,387,000	5,631,000	28.4
8	Roman Catholic	48,391,000	55,259,000	14.2
9	Jews	6,700,000	5,602,000	-16.4
10	Anglican	3,234,000	2,350,000	-27.3

* Based on increases/decreases in membership between 1970 and 1995

TOP 10

LARGEST BUDDHIST POPULATIONS IN THE WORLD

	Country	Total Buddhist population		Country	Total Buddhist population
1	Japan	69,213,191	6	South Korea	12,456,290
2	Thailand	59,722,460	7	Cambodia	8,740,020
3	Myanmar	44,354,408	8	India	8,340,240
4	Vietnam	42,843,480	9	Laos	3,153,303
5	Sri Lanka	13,457,067	10	North Korea	2,253,200

BUDDHA
Buddhism originated in India around 500 BC, and has spread throughout southern Asia.

TOP 10

CHRISTIAN DENOMINATIONS IN THE WORLD

	Denomination	Members
1	Roman Catholic	912,636,000
2	Orthodox	139,544,000
3	Pentecostal	105,756,000
4	Lutheran	84,521,000
5	Baptist	67,146,000
6	Anglican	53,217,000
7	Presbyterian	47,972,000
8	Methodist	25,599,000
9	Seventh Day Adventist	10,650,000
10	Churches of Christ	6,400,000

THE TORAH
Sacred scroll of the Jewish religion.

TOP 10

LARGEST CHRISTIAN POPULATIONS IN THE WORLD

	Country	Total Christian population
1	US	182,674,000
2	Brazil	157,973,000
3	Mexico	88,380,000
4	China	73,300,000
5	Philippines	65,217,000
6	Germany	63,332,000
7	Italy	47,403,000
8	France	45,624,000
9	Nigeria	38,969,000
10	Dem. Rep. of Congo	37,922,000

Although Christian communities are found in almost every country in the world, it is difficult to put a precise figure on nominal membership (a declared religious persuasion) rather than active participation (regular attendance at a place of worship). For example, the total Christian population of the UK was estimated to be 37,394,000 in 1995, but it is estimated that the population who regularly attend church services (who could be classified as practicing Christians) is just over 6,000,000. Even taking into account other denominations in the UK, there is clearly a wide gulf between thought and deed.

LARGEST HINDU POPULATIONS IN THE WORLD

	Country	Total Hindu population
1	India	814,632,942
2	Nepal	21,136,118
3	Bangladesh	14,802,899
4	Indonesia	3,974,895
5	Sri Lanka	2,713,900

	Country	Total Hindu population
6	Pakistan	2,112,071
7	Malaysia	1,043,500
8	US	798,582
9	South Africa	649,980
10	Mauritius	587,884
	World	*865,564,992*

LARGEST JEWISH POPULATIONS IN THE WORLD

	Country	Total Jewish population
1	US	6,122,462
2	Israel	4,354,900
3	France	640,156
4	Russia	460,266
5	Ukraine	424,136
6	UK	345,054
7	Canada	342,096
8	Argentina	253,666
9	Brazil	107,692
10	Belarus	107,350
	World	*15,050,000*

The Diaspora, or scattering of Jewish people, has been in progress for nearly 2,000 years, and today Jewish communities are found in virtually every country in the world.

BRAHMA THE CREATOR *The supreme being of the Hindu religion. Some 99 percent of the world's Hindu population is in Asia, with 94 percent in India, its birthplace.*

LARGEST MUSLIM POPULATIONS IN THE WORLD

	Country	Total Muslim population
1	Pakistan	157,349,290
2	Indonesia	156,213,374
3	Bangladesh	133,873,621
4	India	130,316,250
5	Iran	74,087,700
6	Turkey	66,462,107
7	Russia	64,624,770
8	Egypt	57,624,098
9	Nigeria	46,384,120
10	Morocco	33,542,780
	World	*1,340,743,499*

CHRISTIAN DENOMINATIONS IN THE US

	Denomination	Members
1	The Roman Catholic Church	61,207,914
2	Southern Baptist Convention	15,691,964
3	The United Methodist Church	8,495,378
4	National Baptist Convention, US, Inc.	8,200,000
5	Church of God in Christ	5,499,875
6	Evangelical Lutheran Church in America	5,180,910
7	Church of Jesus Christ of Latter-day Saints	4,800,000
8	Presbyterian Church (US)	3,637,375
9 =	African Methodist Episcopal Church	3,500,000
=	National Baptist Convention of America	3,500,000

Source: 1998 Yearbook of American and Canadian Churches, © National Council of the Churches of Christ in the USA.

ORGANIZED RELIGIOUS GROUPS IN THE WORLD

	Religion	Members*
1	Roman Catholic	1,061,896,000
2	Sunni Muslim	1,061,393,000
3	Hindu	767,424,000
4	Buddhist	364,872,000
5	Orthodox Christian	224,770,000

	Religion	Members*
6	Shi'ite Muslim	117,933,000
7	Anglican	55,077,000
8	Baptist	54,236,000
9	Sikh	22,874,000
10	Jewish	15,050,000

* *Estimated projections to mid-1998*

THE BIBLE

NAMES MOST MENTIONED IN THE BIBLE

	Name	OT*	NT*	Total
1	David	1,005	59	1,064
2	Jesus		984	984
3	Moses	767	80	847
4	Jacob	350	27	377
5	Aaron	347	5	352
6	Solomon	293	12	305
7=	Joseph	215	35	250
=	Abraham	176	74	250
9	Ephraim	182	1	183
10	Benjamin	162	2	166

* Occurrences in verses in the King James Bible (Old and New Testaments), including possessive uses, such as "John's"

In addition to these personal names, "God" is referred to on 4,105 occasions (2,749 Old Testament; 1,356 New Testament). The name Judah also appears 816 times, but the total includes references to the territory as well as the individual with that name. At the other end of the scale, there are many names that – perhaps fortunately – appear only once or twice, among them Berodachbaladan and Tilgathpilneser. The most mentioned place names produce few surprises, with Israel heading the list (2,600 references).

ANIMALS MOST MENTIONED IN THE BIBLE

	Animal	OT*	NT*	Total
1	Sheep	155	45	200
2	Lamb	153	35	188
3	Lion	167	9	176
4	Ox	156	10	166
5	Ram	165	0	165
6	Horse	137	27	164
7	Bullock	152	0	152
8	Ass	142	8	150
9	Goat	131	7	138
10	Camel	56	6	62

* Occurrences in verses in the King James Bible (Old and New Testaments), including plurals

The sheep are sorted from the goats in this Top 10, in a menagerie of the animals considered most significant in biblical times, either economically or symbolically (as in the many references to the lion's strength). A number of generic terms are also found in abundance: beast (a total of 337 references), cattle (153), fowl (90), fish (56), and bird (41). Some creatures are mentioned only once, in Leviticus 11, which contains a list of animals that are considered "unclean" – the weasel, chameleon, and tortoise, for example – and are never referred to again.

LONGEST WORDS IN THE BIBLE

	Word*	Letters
1=	covenantbreakers (NT only)	16
=	evilfavouredness	16
=	lovingkindnesses	16
=	unprofitableness	16
=	unrighteousness (and NT)	16
=	uprighteousness	16
7=	acknowledgement	15
=	administrations (NT only)	15
=	bloodyguiltness	15
=	confectionaries	15
=	fellowdisciples (NT only)	15
=	fellowlabourers (NT only)	15
=	interpretations	15
=	kneadingtroughs	15
=	notwithstanding (and NT)	15
=	prognosticators	15
=	righteousnesses	15
=	stumblingblocks	15
=	threshingfloors	15

* All Old Testament only (King James Bible) unless otherwise stated

LONGEST BOOKS IN THE BIBLE

	Book	Words
1	Psalms	42,732
2	Jeremiah	42,729
3	Ezekiel	39,442
4	Genesis	38,520
5	Isaiah	37,078
6	Numbers	32,943
7	Exodus	32,767
8	Deuteronomy	28,402
9	II Chronicles	26,123
10	Luke	25,986

King James Bible (Old and New Testaments)

SHORTEST BOOKS IN THE BIBLE

	Book	Words
1	III John	295
2	II John	299
3	Philemon	431
4	Jude	609
5	Obadiah	670
6	Titus	899
7	II Thessalonians	1,023
8	Haggai	1,134
9	Nahum	1,285
10	Jonah	1,323

King James Bible (Old and New Testaments)

TOP 10

LONGEST NAMES OF PEOPLE AND PLACES IN THE BIBLE

	Name	Letters
1	Mahershalalhashbaz (Isaiah's son)	18
2=	Bashanhavothjair (alternative name of Argob)	16
=	Chepharhaammonai (Ammonite settlement)	16
=	Chusharishathaim (king of Mesopotamia)	16
=	Kibrothhattaavah (desert encampment of Israelites)	16
=	Selahammahlekoth (stronghold in Maon)	16
7=	Abelbethmaachah (town near Damascus)	15
=	Almondiblathaim (stopping-place of Israelites)	15
=	Apharsathchites (Assyrian nomadic group)	15
=	Berodachbaladan/Merodachbaladan (king of Babylon)	15
=	Helkathhazzurim (a battlefield)	15
=	Ramathaimzophin (town where Samuel was born)	15
=	Tilgathpilneser (king of Assyria)	15
=	Zaphnathpaaneah (name given to Joseph by Pharaoh)	15

King James Bible (Old Testament)

TOP 10

WORDS MOST MENTIONED IN THE BIBLE

	Word	OT*	NT*	Total
1	The	52,948	10,976	63,924
2	And	40,975	10,721	51,696
3	Of	28,518	6,099	34,617
4	To	10,207	3,355	13,562
5	That	9,152	3,761	12,913
6	In	9,767	2,900	12,667
7	He	7,348	3,072	10,420
8	For	6,690	2,281	8,971
9	I	6,669	2,185	8,854
10	His	7,036	1,437	8,473

* *Occurrences in verses in the King James Bible (Old and New Testaments)*

A century before computers were invented, Thomas Hartwell Horne (1780–1862), a dogged biblical researcher, undertook a manual search of biblical word frequencies and concluded that "and" appeared a total of 35,543 times in the Old Testament and 10,684 times in the New Testament. He was fairly close on the latter – but he clearly missed quite a few in the Old Testament, as a recent computer search of the King James Bible indicates.

THE 10

COMMANDMENTS

1 Thou shalt have no other gods before me.

2 Thou shalt not make unto thee any graven image.

3 Thou shalt not take the name of the Lord thy God in vain.

4 Remember the sabbath day, to keep it holy.

5 Honor thy father and thy mother.

6 Thou shalt not kill.

7 Thou shalt not commit adultery.

8 Thou shalt not steal.

9 Thou shalt not bear false witness against thy neighbor.

10 Thou shalt not covet thy neighbor's house, thou shalt not covet thy neighbor's wife, nor his manservant, nor his maidservant, nor his ox, nor his ass, nor any thing that is thy neighbor's.

Exodus 20.iii (King James Bible)

TOP 10

CROPS MOST MENTIONED IN THE BIBLE

	Crop	OT*	NT*	Total
1	Corn (wheat)	126	23	149
2	Fig	45	21	66
3	Olive	42	19	61
4	Grape	46	3	49
5	Barley	43	3	46
6	Pomegranate	33	0	33
7	Raisin	9	7	16
8	Apple	11	0	11
9	Bean	6	0	6
10	Cucumber	2	0	2

* *Occurrences in verses in the King James Bible (Old and New Testaments), including plurals*

THE PAPACY

THE 10

FIRST POPES

	Pope	Reign
1	St. Peter	c.32–c.64
2	St. Linus	c.66–c.78
3	St. Anacletus (Cletus)	c.79–c.91
4	St. Clement I	c.91–c.101
5	St. Evaristus	c.100–c.109
6	St. Alexander I	c.109–c.116
7	St. Sixtus I	c.116–c.125
8	St. Telesphorus	c.125–c.136
9	St. Hyginus	c.138–c.142
10	St. Pius I	c.142–c.155

The first 10 popes all lived during the first century and a half of the Christian Era. As well as all being revered as Christian saints, they have one other striking feature in common, as is indicated by the approximate dating of their reigns: virtually nothing is known about any of them.

LEADING FAITH
With the Pope as its head, the Roman Catholic Church has maintained its position as one of the world's major religions for almost 2,000 years.

THE 10

LATEST POPES

	Pope	Reign
1	John Paul II	Oct 16, 1978–
2	John Paul I	Aug 26–Sep 28, 1978
3	Paul VI	Jun 21, 1963–Aug 6, 1978
4	John XXIII	Oct 28, 1958–Jun 3, 1963
5	Pius XII	Mar 2, 1939–Oct 9, 1958
6	Pius XI	Feb 6, 1922–Feb 10, 1939
7	Benedict XV	Sep 3, 1914–Jan 22, 1922
8	St. Pius X	Aug 4, 1903–Aug 20, 1914
9	Leo XIII	Feb 20, 1878–Jul 20, 1903
10	Pius IX	Jun 16, 1846–Feb 7, 1878

ST. PETER'S, ROME
Named after the first Pope, St. Peter's and the Vatican are the focus of the Catholic Church.

TOP 10

SHORTEST-SERVING POPES

	Pope	Year in office	Duration (days)
1	Urban VII	1590	12
2	Valentine	827	c.14
3	Boniface VI	896	15
4	Celestine IV	1241	16
5	Sisinnius	708	20
6=	Sylvester III	1045	21
=	Theodore II	897	c.21
8	Marcellus II	1555	22
9	Damasus II	1048	23
10=	Pius III	1503	26
=	Leo XI	1605	26

Eleven popes have reigned for less than a month. Some authorities give Stephen's two- or three-day reign in March 757 as the shortest, but although he was elected, he died before he was consecrated and is therefore not included in the official list of popes. (In fact, his successor was given his title, Stephen II, and reigned for five years – although some call the uncrowned Stephen "Stephen II" and his successors are confusingly known as "Stephen II(III)," and so on.). Urban VII thus holds the record for the shortest-serving pope; he was elected on September 15, caught malaria the following day, and died on September 27, 1590.

TOP 10

MOST COMMON NAMES OF POPES

	Name	Number
1	John	23
2	Gregory	16
3	Benedict	15
4	Clement	14
5=	Innocent	13
=	Leo	13
7	Pius	12
8	Boniface	9
9=	Alexander	8
=	Urban	8

T O P   1 0

COUNTRIES MOST VISITED BY POPE JOHN PAUL II*

Country	Visits
1 = Poland	5
= France	5
= US#	5
4 = Brazil	4
= Spain	4
6 = Germany/West Germany	3
= Kenya	3
= Mexico	3
= Côte d'Ivoire	3
10 = Argentina, Australia, Austria,	
= Belgium, Benin, Cameroon,	
= Canada, Dem. Rep. of Congo,	
= Dominican Republic, Guinea Bissau,	
= Papua New Guinea, Peru, Philippines,	
= Portugal, South Korea,	
= Switzerland, Uruguay	2

* As of May, 1998

\# Includes 1984 stopover in Fairbanks, Alaska

Soon after taking office as Pope in 1978, John Paul II embarked on an extensive series of travels. Prior to his long trips, only one Pope had ever traveled outside Italy (Paul VI went to Israel in 1964), and some never left the Vatican. Up to his visit to Cuba in January 1998, John Paul II had visited 117 countries, 28 of them on more than one occasion. Until 1995, the list was headed by Poland, his native country, but his 1995 and 1996 travels to the US and France made those countries equal Poland.

SNAP FACTS

- After his death in 896, the body of Pope Formosus was dug up and tried for various crimes.
- John VIII (died 882) was the first Pope to be murdered – he was poisoned and then clubbed to death.
- Stephen VI (897), Leo V (904), John X (929), Stephen VIII (942), and John XIV (984) were among a number of popes who were murdered in prison.

PAPAL TOUR
Pope John Paul II's exhaustive travels have taken him to more than 100 countries in the past 10 years.

T O P   1 0

NATIONALITIES OF POPES

	Nationality	Number
1	Roman/Italian	208–209 *
2	French	15–17 #
3	Greek	15–16 †
4	Syrian	6
5	German	4–6 #
6	Spanish	5
7	African	2–3
8	Galilean	2
9 =	Dutch	1
=	English	1
=	Polish	1
=	Portuguese	1

* Gelasius I was Roman, but of African descent; it is unknown whether Miltiades was African or Roman.

\# The Franco-German frontier was variable at the births of two popes; hence, their nationalities are uncertain.

† Theodore I was of Greek descent, but born in Jerusalem.

T O P   1 0

LONGEST-SERVING POPES

	Pope	Period in office	Years
1	Pius IX	Jun 16, 1846–Feb 7, 1878	31
2 =	Leo XIII	Feb 20, 1878–Jul 20, 1903	25
=	Peter	c.32–c.64	c.25
4	Pius VI	Feb 15, 1775–Aug 29, 1799	24
5 =	Adrian I	Feb 1, 772–Dec 25, 795	23
=	Pius VII	Mar 14, 1800–Aug 20, 1823	23
7 =	Alexander III	Sep 7, 1159–Aug 30, 1181	21
=	Sylvester	Jan 31, 314–Dec 31, 335	21
=	Leo I	Sep 29, 440–Nov 10, 461	21
10	Urban VIII	Aug 6, 1623–Jul 29, 1644	20

Popes are usually elected from the ranks of cardinals, who are customarily men of mature years. As a result, it is unusual for a pope to remain in office for more than 20 years. Although St. Peter is generally regarded as the first pope, some authorities doubt the historical accuracy of his leadership. If he is omitted from the list as unauthenticated, then those below him in the list at Nos. 4–10 all move up one place and the 10th position is taken by Clement XI (Sep 23, 1700–Mar 19, 1721, a reign of 20 years). Pius IX, the longest-serving pope in history, was 85 years old at the time of his death.

DISASTERS

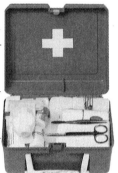

THE 10

MOST COMMON CAUSES OF FATAL CRASHES

	Cause	Total fatalities (1996)
1	Failure to keep in proper lane or running off road	15,883
2	Driving too fast for conditions or in excess of posted speed limit	11,551
3	Failure to yield right of way	5,105
4	Inattention (talking, eating, etc.)	3,704
5	Failure to obey traffic signs, signals, or officer	3,008
6	Operating vehicle in erratic, reckless, careless, or negligent manner	2,921
7	Swerving or avoiding due to wind, slippery surface, vehicle, object, pedestrian in road, etc.	2,267
8	Drowsiness, sleep, fatigue, illness, or blackout	1,792
9	Overcorrecting/oversteering	1,590
10	Making improper turn	1,397

Source: National Highway Traffic Safety Administration

FLAG OF INCONVENIENCE
Until 1896 British drivers had to warn of their presence by having a person precede their car on foot, waving a red flag.

THE 10

US STATES WITH THE MOST MOTOR VEHICLE FATALITIES

	State	Total fatalities (1996)		State	Total fatalities (1996)
1	California	3,989	6	Michigan	1,505
2	Texas	3,741	7	North Carolina	1,493
3	Florida	2,753	8	Illinois	1,477
4	Georgia	1,574	9	Pennsylvania	1,469
5	New York	1,564	10	Ohio	1,395

Source: National Highway Traffic Safety Administration

TOP 10

SAFEST CAR COLORS

	Color	Light reflection percentages
1	White	84.0
2	Cream	68.8
3	Ivory	66.7
4	Light pink	66.5
5	Yellow	57.0
6	Flesh	51.6
7	Buff	51.5
8	Light gray	51.5
9	Light green	45.2
10	Aluminum gray	41.0

Source: Mansell Color Company, Inc., published by the National Safety Council

THE 10 WORST MOTOR VEHICLE AND ROAD DISASTERS IN THE WORLD

	Location/date/incident	No. killed
1	Afghanistan, November 3, 1982	2,000+

Following a collision with a Soviet army truck, a gasoline tanker exploded in the 1.7-mile/2.7-km long Salang Tunnel. Some authorities estimate that the death toll could have been as high as 3,000.

2	Colombia, August 7, 1956	1,200

Seven army ammunition trucks exploded at night in the center of the city of Cali, destroying eight city blocks.

3	Thailand, February 15, 1990	150+

A dynamite truck exploded.

4	Nepal, November 23, 1974	148

Hindu pilgrims were killed when a suspension bridge over the Mahahali River collapsed.

5	Egypt, August 9, 1973	127

A bus drove into an irrigation canal.

6	Togo, December 6, 1965	125+

Two trucks collided with a group of dancers during a festival at Sotouboua.

7	Spain, July 11, 1978	120+

A liquid gas tanker exploded in a campsite at San Carlos de la Rapita.

8	South Korea, April 28, 1995	110

An underground explosion destroyed vehicles and caused about 100 cars and buses to plunge into the pit it created.

9	Gambia, November 12, 1992	c. 100

A bus full of passengers plunged into a river when its brakes failed.

10	Kenya, early December 1992	nearly 100

A bus carrying 112 passengers skidded, hit a bridge, and plunged into a river.

The worst motor racing accident occurred on June 13, 1955, at Le Mans, France, when French driver Pierre Levegh's Mercedes-Benz 300 SLR went out of control, hit a wall, and exploded in mid-air, showering wreckage into the crowd and killing a total of 82 people.

THE 10 AGE GROUPS MOST VULNERABLE TO AUTO ACCIDENTS IN THE US, 1996

	Age group	Deaths	Death rate per 100,000
1	16–20	5,791	31.40
2	21–24	4,112	29.39
3	74+	3,885	25.57
4	25–34	7,610	18.85
5	65–74	3,198	17.10
6	35–44	6,514	15.01
7	55–64	3,019	14.13
8	45–54	4,364	13.48
9	10–15	1,591	6.99
10	0–5	886	4.59

In addition, another 130 people were killed whose ages were unknown, and in the total of 41,907, the gender of three fatalities was unknown.

Source: National Highway Traffic Safety Administration

THE 10 COUNTRIES WITH THE MOST DEATHS BY MOTOR ACCIDENTS

	Country	Death rate per 100,000 population
1	South Africa	99.4
2	Latvia	35.3
3	South Korea	33.1
4	Estonia	26.7
5	Russia	23.6
6	Portugal	22.8
7	Lithuania	22.1
8	Greece	21.3
9	Venezuala	20.7
10=	El Salvador	20.3
=	Kuwait	20.3
	US	*15.8*

SCENE OF THE ACCIDENT
Car crashes in the US kill more than 40,000 people every year, with people under 25 making up a quarter of all fatalities.

THE 10 WORST YEARS FOR ROAD FATALITIES IN THE US

	Year	Total fatalities*
1	1972	54,589
2	1973	54,052
3	1969	53,543
4	1968	52,725
5	1970	52,627
6	1971	52,542
7	1979	51,093
8	1980	51,091
9	1966	50,894
10	1967	50,724

* Traffic fatalities occurring within 30 days of accident

Source: National Highway Traffic Safety Administration

RAILROAD DISASTERS

T H E 1 O

WORST RAILROAD DISASTERS IN THE US

	Location/date/incident	No. killed
1	Nashville, Tennessee July 9, 1918	101

On the Nashville, Chattanooga, and St. Louis Railroad, a head-on collision resulted in a death toll that remains the worst in US history, with 171 injured.

2	Brooklyn, New York November 2, 1918	97

A subway train was derailed in the Malbone Street tunnel.

3 =	Eden, Colorado August 7, 1904	96

A bridge washed away during a flood smashed into Steele's Hollow Bridge as the "World's Fair Express" was crossing.

=	Wellington, Washington March 1, 1910	96

An avalanche swept two trains into a canyon.

5	Bolivar, Texas September 8, 1900	85

A train traveling from Beaumont encountered the hurricane that destroyed Galveston, killing 6,000. Attempts to load the train onto a ferry were abandoned, and it went back, but was destroyed by the storm.

	Location/date/incident	No. killed
6	Woodbridge, New Jersey February 6, 1951	84

A Pennsylvania Railroad commuter train crashed while speeding through a sharply curving detour.

7	Chatsworth, Illinois August 10, 1887	82

A trestle bridge caught fire and collapsed as the Toledo, Peoria & Western train was crossing. As many as 372 were injured.

8	Ashtabula, Ohio December 29, 1876	80

A bridge collapsed in a snowstorm, and the Lake Shore train fell into the Ashtabula River. The death toll may have been as high as 92.

9 =	Frankford Junction, Pennsylvania September 6, 1943	79

Pennsylvania's worst railroad accident: the previous worst had been at Camp Hill, on July 17, 1856, when two trains collided head-on, killing 66 schoolchildren on a school picnic.

=	Richmond Hill, New York November 22, 1950	79

A Long Island Railroad commuter train rammed into the rear of another, leaving 79 dead and 363 injured.

LATE 19TH-CENTURY DISASTER

T H E 1 O

WORST RAIL DISASTERS IN THE UK

	Location	Date	No. killed
1	Quintinshill, near Gretna Green	May 22, 1915	227
2	Harrow and Wealdstone Station, London	October 8, 1952	122
3	Lewisham, London	December 4, 1957	90
4	Tay Bridge, Scotland	December 28, 1879	80
5	Armagh, Northern Ireland	June 12, 1889	78
6	Hither Green, London	November 5, 1967	49
7 =	Bourne End, Hertfordshire	September 30, 1945	43
=	Moorgate Station, London	February 28, 1975	43
9	Castlecary, Scotland	December 10, 1937	35
10 =	Shipton, near Oxford	December 24, 1874	34
=	Clapham Junction, London	December 12, 1988	34

T H E 1 O

WORST UNDERGROUND RAIL DISASTERS IN THE WORLD*

	Location/date	No. killed
1	Baku, Azerbaijan, October 28, 1995	over 300
2	Bethnal Green, London, March 3, 1943	173
3	Bank, London, January 7, 1941	111
4	Brooklyn, New York, November 1, 1918,	97
5	Paris, August 10, 1903	84
6	Balham, London, October 15, 1940	68
7	Moorgate, London, February 28, 1975	43
8	Mexico City, October 20, 1975	34
9	King's Cross, London, November 18, 1987	31
10	Berlin, September 26, 1908	21

* Including disasters caused by bombs, fires, and panics in subway stations

THE 10
WORST RAIL DISASTERS IN EUROPE

Location/date/incident	No. killed
1 Chelyabinsk, Russia, Jun 3, 1989	up to 800

Two passenger trains traveling on the Trans-Siberian Railroad were destroyed by exploding liquid gas from a nearby pipeline.

2 Modane, France, Dec 12, 1917	573

A troop train ran out of control and was derailed. It has been claimed that the train was overloaded and that as many as 1,000 may have died.

3 Balvano, Italy, Mar 12, 1944	521

A heavily loaded train stalled in the Armi Tunnel, asphyxiating many passengers. The true casualty figure was never published.

4 Torre, Spain, Jan 3, 1944	over 500

A double collision and fire in a tunnel resulted in many deaths – some have put the total as high as 800. Wartime secrecy prevented full details from being published.

5 Cireau, Romania, Jan 7, 1917	374

An overcrowded passenger train crashed into a military train and was derailed. In addition to the high death toll, 756 were injured.

6 Pomponne, near Lagny, France, Dec 23, 1933	230

France's second-worst rail disaster resulted from a collision in fog between an express and two stationary trains, all packed with passengers traveling in the Christmas season.

7 Quintinshill, Scotland, May 22, 1915	227

Britain's worst rail disaster involving a troop train, a local passenger train, and an express.

8 Nowy Dwor, Poland, Oct 22, 1949	200

A derailment caused the death of at least 200.

9 Genthin, Germany, Dec 22, 1939	196

A train was hit in the rear by another in Germany's worst-ever rail accident.

10 Zagreb, Yugoslavia, Aug 3, 1974	153

A train was derailed on a curve when the engineer fell asleep.

THE 10
WORST RAIL DISASTERS IN THE WORLD

Location/date/incident	No. killed
1 Bagmati River, India, June 6, 1981	c. 800

The carriages of a train traveling from Samastipur to Banmukhi in Bihar plunged off a bridge over the Bagmati River near Mansi when the engineer braked, apparently to avoid hitting a sacred cow. Although the official death toll is said to have been 268, many authorities have claimed that the train was so massively overcrowded that the actual figure was in excess of 800, making it probably the worst rail disaster of all time.

2 Chelyabinsk, Russia, June 3, 1989	up to 800

Two Trans-Siberian passenger trains, going to and from the Black Sea, were destroyed when liquid gas from a nearby pipeline exploded.

3 Guadalajara, Mexico, January 18, 1915	over 600

A train derailed on a steep incline, but political strife in the country meant that full details of the disaster were suppressed.

4 Modane, France, December 12, 1917	573

A troop train ran out of control and was derailed. It was probably overloaded, and as many as 1,000 people may have died.

5 Balvano, Italy, March 2, 1944	521

A crowded train stalled in the Armi Tunnel, and many passengers were asphyxiated.

6 Torre, Spain, January 3, 1944	over 500

A double collision and fire in a tunnel resulted in many deaths. Like the disaster at Balvano two months later, wartime secrecy prevented full details from being published.

7 Awash, Ethiopia, January 13, 1985	428

A derailment hurled a train into a ravine.

8 Cireau, Romania, January 7, 1917	374

An overcrowded passenger train crashed into a military train and was derailed.

9 Quipungo, Angola, May 31, 1993	355

A train was derailed by UNITA guerrilla action.

10 Sangi, Pakistan, January 4, 1990	306

A diverted train resulted in a fatal collision.

Casualty figures for rail accidents are often extremely imprecise, especially during wartime – and half of the 10 worst disasters occurred during the two World Wars.

OVERCROWDING ON INDIA'S TRAINS
The extremely high death toll in the world's worst railroad accident owed much to this fact of Indian life.

MARINE DISASTERS

WORST MARINE DISASTERS OF THE 20TH CENTURY

	Vessel	Date	Approx. no. killed
1	Wilhelm Gustloff	January 30, 1945	up to 7,800

The German liner, crowded with refugees, was torpedoed off Danzig by a Soviet submarine, S-13, January 30, 1945. The precise death toll remains uncertain, but is in the range 5,348 to 7,800.

2	Goya	April 16, 1945	6,800

A German ship carrying evacuees from Danzig was torpedoed in the Baltic near Cape Rixhöft.

3	Unknown vessel	November 1947	over 6,000

An unidentified Chinese troopship carrying Nationalist soldiers from Manchuria sank off Yingkow. The exact date is unknown.

4	Cap Arcona	May 3, 1945	5,000

A German ship carrying concentration camp survivors was bombed and sunk by British aircraft in Lübeck harbor.

5	Lancastria	June 17, 1940	3,050

A British troopship sank off St. Nazaire.

6	Steuben	February 9, 1945	3,000

German war-wounded and refugees were lost when the ship was torpedoed off Stolpmünde by the same Russian submarine that had sunk the Wilhelm Gustloff.

7	Dona Paz	December 20, 1987	up to 3,000

The ferry Dona Paz was struck by oil tanker MV Victor in the Tabias Strait, Philippines.

8	Kiangya	December 3, 1948	over 2,750

An overloaded steamship carrying refugees struck a Japanese mine off Woosung, China.

9	Thielbeck	May 3, 1945	2,750

A refugee ship sank during the British bombardment of Lübeck harbor in the closing weeks of World War II.

10	Laconia	September 12, 1942	2,279

A British passenger vessel carrying Italian prisoners of war was sunk by German U-boat U-156.

Recent reassessments of the death tolls in some of the World War II marine disasters mean that the most famous of all, the *Titanic*, the British liner that struck an iceberg in the North Atlantic and sank April 15, 1912, with the loss of 1,517 lives, no longer ranks in the Top 10. However, the *Titanic* tragedy remains one of the worst-ever peacetime disasters, along with such notable incidents as that involving the *General Slocum*, an excursion liner that caught fire in the port of New York on June 15, 1904, with the loss of 1,021 lives. Among other disasters that occurred during wartime and resulted in losses of more than 1,000 was the explosion of *Mont Blanc*, a French ammunition ship, following its collision with a Belgian steamer *Imo* off Halifax, Nova Scotia, on December 6, 1917, with 1,635 lives lost.

WORST SUBMARINE DISASTERS OF ALL TIME

(Excluding those as a result of military action)

	Submarine	Date	No. killed
1	Le Surcourf	February 18, 1942	159

The French submarine was accidentally rammed by a US merchant ship.

2	Thresher	April 10, 1963	129

The three-year-old US nuclear submarine, worth $45,000,000, sank in the North Atlantic, 220 miles/350 km east of Boston, Mass.

3	I-12	January 1945	114

The Japanese submarine sank in the Pacific in unknown circumstances.

4	I-174	April 3, 1944	107

A Japanese submarine sank in the Pacific in unknown circumstances.

5	I-26	October 1944	105

This Japanese submarine sank east of Leyte, cause and date unknown.

6	I-169	April 4, 1944	103

A Japanese submarine flooded and sank while in harbor at Truk.

7	I-22	October 1942	100

A Japanese submarine sank off the Solomon Islands, exact date unknown.

8 =	Seawolf	October 3, 1944	99

A US submarine was sunk in error by USS Rowell off Morotai.

=	Scorpion	May 21, 1968	99

This US nuclear submarine was lost in the North Atlantic, southwest of the Azores. The wreck was located on October 31 of that year.

9	I-67	August 29, 1940	89

This Japanese submarine foundered in storms off Bonin Island, to the south of Japan.

The loss of the *Thresher* is the worst accident ever involving a nuclear submarine. It sank while undergoing tests off the US coast and was located by the bathyscaphe *Trieste*. The remains of the submarine were scattered over the ocean floor at a depth of 8,400 ft/2,560 m. The cause of the disaster remains a military secret.

SNAP FACT

• A rare example of a liner destroying a warship occurred on October 2, 1942, when the *Queen Mary*, carrying 10,000 US troops, sliced the British cruiser *Curaçao* in half, killing 338.

THE 10
WORST PRE-20TH-CENTURY MARINE DISASTERS

	Location/date/incident	Approx. no. killed
1	Off the British coast, August to October, 1588, Spanish Armada	4,000
2 =	Off Egg Island, Labrador, August 22, 1711, British fleet	over 2,000
=	December 4, 1811, *St. George, Defence,* and *Hero*	over 2,000
4	Near Memphis, Tennessee, April 27, 1865, *Sultana*	1,547
5	Off the Florida coast, July 31, 1715, *Capitanas*	over 1,000
6	Off Spithead, UK, August 29, 1782, *Royal George*	over 900
7	River Thames near Woolwich, UK, September 3, 1878, *Princess Alice*	786
8	Livorno harbor, Italy, March 17, 1800, *Queen Charlotte*	over 700
9	Ertogrul, off the Japanese coast, September 19, 1890	587
10	Off Gibraltar, March 17, 1891, *Utopia*	576

THE 10
WORST PEACETIME OIL TANKER SPILLS OF ALL TIME

	Tanker	Location	Date	Approx. spillage (tons)
1	Atlantic Empress and Aegean Captain	Trinidad	July 19, 1979	331,000
2	Castillio de Bellver	Cape Town, South Africa	August 6, 1983	281,000
3	Olympic Bravery	Ushant, France	January 24, 1976	276,000
4	Showa-Maru	Malacca, Malaya	June 7, 1975	261,000
5	Amoco Cadiz	Finistère, France	March 16, 1978	246,000
6	Odyssey	Atlantic, off Canada	November 10, 1988	154,000
7	Torrey Canyon	Scilly Isles, UK	March 18, 1967	132,000
8	Sea Star	Gulf of Oman	December 19, 1972	127,000
9	Irenes Serenada	Pilos, Greece	February 23, 1980	112,000
10	Urquiola	Corunna, Spain	May 12, 1976	111,000

The grounding of the *Exxon Valdez* in Prince William Sound, Alaska, on March 24, 1989, ranks outside the 10 worst spills at about 35,000 tons of oil spilled, but resulted in major ecological damage. All the accidents in this Top 10 were caused by collision, grounding, fire, or explosion, but worse tanker oil spills have been caused by military action. Between January and June 1942, for example, German U-boats torpedoed a number of tankers off the east coast of the US with a loss of about 650,000 tons of oil, and in June 1991, during the Gulf War, various tankers were sunk in the Persian Gulf, spilling a total of more than 1,100,000 tons of oil.

FIRE DESTROYS SHIP ON GREAT LAKES

Canada suffered its greatest ship loss since the *Titanic* 50 years ago when a giant liner, the *Noronic*, burst into flames in the early hours of the morning of September 17, 1949, while docked at the Ontario Pier in Toronto. The cause of the fire has never been established. Most of the passengers and crew aboard the giant liner ran terrified to the starboard side of the ship, causing it to crash into the pier. The fire gutted the ship in 15 minutes, allowing no time to lower the lifeboats, which burned with the ship. Of the 511 on board that night, 207 died. Only four years earlier, the *Noronic's* sister ship, the *Hamonic* was also destroyed by fire. However, in that case only one person was killed in the blaze.

50 YEARS AGO

AIR DISASTERS

LOCKERBIE AIR CRASH AFTERMATH

THE 10 WORST AIR DISASTERS IN THE WORLD
(No. killed)

❶ Tenerife, Canary Islands, March 27, 1977 (583) ❷ Mt. Ogura, Japan, August 12, 1985 (520) ❸ Charkhi Dadri, India, November 12, 1996 (349) ❹ France, Paris, March 3, 1974 (346) ❺ Off the Irish coast, June 23, 1985 (329) ❻ Riyadh, Saudi Arabia, August 19, 1980 (301) ❼ Kinshasa, Dem. Rep. of Congo, January 8, 1996 (300) ❽ Off the Iranian coast, July 3, 1988 (290) ❾ Chicago, May 25, 1979 (273) ❿ Lockerbie, Scotland, December 21, 1988 (270)

THE 10
WORST AIR COLLISIONS IN THE WORLD

	Location/date/incident	No. killed
1	Charkhi Dadrio, India, November 12, 1996	349
	(See The 10 Worst Air Disasters in the World, No. 3.)	
2	Near Gaj, Yugoslavia, September 10, 1976	177
	A British Airways Trident and a Yugoslav DC-9 collided.	
3	Near Dneprodzerzhinsk, Ukraine, USSR, August 11, 1979	173
	Two Soviet Tupolev-134 Aeroflot airliners collided in midair.	
4	Morioko, Japan, July 30, 1971	162
	An air collision occurred between an All Nippon Boeing 727 and Japanese Air Force F-86F.	
5	Near Souq as-Sabt, Libya, December 22, 1992	157
	A Libyan Boeing 747 and a Libyan Air Force MiG-23 fighter collided.	
6	San Diego, California, September 25, 1978	144
	A Pacific Southwest Boeing 727 collided in the air with a Cessna 172 light aircraft with a student pilot, killing 135 in the airliner.	
7	New York City, December 16, 1960	134
	A United Airlines DC-8 and a TWA Super Constellation collided.	
8	Tehran, Iran, February 8, 1993	132
	As it took off, a passenger aircraft was struck by a military aircraft.	
9	Grand Canyon, Arizona, June 30, 1956	128
	A United Airlines DC-7 and a TWA Super Constellation collided.	
10	Ankara, Turkey, February 1, 1963	104
	A Middle East Airlines Viscount 754 and a Turkish Air Force C-47 collided.	

THE 10
WORST AVIATION DISASTERS WITH GROUND FATALITIES

	Location/date/incident	Ground fatalities
1	Kinshasa, Dem. Rep. of Congo, January 8, 1996	300
	An Antonov-32 cargo plane crashed shortly after takeoff.	
2	Santa Cruz, Bolivia, October 13, 1976	110
	A Lloyd A. Boliviana B-707 crashed on takeoff.	
3	Dar Nang, South Vietnam, December 24, 1966	107
	A Canadair CL-44 crash-landed into a village.	
4	Ankara, Turkey, February 1, 1963	87
	A Vickers Viscount 754 and a Turkish Air Force Douglas C-47 collided and fell into the city.	
5	Maracaibo, Venezuela, March 16, 1969	71
	A DC-9 crashed into the city after hitting power lines.	
6	Ramstein US Air Force base, Germany, August 28, 1988	67
	Three fighters in an Italian aerobatic team crashed into a crowd.	
7	Irkutsk, Russia, December 6, 1997	63
	An Antonov An-124 cargo aircraft suffered engine failure.	
8	Campo de Marte, Bogota, Colombia, July 24, 1938	53
	A low-flying stunt plane crashed into a stand, broke up, and hurled blazing wreckage into the crowd.	
9	Freckelton, Lancashire, UK, August 23, 1944	51
	A B-24 bomber crashed into a school.	
10	Mexico City, Mexico, August 1, 1987	44
	An overloaded Belize Air B-377 crashed on takeoff.	

THE 10

WORST AIRSHIP DISASTERS IN THE WORLD

Location/date/incident	No. killed
1 Off the Atlantic coast, US, April 4, 1933	73

US Navy airship Akron *crashed into the sea in a storm.*

| **2** Over the Mediterranean, December 21, 1923 | 52 |

French airship Dixmude *is assumed to have been struck by lightning.*

| **3** Near Beauvais, France, October 5, 1930 | 50 |

British airship R101 crashed into a hillside.

| **4** Off the coast near Hull, UK, August 24, 1921 | 44 |

Airship R38 broke in two on a training and test flight.

| **5** Lakehurst, New Jersey, May 6, 1937 | 36 |

German Zeppelin Hindenburg *caught fire when mooring.*

| **6** Hampton Roads, Virginia, February 21, 1922 | 34 |

Roma *crashed killing all but 11 people on board.*

| **7** Berlin, Germany, October 17, 1913 | 28 |

German airship LZ18 crashed after engine failure during a test flight.

| **8** Baltic Sea, March 30, 1917 | 23 |

German airship SL9 was struck by lightning on a flight.

| **9** Mouth of the River Elbe, Germany, September 3, 1915 | 19 |

German airship L10 was struck by lightning and plunged into the sea.

| **10=** Off Heligoland, September 9, 1913 | 14 |

German Navy airship L1 crashed into the sea.

| **=** Caldwell, Ohio, September 3, 1925 | 14 |

US dirigible Shenandoah *broke up in a storm, scattering sections over many miles of the Ohio countryside.*

THE 10

WORST AIR DISASTERS IN THE US

Location/date/incident	No. killed
1 Chicago, Illinois, May 25, 1979	273

An engine fell off a DC-10 as it took off from Chicago's O'Hare Airport, killing all 271 on board and two on the ground.

| **2** Off Long Island, New York, July 17, 1996 | 230 |

Soon after takeoff from JFK, a TWA Boeing 747-100 en route for Paris exploded in midair and crashed into the Atlantic Ocean 9 miles (14.5 km) south of Moriches Inlet, Long Island, killing all on board.

| **3** Romulus, Michigan, August 16, 1987 | 156 |

A Northwest Airlines McDonnell Douglas DC-9 crashed onto a road following an engine fire after takeoff from Detroit.

| **4** Kenner, Louisiana, July 9, 1982 | 153 |

A Pan American Boeing 727 crashed after takeoff from New Orleans for Las Vegas, killing all on board (137 passengers and the crew of eight) and eight on the ground.

| **5** San Diego, California, September 25, 1978 | 144 |

A Pacific Southwest Airline Boeing 727 collided in the air with a Cessna 172 light aircraft, killing 135 in the airliner, two in the Cessna, and seven on the ground.

| **6** Dallas-Ft. Worth Airport, Texas, August 2, 1985 | 137 |

A Delta Airlines TriStar crashed when a severe down draft affected it during landing, killing 136 on board and a truck driver on the ground.

| **7** New York, December 16, 1960 | 134 |

A United Air Lines DC-8 with 77 passengers and seven crew and a TWA Super Constellation with 39 passengers and five crew collided in a snow-storm. The DC-8 crashed in Brooklyn, killing six on the ground; the Super Constellation crashed in Staten Island harbor, killing all on board.

| **8** Pittsburgh, Pennsylvania, September 8, 1994 | 132 |

A US Air Boeing 737-400 en route from Chicago to West Palm Beach, Florida, crashed 7 miles (11.25 km) from Pittsburgh airport, killing all the passengers and crew.

| **9** Grand Canyon, Arizona, June 30, 1956 | 128 |

A United Airlines DC-7 and a TWA Super Constellation collided in the air, killing all on board both planes in the worst civil aviation disaster to that date.

| **10** JFK Airport, New York, June 24, 1975. | 115 |

An Eastern Airlines Boeing 727 on a flight from New Orleans crashed while attempting to land during a storm.

DEADLY HIJACK
On November 23, 1996, an Ethiopian Airlines Boeing 767 was hijacked and ditched in the sea off the Comoros Islands, killing 158 of the 175 on board.

ACCIDENTS AT WORK & HOME

LATEST YEARS OF HOME FATALITIES IN THE US CAUSED BY FIRE

Year	Deaths	Fires	Year	Deaths	Fires
1996	4,035	417,000	1991	3,500	464,500
1995	3,640	414,000	1990	4,050	454,500
1994	3,425	488,000	1989	4,335	498,500
1993	3,720	458,000	1988	4,955	538,500
1992	3,705	459,000	1987	4,570	536,500

Source: National Fire Protection Association

CAUSES OF FATALITIES AT WORK IN THE US

	Accident	Total (1995)
1	Highway traffic incidents	1,329
2	Assaults and violent acts by persons	1,024
3	Fall to lower level	573
4	Struck by object	546
5	Nonhighway incident, except rail, air, water	388
6	Nonpassenger struck by vehicle, mobile equipment	385
7	Contact with electric current	347
8	Aircraft incident	278
9	Caught in or compressed by equipment or object	255
10	Self-inflicted injury	215

Other causes of fatal accidents at work include explosion; exposure to caustic, noxious, or allergenic substances; caught in or crushed in collapsing materials; fire; oxygen deficiency; water vehicle incident; and railroad incident.

Source: National Safety Council/Bureau of Labor Statistics, Census of Fatal Occupational Injuries data

MOST ACCIDENT-PRONE COUNTRIES

	Country	Accidental death rate (per 100,000 population)
1	Estonia	153.5
2	Lithuania	120.7
3	South Africa	99.4
4	Hungary	74.3
5	Moldova	72.1
6	Latvia	71.7
7	Czech Republic	60.7
8	South Korea	59.9
9	Romania	57.1
10	Slovenia	55.2
	US	35.0

ARTICLES MOST FREQUENTLY INVOLVED IN ACCIDENTS IN THE HOME

	Article	Accidents per annum*		Article	Accidents per annum*
1	Construction feature	775,000	6	Building/raw materials	159,000
2	Furniture	329,000	7	Furnishings	145,000
3	Person	230,000	8	Cooking/kitchen equipment	134,000
4	Outdoor surface	194,000	9	Animal/insect	113,000
5	Clothing/footwear	191,000	10	Food/drink	109,000
				Total	2,502,000

* *National estimates based on actual Home Accident Surveillance System figures for sample population*

THE 10

MOST COMMON CAUSES OF DOMESTIC FIRE IN THE US*

	Major cause	Fires
1	Cooking equipment	99,300
2	Heating equipment	74,400
3	Incendiary or suspicious causes	55,000
4	Other equipment	44,500
5	Electrical distribution system	39,400
6	Appliance, tool, or air-conditioning	30,700
7	Smoking materials	23,800
8	Child playing	21,900
9	Open flame, torch	20,800
10	Exposure (to other hostile fire)	17,200

* Survey conducted by the NFIRS and NFPA covering the period 1991–95.

Source: National Fire Protection Association

PERILOUS WORK
Since the 19th century, most countries have introduced laws designed to make working conditions in factories less hazardous.

THE 10

INDUSTRIES WITH THE MOST INJURIES IN THE US

	Industry	Injury rate*
1	Meat-packing	36.6
2	Shipbuilding and repairing	32.7
3	Motor vehicles and car bodies	31.5
4	Truck trailers	31.2
5=	Gray and ductile iron foundries	29.2
=	Iron foundries	29.2
7	Secondary nonferrous metals	26.1
8	Malleable iron foundries	26.0
9	Mobile homes	24.3
10	Automotive stampings	23.8

* Nonfatal, per 100 employees, 1995

Source: US Bureau of Labor Statistics

THE 10

MOST COMMON CAUSES OF INJURY AT WORK IN THE US*

	Cause	Days lost
1	Contact with objects, equipment	27,500,000
2	Overexertion	27,400,000
3	Fall to same level	11,000,000
4=	Fall to lower level	5,100,000
=	Exposure to harmful substances	5,100,000
6	Repetitive motion	4,000,000
7	Transportation accidents	3,600,000
8	Slips, trips	2,900,000
9	Assault, violent act by person	1,100,000
10	Fires, explosions	200,000

* 1995, based on injuries and illnesses involving days away from work

Source: National Safety Council/Bureau of Labor Statistics

THE 10

MOST COMMON CAUSES OF ACCIDENTAL DEATH IN THE US

	Cause	Total (1994)
1	Motor vehicle	42,524
2	Falls	13,450
3	Poisoning by solids and liquid	8,309
4	Fires and flames	3,475
5	Drowning	3,404
6	Suffocation by ingested object	3,065
7	Complications, misadventures, and surgical, medical care	2,616
8	Natural and environmental factors	1,474
9	Firearms	1,356
10	Mechanical suffocation	1,078

Source: National Safety Council

THE 10

MOST DANGEROUS JOBS IN THE US

	Job sector	Fatalities
1	Agriculture, forestry, and fishing	793
2	Special trade contractors	613
3	Trucking and warehousing	462
4	Wholesale trade	254
5	Heavy construction, other than building	245
6	Business services	211
7	Food stores	188
8	Lumber and wood products	182
9	General building contractors	175
10	Eating and drinking places	164

In 1995 a total of 6,210 people received fatal occupational injuries. Of these, 5,438 were employed in private industry and 772 in state or federal government.

Source: US Bureau of Labor Statistics

INDUSTRIAL & OTHER DISASTERS

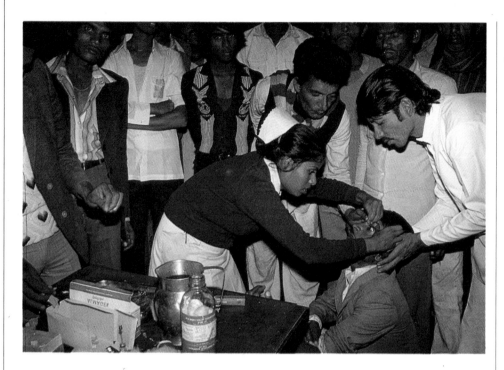

The leak of toxic gas at a chemical plant in a heavily populated area resulted in nearly 3,000 deaths, with up to 200,000 people injured.

THE 10
WORST MINING DISASTERS

	Location	Date	No. killed
1	Hinkeiko, China	Apr 26, 1942	1,549
2	Courrières, France	Mar 10, 1906	1,060
3	Omuta, Japan	Nov 9, 1963	447
4	Senghenydd, UK	Oct 14, 1913	439
5	Coalbrook, South Africa	Jan 21, 1960	437
6	Wankie, Rhodesia	Jun 6, 1972	427
7	Dharbad, India	May 28, 1965	375
8	Chasnala, India	Dec 27, 1975	372
9	Monongah, US	Dec 6, 1907	362
10	Barnsley UK	Dec 12, 866	361*

* Including 27 killed the following day while searching for survivors

THE 10
WORST DISASTERS AT SPORTS VENUES IN THE 20TH CENTURY

	Location/incident	Date	No. killed
1	Hong Kong Jockey Club (stand collapse and fire)	February 26, 1918	604
2	Lenin Stadium, Moscow (stampede in soccer stadium)	October 20, 1982	340
3	Lima, Peru (soccer stadium riot)	May 24, 1964	320
4	Sinceljo, Colombia (bullring stand collapse)	January 20, 1980	222
5	Hillsborough, Sheffield, UK (stampede in soccer stadium)	April 15, 1989	96
6	Guatemala City, Guatemala (stampede in Mateo Flores National Stadium during World Cup soccer qualifying match, Guatemala *vs.* Costa Rica, with 127 injured)	October 16, 1996	83
7	Le Mans, France (race-car crash)	June 11, 1955	82
8	Katmandu, Nepal (stampede in soccer stadium)	March 12, 1988	80
9	Buenos Aires, Argentina (riot in soccer stadium)	May 23, 1968	74
10	Ibrox Park, Glasgow, Scotland (barrier collapse in soccer stadium)	January 2, 1971	66

A mine disaster at the Fushun mines, Manchuria, in February 1931, may have resulted in up to 3,000 deaths, but information was suppressed by the Chinese government. Soviet security was responsible for obscuring details of an explosion at the Johanngeorgendstadt uranium mine in East Germany on November 29, 1949, when as many as 3,700 may have died. Among the most tragic disasters of this century, that at Aberfan, Wales, on October 20, 1966, was a mine disaster that affected the mining community rather than the miners. Waste from the local mine had built up for many years to become a heap some 800 ft/244 m high. Weakened by the presence of a spring, a huge volume of slurry suddenly flowed down and engulfed the local school, killing 144, of whom 116 were children.

Before the Ibrox Park disaster, the worst accident at a British stadium was caused by the collapse of a stand at Burnden Park, Bolton, on March 9, 1946, which left 33 dead and 400 injured. If stunt-flying is included as a "sport," the worst airshow disaster of all time occurred at the Ramstein US Air Force base, Germany, on August 28, 1988, when three fighters in an Italian aerobatic team collided, one of them crashing into the crowd, leaving 70 dead and 150 injured. Such tragedies are not an exclusively modern phenomenon: during the reign of Roman Emperor Antoninus Pius (AD 138–161), a stand at the Circus Maximus collapsed during a gladiatorial spectacle, and 1,162 spectators were killed.

THE 10

WORST EXPLOSIONS*

	Location/incident	Date	No. killed[#]
1	Lanchow, China (arsenal)	Oct 26, 1935	2,000
2	Halifax, Nova Scotia (ammunition ship *Mont Blanc*)	Dec 6, 1917	1,635
3	Memphis, Tennessee (steamboat *Sultana* boiler explosion)	Apr 27, 1865	1,547
4	Bombay, India (ammunition ship *Fort Stikine*)	Apr 14, 1944	1,376
5	Cali, Colombia (ammunition trucks)	Aug 7, 1956	1,200
6	Salang Tunnel, Afghanistan (gasoline tanker collision)	Nov 2, 1982	over 1,100
7	Chelyabinsk, USSR (liquid gas beside railroad)	Jun 3, 1989	up to 800
8	Texas City, Texas (ammonium nitrate on *Grandcamp* freighter)	Apr 16, 1947	752
9	Oppau, Germany (chemical plant)	Sep 21, 1921	561
10	Mexico City, Mexico (PEMEX gas plant)	Nov 20, 1984	540

* *Excluding mining disasters, and terrorist and military bombs*

All these "best estimate" figures should be treated with caution, since – as with fires and shipwrecks – body counts are notoriously unreliable.

THE 10

WORST FIRES OF THE 20TH CENTURY*

	Location/incident	Date	No. killed
1	Kwanto, Japan (following earthquake)	Sep 1, 1923	60,000
2	Chungking, China (docks)	Sep 2, 1949	1,700
3	Cloquet, Minnesota (forest)	Oct 12, 1918	800
4	Mandi Dabwali, India (school tent)	Dec 23, 1995	over 500
5	Hoboken, New Jersey (docks)	Jun 30, 1900	326
6=	Brussels, Belgium (department store)	May 22, 1967	322
=	Ohio State Penitentiary, Columbus, Ohio	Apr 21, 1930	322
8	London High School, London, Texas	Mar 18, 1937	294
9	Guatemala City, Guatemala (mental hospital)	July 14, 1960	225
10	São Paulo, Brazil (city fire)	Feb 1, 1974	220

* *Excluding sports and entertainment venues, mining disasters, and the results of military action*

THE 10

WORST COMMERCIAL AND INDUSTRIAL DISASTERS*

	Location/date/incident	No. killed
1	Bhopal, India, December 3, 1984 (methyl isocyante gas escape at Union Carbide plant)	up to 3,000
2	Seoul, Korea, June 29, 1995 (collapse of Sampoong Department Store)	640
3	Oppau, Germany, September 21, 1921 (chemical plant explosion)	561
4	Mexico City, Mexico, November 20, 1984 (explosion at a PEMEX liquified petroleum gas plant)	540
5	Brussels, Belgium, May 22, 1967 (fire in L'Innovation department store)	322
6	Novosibirsk, USSR, April 1979 (anthrax infection following accident at biological and chemical warfare plant)	up to 300
7	Guadalajara, Mexico, April 22, 1992 (explosions caused by gas leak into sewers)	230
8	São Paulo, Brazil, February 1, 1974 (fire in Joelma bank and office building)	227
9	Oakdale, Pennsylvania, May 18, 1918 (chemical plant explosion)	193
10	Bangkok, Thailand, May 10, 1993 (fire engulfed a four-story doll factory)	187

* *Including industrial sites, factories, offices, and stores; excluding military, mining, marine and other transportation disasters*

THE 10

WORST DISASTERS AT THEATER AND ENTERTAINMENT SITES*

	Location	Date	No. killed
1	Canton, China (theater)	May 25, 1845	1,670
2	Shanghai, China (theater)	Jun 1871	900
3	Lehmann Circus, Russia,	Feb 14, 1836	800
4	Antoung, China (movie theater)	Feb 13, 1937	658
5	Ring Theater, Vienna	Dec 8, 1881	620
6	Iroquois Theater, Chicago	Dec 30, 1903	591
7	Cocoanut Grove Night Club, Boston	Nov 28, 1942	491
8	Abadan, Iran (theater)	Aug 20, 1978	422
9	Niteroi, Brazil (circus)	Dec 17, 1961	323
10	Brooklyn Theater, New York	Dec 5, 1876	295

* *19th and 20th centuries, excluding sports stadiums and racetracks*

NATURAL DISASTERS

WORST FLOODS AND STORMS OF THE 20TH CENTURY

	Location	Date	Estimated no. killed
1	Huang He River, China	Aug 1931	3,700,000
2	Bangladesh	Nov 13, 1970	300–500,000
3	Henan, China	Sep 1939	over 200,000
4	Chang Jiang River, China	Sep 1911	100,000
5	Bengal, India	Nov 15–16, 1942	40,000
6	Bangladesh	Jun 1–2, 1965	30,000
7	Bangladesh	May 28–29, 1963	22,000
8	Bangladesh	May 11–12, 1965	17,000
9	Morvi, India	Aug 11, 1979	5,000-15,000
10=	Hong Kong	Sep 18, 1906	10,000
=	Bangladesh	May 25, 1985	10,000

WORST EARTHQUAKES OF THE 20TH CENTURY

	Location	Date	Estimated no. killed
1	Tang-shan, China	Jul 28, 1976	242,419
2	Nan-shan, China	May 22, 1927	200,000
3	Kansu, China	Dec 16, 1920	180,000
4	Messina, Italy	Dec 28, 1908	160,000
5	Tokyo/Yokohama, Japan	Sep 1, 1923	142,807
6	Kansu, China	Dec 25, 1932	70,000
7	Yungay, Peru	May 31, 1970	66,800
8	Quetta, India*	May 30, 1935	50–60,000
9	Armenia	Dec 7, 1988	over 55,000
10	Iran	Jun 21, 1990	over 40,000

* Now Pakistan

There are some discrepancies between the "official" death tolls of many of the world's worst earthquakes and the estimates of other authorities: a figure of 750,000 is sometimes quoted for the Tang-shan earthquake of 1976, for example. The earthquake that struck Kobe, Japan (now officially known as the Hyougo-ken Nanbu earthquake) at 5:46 a.m. on January 17, 1995, was precisely monitored. It left a total of 3,842 dead and 14,679 injured. Another 114,679 people were immediately evacuated.

KOBE EARTHQUAKE DAMAGE
Reaching 7.2 on the Richter scale, the initial shock completely destroyed 54,949 buildings and damaged 31,783 more.

WORST EPIDEMICS OF ALL TIME

	Epidemic	Location	Date	Estimated no. killed
1	Black Death	Europe/Asia	1347–51	75,000,000
2	Influenza	Worldwide	1918–20	21,640,000
3	AIDS	Worldwide	1981–	6,400,000
4	Plague	India	1896–1907	5,000,000
5=	"Plague of Justinian"	Rome	541–590	millions*
=	Cholera	Worldwide	1846–60	millions*
=	Cholera	Europe	1826–37	millions*
=	Cholera	Worldwide	1893–94	millions*
=	Plague	China, India	1910–13	millions*
=	Smallpox	Mexico	1530–45	over 1,000,000

* No precise figures available

THE 10

WORST AVALANCHES AND LANDSLIDES OF THE 20TH CENTURY*

	Location	Incident	Date	Estimated no. killed
1	Yungay, Peru	Landslide	May 31, 1970	17,500
2	Italian Alps	Avalanche	Dec 13 , 1916	10,000
3	Huarás, Peru	Avalanche	Dec 13, 1941	5,000
4	Nevada Huascaran, Peru	Avalanche	Jan 10, 1962	3,500
5	Medellin, Colombia	Landslide	Sep 27, 1987	683
6	Chungar, Peru	Avalanche	Mar 19, 1971	600
7	Rio de Janeiro, Brazil	Landslide	Jan 11,1966	550
8=	Northern Assam, India	Landslide	Feb 15, 1949	500
=	Grande Rivière du Nord, Haiti	Landslide	Nov 13/14, 1963	500
10	Blons, Austria	Avalanche	Jan 11, 1954	411

* Excluding those where most deaths resulted from flooding, earthquakes, etc., associated with landslides

The worst incident of all, the destruction of Yungay, Peru, in May 1970, was only part of a much larger cataclysm that left a vast total of up to 70,000 people dead.

THE 10

WORST TSUNAMIS OF THE 20TH CENTURY

	Locations affected	Date	Estimated no. killed
1	Agadir, Morocco*	Feb 29, 1960	12,000
2=	Philippines	Aug 17, 1976	5,000
=	Chile/Pacific islands/Japan	May 22, 1960	5,000
4	Japan/Hawaii	Mar 2, 1933	3,000
5	Japan*	Dec 21, 1946	1,088
6	Japan	Dec 4, 1944	998
7	Lomblem Island, Indonesia	Jul 22, 1979	700
8	Colombia	Dec 12, 1979	500
9	Hawaii/Aleutians/California	Apr 1, 1946	173
10	Alaska/Aleutians/California*	Mar 27, 1964	122

* Combined effect of earthquake and tsunamis

Tsunamis (from the Japanese tsu [port] and nami [wave]) are powerful waves caused by undersea disturbances such as earthquakes or volcanic eruptions. Tsunamis can be so intense that they frequently cross entire oceans, devastating any islands and coastal regions that lie in their paths.

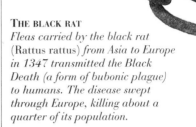

THE BLACK RAT
Fleas carried by the black rat (Rattus rattus) from Asia to Europe in 1347 transmitted the Black Death (a form of bubonic plague) to humans. The disease swept through Europe, killing about a quarter of its population.

THE 10

WORST 20TH CENTURY VOLCANIC ERUPTIONS

	Location/date	Estimated no. killed
1	Mt. Pelée, Martinique, May 8, 1902	up to 40,000

After lying dormant for centuries, Mt. Pelée began to erupt in April 1902. When the volcano burst apart at 7:30 a.m. on May 8th, it showered the port with molten lava, ash, and gas, destroying all life and property.

| 2 | Nevado del Ruiz, Colombia, November 13, 1985 | 22,940 |

The Andean volcano gave warning signs of erupting, but by the time it was decided to evacuate the local inhabitants, it was too late. The hot steam, rocks, and ash ejected from Nevado del Ruiz melted its icecap, resulting in a mudslide that completely engulfed the town of Armero.

| 3 | Keluit, Java, May 19, 1919 | 5,110 |

One of the most remarkable of all volcanic eruptions on record, water pouring from Keluit's crater lake drowned inhabitants on the lower slopes.

| 4 | Santa Maria, Guatemala, October 24, 1902 | 4,500 |

Some 1,500 died as a direct consequence of the volcanic eruption, and another 3,000 as a result of its aftereffects.

| 5 | Mt. Lamington, New Guinea, January 21, 1951 | 2,942 |

Mt. Lamington erupted with hardly any warning, with a huge explosion that was heard up to 200 miles/320 km away.

| 6 | El Chichón, Mexico, March 29, 1982 | 1,879 |

Of these, 1,755 people were reported missing and 124 confirmed killed.

| 7 | Lake Nyos, Cameroon, August 21, 1986 | more than 1,700 |

A volcano erupted beneath the lake, and gases killed sleeping villagers.

| 8 | La Soufrière, St. Vincent, May 7–8, 1902 | 1,565 |

The day before the cataclysmic eruption of Mt. Pelée (No. 1), La Soufrière erupted and engulfed the local inhabitants in ash flows.

| 9 | Merapi, Java, December 18, 1931 | 1,369 |

In addition to the human casualties, 2,140 cattle were killed.

| 10 | Taal, Philippines, January 30, 1911 | 1,335 |

Taal has erupted frequently, with the 1911 incident the worst of several this century.

TOWN & COUNTRY

NEW YORK

TOP 10

LEAST POPULATED COUNTRIES IN THE WORLD

	Country	Population
1	Vatican City	840
2	San Marino	25,000
3	Monaco	27,000
4	Liechtenstein	28,000
5	Marshall Islands	45,000
6	Dominica	72,000
7	Kiribati	73,000
8	Seychelles	74,000
9	Grenada	89,000
10	Tonga	93,000

Source: United Nations

THEN & NOW

TOP 10 MOST HIGHLY POPULATED COUNTRIES IN THE WORLD

Population 1987	Country		Country	Population 1997
1,104,193,000	China	1	China	1,243,738,000
783,730,000	India	2	India	960,178,000
388,100,000	USSR	3	US	271,648,000
242,836,000	US	4	Indonesia	203,479,000
172,010,000	Indonesia	5	Brazil	163,132,000
137,267,000	Brazil	6	Russia	147,709,000
122,069,000	Japan	7	Pakistan	143,831,000
102,705,000	Pakistan	8	Japan	125,638,000
102,563,000	Bangladesh	9	Bangladesh	122,013,000
101,408,000	Nigeria	10	Nigeria	118,369,000
5,026,319,000	*World*		*World*	5,847,465,000

The population of China is now more than 4½ times that of the US and represents a percentage of the total population of the world that proves the commonly stated statistic that "one person in five is Chinese." The Top 10, which accounts for about 60 percent of the world's population, remains largely the same from year to year, and contains every country with a population of more than 100,000,000. The main changes between 1987 and 1997 are the positions of Pakistan and Brazil which, with their rapidly growing populations, have swapped places with Japan and Russia, respectively. Also, because of the Soviet breakup in 1991, the USSR has been replaced in this list by Russia.

Source: United Nations

TOP 10
COUNTRIES OF ORIGIN OF US IMMIGRANTS, 1820–1996

	Country of last residence	No. of immigrants
1	Germany	7,142,393
2	Mexico*	5,542,625
3	Italy	5,427,298
4	UK	5,225,701
5	Ireland	4,778,159
6	Canada	4,423,066
7	USSR#	3,752,811
8	Austria†	1,841,068
9	Hungary†	1,673,579
10	Philippines	1,379,403

* Unreported 1886–93

\# Russia before 1917

† Unreported before 1861; combined 1861–1905; separately 1905; Austria included with Germany 1938–45

For many years the United States has been the magnet that attracted vast numbers of immigrants: in 1903–15, for example, an average of 982,655 arrived every year. From 1820, when detailed records were first kept, until 1996, the total number of immigrants recorded was 63,140,227.

Source: US Immigration and Naturalization Service

TOP 10
COUNTRIES WITH THE YOUNGEST POPULATIONS

	Country	Percentage of pop. under 15
1	Cote d'Ivoire	49.1
2	Uganda	48.8
3	Comoros	48.7
4	Niger	48.4
5	Dem. Rep. of Congo	48.0
6	Kenya	47.7
7=	Oman	47.5
=	Somalia	47.5
9=	Benin	47.4
=	Mali	47.4
=	Zambia	47.4
	US	22.0

Source: World Health Organization

TOP 10
FASTEST-GROWING COUNTRIES IN THE WORLD

	Country	Population growth rate (percent per annum)
1	Liberia	8.56
2	Rwanda	7.85
3	Afghanistan	5.27
4	Oman	4.16
5	Bosnia and Herzegovina	3.90
6	Somalia	3.89
7	Yemen	3.74
8	Eritrea	3.66
9	Marshall Islands	3.51
10	Maldives	3.44
	US	0.79

Source: United Nations

TOP 10
FASTEST-SHRINKING COUNTRIES IN THE WORLD

	Country	Population growth rate (percent per annum)		Country	Population growth rate (percent per annum)
1	Latvia	-1.13	6	Russia	-0.31
2	Estonia	-0.96	7	Lithuania	-0.25
3	Hungary	-0.59	8	Romania	-0.20
4	Bulgaria	-0.48	9=	Belarus	-0.13
5	Ukraine	-0.37	=	Czech Republic	-0.13
				US	0.7

Source: United Nations

COUNTRIES OF THE WORLD

TOP 10

COUNTRIES WITH THE MOST NEIGHBORS

Country/neighbors	No. of neighbors
1 China	15

Afghanistan, Bhutan, India, Kazakhstan, Kyrgyzstan, Laos, Macau, Mongolia, Myanmar, Nepal, North Korea, Pakistan, Russia, Tajikistan, Vietnam

2 Russia	14

Azerbaijan, Belarus, China, Estonia, Finland, Georgia, Kazakhstan, Latvia, Lithuania, Mongolia, North Korea, Norway, Poland, Ukraine

3 Brazil	10

Argentina, Bolivia, Colombia, French Guiana, Guyana, Paraguay, Peru, Surinam, Uruguay, Venezuela

4= Germany	9

Austria, Belgium, Czech Republic, Denmark, France, Luxembourg, Netherlands, Poland, Switzerland

= Sudan	9

Central African Republic, Chad, Dem. Rep. of Congo, Egypt, Eritrea, Ethiopia, Kenya, Libya, Uganda

= Dem. Rep. of Congo	9

Angola, Burundi, Central African Republic, Rep. of Congo, Rwanda, Sudan, Tanzania, Uganda, Zambia

7= Austria	8

Czech Republic, Germany, Hungary, Italy, Liechtenstein, Slovakia, Slovenia, Switzerland

= France	8

Andorra, Belgium, Germany, Italy, Luxembourg, Monaco, Spain, Switzerland

= Saudi Arabia	8

Iraq, Jordan, Kuwait, Oman, People's Democratic Republic of Yemen, Qatar, United Arab Emirates, Yemen Arab Republic

= Tanzania	8

Burundi, Dem. Rep. of Congo, Kenya, Malawi, Mozambique, Rwanda, Uganda, Zambia

= Turkey	8

Armenia, Azerbaijan, Bulgaria, Georgia, Greece, Iran, Iraq, Syria

TOP 10

LONGEST BORDERS IN THE WORLD

	Country	Length km	miles
1	China	22,143	13,759
2	Russia	20,139	12,514
3	Brazil	14,691	9,129
4	India	14,103	8,763
5	US	12,248	7,611
6	Dem. Rep. of Congo	10,271	6,382
7	Argentina	9,665	6,006
8	Canada	8,893	5,526
9	Mongolia	8,114	5,042
10	Sudan	7,697	4,783

This list represents the total length of borders, compiled by adding together the lengths of individual land borders. The 7,611 miles/12,248 km of the US's borders include those shared with Canada (3,987 miles/6,416 km of which comprise the longest continuous border in the world), the 1,539-mile/2,477-km boundary between Canada and Alaska, that with Mexico (2,067 miles/3,326 km), and between the US naval base at Guantánamo and Cuba (18 miles/ 29 km).

TOP 10

LARGEST COUNTRIES IN EUROPE

	Country	Area sq km	sq miles
1	Russia (in Europe)	4,710,227	1,818,629
2	Ukraine	603,700	233,090
3	France	547,026	211,208
4	Spain*	504,781	194,897
5	Sweden	449,964	173,732
6	Germany	356,999	137,838
7	Finland	337,007	130,119
8	Norway	324,220	125,182
9	Poland	312,676	120,725
10	Italy	301,226	116,304

* Including offshore islands

The United Kingdom falls just outside the Top 10 with an area of 94,247 sq miles/ 244,101 sq km, excluding the Isle of Man and the Channel Islands.

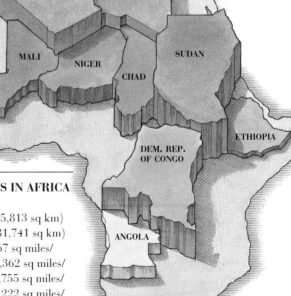

TOP 10 LARGEST COUNTRIES IN AFRICA
(Area)

❶ Sudan (967,500 sq miles/2,505,813 sq km)
❷ Algeria (919,595 sq miles/2,381,741 sq km)
❸ Dem. Rep. of Congo (905,567 sq miles/ 2,345,409 sq km) ❹ Libya (679,362 sq miles/ 1,759,540 sq km) ❺ Chad (495,755 sq miles/ 1,284,000 sq km) ❻ Niger (489,222 sq miles/ 1,267,080 sq km) ❼ Angola (481,354 sq miles/ 1,246,700 sq km) ❽ Mali (478,767 sq miles/ 1,240,000 sq km) ❾ Ethiopia (435,609 sq miles/ 1,128,121 sq km) ❿ South Africa (471,445 sq miles/1,221,031 sq km)

TOP 10 LARGEST COUNTRIES IN THE WORLD
(Area)

❶ Russia (6,590,876 sq miles/17,070,289 sq km) ❷ Canada (3,849,670 sq miles/ 9,970,599 sq km) ❸ China (3,705,408 sq miles/9,596,961 sq km) ❹ US (3,540,321 sq miles/9,169,389 sq km) ❺ Brazil (3,286,488 sq miles/8,511,965 sq km) ❻ Australia (2,967,909 sq miles/7,686,848 sq km) ❼ India (1,269,346 sq miles/ 3,287,590 sq km) ❽ Argentina (1,073,512 sq miles/2,780,400 sq km) ❾ Kazakhstan (1,049,156 sq miles/2,717,300 sq km) ❿ Sudan (967,500 sq miles/2,505,813 sq km)

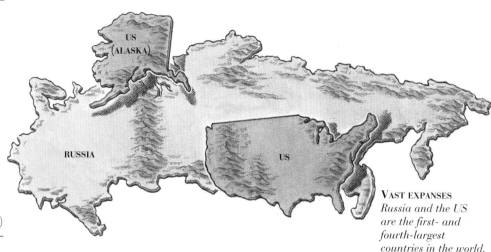

VAST EXPANSES
Russia and the US are the first- and fourth-largest countries in the world.

TOP 10
LARGEST COUNTRIES IN ASIA

	Country	Area sq km	sq miles
1	Russia (in Asia)	12,360,062	4,772,247
2	China	9,596,961	3,705,408
3	India	3,287,590	1,269,346
4	Kazakhstan	2,717,300	1,049,156
5	Saudi Arabia	2,149,640	830,000
6	Indonesia	1,904,569	735,358
7	Iran	1,648,000	636,296
8	Mongolia	1,565,000	604,250
9	Pakistan	803,950	310,407
10	Turkey (in Asia)	790,200	305,098

TOP 10
LARGEST COUNTRIES IN THE AMERICAS

	Country	Area sq km	sq miles
1	Canada	9,970,599	3,849,670
2	US	9,169,389	3,540,321
3	Brazil	8,511,965	3,286,488
4	Argentina	2,780,400	1,073,512
5	Mexico	1,958,201	756,066
6	Peru	1,285,216	496,225
7	Colombia	1,138,914	439,937
8	Bolivia	1,098,581	428,165
9	Venezuela	912,050	352,145
10	Chile	756,626	292,134

Geographically, Greenland (the largest island in the world) is considered part of the Americas but does not qualify as a country since it is under Danish control.

TOP 10
LARGEST COUNTRIES IN OCEANIA

	Country	Area sq km	sq miles
1	Australia	7,686,848	2,967,909
2	Papua New Guinea	461,691	178,260
3	New Zealand	268,676	103,736
4	Solomon Islands	28,446	10,983
5	New Caledonia	19,058	7,358
6	Fiji	18,274	7,055
7	Vanuatu	12,190	4,706
8	French Polynesia	4,000	1,544
9	Western Samoa	2,842	1,097
10	Kiribati	728	281

Australia is over nine times as large as the combined areas of the rest of the Top 10 Oceanian countries.

TOP 10
SMALLEST COUNTRIES IN THE WORLD

	Country	Area sq km	sq miles
1	Vatican City	0.44	0.17
2	Monaco	1.81	0.7
3	Gibraltar	6.47	2.5
4	Macau	16.06	6.2
5	Nauru	21.23	8.2
6	Tuvalu	25.90	10.0
7	Bermuda	53.35	20.6
8	San Marino	59.57	23.0
9	Liechtenstein	157.99	61.0
10	Antigua	279.72	108.0

The government, defense, currency, and other features of several of these microstates are often intricately linked with those of larger countries: the Vatican City with Italy, and Monaco with France, for example, while Gibraltar and Bermuda are dependent territories of the UK.

● Since the independence of Nauru in 1968, the landlocked state of San Marino has lost its status as the smallest republic. However, it remains the world's oldest republic, having been founded during the fourth century.

SNAP FACT

WORLD CITIES

MOST HIGHLY POPULATED CITIES IN SOUTH AMERICA

	City/country	Population
1	São Paulo, Brazil	18,701,000
2	Rio de Janeiro, Brazil	11,688,000
3	Buenos Aires, Argentina	11,657,000
4	Lima, Peru	6,815,000
5	Bogotá, Colombia	5,913,000
6	Santiago, Chile	5,378,000
7	Belo Horizonte, Brazil	3,812,000
8	Caracas, Venezuela	3,217,000
9	Pôrto Alegre, Brazil	3,114,000
10	Salvador, Brazil	2,298,000

HIGHEST TOWNS AND CITIES IN THE WORLD

	City/country	Height m	ft
1	Wenchuan, China	5,099	16,730
2	Potosí, Bolivia	3,976	13,045
3	Oruro, Bolivia	3,702	12,146
4	La Paz, Bolivia	3,632	11,916
5	Lhasa, Tibet	3,684	12,087
6	Cuzco, Peru	3,399	11,152
7	Huancayo, Peru	3,249	10,660
8	Sucre, Bolivia	2,835	9,301
9	Tunja, Colombia	2,820	9,252
10	Quito, Ecuador	2,819	9,249

Lhasa was formerly the highest capital city in the world, a role now occupied by La Paz, the capital of Bolivia. Wenchuan in China is more than half the elevation of Everest.

TOP 10 COUNTRIES WITH THE MOST MILLION-PLUS CITIES*
(No. of cities)
❶ China# (48) ❷ US (35) ❸ India (29)
❹ Germany (16) ❺= Brazil, Russia (13)
❼ Indonesia (9) ❽ Pakistan (8) ❾= Japan, Mexico, South Korea (6)
* Based on urban agglomeration
 # Includes Hong Kong

MOST DENSELY POPULATED CITIES IN THE WORLD*

	City/country	Population per sq km	sq mile
1	Hong Kong, China	98,053	253,957
2	Lagos, Nigeria	67,561	174,982
3	Dhaka, Bangladesh	63,900	165,500
4	Jakarta, Indonesia	56,650	146,724
5	Bombay, India	54,997	142,442
6	Ahmadabad, India	50,676	131,250
7	Ho Chi Minh City, Vietnam	50,617	131,097
8	Shenyang, China	44,125	114,282
9	Bangalore, India	43,583	112,880
10	Cairo, Egypt	41,413	107,260

* Includes only cities with populations of over 2,000,000

MOST HIGHLY POPULATED CITIES IN OCEANIA

	City/country	Population
1	Sydney, NSW, Australia	3,656,000
2	Melbourne, Vic., Australia	3,080,800
3	Brisbane, Qsl., Australia	1,310,650
4	Perth, W.Aus., Australia	1,193,130
5	Adelaide, S.Aus., Australia	1,049,875
6	Auckland, New Zealand	885,600
7	Newcastle, NSW, Australia	428,760
8	Honolulu, Hawaii	365,272
9	Wellington, New Zealand	325,682
10	Christchurch, New Zealand	307,200

MOST HIGHLY POPULATED CITIES IN EUROPE

	City/country	Population
1	Moscow*, Russia	10,769,000
2	London*, UK	8,897,000
3	Paris*, France	8,764,000
4	Istanbul#, Turkey	7,624,000
5	Essen, Germany	7,364,000
6	Milan, Italy	4,795,000
7	Madrid*, Spain	4,772,000
8	St. Petersburg, Russia	4,694,000
9	Barcelona, Spain	4,492,000
10	Manchester, UK	3,949,000

* Capital city
 # Located in the European part of Turkey

The problem of defining a city's boundaries means that population figures generally relate to "urban agglomerations," which often include large suburbs sprawling over enormous areas.

MOST POPULATED CHINESE CITY
China is the most populous country on the Earth, with Shanghai, its foremost port and industrial center, its largest city, with a total population of 15,082,000.

TOP 10

MOST HIGHLY POPULATED CITIES IN ASIA

	City	Country	Population*
1	Tokyo	Japan	26,836,000
2	Bombay	India	15,093,000
3	Shanghai	China	15,082,000
4	Beijing	China	12,362,000
5	Calcutta	India	11,673,000
6	Seoul	South Korea	11,641,000
7	Jakarta	Indonesia	11,500,000
8	Tianjin	China	10,687,000
9	Osaka	Japan	10,601,000
10	Delhi	India	9,882,000

* Of urban agglomeration
Source: United Nations

THE COLOSSEUM, ROME

TOP 10

MOST HIGHLY POPULATED CITIES IN AFRICA

	City/country	Population*		City/country	Population*
1	Lagos, Nigeria	10,287,000	6	Casablanca, Morocco	3,289,000
2	Cairo, Egypt	9,656,000	7	Tripoli, Libya	3,272,000
3	Kinshasa, Dem. Rep. of Congo	4,214,000	8	Abidjan, Côte d'Ivoire	2,797,000
4	Algiers, Algeria	3,702,000	9	Cape Town, South Africa	2,671,000
5	Alexandria, Egypt	3,577,000	10	Khartoum, Sudan	2,429,000

* Of urban agglomeration   *Source: United Nations*

THE 10 FIRST CITIES WITH POPULATIONS OF MORE THAN ONE MILLION

❶ Rome, Italy ❷ Angkor, Cambodia
❸ Hangchow (Hangzhou), China ❹ London, UK ❺ Paris, France ❻ Peking, China
❼ Canton, China ❽ Berlin, Prussia
❾ New York, US ❿ Vienna, Austria

TOP 10

LARGEST CITIES IN THE US*

	City/state	Population
1	New York, New York	7,380,906
2	Los Angeles, California	3,553,638
3	Chicago, Illinois	2,721,547
4	Houston, Texas	1,744,058
5	Philadelphia, Pennsylvania	1,478,002
6	San Diego, California	1,171,121
7	Phoenix, Arizona	1,159,014
8	San Antonio, Texas	1,067,816
9	Dallas, Texas	1,053,292
10	Detroit, Michigan	1,000,272

* Estimated figures up to July 1, 1996 for central city areas only, not for the total metropolitan areas

Source : US Bureau of the Census

TOP 10

MOST HIGHLY POPULATED CITIES IN THE WORLD, 1990/2000*

	City, country	1990 Population	2000 Population
1	Tokyo-Yokohama, Japan	26,952,000	29,971,000
2	Mexico City, Mexico	20,207,000	27,872,000
3	São Paulo, Brazil	18,052,000	25,354,000
4	Seoul, South Korea	16,268,000	21,976,000
5	Bombay, India	11,777,000	15,357,000
6	New York, US	14,622,000	14,648,000
7	Osaka-Kobe-Kyoto, Japan	13,826,000	14,287,000
8	Tehran, Iran	9,354,000	14,251,000
9	Rio de Janeiro, Brazil	11,428,000	14,169,000
10	Calcutta, India	11,663,000	14,088,000

* Based on US Bureau of the Census method of calculating urban agglomeration

US PLACES & PEOPLES

THE 10

LARGEST STATES IN THE US

	State	Area* sq km	sq miles		State	Area* sq km	sq miles
1	Alaska	1,700,130	656,424	6	Arizona	295,274	114,006
2	Texas	695,673	268,601	7	Nevada	286,367	110,567
3	California	423,999	163,707	8	Colorado	269,618	104,100
4	Montana	380,847	147,046	9	Oregon	254,819	98,386
5	New Mexico	314,937	121,598	10	Wyoming	253,347	97,818

* Total, including water

THE 10

FIRST STATES ADMITTED TO THE US

	State	Entered Union		State	Entered Union
1	Delaware	December 7, 1787	6	Massachusetts	February 6, 1788
2	Pennsylvania	December 12, 1787	7	Maryland	April 28, 1788
3	New Jersey	December 18, 1787	8	South Carolina	May 23, 1788
4	Georgia	January 2, 1788	9	New Hampshire	June 21, 1788
5	Connecticut	January 9, 1788	10	Virginia	June 25, 1788

THE 10

LATEST STATES ADMITTED TO THE US

	State	Entered Union		State	Entered Union
1	Hawaii	August 21, 1959	6	Utah	January 4, 1896
2	Alaska	January 3, 1959	7	Wyoming	July 10, 1890
3	Arizona	February 14, 1912	8	Idaho	July 3, 1890
4	New Mexico	January 6, 1912	9	Washington	November 11, 1889
5	Oklahoma	November 16, 1907	10	Montana	November 8, 1889

FIRE AND ICE

On March 2, 1899, Mount Rainier National Park, Washington, became only the fifth National Park in the US. Created by an Act of Congress, it comprises 378 square miles of fir forests and meadows radiating from a central point, Mount Rainier, a 14,411-ft dormant volcano down which an intricate network of glaciers flows, the greatest single–peak glacial system in the whole US. Situated 98 miles from Seattle, the park is a popular venue for hiking, winter sports, and other recreations. Mount Rainier itself was named in 1792 by Captain George Vancouver for his friend Rear Admiral Peter Rainier – who never saw "his" mountain.

100 YEARS AGO

THE 10

SMALLEST STATES IN THE US

	State	Area* sq km	sq miles
1	Rhode Island	4,002	1,545
2	Delaware	6,447	2,489
3	Connecticut	14,358	5,544
4	New Jersey	22,590	8,722
5	New Hampshire	24,219	9,351
6	Vermont	24,903	9,615
7	Massachusetts	27,337	10,555
8	Hawaii	28,313	10,932
9	Maryland	32,135	12,407
10	West Virginia	62,759	24,231

* Total, including water

TOP 10

MOST VISITED NATIONAL PARKS IN THE US

	Park/location	Visitors (1996)
1	Great Smoky Mountains National Park, North Carolina/Tennessee	9,265,667
2	Grand Canyon National Park, Arizona	4,537,703
3	Yosemite National Park, California	4,046,207
4	Olympic National Park, Washington	3,348,723
5	Yellowstone National Park, Wyoming	3,012,171
6	Rocky Mountain National Park, Colorado	2,923,755
7	Grand Teton National Park, Wyoming	2,733,439
8	Acadia National Park, Maine	2,704,831
9	Zion National Park, Utah	2,498,001
10	Mammoth Cave, Kentucky	1,896,829

The total number of visitors to US National Parks in 1996 was 63,061,828. Figures for Katmai, Alaska, and Samoa and American Samoa were unavailable.

TOP 10

LARGEST NATIVE AMERICAN TRIBES

	Tribe	Population
1	Cherokee	308,132
2	Navajo	219,198
3	Chippewa	103,826
4	Sioux	103,255
5	Choctaw	82,299
6	Pueblo	52,939
7	Apache	50,051
8	Iroquois	49,038
9	Lumbee	48,444
10	Creek	43,550

The 1990 Census found the total Native American population to be 1,878,285. Different authorities have estimated that the total North American population at the time of the first European arrivals in 1492 was anything from 1,000,000 to 10,000,000. This declined to a low in 1890 of about 90,000, but has experienced a subtantial resurgence in the past century.

TOP 10

LARGEST NATIVE AMERICAN RESERVATIONS

	Reservation/state	Population
1	Navajo, Arizona/New Mexico/Utah	143,405
2	Pine Ridge, Nebraska/South Dakota	11,182
3	Fort Apache, Arizona	9,825
4	Gila River, Arizona	9,116
5	Papago, Arizona	8,480
6	Rosebud, South Dakota	8,043
7	San Carlos, Arizona	7,110
8	Zuni Pueblo, Arizona/New Mexico	7,073
9	Hopi, Arizona	7,061
10	Blackfeet, Montana	7,025

THE 10

FIRST NATIONAL MONUMENTS IN THE US

	National Monument	Established
1	Little Big Horn Battlefield, Montana	Jan 29, 1879
2	Casa Grande Ruins, Arizona	Mar 2, 1889
3	Devils Tower, Wyoming	Sep 24, 1906
4=	El Morro, New Mexico	Dec 8, 1906
=	Montezuma Castle, Arizona	Dec 8, 1906
6	Gila Cliff Dwellings, New Mexico	Nov 16, 1907
7	Tonto, Arizona	Dec 19, 1907
8	Muir Woods, California	Jan 9, 1908
9	Grand Canyon, Arizona	Jan 11, 1908
10	Pinnacles, California	Jan 16, 1908

THE 10

FIRST NATIONAL HISTORIC SITES IN THE US

	National Historic Site	Established*
1	Ford's Theater, Washington DC	Apr 7, 1866
2	Abraham Lincoln Birthplace, Kentucky	Jul 17, 1916
3	Andrew Johnson, Tennessee	Aug 29, 1935
4	Jefferson National Expansion Memorial, Missouri	Dec 20, 1935
5	Whitman Mission, Washington	Jun 29, 1936
6	Salem Maritime, Massachusetts	Mar 17, 1938
7	Fort Laramie, Wyoming	Jul 16, 1938
8	Hopewell Furnace, Pennsylvania	Aug 3, 1938
9	Vanderbilt Mansion, New York	Dec 18, 1940
10	Fort Raleigh, North Carolina	Apr 5, 1941

* Dates include those for locations originally assigned other designations but later authorized as Historic Sites

THE 10

FIRST NATIONAL PARKS IN THE US

	National Park	Established
1	Yellowstone, Wyoming/Montana/Idaho	Mar 1, 1872
2	Sequoia, California	Sep 25, 1890
3=	Yosemite, California	Oct 1, 1890
=	General Grant, California*	Oct 1, 1890
5	Mount Rainier, Washington	Mar 2, 1899
6	Crater Lake, Oregon	May 22, 1902
7	Wind Cave, South Dakota	Jan 9, 1903
8	Mesa Verde, Colorado	Jun 29, 1906
9	Glacier, Montana	May 11, 1910
10	Rocky Mountain, Colorado	Jan 26, 1915

* Name changed to Kings Canyon National Park, March 4, 1940

THE 10

FIRST UNESCO HERITAGE SITES IN THE US

	Site	Year
1=	Mesa Verde National Park, Colorado	1978
=	Yellowstone National Park, Wyoming/Idaho/Montana	1978
3=	Everglades National Park, Florida	1979
=	Grand Canyon National Park, Arizona	1979
=	Independence Hall, Pennsylvania	1979
6	Redwood National Park, California	1980
7=	Mammoth Cave National Park, Kentucky	1981
=	Olympic National Park, Washington State	1981
9	Cahokia Mounds State Historic Site, Illinois	1982
10	Great Smokey Mountains National Park, North Carolina/Tennessee	1983

104

PLACE NAMES

TOP 10

MOST COMMON STREET NAMES IN THE US

1 Second Street
2 Park Street
3 Third Street
4 Fourth Street
5 Fifth Street
6 First Street
7 Sixth Street
8 Seventh Street
9 Washington Street
10 Maple Street

The list continues with Oak, Eighth, Elm, Lincoln, Ninth, Pine, Walnut, Tenth, and Cedar. Oddly, First is not first, because many streets that would be so designated are instead called Main.

TOP 10

MOST COMMON PLACE NAMES IN THE US

	Name	Occurrences
1	Fairview	287
2	Midway	252
3	Riverside	180
4	Oak Grove	179
5	Five Points	155
6	Oakland	149
7	Greenwood	145
8 =	Bethel	141
=	Franklin	141
10	Pleasant Hill	140

TOP 10

LONGEST PLACE NAMES IN THE US*

	Name	Letters
1	Chargoggagoggmanchauggagogg-chaubunagungamaugg (See The 10 Longest Place Names in the World, No. 6.)	45
2	Winchester-on-the-Severn, Maryland	21
3	Scraper-Moechereville, Illinois	20
4	Linstead-on-the-Severn, Maryland	19
5 =	Kentwood-in-the-Pines, California	18
=	Lauderdale-by-the-Sea, Florida	18
=	Vermilion-on-the-Lake, Ohio	18
8 =	Chippewa-on-the-Lake, Ohio	17
=	Fairhaven-on-the-Bay, Maryland	17
=	Highland-on-the-Lake, New York	17
=	Kleinfeltersville, Pennsylvania	17
=	Mooselookmeguntic, Maine	17
=	Palermo-by-the-Lakes, Ohio	17
=	Saybrook-on-the-Lake, Ohio	17

* Including only single-word and hyphenated names (not counting hyphens as characters)

TOP 10

COUNTRIES WITH THE LONGEST OFFICIAL NAMES

	Official name*	Common English name	Letters
1	Al Jamāhīrīyah al ʾArabīyah al Lībīyah ash Shaʾbīyah al Ishtirakīyah	Libya	56
2	Al Jumhūrīyah al Jazāʾirīyah ad Dīmuqrāṭīyah ash Shaʾbīyah	Algeria	49
3	United Kingdom of Great Britain and Northern Ireland	United Kingdom	45
4	Sri Lankā Prajathanthrika Samajavadi Janarajaya	Sri Lanka	43
5	Jumhūrīyat al-Qumur al-Ittihādīyah al-Islāmīyah	The Comoros	41
6 =	Al Jumhūrīyah al Islāmīyah al Mūrītānīyah	Mauritania	36
=	The Federation of St. Christopher and Nevis	St. Kitts and Nevis	36
8	Jamhuuriyadda Dimuqraadiga Soomaaliya	Somalia	35
9 =	al-Mamlakah al-Urdunnīyah al-Hāshimīyah	Jordan	34
=	Repoblika Demokratika n' i' Madagasikara	Madagascar	34

* Some official names have been transliterated from languages that do not use the Roman alphabet; their lengths may vary according to the method of transliteration used

There is clearly no connection between the lengths of names and the longevity of the nation states that bear them. Since this list was first published in 1991, the following three countries have ceased to exist: Socijalisticka Federativna Republika Jugoslavija (Yugoslavia, 45 letters), Soyuz Sovetskikh Sotsialisticheskikh Respublik (USSR, 43), and Ceskoslovenská Socialistická Republika (Czechoslovakia, 36). Uruguay's official name of La República Oriental del Uruguay (29 letters) is sometimes given in full as the 38-letter La República de la Banda Oriental del Uruguay, which would place it in 6th position.

TOP 10

MOST COMMON CITY NAMES IN THE US

	Name	Occurrences*
1	Fairview	66
2	Midway	52
3	Oak Grove	44
4 =	Franklin	40
=	Riverside	40
6	Centerville	39
7	Mount Pleasant	38
8	Georgetown	37
9	Salem	36
10	Greenwood	34

* Incorporated city status only

MOST COMMON PLACE NAMES OF BIBLICAL ORIGIN IN THE US

	Name/meaning	Occurrences
1	Bethel (house of God)	141
2	Salem (peace)	134
3	Eden (pleasure)	101
4	Shiloh (peace)	98
5	Paradise (pleasure ground)	94
6	Antioch (named for Antiochus, king of Syria)	83
7	Sharon (plain)	72
8	Jordan (descender)	65
9=	Bethany/Bethania (house of affliction)	59
=	Zion (mount, sunny)	59

This list takes account of all populated places (cities, towns, and villages) in the US and includes compound names, such as Salemville and Salem Height.

MOST COMMON STREET NAMES IN THE UK

1	High Street	6	Station Approach
2	Station Road	7	Green Lane
3	Church Road	8	The Avenue
4	Park Road	9	London Road
5	The Drive	10	Church Lane

LONGEST PLACE NAMES IN THE WORLD*

Name	Letters
1 Krung thep mahanakhon bovorn ratanakosin mahintharayutthaya mahadilok pop noparatratchathani burirom udomratchanivetma hasathan amornpiman avatarnsa thit sakkathattiyavisnukarmprasit	167

When the poetic name of Bangkok, capital of Thailand, is used, it is usually abbreviated to "Krung Thep" (City of Angels).

Name	Letters
2 Taumatawhakatangihangakoauau-otamateaturipukakapikimaunga-horonukupokaiwhenuakitanatahu	85

This is the longer version (the other has a mere 83 letters) of the Maori name of a hill in New Zealand. It translates as "The place where Tamatea, the man with the big knees, who slid, climbed, and swallowed mountains, known as land-eater, played on the flute to his loved one."

Name	Letters
3 Gorsafawddacha`idraigodanhed-dogleddollônpenrhynareur-draethcere digion	67

A name contrived by the Fairbourne Steam Railway, Gwynedd, North Wales, UK, for publicity purposes and in order to out-do its rival, No. 4. It means "The Mawddach station and its dragon teeth at the Northern Penrhyn Road on the golden beach of Cardigan Bay."

Name	Letters
4 Llanfairpwllgwyngyllgogerychwyrn-drobwllllantysiliogogogoch	58

This is the place in Gwynedd, UK, known especially for the length of its train tickets. It means "St. Mary's Church in the hollow of the white hazel near to the rapid whirlpool of Llantysilio of the Red Cave." Its official name consists of only the first 20 letters.

Name	Letters
5 El Pueblo de Nuestra Señora la Reina de los Angeles de la Porciuncula	57

The site of a Franciscan mission and the full Spanish name of Los Angeles, it means "the town of Our Lady the Queen of the Angels of the Little Portion."

Name	Letters
6 Chargoggagoggmanchauggagogg-chaubunagungamaugg	45

This is a lake near Webster, Massachusetts. Its Native American name loosely means "You fish on your side, I'll fish on mine, and no one fishes in the middle." An invented extension of its real name (Chagungungamaug Pond, or "boundary fishing place"), this name was devised in the 1920s by Larry Daly, editor of the Webster Times.

Name	Letters
7= Lower North Branch Little Southwest Miramichi	40

Canada's longest place name belongs to a short river in New Brunswick.

Name	Letters
7= Villa Real de la Santa Fe de San Francisco de Asis	40

The full Spanish name of Santa Fe, New Mexico, translates as "Royal city of the holy faith of St. Francis of Assisi."

Name	Letters
9 Te Whakatakanga-o-te-ngarehu-o-te-ahi-a-Tamatea	38

The Maori name of Hammer Springs, New Zealand, like the 2nd name in this list, refers to a legend of Tamatea, explaining how the springs were warmed by "the falling of the cinders of the fire of Tamatea."

Name	Letters
10 Meallan Liath Coire Mhic Dhubhghaill	32

The longest multiple name in Scotland, this is the name of a place near Aultanrynie, Highland, alternatively spelled Meallan Liath Coire Mhic Dhughaill.

* *Including single-word, hyphenated, and multiple names*

THE LONG SIDE OF THE TRACKS

For the benefit of its many visitors, the original 58-letter version of the name of this Welsh village is spelled phonetically on its station signboard. It is of dubious origin, however, the modern invention of local poet John Evans, and today ranks only as the world's second longest train station name, having been overtaken by a similarly contrived Welsh place name.

TALLEST INHABITED BUILDINGS

TOP 10 TALLEST HABITABLE BUILDINGS IN THE WORLD

Building/location/year	Height m	ft		Height m	ft	Building/location/year
1987						**1997**
Sears Tower, Chicago (1974)	443	1,454	**1**	452	1,482	Petronas Towers, Kuala Lumpur, Malaysia (1996)
World Trade Center, New York (1973)	417	1,368	**2**	443	1,454	Sears Tower, Chicago (1974)
Empire State Building, New York (1931)	381	1,250	**3**	417	1,368	World Trade Center, New York (1973)
Amoco Building, Chicago (1973)	346	1,136	**4**	382	1,255	Jin Mao Building, Shanghai, China (1997)
John Hancock Center, Chicago (1968)	344	1,127	**5**	381	1,250	Empire State Building, New York (1931)
Chrysler Building, New York (1930)	319	1,046	**6**	348	1,142	T & C Tower, Kao-hsiung, Taiwan (1997)
Texas Commerce Tower, Houston (1981)	305	1,002	**7**	346	1,136	Amoco Building, Chicago (1973)
Allied Bank Plaza, Houston (1983)	302	992	**8**	344	1,127	John Hancock Center, Chicago (1968)
First Canadian Place, Toronto, Canada (1975)	290	952	**9**	330	1,082	Shun Hing Square, Shenzen, China (1996)
International Building, New York (1932)	289	950	**10**	323	1,060	Sky Central Plaza, Guangzhou, China (1996)

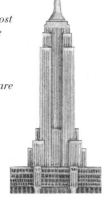

EMPIRE STATE BUILDING
Completed in 1931 at a cost of $25 million, the Empire State Building contains 60,000 tons of steel and 6,500 windows. Its 2,248,000 sq ft of offices are served by 73 elevators.

WORLD CITIES WITH THE MOST SKYSCRAPERS*

	City	Skyscrapers
1	New York City	140
2	Chicago	68
3 =	Hong Kong, China	36
=	Houston	36
5	Kuala Lumpur, Malaysia	25
6	Los Angeles	24
7	Dallas	22
8 =	San Francisco	20
=	Shanghai, China	20
10 =	Singapore, Singapore	18
=	Sydney, Australia	18

* Habitable buildings of over 500 ft/152 m

The word "skyscraper" was first used in the 18th century to mean a high-flying flag on a ship, and later to describe a tall horse or person. It was not used to describe buildings until the 1880s, when the first tall office blocks of 10 stories or more were built in Chicago and New York, with the Eiffel Tower following at the end of the decade. The first modern, steel-framed skyscraper was the Woolworth Building, New York, built in 1913.

REACHING FOR THE SKY

Apart from the Eiffel Tower and the Washington Memorial, the majority of tall buildings erected before the 1890s were religious structures. The six-story 130-ft Equitable Life Building, New York, completed in 1870, the first building with an elevator, marked the beginning of the rise of the city's skyline. In 1895, the skyline reached new heights when it was taken to 306 ft by the 21-story American Surety Building, followed in 1899 by the St. Paul Building on Broadway and Ann Street, a 16-story structure measuring 310 ft, and the Park Row Building, which at 29 stories and 386 ft briefly held the record as the tallest building in the world.

100 YEARS AGO · YEARS AGO · YEARS AGO

SNAP FACTS

- The Woolworth Building cost $13.5 million – which F.W. Woolworth paid in cash.
- A gargoyle on the building depicts its designer, Cass Gilbert.
- Its 29 elevators were the world's fastest.

TOP 10

TALLEST BUILDINGS IN THE WORLD ERECTED MORE THAN 100 YEARS AGO

	Building/location	Year completed	Height m	ft
1	Eiffel Tower, Paris, France	1889	300	984
2	Washington Monument, Washington, DC	1885	169	555
3	Ulm Cathedral, Ulm, Germany	1890	161	528
4	Lincoln Cathedral, Lincoln, England (destroyed 1548)	c.1307	160	525
5	Cologne Cathedral, Cologne, Germany	1880	156.4	513
6	Rouen Cathedral I, Rouen, France (destroyed 1822)	1530	156	512
7	St. Pierre Church, Beauvais, France (collapsed 1573)	1568	153	502
8	Lin-He Pagoda, Hang Zhoc, China (destroyed 1121)	970	150	492
9	St. Paul's Cathedral, London, England (destroyed 1561)	1315	149	489
10	Rouen Cathedral II, Rouen, France	1876	148	485

TOP 10

TALLEST HOTELS IN THE WORLD

	Building/location	Stories	Height m	ft
1	Baiyoke II Tower, Bangkok, Thailand	89	319	1,046
2	Yu Kyong, Pyong Yang, North Korea	105	300	985
3	Emirates Tower 2, Dubae, UAE	50	262	858
4	Shangri-la, Hong Kong, China	60	228	748
5	Raffles Western Hotel, Singapore	73	226	742
6	Westin Peachtree, Hotel, Atlanta, GA	71	220	723
7	Westin Hotel, Detroit, MI	71	219	720
8	Four Seasons Hotel, New York, NY	52	208	682
9	Trump International Hotel, New York, NY	45	207	679
10	Trump Tower, New York, NY	68	202	664

TOP 10

TALLEST APARTMENT BUILDINGS IN THE WORLD

	Building	Location	Stories	Height m	ft
1	Lake Point Tower	Chicago	70	197	645
2	Central Park Place	New York City	56	191	628
3	Olympic Tower	New York City	51	189	620
4	May Road Apartments	Hong Kong	58	180	590
5	Marina City Apartments	Chicago	61	179	588
6	North Pier Apartments	Chicago	61	177	581
7	Onterie Center	Chicago	58	174	570
8	30 Broad Street	New York City	48	171	562
9	Huron Apartments	Chicago	58	170	560
10	Harbor Point	Chicago	59	170	558

TOP 10

TALLEST HABITABLE BUILDINGS IN 2001

	Building/location/year*	Height m	ft
1	Shanghai World, Finance Center Shanghai, China, 2001	460	1,508
2	Chongqing Tower, Chongqing, China, 2000	457	1,500
3	Petronas Towers, Kuala Lumpur, Malaysia, 1997	452	1,482
4	Sears Tower, Chicago, IL, 1974	443	1,454
5	Tour Sans Fin, Paris, France, 2000	419	1,377
6	World Trade Center, New York, NY, 1973	417	1,368
7=	Daewoo Corporation, Puxi, Shanghai, China, 2000	400	1,310
=	International Finance Tower, Hong Kong, China, 2002	400	1,310
9	Jin Mao Building, Shanghai, China, 1998	382	1,255
10	Empire State Building, New York, NY, 1931	381	1,250

* *Opened or expected completion year*

CHICAGO SKYLINE

TALLEST UNINHABITED BUILDINGS

COLOGNE CATHEDRAL

TALLEST TELECOMMUNICATIONS TOWERS IN THE WORLD

	Tower/location	Year	Height m	ft
1	CN Tower, Toronto, Canada	1975	555	1,821
2	Ostankino Tower, Moscow, Russia	1967	537	1,762
3	Oriental Pearl Broadcasting Tower, Shanghai, China	1995	468	1,535
4	Telecom Tower, Kuala Lumpur, Malaysia	1995	420	1,380
5	Central Radio and TV Tower, Beijing, China	1994	405	1,328
6	Liberation Tower, Kuwait City, Kuwait	1998	372	1,220
7	Alma-Ata Tower, Kazakhstan	1983	370	1,214
8	TV Tower, Berlin, Germany	1969	365	1,198
9	TV Tower, Tashkent, Uzbekistan	1983	357	1,171
10	Stratosphere Tower, Las Vegas, NV	1996	350	1,149

All the towers listed are self-supporting, rather than masts braced with guy wires, and all have observation facilities. The Menara Jakarta, a tower under construction in Jakarta, Indonesia, scheduled for completion in 2001 but currently "on hold," is intended to be 1,831 ft/558 m tall, making it the tallest tower in the world.

TALLEST CHIMNEYS IN THE WORLD

	Chimney/location	Height m	ft
1	Ekibastuz power station, Kazakhstan	420	1,377
2	International Nickel Company, Copper Hill, Sudbury, Ontario, Canada	381	1,250
3	Pennsylvania Electric Company, Homer City, Pennsylvania	371	1,216
4	Kennecott Copper Corporation, Magna, Utah	370	1,215
5	Ohio Power Company, Cresap, West Virginia	368	1,206
6	Zasavje power station, Trboulje, Yugoslavia	360	1,181
7	Empresa Nacional de Electricidad SA, Puentes de Garcia Rodriguez, Spain	356	1,169
8	Appalachian Power Company, New Haven, West Virginia	336	1,103
9	Indiana and Michigan Electric Company, Rockport, Indiana	316	1,037
10	West Penn Power Company, Reesedale, Pennsylvania	308	1,012

Numbers 2 to 5 and 7 to 10 in the list were all built by Pullman Power Products Corporation (formerly a division of M. W. Kellogg), an American engineering company that has been in business since 1902 and has built many of the world's tallest chimneys. The largest internal volume is No. 7 – 6,700,000 cubic feet. The diameter of No. 1, completed in 1991, tapers from 144 ft/44 m at the base to 47 ft/14 m at the top; the outside diameter of No. 4, built in 1974 and formerly the world's largest, is 124 ft/38 m at the base, tapering to 40 ft/12 m at the top.

TALLEST MASTS IN THE WORLD

	Mast/location	Height m	ft
1	KTHI-TV Mast, Fargo, ND	629	2,063
2	KSLA-TV Mast, Shreveport, LA	579	1,898
3 =	WBIR-TV Mast, Knoxville, TN	533	1,749
=	WTVM and WRBL Television Mast, Columbus, GA	533	1,749
5	KFVS Television Mast, Cape Girardeau, MO	511	1,676
6	WPSD-TV Mast, Paducah, KY	499	1,638
7	WGAN Television Mast, Portland, ME	493	1,619
8	KWTV Television Mast, Oklahoma City, OK	479	1,572
9	BREN Tower, Nye County, NV	464	1,521
10	Omega Base Navigational Mast, Gippsland, Victoria, Australia	426	1,400

On August 10, 1991, the former No. 1, the Warszawa Radio Mast, Konstantynow, Poland, which measured 2,120 ft/646 m, collapsed during renovation. As a result, all but the last entry of the Top 10 consists of masts located in the US.

T O P   1 0
HIGHEST PUBLIC OBSERVATORIES IN THE WORLD

	Building/location/observatory	Year	Height m	ft
1	CN Tower, Toronto, Canada (space deck)	1975	447	1,465
2	World Trade Center, New York, NY (rooftop Tower B)	1973	415	1,360
3	Sears Tower, Chicago, IL (103rd floor)	1974	412	1,353
4	Empire State Building, New York, NY (102nd floor) (outdoor observation deck)	1931	381 320	1,250 1,050
5	Ostankino Tower, Moscow, Russia (5th floor turret)	1967	360	1,181
6	Oriental Pearl Broadcasting Tower, Shanghai, China (VIP observation level) (public observation level)	1995	350 263	1,148 863
7	Jin Mao Building, Shanghai, China (88th floor)	1997	340	1,115
8	John Hancock Center, Chicago, IL (94th floor)	1968	314	1,030
9	Sky Central Plaza, Guanghshou, China (90th-floor observatory)	1996	310	1,016
10	KL Tower, Kuala Lumpur, Malaysia (revolving restaurant) (public observation level)	1995	282 276	925 907

The opportunity to ascend to a great height and look out over vast distances is a feature of towers and buildings the world over. The Eiffel Tower, constructed for this purpose and as a symbol of the technological skills of the French people, was built between 1887 and 1889 as the centerpiece of the Paris Exhibition. At 900 ft/274 m, it was the world's highest viewing platform in a man-made structure for 42 years, until the opening of the Empire State Building. From the 1930s onward, US observatories dominated the world, but have been steadily losing ground to Asian buildings, with the KL Tower, Kuala Lumpur, recently joining the list. For the first time, more than half the Top 10 are outside the US.

T H E   1 0
TALLEST CHURCHES IN THE WORLD

	Church	Location	Year completed	Height m	ft
1	Chicago Methodist Temple	Chicago, Ilinois	1924	173	568
2	Ulm Cathedral	Ulm, Germany	1890	161	528
3	Notre Dame de la Paix	Yamoussoukro, Côte d'Ivoire	1989	158	519
4	Cologne Cathedral	Cologne, Germany	1880	156	513
5	Rouen Cathedral	Rouen, France	1876	148	485
6	St. Nicholas	Hamburg, Germany	1847	145	475
7	Notre Dame	Strasbourg, France	1439	142	465
8	St. Peter's Basilica	Rome, Italy	1612	140	458
9	St. Stephen's Cathedral	Vienna, Austria	1433	136	446
10=	Amiens Cathedral	Amiens, France	1260	134	440
=	St. Michael	Hamburg, Germany	1906	134	440

T O P   1 0
TALLEST LIGHTHOUSES IN THE US

	Lighthouse/location	Height* m	ft
1	Cape Hatteras, NC	59.7	196
2	Cape Charles, VA	58.2	191
3	Pensacola, FL	52.1	171
4 =	Cape May, NJ	51.8	170
=	Absecon, NJ	51.8	170
6	Lookout, NC	51.5	169
7	Ponce de Leon Inlet, FL	51.2	168
8	Fire Island, NY	50.9	167
9	"New" Cape Henry, NC	50.3	165
10=	Currituck, NC	49.7	163
=	Bodie Island, NC	49.7	163

* *Measurement taken from ground level to the top of the lantern*

Source: US Lighthouse Society

THE SEARS TOWER
Chicago's tallest building has one of the highest public observatories in the world on its 103rd floor.

BRIDGES & TUNNELS

T O P · 1 0

LONGEST SUSPENSION BRIDGES IN THE WORLD

	Bridge/location	Year completed	Length of main span m	ft
1	AkasHi-Kaiko, Kobe-Naruto, Japan	1998	1,990	6,529
2	Great Belt, Denmark	1997	1,624	5,328
3	Jiangyin, China	1998	1,624	5,328
4	Humber Estuary, UK	1980	1,410	4,626
5	Tsing Ma, Hong Kong, China	1997	1,377	4,518
6	Verrazano Narrows, New York	1964	1,298	4,260
7	Golden Gate, San Francisco	1937	1,280	4,200
8	Höga Kusten, Veda, Sweden	1997	1,210	3,970
9	Mackinac Straits, Michigan	1957	1,158	3,800
10	Minami Bisan-seto, Kojima-Sakaide, Japan	1988	1,100	3,609

T O P · 1 0

LONGEST CABLE-STAYED BRIDGES IN THE WORLD

	Bridge/location	Year Completed	Length of main span m	ft
1	Pont de Normandie, Le Havre, France	1994	856	2,808
2	Qunghzhou Minjiang, Fozhou, China	1996	605	1,985
3	Yangpu, Shanghai, China	1993	602	1,975
4 =	Meiko-Chuo, Nagoya, Japan	1997	590	1,936
=	Xupu, Shanghai, China	1997	590	1,936
6	Skarnsundet, Trondheim, Fjord, Norway	1991	530	1,739
7	Ikuchi, Onomichi-Imabari, Japan	1994	490	1,608
8	Higashi-Kobe, Kobe, Japan	1992	485	1,591
9	Ying Kau, Hong Kong, China	1997	475	1,558
10	Seohae Grand, Asan Man, South Korea	1997	470	1,542

T O P · 1 0

LONGEST RAIL TUNNELS IN THE WORLD

	Tunnel/location	Year completed	Length km	miles
1	Seikan, Japan	1988	53.90	33.49
2	Channel Tunnel, France/England	1994	49.94	31.03
3	Moscow Metro (Medvedkovo/ Belyaevo section), Russia	1979	30.70	19.07
4	London Underground (East Finchley/ Morden Northern Line), UK	1939	27.84	17.30
5	Dai-Shimizu, Japan	1982	22.17	13.78
6	Simplon II, Italy/Switzerland	1922	19.82	12.31
7	Simplon I, Italy/Switzerland	1906	19.80	12.30
8	Shin-Kanmon, Japan	1975	18.68	11.61
9	Apennine, Italy	1934	18.52	11.50
10	Rokko, Japan	1972	16.25	10.10

T O P · 1 0

TALLEST RAIL BRIDGES IN THE WORLD

	Bridge	Location	Year completed	Height m	ft
1	Mala Reka Viaduct	Yugoslavia	1976	198	650
2	Vresk	Iran	1938	152	500
3	Fades Viaduct	France	1909	133	435
4	Khotur	Iran	1973	131	430
5	Victoria Falls	Zimbabwe	1904	128	420
6	Pfaffenberg-Zwenberg	Austria	1971	120	394
7	Viaur	France	1902	116	381
8	Garabit Viaduct	France	1884	112	367
9	Müngstner	Germany	1897	107	350
10 =	Rio Grande	Costa Rica	1890	105	346
=	Vance Creek	US	1928	105	346

T O P · 1 0

LONGEST CANTILEVER BRIDGES IN THE WORLD

	Bridge/location	Longest span m	ft
1	Pont de Québec, Canada	549	1,800
2	Firth of Forth, Scotland	521	1,710
3	Minato, Osaka, Japan	510	1,673
4	Commodore John Barry, Pennsylvania	494	1,622
5 =	Greater New Orleans 1, Louisiana	480	1,575

	Bridge/location	Longest span m	ft
=	Greater New Orleans 2, Louisiana	480	1,575
7	Howrah, Calcutta, India	457	1,500
8	Gramercy, Gramercy, Louisiana	445	1,460
9	Transbay, San Francisco	427	1,400
10	Baton Rouge, Louisiana	376	1,235

TOP 10
LONGEST ROAD TUNNELS IN THE WORLD

	Tunnel/location	Year completed	km	miles
1	St. Gotthard, Switzerland	1980	16.32	10.14
2	Arlberg, Austria	1978	13.98	8.69
3=	Fréjus, France/Italy	1980	12.90	8.02
=	Pinglin Highway, Taiwan	u/c*	12.90	8.02
5	Mt. Blanc, France/Italy	1965	11.60	7.21
6	Gudvangen, Norway	1992	11.40	7.08
7	Leirfjord, Norway	u/c*	11.11	6.90
8	Kan–Etsu, Japan	1991	11.01	6.84
9	Kan–Etsu, Japan	1985	10.93	6.79
10	Gran Sasso, Italy	1984	10.17	6.32

* *Under construction*

TOP 10
LONGEST ROAD AND RAIL TUNNELS IN THE US*

	Tunnel/location	Year completed	km	miles
1	Cascade (rail), Washington	1929	12.54	7.79
2	Flathead (rail), Montana	1970	12.48	7.78
3	Moffat (rail), Colorado	1928	10.00	6.21
4	Hoosac (rail), Massachusetts	1875	7.56	4.70
5	BART Trans-Bay Tubes (rail), San Francisco, California	1974	5.79	3.60
6	Brooklyn-Battery (road), New York	1950	2.78	1.73
7	E. Johnson Memorial (road), Colorado	1979	2.74	1.70
8	Eisenhower Memorial (road), Colorado#	1973	2.72	1.69
9	Holland Tunnel (road), New York	1927	2.61	1.62
10	Lincoln Tunnel I (road), New York	1937	2.51	1.56

* *Excluding subways* # *Highest elevation highway tunnel in the world*

TOP 10
LONGEST STEEL ARCH BRIDGES IN THE WORLD

	Bridge	Year completed	m	ft
1	New River Gorge, Fayetteville, West Virginia	1977	518	1,700
2	Kill Van Kull, Bayonne, New Jersey/ Staten Island, New York	1931	504	1,654
3	Sydney Harbour, Australia	1932	503	1,650
4	Fremont, Portland, Oregon	1973	383	1,257
5	Port Mann, Vancouver, Canada	1964	366	1,200
6	Thatcher Ferry, Panama Canal	1962	344	1,128
7	Laviolette, Quebec, Canada	1967	335	1,100
8=	Runcorn-Widnes, UK	1961	330	1,082
=	Zdákov, Lake Orlik, Czech Republic	1967	330	1,082
10=	Birchenough, Fort Victoria, Zimbabwe	1935	329	1,080
=	Roosevelt Lake, Arizona	1990	329	1,080

TOP 10 LONGEST UNDERWATER TUNNELS IN THE WORLD
(Length)

❶ Seikan, Japan (33.49 miles/53.90 km) ❷ Channel Tunnel, France/England (31.03 miles/49.94 km) ❸ Dai-Shimizu, Japan (13.78 miles/22.17 km) ❹ Shin-Kanmon, Japan (11.61 miles/ 18.68 km) ❺ Great Belt Fixed Link (Eastern Tunnel), Denmark (4.97 miles/8.00 km) ❻ Severn, UK (4.46 miles/7.01 km) ❼ Haneda, Japan (3.72 miles/5.98 km) ❽ BART, San Francisco (3.62 miles/5.83 km) ❾ Kammon, Japan (2.24 miles/3.60 km) ❿ Kammon, Japan (2.15 miles/3.46 km)

THE CHANNEL TUNNEL
First proposed almost 200 years ago, the Channel Tunnel was finally opened in 1994. It is Europe's longest and the world's second longest undersea rail tunnel.

OTHER STRUCTURES

T O P   1 0

HIGHEST DAMS IN THE WORLD

	Dam	Location	Completed	Height m	ft
1	Rogun	Vakhsh, Tajikistan	u/c*	335	1,099
2	Nurek	Vakhsh, Tajikistan	1980	300	984
3	Grand Dixence	Dixence, Switzerland	1961	285	935
4	Inguri	Inguri, Georgia	1980	272	892
5	Chicoasén	Grijalva, Mexico	u/c*	261	856
6	Tehri	Bhagirathi, India	u/c*	261	856
7	Kishau	Tons, India	u/c*	253	830
8	Ertan	Yangtse-kiang, China	u/c*	245	804
9	Sayano-Shushensk	Yeniesei, Russia	u/c*	245	804
10	Guavio	Guavio, Colombia	u/c*	243	797

* *Under construction*

HIGH ASWAN DAM AND LAKE
Containing 18 times the amount of material used in the Great Pyramid of Cheops, the High Aswan Dam has created the third largest artificial lake in the world.

T O P   1 0

LARGEST-VOLUME DAMS IN THE WORLD

(Ranked according to the volume of material used in construction)

	Dam/location	Completed	Volume (yd³)
1	Syncrude Tailings, Alberta, Canada	1992	706,293,324
2	Pati, Paraná, Argentina	1990	301,064,069
3	New Cornelia, Ten Mile Wash, Tailings, Arizona	1973	274,015,651
4	Tarbela, Indus, Pakistan	1976	138,540,743
5	Fort Peck, Missouri, Montana	1937	125,628,655
6	Lower Usuma, Usuma, Nigeria	1990	121,639,406
7	Atatürk, Euphrates, Turkey	1990	110,521,826
8	Yacyreta-Apipe, Paraná, Paraguay/Argentina	1991	105,943,999
9	Guri (Raul Leoni), Caroni, Venezuela	1986	101,982,216
10	Rogun, Vakhsh, Tajikistan	1987	98,750,270

Numerous major projects are in development for completion by the end of the century, by which time this Top 10 will contain some exciting new entries throughout the world.

T O P   1 0

LARGEST MAN-MADE LAKES IN THE WORLD*

	Dam/lake	Location	Completed	Volume (yd³)
1	Owen Falls	Uganda	1954	267,868,000,000
2	Bratsk	Russia	1964	222,221,000,000
3	High Aswan	Egypt	1970	211,888,000,000
4	Kariba	Zimbabwe	1959	209,753,000,000
5	Akosombo	Ghana	1965	193,524,000,000
6	Daniel Johnson	Canada	1968	185,534,000,000
7	Guri (Raul Leoni)	Venezuela	1986	176,573,000,000
8	Krasnoyarsk	Russia	1967	95,873,000,000
9	W.A.C. Bennett	Canada	1967	91,961,000,000
10	Zeya	Russia	1978	89,464,000,000

* *Includes only those formed as a result of dam construction*

The enlargement of the existing natural lake that resulted from the construction of the Owen Falls created not only the largest reservoir in the world, but also the man-made lake with the greatest surface area: at 26,828 sq miles/69,484 sq km, it is almost as large as the Republic of Ireland. The building of the Akosombo Dam on the River Volta, Ghana, created a lake that occupies about four percent of the entire area of the country.

TOP 10

LONGEST FLIGHTS OF STAIRS IN THE WORLD

	Stairs/location	Steps
1	Niesenbahn funicular railway, Spiez, Switzerland	11,674
2	T'ai Chan Temple, China	6,600
3	Mår Power Station, Norway	3,875
4	Aura Power Station, Norway	3,715
5	CN Tower, Toronto, Canada	3,642
6	Ostankino Tower, Moscow, Russia	3,544
7	World Trade Center, New York, NY	3,140
8	Empire State Building, New York, NY	2,908
9	Sears Tower, Chicago, IL	2,906
10	Tokyo Tower, Tokyo, Japan	2,184

TOP 10

OLDEST CHURCHES IN THE US*

	Church/location	Built
1	Convento de Porta Coeli, San German, PR	1609
2	San Estevan del Rey Mission, Valencia County, NM	1629
3	St. Luke's Church, Isle of Wight County, VA	1632
4	First Church of Christ, Hartford County, CT	1640
5	St. Ignatius Catholic Church, St. Mary's County, MD	1641
6	Merchant's Hope Church, Prince George County, VA	1657
7	Flatlands Dutch Reformed Church, King's County, NY	1660
8=	Claflin-Richards House, Essex County, MA	1661
=	Church San Blas de Illesces of Coamo, Ponce, PR	1661
=	St. Mary's Whitechapel, Lancaster County, VA	1661

* Source: US National Register of Historic Sights, which for its purposes includes Puerto Rico in its list of locations of historic sights.

TOP 10

LARGEST BELLS IN THE WESTERN WORLD

	Bell/location	Year cast	Weight (tons)
1	*Tsar Kolokol*, Kremlin, Moscow, Russia	1735	222.56
2	*Voskresenskiy (Resurrection)*, Ivan the Great Bell Tower, Kremlin, Moscow, Russia	1746	72.20
3	*Petersglocke*, Cologne Cathedral, Germany	1923	28.00
4	Lisbon Cathedral, Portugal	post-1344	26.90
5	St. Stephen's Cathedral, Vienna, Austria	1957	23.58
6	Bourdon, Strasbourg Cathedral, France	1521	22.05
7	*Savoyarde*, Sacre-Coeur Basilica, Paris, France	1891	20.78
8	Bourdon, Riverside Church, New York, NY	1931	20.44
9	Olmütz, Czech Republic	1931	20.05
10	*Campagna gorda*, Toledo Cathedral, Spain	1753	19.04

The largest bell in the world is the 20-ft 2-in/6.14-m high 21-ft 8-in/6.6-m diameter *Tsar Kolokol*, cast in Moscow for the Kremlin. It cracked before it had been installed and has remained there, unrung, ever since. New York's Riverside Church bell (the largest ever cast in England) is the bourdon (that sounding the lowest note) of the 74-bell Laura Spelman Rockefeller Memorial Carillon.

TOP 10

LARGEST SPORTS STADIUMS IN THE WORLD

	Stadium	Location	Capacity
1	Strahov Stadium	Prague, Czech Republic	240,000
2	Maracaña Municipa Stadium	Rio de Janeiro, Brazil	205,000
3	Rungrado Stadium	Pyungyang, North Korea	150,000
4	Estadio Maghalaes Pinto	Belo Horizonte, Brazil	125,000
5=	Estadio Morumbi	São Paulo, Brazil	120,000
=	Estadio da Luz	Lisbon, Portugal	120,000
=	Senayan Main Stadium	Jakarta, Indonesia	120,000
=	Yuba Bharati Krirangan	nr. Calcutta, India	120,000
9	Estadio Castelão	Fortaleza, Brazil	119,000
10=	Estadio Arrudão	Recife, Brazil	115,000
=	Estadio Azteca	Mexico City, Mexico	115,000
=	Nou Camp	Barcelona, Spain	115,000

The Aztec Stadium, Mexico City, holds 107,000, with most of the seats under cover. The New Orleans Superdome is the largest indoor stadium, with a capacity of 97,365. The largest stadium in the United Kingdom is Wembley Stadium with a capacity of 80,000.

CULTURE & LEARNING

TOP 10

COUNTRIES WITH THE HIGHEST PROPORTION OF WOMEN IN UNIVERSITY EDUCATION

	Country	Percentage of women*
1	United Arab Emirates	78
2	Cyprus	77
3	Qatar	72
4	Mongolia	70
5	Kuwait	66
6	Myanmar	64
7	Barbados	63
8	Bulgaria	61
9 =	Cuba	60
=	Panama	60
	US	53

* Percentage of women out of the total number of university students

TOP 10

COUNTRIES THAT SPEND THE MOST ON EDUCATION

	Country	Annual expenditure (as percentage of GNP)
1	Uzbekistan	11.0
2	Tajikistan	9.5
3	Norway	9.2
4	Namibia	8.7
5 =	Botswana	8.5

US 5.5

	Country	Annual expenditure (as percentage of GNP)
=	Denmark	8.5
7 =	Finland	8.4
=	Sweden	8.4
9 =	Rep. of Congo	8.3
=	Zimbabwe	8.3

Source: UNESCO

Since the list ranks countries spending the most on education as a percentage of Gross National Product, it includes several African countries with very small GNPs. Also figuring prominently in this and just outside the Top 10 are several former Soviet countries that have inherited a relatively highly developed and expensive education system, but whose GNPs have collapsed following the breakup of the Soviet Union. As these countries adapt to new economic and political situations, their GNP's are likely to increase, and spending on education as a percentage of GNP will shrink, so they may disappear from the list.

ST. JOHN'S COLLEGE, CAMBRIDGE UNIVERSITY, UK

TOP TEN COUNTRIES WITH THE MOST UNIVERSITY STUDENTS

(No. of students per 100,000 population)

❶ Canada (6,980) ❷ US (5,546)

❸ Korea (4,756) ❹ New Zealand (4,675)

❺ Norway (4,111) ❻ Finland (3,902)

❼ Spain (3,719) ❽ Armenia (3,711)

❾ France (3,623) ❿ Netherlands (3,352)

Source: UNESCO

TOP 10

LARGEST UNIVERSITIES IN THE WORLD

	University	Students
1	University of Paris, France	308,904
2	University of Calcutta, India	300,000
3	University of Bombay, India	262,350
4	University of Mexico, Mexico	261,693
5	University of Guadalajara, Mexico	214,986
6	University of Buenos Aires, Argentina	206,658
7	University of Rome, Italy	184,000
8	University of Rajasthan, India	175,000
9	University of Wisconsin	154,620
10	State University of New York	146,873

The huge number of university institutions in India reflects the country's population and the high value placed on education in Indian culture, but also the inclusion of many "Affiliating and Teaching" colleges attached to universities. Several other universities in the US, India, Egypt, and Italy have more than 100,000 students.

TOP 10

COUNTRIES WITH THE LONGEST SCHOOL YEARS

	Country	School year (days)
1	China	251
2	Japan	243
3	Korea	220
4	Israel	215
5 =	Germany	210
=	Russia	210
7	Switzerland	207
8 =	Netherlands	200
=	Scotland	200
=	Thailand	200
	US	*180*

TOP 10

MOST EXPENSIVE UNIVERSITIES AND COLLEGES IN THE US, 1997/98

	University	Tuition fees*($)
1	Landmark College, VT	30,000
2	New York University, NY	28,278
3	Brown University, RI	27,939
4	Brandeis University, MA	27,885
5	Barnard College, NY	27,652
6	Yale University, CT	27,630
7	Harvard University, MA	27,575
8	Sarah Lawrence College, NY	27,550
9	Hampshire College, MA	27,485
10	University of Pennsylvania, PA	27,398

* Excluding room and board (for a 4-year undergraduate)

TOP 10

COUNTRIES WITH THE MOST SECONDARY-SCHOOL STUDENTS

	Country	Secondary-school students		Country	Secondary-school students
1	India	64,115,978	6	Japan	10,202,510
2	China	53,837,300	7	Germany	7,796,256
3	US	20,578,000	8	Iran	7,652,829
4	Russia	13,732,000	9	Mexico	7,264,650
5	Indonesia	11,360,349	10	Egypt	6,138,263

Source: UNESCO

BOOK RECORDS

US CITIES WITH THE MOST INDEPENDENT BOOKSTORES

	City	Bookstores
1	New York, NY	88
2	Chicago, IL	59
3	San Francisco, CA	49
4=	Seattle, WA	44
=	Washington, DC	44
6	Los Angeles, CA	35
7	Atlanta, GA	28
8	Portland, OR	25
9	Minneapolis, MN	24
10=	Berkeley, CA	23
=	Houston, TX	23
=	Philadelphia, PA	23

Source: American Booksellers Association

STATES WITH THE MOST INDEPENDENT BOOKSTORES

	State	Bookstores
1	California	606
2	New York	296
3	Illinois	174
4	Massachusetts	173
5	Pennsylvania	162
6	District of Columbia	144
7	Texas	142
8	Florida	135
9	Ohio	134
10	Michigan	128

Source: American Booksellers Association

MOST EXPENSIVE BOOKS/MANUSCRIPTS EVER SOLD AT AUCTION

	Book/manuscript/sale	Price ($)*
1	*The Codex Hammer,* Christies, New York, November 11, 1994	$30,800,000

This is one of Leonardo da Vinci's notebooks, which includes many scientific drawings and diagrams. It was purchased by Bill Gates, the billionaire founder of Microsoft.

2	*The Gospels of Henry the Lion,* c.1173-75, Sotheby's, London, December 6, 1983	$10,841,000

At the time of its sale, it became the most expensive manuscript, book, or work of art other than a painting ever sold.

3	*The Gutenberg Bible,* 1455, Christie's, New York, October 22, 1987	$5,390,000

One of the first books ever printed, by Johann Gutenberg and Johann Fust in 1455, it holds the record for the most expensive printed book.

4	*The Northumberland Bestiary,* c.1250–60, Sotheby's, London, November 29, 1990	$5,049,000

The highest price ever paid for an English manuscript.

5	Autographed manuscript of nine symphonies by Wolfgang Amadeus Mozart, c.1773–74, Sotheby's, London, May 22, 1987	$3,854,500

The record for a music manuscript.

* Excluding premiums

	Book/manuscript/sale	Price ($)*
6	John James Audubon's *The Birds of America,* 1827–38, Sotheby's, New York, June 6, 1989	$3,600,000

The record for any natural history book. Additional copies of the same book, a collection of more than 400 large, hand-colored engravings, have also fetched high prices. A facsimile reprint of Audubon's The Birds of America, *published in 1985 by Abbeville Press, New York, is listed at $30,000 – the most expensive book ever published.*

7	*The Bible in Hebrew,* Sotheby's, London, December 5, 1989	$2,932,000

A manuscript written in Iraq, Syria, or Babylon in the ninth or tenth century, it holds the record for any Hebrew manuscript.

8	*The Monypenny Breviary,* illuminated manuscript, c.1490–95, Sotheby's, London, June 19, 1989	$2,639,000

The record for any French manuscript.

9	*The Hours and Psalter of Elizabeth de Bohun, Countess of Northampton,* c.1340–45, Sotheby's, London, June 21, 1988	$2,530,000

10	*Biblia Pauperum* Christie's, New York, October 22, 1987	$2,200,000

A block-book bible printed in the Netherlands c.1460 (the pages of block-books were printed from single carved woodblocks rather than moveable type).

100 YEARS OF BOOK BLURBS

Two New York publishers, Harper and Dodd Mead, first featured descriptions on the jackets of their book in 1899, but it was several years before these were given a name. At a booksellers' dinner in 1907, as a publicity gimmick, the humor author Frank Gelett Burgess (1866–1951) distributed copies of his latest book, entitled *Are You a Bromide?*, with a specially designed cover featuring an imaginary authoress called "Miss Belinda Blurb," who he claimed had written the "sensation of the year." The outcome was that Burgess invented the word "blurb," which is what these often lavish summaries have been called ever since.

YEARS AGO • YEARS AGO • YEARS AGO • YEARS AGO

100

T O P   1 0

TRADE BOOK PUBLISHERS IN THE US*

1 Random House

2 Simon and Schuster

3 Bantam Doubleday Dell

4 HarperCollins

5 Penguin

6 Time Warner (Warner Books, Little, Brown)

7 Putnam Berkley

8 Georg von Holtzbrinck (St. Martin's Press, Henry Holt, Farrar, Straus and Giroux)

9 Hearst Book Group (William Morrow, Avon Books)

10 Thomas Nelson

* *Based on 1996 revenues*

Source: Cowles/Simba Information

T O P   1 0

LARGEST BOOKSTORE CHAINS IN THE US*

Chain	Book stores
1 Waldenbooks	950
2 B. Dalton	577
3 Fowletts	518
4 Barnes and Noble	431
5 Barnes and Noble College Bookstores	305
6 Crown	174
7 Borders	157
8 Books-A-Million	150
9 Lauriats	130
10 Hastings	119

* *Waldenbooks is a subsidiary of Borders, and B. Dalton a subsidiary of Barnes & Noble.*

Source: Book Publishing Report/National Association of College Bookstores

T H E   1 0

FIRST BOOKS PUBLISHED IN THE US

Book	Year
1 *Massachusetts Bay Colony: The Oath of a Free-Man*	1638
2 *An Almanack for the Year of our Lord 1639*	1639
3 *An Almanack for the Year of our Lord 1640*	1640
4 *Bay Psalm Book*	1640
5 *An Almanack for the Year of our Lord 1641*	1641
6 *Massachusetts Bay Colony: The Liberties of the Massachusetts Colonie in New England*	1641
7 *A Short Catechism, Agreed Upon by the Elders at the Desire of the General Court*	1641
8 *An Almanack for the Year of our Lord 1642*	1642
9 *Harvard College: Theses Philologicas, Theses Philosophicas*	1642
10 *Massachusetts Bay Colony: By the Court – In the Yeares 1641, 1642. Capital Lawes, Established Within the Jurisdiction of Massachusetts. The Oath of a Free-Man*	1642

Source: Charles Evans, The American Bibliography of Charles Evans, 1903–34

PRINTING PRESS
The first mechanized printing presses began to be used early in the 17th century.

WORD POWER

TOP 10

LONGEST WORDS IN THE *OXFORD ENGLISH DICTIONARY**

	Word (first used)	Letters
1	Pneumonoultramicroscopicsilico-volcanoconiosis (1936)	45
2	Supercalifragilisticexpialidocious (1964)	34
3	Pseudopseudohypoparathyroidism (1952)	30
4	Floccinaucinihilipilification (17+1)	29
5 =	Antidisestablishmentarianism (1923)	28
=	Hepaticocholangiogastrostomy (1933)	28
=	Octamethylcyclotetrasiloxane (1946)	28
=	Tetrachlorodibenzoparadioxin (1959)	28
9 =	Radioimmunoelectrophoresis (1962)	26
=	Radioimmunoelectrophoretic (1962)	26

* Words that are hyphenated, including compound words, have not been included

TOP 10

MOST STUDIED FOREIGN LANGUAGES IN THE US*

	Language	Registrations
1	Spanish	606,286
2	French	205,351
3	German	96,263
4	Japanese	44,723
5	Italian	43,760
6	Chinese	26,471
7	Latin	25,897
8	Russian	24,729
9	Ancient Greek	16,272
10	Hebrew	13,127#

* In US institutions of higher education

 # Made up of 5,648 registrations in Biblical Hebrew and 7,479 in Modern Hebrew

These figures are from the most recent survey conducted every five years, from colleges and universities in the fall of 1995, which indicated a total of 1,138,772 foreign language registrations.

Source: Modern Language Association of America

TOP 10

MOST WIDELY SPOKEN LANGUAGES IN THE EUROPEAN UNION

	Language	Approx. no. of speakers*
1	German	86,562,000
2	English	59,735,000
3	French	58,084,000
4	Italian	55,320,000
5	Spanish (Castilian)	31,398,000
6	Dutch	20,711,000
7	Portuguese	10,622,000
8	Greek	10,411,000
9	Swedish	8,207,000
10	Catalan	5,120,000

* As a "first language," including speakers resident in EC countries other than those where it is the main language, such as German-speakers living in France

Sweden's joining the European Union on January 1, 1995, means that Danish has dropped out of this list.

TOP 10

WORDS WITH THE MOST MEANINGS IN THE *OXFORD ENGLISH DICTIONARY*

	Word	Meanings
1	Set	464
2	Run	396
3	Go	368
4	Take	343
5	Stand	334
6	Get	289
7	Turn	288
8	Put	268
9	Fall	264
10	Strike	250

TOP 10

LETTERS OF THE ALPHABET WITH MOST ENTRIES IN THE *OXFORD ENGLISH DICTIONARY*

	Letter	Entries
1	S	34,556
2	C	26,239
3	P	24,980
4	M	17,495
5	A	15,880
6	T	15,497
7	R	15,483
8	B	14,633
9	D	14519
10	U	12,943

TOP 10

MOST STUDIED FOREIGN LANGUAGES IN THE UK

1	French
2	Spanish
3	Arabic
4	Chinese (Mandarin)
5	German
6	Italian
7	Russian
8	Japanese
9	Dutch
10	Portuguese

This ranking is based on language courses studied at the School of Languages at the University of Westminster, the largest source of language teaching in the public sector in all of Europe.

TOP 10
MOST USED LETTERS IN WRITTEN ENGLISH

	i	ii
1	e	e
2	t	t
3	a	a
4	o	i
5	i	n
6	n	o
7	s	s
8	r	h
9	h	r
10	l	d

Column i is the order as indicated by a survey across approximately 1,000,000 words appearing in a wide variety of printed texts. Column ii is the order estimated by Samuel Morse, the inventor in the 1830s of Morse Code, based on his calculations of the respective quantities of type used by a printer.

TOP 10
MOST WIDELY SPOKEN LANGUAGES IN THE WORLD

	Country	Approximate no. of speakers
1	Chinese (Mandarin)	1,034,000,000
2	English	500,000,000
3	Hindi	478,000,000
4	Spanish	413,000,000
5	Russian	280,000,000
6	Arabic	230,000,000
7	Bengali	204,000,000
8	Portuguese	186,000,000
9	Malay-Indonesian	164,000,000
10=	French	126,000,000
=	Japanese	126,000,000

According to 1997 estimates by Sidney S. Culbert of the University of Washington, there are only two other languages spoken by more than 100,000,000 people: German (124,000,000) and Urdu (104,000,000).

TOP 10
MOST WIDELY SPOKEN "FIRST" LANGUAGES IN THE US

	Language	Approximate no. of speakers
1	English	198,601,000
2	Spanish	17,339,172
3	French	1,702,176
4	German	1,547,099
5	Italian	1,308,648
6	Chinese	1,249,213
7	Tagalog	843,251
8	Polish	723,483
9	Korean	626,478
10	Vietnamese	507,069

Source: US Bureau of the Census

TOP 10
MOST COMMON WORDS IN ENGLISH

Spoken English		Written English
the	1	the
and	2	of
I	3	to
to	4	in
of	5	and
a	6	a
you	7	for
that	8	was
in	9	is
it	10	that

Various surveys have been conducted to establish the most common words in spoken English of various types, from telephone conversations to broadcast commentaries. Beyond the Top 10, many other words, such as "yes" and "well," also appear with far greater frequency in everyday speech than in the comparative list of the most common words in written English, which is based on a survey of newspaper usages.

TOP 10
COUNTRIES WITH THE MOST ENGLISH-LANGUAGE SPEAKERS

	Country	Approximate no. of speakers
1	US	228,770,000
2	UK	57,190,000
3	Canada	18,112,000
4	Australia	15,538,000
5	South Africa	3,800,000
6	Irish Republic	3,540,000
7	New Zealand	3,290,000
8	Jamaica	2,390,000
9	Trinidad and Tobago	1,189,000
10	Guyana	692,000

This Top 10 represents countries with the greatest numbers of inhabitants who are considered English speakers in their daily working lives. Many people who use English in the workplace conduct their home lives in another language – hence, the lower number of English speakers in the adjacent list.

TOP 10
LANGUAGES OFFICIALLY SPOKEN IN THE MOST COUNTRIES

	Language	Countries
1	English	54
2	French	33
3	Arabic	24
4	Spanish	21
5	Portuguese	8
6	German	5
7 =	Malay	4
=	Dutch	4
9	Chinese (Mandarin)	3
10=	Italian	2
=	Russian	2
=	Tamil	2

LIBRARIES OF THE WORLD

TOP 10
LARGEST LIBRARIES IN THE WORLD

	Library	Location	Founded	Books
1	Library of Congress	Washington, DC	1800	23,041,334
2	National Library of China	Beijing, China	1909	15,980,636
3	National Library of Canada	Ottawa, Canada	1953	14,500,000
4	Deutsche Bibliothek*	Frankfurt, Germany	1990	14,350,000
5	British Library#	London, UK	1753	13,000,000
6	Harvard University Library	Cambridge, Massachusetts	1638	12,877,360
7	Russian State Library†	Moscow, Russia	1862	11,750,000
8	National Diet Library	Tokyo, Japan	1948	11,304,139
9	New York Public Library	New York, New York	1895★	10,505,079
10	Yale University Library	New Haven, Connecticut	1701	9,485,823

* *Formed in 1990 through the unification of the Deutsche Bibliothek, Frankfurt (founded 1947), and the Deutsche Bücherei, Leipzig*

\# *Founded as part of the British Museum in 1753; became an independent body in 1973*

† *Founded 1862 as Rumyantsev Library, formerly State V.I. Lenin Library*

★ *Astor Library founded 1848, consolidated with Lenox Library and Tilden Trust to form New York Public Library in 1895*

The figures for books in such vast collections as held by the libraries listed above represent only a fraction of the total collections, which include manuscripts, microfilms, maps, prints, and records. The Library of Congress has perhaps more than 100,000,000 cataloged items and the New York Public Library more than 26,000,000 manuscripts, maps, audiovisual, and other catalogued items in addition to books.

TOP 10
LARGEST PUBLIC LIBRARIES IN THE US

	Library/ no. of branches	Location	Founded	Books
1	New York Public Library (The Branch Libraries) (82)	New York, NY	1895*	10,505,079 #
2	Queens Borough Public Library (62)	Jamaica, NY	1896	9,681,898
3	Chicago Public Library (81)	Chicago, IL	1872	6,840,109
4	Boston Public Library (26)	Boston, MA	1852	6,529,998
5	Carnegie Library of Pittsburgh (18)	Pittsburgh, PA	1895	6,409,300
6	County of Los Angeles Public Library (147)	Los Angeles, CA	1872	6,102,920
7	Free Library of Philadelphia (52)	Philadelphia, PA	1891	5,933,711
8	Public Library of Cincinnati and Hamilton County (41)	Cincinnati, OH	1853	4,655,050
9	Houston Public Library (37)	Houston, TX	1901	4,113,095
10	Buffalo and Erie County Public Library (53)	Buffalo, NY	1836	4,096,516

* *Astor Library founded 1848; consolidated with Lenox Library and Tilden Trust to form New York Public Library, 1895*

\# *Lending library and reference library holdings available for loan*

Source: American Library Association

THE NEW BRITISH LIBRARY
After controversy over the expense of the building, the New British Library finally opened in November 1997. It will take until the turn of the century to complete the move of about 13 million books.

LIBRARIES OF THE WORLD

THE 10
LARGEST TYPES OF LIBRARIES IN THE US*

	Library	Total
1	Public libraries excluding branches	9,123
2	Public library branches	6,223
3	Medical libraries	2,443
4	Government libraries	1,864
5	Law libraries	1,763
6	University and College Departmental libraries	1,666
7	Academic libraries – Junior College	1,261
8	Religious libraries	1,116
9	Army libraries	177
10	Navy libraries	145

Excluding elementary and secondary school libraries

Source: American Library Directory

THE 10
LARGEST UNIVERSITY LIBRARIES IN THE US

	Library	Books
1	Harvard University	12,877,360
2	Yale University	9,485,823
3	University of Illinois-Urbana	8,474,737
4	University of California-Berkeley	8,078,685
5	University of Texas	7,019,508
6	University of Michigan	6,664,081
7	Columbia University	6,532,066
8	University of California-Los Angeles	6,460,391
9	Stanford University	6,409,239
10	University of Chicago	5,710,003

Source: American Library Association

THE 10
STATES WITH MOST LIBRARIES*

	State	Libraries
1	New York	436
2	Illinois	366
3	Pennsylvania	317
4	Iowa	293
5	Michigan	263
6	Texas	261
7	Massachusetts	257
8	New Jersey	235
9	Wisconsin	231
10	Ohio	207

A total of 5,638 libraries reporting annual acquisition expenditures

Source: American Library Directory

THE 10
FIRST PUBLIC LIBRARIES IN THE US

	Library	Founded
1	Peterboro Public Library, Peterboro, New Hampshire	1833
2	New Orleans Public Library, New Orleans, Louisiana	1843
3	Boston Public Library, Boston, Massachusetts	1852
4	Public Library of Cincinnati and Hamilton County, Cincinnati, Ohio	1853
5	Springfield City Library, Springfield, Massachusetts	1857
6	Worcester Public Library, Worcester, Massachusets	1859
7	County Library, Portland, Oregon	1864
8=	Detroit Public Library, Detroit, Michigan	1865
=	St. Louis Public Library, St. Louis, Missouri	1865
10	Atlanta-Fulton Public Library, Atlanta, Georgia	1867

Source: Public Library Association

THE 10
FIRST CARNEGIE LIBRARIES IN THE US*

	Library/year opened	Amount of grant ($)
1	Allegheny, PA, 1886	481,012
2	Johnstown, PA, May 9, 1890	55,332
3	Fairfield, IA, Jan 15, 1892	30,000
4	Braddock, PA, Dec 31, 1895	357,782
5	Homestead, PA, Nov 27, 1896	332,067
6	Carnegie, PA, Apr 26, 1898	310,000
7	Pittsburg, TX, Apr 30, 1898	5,000
8	Atlanta, GA (4), Oct 3, 1898	202,000
9	Oakmont, PA, Jan 24, 1899	25,000
10	McKeesport, PA, Apr 2, 1899	50,000

Excludes towns with libraries established before grant

Source: Carnegie Libraries: Their History and Impact on American Public Library Development

TOP 10
LARGEST LIBRARIES IN THE US

	Library	Books
1	Library of Congress	23,041,334
2	Harvard University	12,877,360
3	New York Public	10,505,079
4	Queens Borough Public Library	9,681,898
5	Yale University	9,485,823
6	University of Illinois-Urbana	8,474,737
7	University of California-Berkeley	8,078,685
8	University of Texas	7,019,508
9	Chicago Public Library	6,840,109
10	University of Michigan	6,664,081

Source: American Library Association

ENGLISH-LANGUAGE BESTSELLERS

TOP 10 US HARDBACK NONFICTION BESTSELLERS

1987 Author/title		1997 Author/title
Peter Wright with Paul Greengrass, *Spycatcher*	1	Frank McCourt, *Angela's Ashes*
Allan Bloom, *The Closing of the American Mind*	2	Sarah Ban Breathnach, *Simple Abundance*
Bill Cosby, *Time Flies*	3	John Berendt, *Midnight in the Garden of Good and Evil*
Rick Smolan and David Cohen, *A Day in the Life of America*	4	Kitty Kelley, *The Royals*
Erma Bombeck, *Family: The Ties That Bind ... and Gag*	5	Irma S. Rombauer, Marion Rombauer Becker, and Ethan Becker, *Joy of Cooking*
Ravi Batra, *The Great Depression of 1990*	6	Andrew Morton, *Diana: Her True Story*
Tip O'Neill with William Novak, *Man of the House: The Life and Political Memoirs of Speaker Tip O'Neill*	7	Jon Krakauer, *Into Thin Air*
Bernie S. Siegel, *Love, Medicine and Miracles*	8	Neale Donald Walsch, *Conversations with God, Book 1*
Bob Woodward, *Veil*	9	John Gray, *Men are from Mars, Women are from Venus*
John Feinstein, *A Season on the Brink*	10	Andrew Weil, *Eight Weeks to Optimum Health*

Source: Publishers Weekly

US ALMANACS, ATLASES, AND ANNUALS OF 1997

1	*The World Almanac and Book of Facts 1998*
2	*Ernst and Young Tax Guide 1997*
3	*The World Almanac and Book of Facts 1997*
4	*The Old Farmer's Almanac 1998*
5	*Birnbaum's Walt Disney World 1998*
6	*The Wall Street Journal Almanac 1998*
7	*Taxes for Dummies, 98 Edition*
8	*Christmas Ideals 97*
9	*Sports Illustrated, Almanac 98*
10	*The New York Times Almanac 1998*

Source: Publishers Weekly

SNAP FACT

• Although there were bestsellers before 1889, none was so called until Thursday, April 25 of that year, when the US newspaper the *Kansas Times and Star* listed six books as the "best sellers here last week" – the first occasion the phrase appeared in print.

CHILDREN'S BOOKS IN THE US, 1997

	Author/title	Sales
1	*Disney's Pooh: Thank You, Pooh!*	598,820
2	*Hercules*	558,992
3	*Disney's Pooh: A Grand and Wonderful Day*	494,300
4	Sam McBratney, *Guess How Much I Love You*	481,488
5	Margaret Wise Brown, *Goodnight Moon*	468,240
6	*Disney's 101 Dalmatians*	448,930
7	Bill Martin, Jr., *Brown Bear, Brown Bear, What Do You See?*	441,709
8	*Disney's Pooh: The Sweetest Christmas*	433,130
9	Dr. Seuss, *Oh, The Places You'll Go!*	408,779
10	*Anastasia*	396,360

Source: Publishers Weekly

FROM BLANK PAGES TO BESTSELLER

American author Elbert Hubbard (1856–1915) can be credited with writing both the shortest and one of the bestselling books of all time. In 1898 he published his *Essay on Silence*, a book containing only blank pages. Then, in 1899, he turned his essay *A Message to García* into a pamphlet that was to become one of the bestselling works ever. Now largely forgotten, Hubbard's polemic on the subject of labor relations achieved phenomenal sales at the time, primarily because many employers purchased bulk supplies to distribute to their employees. The literary career of Elbert Hubbard was cut short on May 7, 1915, when he went down with the British passenger liner *Lusitania*, torpedoed by a German submarine with the loss of 1,198 civilians.

100 YEARS AGO

THEN & NOW

TOP 10 US HARDBACK FICTION BESTSELLERS

1987 Author/title		1997 Author/title
Stephen King, *The Tommyknockers*	**1**	John Grisham, *The Partner*
Scott Turow, *Presumed Innocent*	**2**	Charles Frazier, *Cold Mountain*
Tom Clancy, *Patriot Games*	**3**	Danielle Steel, *The Ghost*
Stephen King, *Misery*	**4**	Danielle Steel, *The Ranch*
Sidney Sheldon, *Windmills of the Gods*	**5**	Danielle Steel, *Special Delivery*
Danielle Steel, *Kaleidoscope*	**6**	Patricia Cornwell, *Unnatural Exposure*
Danielle Steel, *Fine Things*	**7**	Sidney Sheldon, *The Best Laid Plans*
Garrison Keillor, *Leaving Home*	**8**	Mary Higgins Clark, *Pretend You Don't See Her*
Stephen King, *The Eyes of the Dragon*	**9**	James Patterson, *Cat and Mouse*
Tom Wolfe, *The Bonfire of the Vanities*	**10**	Patricia Cornwell, *Hornet's Nest*

Source: Publishers Weekly

TOP 10

BESTSELLING BOOKS OF ALL TIME

	Book	Approximate sales
1	*The Bible*	6,000,000,000
2	*Quotations from the Works of Mao Tse-tung*	800,000,000
3	*American Spelling Book*, Noah Webster	100,000,000
4	*The Guinness Book of Records*	80,000,000 *
5	*The McGuffey Readers*, William Holmes McGuffey	60,000,000
6	*A Message to Garcia*, Elbert Hubbard	40–50,000,000
7	*World Almanac*	over 40,000,000 *
8	*The Common Sense Book of Baby and Child Care*, Benjamin Spock	over 39,200,000
9	*Valley of the Dolls*, Jacqueline Susann	30,000,000
10	*In His Steps: "What Would Jesus Do?"* Rev. Charles Monroe Sheldon	28,500,000

* *Aggregate sales of annual publication*

MICHAEL CRICHTON
US author Michael Crichton's Jurassic Park *has remained at the top of the list of bestselling novels of the 1990s in the UK, with sales of over three-quarters of a million copies.*

TOP 10

US TRADE PAPERBACK BESTSELLERS OF 1997

	Author/title	Sales
1	Richard Carlson, *Don't Sweat The Small Stuff and it's All Small Stuff*	4,506,683
2	Jack Canfield, Mark Victor Hansen *et al*, *Chicken Soup for the Woman's Soul*	2,228,000
3	Wally Lamb, *She's Come Undone*	Unavailable
4	Jack Canfield, Mark Victor Hansen *et al*, *Chicken Soup for the Mother's Soul*	1,406,739
5	Stephen King, *Wizard and Glass*	1,298,664
6	Ursula Hegi, *Stones from the River*	1,285,000
7	James F. and Phyllis A. Balch, *Prescription for Nutritional Healing*	1,275,000
8	Andy Rathbone, *Windows95 for Dummies, 2nd edition*	1,148,107
9	Jack Canfield, Mark Victor Hansen *et al*, *Chicken Soup for the Christian Soul*	1,263,328
10	Mary McGarry Morris, *Songs in Ordinary Time*	1,120,000

Source: Publishers Weekly

TOP 10 NOVELS OF THE 1990s IN THE UK
(Sales)

❶ *Jurassic Park*, Michael Crichton (769,981)
❷ *The Chamber*, John Grisham (760,495)
❸ *The Client*, John Grisham (722,195)
❹ *Bravo Two Zero*, Andy McNab (715,406)
❺ *The Glass Lake*, Maeve Binchy (683,270)
❻ *Schindler's Ark/List*, Thomas Keneally (601,308) ❼ *Polo*, Jilly Cooper (597,562)
❽ *The Negotiator*, Frederick Forsyth (553,380) ❾ *The Man Who Made Husbands Jealous*, Jilly Cooper (526,591) ❿ *As the Crow Flies*, Jeffrey Archer (515,867)

LITERARY PRIZES

THE 10

LATEST WINNERS OF THE PULITZER PRIZE FOR FICTION

Year	Author	Novel
1998	Philip Roth	*American Pastoral*
1997	Steven Millhauser	*Martin Dressler: The Tale of an American Dreamer*
1996	Richard Ford	*Independence Day*
1995	Carol Shields	*The Stone Diaries*
1994	E. Annie Proulx	*The Shipping News*
1993	Robert Olen Butler	*A Good Scent from a Strange Mountain: Stories*
1992	Jane Smiley	*A Thousand Acres*
1991	John Updike	*Rabbit at Rest*
1990	Oscar Hijuelos	*The Mambo Kings Play*
1989	Anne Tyler	*Breathing Lessons*

THE 10

LATEST BOOKER PRIZE WINNERS

Year	Author	Novel
1997	Arundhati Roy	*The God of Small Things*
1996	Graham Swift	*Last Orders*
1995	Pat Barker	*The Ghost Road*
1994	James Kelman	*How Late It Was, How Late*
1993	Roddy Doyle	*Paddy Clarke Ha Ha Ha*
1992 =	Michael Ondaatje	*The English Patient*
=	Barry Unsworth	*Sacred Hunger*
1991	Ben Okri	*Famished Road*
1990	A.S. Byatt	*Possession: A Romance*
1989	Kazuo Ishiguro	*The Remains of the Day*

THE 10

LATEST WINNERS OF THE NATIONAL BOOK CRITICS CIRCLE AWARD FOR FICTION

Year	Author/title	Year	Author/title
1997	Penelope Fitzgerald, *The Blue Flower*	1992	Cormac McCarthy, *All the Pretty Horses*
1996	Gina Berriault, *Women in Their Beds*	1991	Jane Smiley, *A Thousand Acres*
1995	Stanley Elkin, *Mrs. Ted Bliss*	1990	John Updike, *Rabbit at Rest*
1994	Carol Shields, *The Stone Diaries*	1989	E. L. Doctorow, *Billy Bathgate*
1993	Ernest J. Gaines, *A Lesson Before Dying*	1988	Bharati Mukherjee, *The Middleman and Other Stories*

The National Book Critics Circle was founded in 1974 and consists of almost 700 active reviewers. The Circle presents annual awards in five categories: fiction, general nonfiction, biography and autobiography, poetry, and criticism. Awards are made in March each year.

THE 10

LATEST WINNERS OF THE PEN/FAULKNER AWARD

Year	Author/title	Year	Author/title
1997	Gina Berriault, *Women in Their Beds*	1992	Don Delillo, *Mao II*
1996	Richard Ford, *Independence Day*	1991	John Edgar Wideman, *Phildelphia Fire*
1995	David Guterson, *Snow Falling on Cedars*	1990	E. L. Doctorow, *Billy Bathgate*
1994	Philip Roth, *Operation Shylock*	1989	James Salter, *Dusk*
1993	E. Annie Proulx, *Postcards*	1988	T. Coraghessan Boyle, *World's End*

THE 10

LATEST WINNERS OF HUGO AWARDS FOR BEST SCIENCE FICTION NOVEL

Year	Author/novel
1997	Kim Stanley Robinson, *Blue Mars*
1996	Neal Stephenson, *The Diamond Age*
1995	Lois McMaster Bujold, *Mirror Dance*
1994	Kim Stanley Robinson, *Green Mars*
1993 =	Vernor Vinge, *A Fire Upon the Deep*
=	Connie Willis, *Doomsday Book*
1992	Lois McMaster Bujold, *Barrayar*
1991	Lois McMaster Bujold, *The Vor Game*
1990	Dan Simmons, *Hyperion*
1989	C.J. Cherryh, *Cyteen*

Hugo Awards for science fiction novels, short stories, and other fiction and non-fiction works are presented by the World Science Fiction Society. They were established in 1953 as "Science Fiction Achievement Awards for the best science fiction writing." The prize in the Awards' inaugural year was presented to Alfred Bester for *The Demolished Man*.

THE 10

LATEST WINNERS OF THE NATIONAL BOOK AWARD FOR FICTION

Year	Author	Title
1997	Charles Frazier	Cold Mountain
1996	Andrea Barrett	Ship Fever and Other Stories
1995	Philip Roth	Sabbath's Theater
1994	William Gaddis	A Frolic of His Own
1993	E. Annie Proulx	The Shipping News
1992	Cormac McCarthy	All the Pretty Horses
1991	Norman Rush	Mating
1990	Charles Johnson	Middle Passage
1989	John Casey	Spartina
1988	Pete Dexter	Paris Trout

The National Book Award is presented by the National Book Foundation as part of its program to foster reading in the United States through such activities as author events and fund-raising for literacy campaigns. Award winners are announced each November and receive $10,000. Past recipients include many books that are now regarded as modern classics, some of which have since been filmed, among them William Styron's *Sophie's Choice* and John Irving's *The World According to Garp*, joint winners in 1980, and Alice Walker's *The Color Purple*, co-winner in 1983.

THE 10

LATEST WINNERS OF THE EDGAR ALLAN POE AWARD

Year	Author	Title
1997	Thomas A. Cook	The Chatham School Affair
1996	Dick Francis	Come to Grief
1995	Mary Willis Walker	The Red Scream
1994	Minette Walters	The Sculptress
1993	Margaret Maron	Bootlegger's Daughter
1992	Lawrence Block	A Dance at the Slaughterhouse
1991	Julie Smith	New Orleans Mourning
1990	James Lee Burke	Black Cherry Blues
1989	Stuart M. Kaminsky	A Cold Red Sunrise
1988	Aaron Elkins	Old Bones

Popularly called the "Edgar," this award has been presented by the Mystery Writers of America since 1954 for novels in the following three genres: suspense, detective, and spy fiction. It is named after the great American mystery writer Edgar Allan Poe, a ceramic bust of whom is presented to the winner.

THE 10

LATEST WINNERS OF THE JOHN NEWBERY MEDAL

Year	Author	Title
1998	Karen Hesse	Out of the Dust
1997	E. L. Konigsburg	The View from Saturday
1996	Karen Cushman	The Midwife's Apprentice
1995	Sharon Creech	Walk Two Moons
1994	Lois Lowry	The Giver
1993	Cynthia Rylant	Missing May
1992	Phyllis Reynolds Naylor	Shiloh
1991	Jerry Spinelli	Maniac Magee
1990	Lois Lowry	Number the Stars
1989 =	Paul Fleischman	Joyful Noise
=	Walter Myers	Scorpions

The John Newbery Medal is awarded for "the most distinguished contribution to American literature for children." Its first winner in 1923 was Hugh Lofting's *The Voyages of Doctor Dolittle*. The medal is named after John Newbery (1713–67), a London bookseller and publisher who specialized in children's books.

THE 10

LATEST RANDOLPH CALDECOTT MEDAL WINNERS

Year	Author	Title
1998	Paul O. Zelinsky	Rapunzel
1997	David Wisniewski	Golem
1996	Peggy Rathman	Officer Buckle and Gloria
1995	Eve Bunting (illustrated by David Diaz)	Smoky Night
1994	Allen Say	Grandfather's Journey
1993	Emily McCully Honor	Mirette on High Wire
1992	David Weisner	Tuesday
1991	David Macauley	Black and White
1990	Ed Young	Lon Po Po
1989	Stephen Gammell	Song and Dance Man

The Randolph Caldecott Medal, named after the English illustrator (1846–86), has been awarded annually since 1938 "to the artist of the most distinguished American picture book for children published in the United States during the preceding year." The winner in the debut year was Helen Dean Fish's *Animals of the Bible*, illustrated by Dorothy P. Lethrop. In subsequent years many books have been honored that have gone on to be regarded as modern classics, among them Maurice Sendak's *Where the Wild Things Are*, the Medal winner in 1964.

THE PRESS

FIRST COMICS PUBLISHED IN THE US

	Comic	Year
1=	*The Yellow Kid in McFadden Flats*	1897
=	*The Yellow Kid #1–9* (magazine)	1897
3	*Funny Folk*	1899
4	*Vaudeville and Other Things*	1900
5=	*The Blackberries*	1901
=	*Foxy Grampa*	1901
7=	*The Latest Larks of Foxy Grampa*	1902
=	*The Many Adventures of Foxy Grampa*	1902
=	*Pore Li'l Mose*	1902
10	*Alphonse and Gaston and Leon*	1903

Source: Gemstone Publishing

LONGEST-RUNNING MAGAZINES IN THE US

	Magazine	First published
1	*Scientific American*	1845
2	*Town and Country*	1846
3	*Harper's**	1850
4	*The Moravian*	1856
5	*The Atlantic#*	1857
6	*Armed Forces Journal†*	1863
7	*The Nation*	1865
8	*American Naturalist*	1867
9	*Harper's Bazaar*	1867
10	*Animals★*	1868

* *Originally* Harper's New Monthly Magazine

\# *Originally* The Atlantic Monthly

† *Originally* Army and Navy Journal

★ *Originally* Our Dumb Animals

Source: Magazine Publishers of America

THE FIRST OCEAN NEWSPAPER

The first newspaper published at sea using messages transmitted by the latest wireless technology pioneered by Guglielmo Marconi was published by Marconi himself. On November 15, 1899, on board the 11,600-ton American liner S.S. *St. Paul*, he set up a receiver on which he picked up news transmitted from a station on the Isle of Wight. This was then printed in a four-page newspaper, the *Transatlantic Times*, which was sold to passengers for the then enormous price of one dollar (although the proceeds from its sales were donated to the Seaman's Fund). The first daily ocean newspaper was the *Cunard Daily Bulletin*, published in October 1902 on board the S.S. *Campania* and S.S. *Lucania*, then the two largest liners afloat, receiving wireless news from stations in England and Canada.

100 YEARS AGO · YEARS AGO · YEARS AGO

LONGEST-RUNNING COMIC STRIPS IN THE US

	Strip	First published
1	*Gasoline Alley*	1918
2	*Winnie Winkle*	1920
3	*Tarzan*	1929
4	*Blondie*	1930
5	*Dick Tracy*	1931
6	*Alley Oop*	1933
7	*Li'l Abner*	1934
8	*The Phantom*	1936
9	*Prince Valiant*	1937
10	*Nancy*	1938

Source: Gemstone Publishing

FIRST COMIC BOOKS IN THE US

	Comic	First published
1	*Famous Funnies: Series 1*	Feb 1934

35,000 copies of this 64-page comic book sold at 10c each mark the beginning of the comic book era.

2	*Famous Funnies No. 1*	Jul 1934

The first monthly comic ("The Nation's Comic Monthly"), it ran for 21 years (218 issues).

3	*New Fun*	Feb 1935

Became More Fun *after the 6th issue.*

4	*Mickey Mouse Magazine*	Jun 1935

Became Walt Disney's Comics and Stories *in October 1940.*

5	*New Comics*	Dec 1935

Became New Adventure Comics *after No. 12.*

6	*Popular Comics*	Feb 1936
7=	*King Comics*	Apr 1936
=	*Tip Top Comics*	Apr 1936

One of the longest-running of the early comic books, it ceased publication in May 1961 with its 225th issue.

9	*The Funnies*	Oct 1936

Became The New Funnies *with issue No. 65.*

10	*Detective Picture Stories*	Dec 1936

The first thematic comic book, in July 1938 its title was changed to Keen Detective Funnies.

* *First published commercially: some earlier comic books were given away as promotional items*

TOP 10

SUNDAY NEWSPAPERS IN THE US

	Newspaper	Average Sunday circulation*
1	New York Times	1,658,718
2	Los Angeles Times	1,361,748
3	Washington Post	1,102,329
4	Chicago Tribune	1,023,736
5	Philadelphia Inquirer	878,660
6	Detroit Free Press	829,178
7	New York News	807,788
8	Dallas News	789,004
9	Boston Globe	758,843
10	Houston Chronicle	748,036

* Through September 30, 1997

Source: Audit Bureau of Circulations

TOP 10

COUNTRIES WITH THE MOST DAILY NEWSPAPERS

	Country	No. of daily newspapers
1	India	1,802
2	US	1,533
3	Germany	406
4	Turkey	400
5	Brazil	320
6	Mexico	310
7	Russia	292
8	Pakistan	223
9	Argentina	190
10	Greece	168

Source: UNESCO

MODERN PRINTING PRESS

TOP 10

OLDEST NEWSPAPERS IN THE US

	Newspaper	Year established
1	The Hartford Courant, Hartford, CT	1764
2=	Poughkeepsie Journal, Poughkeepsie, NY	1785
=	The Augusta Chronicle, Augusta, GA	1785
=	Register-Star, Hudson, NY	1785
5=	Pittsburgh Post Gazette, Pittsburgh, PA	1786
=	Daily Hampshire Gazette, Northampton, MA	1786
7	The Berkshire Eagle, Pittsfield, MA	1789
8	Norwich Bulletin, Norwich, CT	1791
9	The Recorder, Greenfield, MA	1792
10	Intelligencer Journal, Lancaster, PA	1794

Source: Editor and Publisher Year Book

TOP 10

MAGAZINES IN THE US

	Magazine/ no. of issues a year	Circulation*
1	NRTA/AARP Bulletin (10)	20,415,981
2	Modern Maturity (36)	20,390,755
3	Reader's Digest (12)	15,038,708
4	TV Guide (52)	13,103,187
5	National Geographic Magazine (12)	9,012,074
6	Better Homes and Gardens (12)	7,605,187
7	Family Circle (17)	5,107,477
8	Good Housekeeping (12)	4,739,592
9	Ladies Home Journal (12)	4,590,155
10	Woman's Day (17)	4,461,023

* Average for last six months of 1997

National Geographic, the official publication of the National Geographic Society (founded by Gardiner Greene Hubbard, the father-in-law of the great American inventor Alexander Graham Bell), was first published as a monthly magazine in 1896.

Source: Magazine Publishers of America

TOP 10

DAILY NEWSPAPERS IN THE US

	Newspaper	Average daily circulation*
1	Wall Street Journal	1,774,880
2	USA Today	1,629,665
3	New York Times	1,074,741
4	Los Angeles Times	1,050,176
5	Washington Post	775,894
6	New York Daily News	721,256
7	Chicago Tribune	653,554
8	Long Island Newsday	568,914
9	Houston Chronicle	549,101
10	Dallas Morning News	484,379

* Through September 30, 1997

Apart from the Wall Street Journal, which focuses mainly on financial news, USA Today remains the United States' only true national daily newspaper.

Source: Audit Bureau of Circulations

ART AT AUCTION

RISING SUN
*The sale of van Gogh's Sunflowers
in 1987 established a new world
record price for a painting.*

TOP 10
MOST EXPENSIVE OLD MASTER PAINTINGS EVER SOLD AT AUCTION

	Work/artist/sale	Price ($)
1	*Portrait of Duke Cosimo I de Medici*, Jacopo da Carucci (Pontormo) (Italian; 1493–1558), Christie's, New York, May 31, 1989	32,000,000
2	*The Old Horse Guards, London, from St. James's Park*, Canaletto (Italian; 1697–1768), Christie's, London, April 15, 1992 (£9,200,000)	16,008,000
3	*View of the Giudecca and the Zattere, Venice*, Francesco Guardi (Italian; 1712–93), Sotheby's, Monaco, December 1, 1989 (F.FR85,000,000)	13,943,218
4	*Venus and Adonis*, Titian (Italian; *c.*1488–1576), Christie's, London, December 13, 1991 (£6,800,000)	12,376,000
5	*Le Retour du Bucentaure le Jour de l'Ascension*, Canaletto, Ader Tajan, Paris, December 15, 1993 (F.FR66,000,000)	11,316,457
6	*View of Molo from Bacino di San Marco, Venice* and *View of the Grand Canal Facing East from Campo di Santi, Venice* (pair), Canaletto, Sotheby's, New York, June 1, 1990	10,000,000
7	*Adoration of the Magi*, Andrea Mantegna (Italian; 1431–1606), Christie's, London, April 18, 1985	9,525,000
8	*Portrait of a Girl Wearing a Gold–trimmed Cloak*, Rembrandt (Dutch; 1606–69), Sotheby's, New York, December 10, 1986	9,372,000
9	*Portrait of Bearded Man in Red Coat*, Rembrandt, Sotheby's, New York, January 30, 1998	8,250,000
10	*Study for Head and Hand of an Apostle*, Raphael (Italian; 1483–1520), Christie's, London, December 13, 1996	7,920,000

TOP 10
MOST EXPENSIVE PAINTINGS BY WOMEN ARTISTS EVER SOLD AT AUCTION

	Work/artist/sale	Price ($)
1	*The Conversation*, Mary Cassatt (American; 1845–1926), Christie's, New York, May 11, 1988	4,100,000
2	*In the Box*, Mary Cassatt, Christie's, New York, May 23, 1996	3,700,000
3	*Mother, Sara and the Baby*, Mary Cassatt, Christie's, New York, May 10, 1989	3,500,000
4	*Après le déjeuner*, Berthe Morisot (French; 1841–1895), Christie's, New York, May 14, 1997	3,250,000
5	*From the Plains*, Georgia O'Keeffe (American; 1887–1986), Sotheby's, New York, December 3, 1997	3,300,000
6	*Autoretrato con chango y loro*, Frida Kahlo (Mexican; 1907–54), Sotheby's, New York, May 17, 1995	2,900,000
7	*Augusta Reading to her Daughter*, Mary Cassatt, Sotheby's, New York, May 9, 1989	2,800,000
8	*Sara Holding her Dog*, Mary Cassatt, Sotheby's, New York, November 11, 1988	2,500,000
9	*Young Lady in a Loge, Gazing to the Right*, Mary Cassatt, Sotheby's, New York, November 10, 1992	2,300,000
10	*Madame H. de Fleury and her Child*, Mary Cassatt, Sotheby's, New York, May 25, 1988	1,900,000

TOP 10

MOST EXPENSIVE PAINTINGS EVER SOLD AT AUCTION

Work/artist/sale	Price ($)
1 *Portrait of Dr. Gachet*, Vincent van Gogh (Dutch; 1853–90), Christie's, New York, May 15, 1990	75,000,000

Both this painting and the one in the No. 2 position were bought by Ryoei Saito, head of Japanese Daishowa Paper Manufacturing.

2 *Au Moulin de la Galette*, Pierre-Auguste Renoir (French; 1841–1919), Sotheby's, New York, May 17, 1990	71,000,000
3 *Les Noces de Pierrette*, Pablo Picasso (Spanish; 1881–1973), Binoche et Godeau, Paris, Nov 30, 1989 (F.Fr315,000,000)	51,671,920

The painting was sold by Swedish financier Fredrik Roos to Tomonori Tsurumaki, a property developer, who bid for it by telephone from Tokyo.

4 *Irises*, Vincent van Gogh, Sotheby's, New York, Nov 11, 1987	49,000,000

After much speculation, its purchaser was confirmed as businessman Alan Bond. However, he was unable to pay for it in full, so its former status as the world's most expensive work of art has been disputed.

5 *Le Rêve*, Pablo Picasso, Christie's, New York, Nov 10, 1997	44,000,000

Picasso's Le Rêve (The Dream), a portrait of Marie Thérèse Walter from the Ganz collection, is the highest priced painting sold since 1990.

6 *Self Portrait: Yo Picasso*, Pablo Picasso, Sotheby's, New York, May 9, 1989	43,500,000

The purchaser has remained anonymous, but unconfirmed reports have identified him as Stavros Niarchos, the Greek shipping magnate.

7 *Au Lapin Agile*, Pablo Picasso, Sotheby's, New York, Nov 15, 1989	37,000,000

The painting depicts Picasso as a harlequin at the bar of the Café Lapin. In 1989 it was bought by the Walter Annenberg Foundation.

8 *Sunflowers*, Vincent van Gogh, Christie's, London, Mar 30, 1987 (£22,500,000)	36,225,000

At the time, this was the most expensive picture ever sold. It was bought by the Yasuda Fire and Marine Insurance Company of Tokyo.

9 *Acrobate et Jeune Arlequin*, Pablo Picasso, Christie's, London, Nov 28, 1988 (£19,000,000)	35,530,000

Until the sale of Yo Picasso, this held the world record for a 20th-century painting. It was bought by Mitsukoshi, a Japanese department store (in Japan, many major stores have important art galleries).

10 *Portrait of Duke Cosimo I de Medici*, Jacopo da Carucci (Pontormo) (Italian; 1494–1556/7), Christie's, New York, May 31, 1989	32,000,000

This is the record price paid for an Old Master – and the only one in this Top 10. It was bought by the J. Paul Getty Museum, Malibu, CA.

TOP 10 ARTISTS WITH THE MOST WORKS SOLD FOR MORE THAN ONE MILLION DOLLARS

(No. of works sold)

❶ Pablo Picasso (211) ❷ Pierre Auguste Renoir (168) ❸ Claude Monet (163) ❹ Edgar Degas (88) ❺= Paul Cézanne (63), Marc Chagall (63) ❼ Camille Pissaro (60) ❽ Henri Matisse (59) ❾= Amedeo Modigliani (44), Vincent van Gogh (44)

TOP 10

MOST EXPENSIVE PAINTINGS EVER SOLD IN THE US

Work/artist/sale	Price ($)
1 *Portrait of Dr. Gachet*, Vincent van Gogh, Christie's, New York, May 15, 1990	75,000,000
2 *Au Moulin de la Galette*, Pierre-Auguste Renoir, Sotheby's, New York, May 17, 1990	71,000,000
3 *Irises*, Vincent van Gogh, Sotheby's, New York, November 11, 1987	49,000,000
4 *Le Rêve*, Pablo Picasso, Christie's, New York, November 10, 1997	44,000,000
5 *Self Portrait: Yo Picasso*, Pablo Picasso, Sotheby's, New York, May 9, 1989	43,500,000
6 *Au Lapin Agile*, Pablo Picasso, Sotheby's, New York, November 15, 1989	37,000,000
7 *Portrait of Duke Cosimo I de Medici*, Jacopo da Carucci (Pontormo), Christie's, New York, May 31, 1989	32,000,000
8 *Les femmes d'Alger*, Pablo Picasso, Christie's, New York, November 10, 1997	29,000,000
9 *Angel Fernandez de Soto*, Pablo Picasso, Sotheby's, New York, May 8, 1995	26,500,000
10 *Nature morte – les grosses pommes*, Paul Cézanne, Sotheby's, New York, May 1, 1993	26,000,000

20TH-CENTURY ARTISTS

DAVID HOCKNEY
Although a British artist, many of his works depict scenes in California, where he lives, and have achieved high prices among American collectors.

TOP 10 MOST EXPENSIVE PAINTINGS BY DAVID HOCKNEY
(Prices in $)

❶ *Grand procession of Dignitaries in the semi-Egyptian style* (2,00,000) ❷ *Deep and wet water* (1,300,000) ❸ *Henry Geldzahler and Christopher Scott* (1,000,000) ❹ *California art collector* (925,000) ❺ *The Room, Manchester Street* (800,000) ❻ *A neat lawn* (598,400) ❼ *Berlin, a souvenir* (575,000) ❽ *Different kinds of water pouring into swimming pool, Santa Monica* (460,000) ❾ *The Room, Tarzana* (447,200) ❿ *The Actor* (386,400)

TOP 10

MOST EXPENSIVE PAINTINGS BY WASSILY KANDINSKY

	Work/sale	Price ($)
1	*Fugue* Sotheby's, New York, May 17, 1990	19,000,000
2	*Sketch for Composition VII – Entwurf I zu Komposition VII* Sotheby's, London, December 1, 1992 (£5,000,000)	7,900,000
3	*Dans le cercle noir* Guy Loudmer, Paris, November 22, 1993 (F.FR36,000,000)	6,089,143
4	*Das jungste Gericht* Sotheby's, New York, November 8, 1995	4,750,000
5	*Engel des jungsten Gerichts* Christie's, New York, May 10, 1989	4,200,000
6	*Milieu accompagné* Sotheby's, London, June 22, 1993 (£2,750,000)	4,097,500
7	*Skizze für Improvisation 4* Sotheby's, London, June 27, 1995 (£2,500,000)	3,975,000
8	*Herbstlandschaft* Sotheby's, New York, May 9, 1989	3,600,000
9	*Herbstlandschaft mit Booten* Christie's, New York, November 13, 1996	3,500,000
10	*Murnau - Landschaft mit Kirche I* Christie's, New York, November 2, 1993	2,500,000

TOP 10

MOST EXPENSIVE PAINTINGS BY JASPER JOHNS

	Work/sale	Price ($)
1	*False start* Sotheby's, New York, November 10, 1988	15,500,000
2	*Two flags* Sotheby's, New York, November 8, 1989	11,000,000
3	*Corpse and Mirror* Christie's, New York, November 10, 1997	7,600,000
4	*White Numbers* Christie's, New York, November 10, 1997	7,200,000
5	*White flag* Christie's, New York, November 9, 1988	6,400,000
6	*Jubilee* Sotheby's, New York, November 13, 1991	4,500,000
7=	*Device circle* Christie's, New York, November 12, 1991	4,000,000
=	*Decoy* Christie's, New York, November 10, 1997	4,000,000
9	*Gray rectangles* Sotheby's, New York, November 10, 1988	3,900,000
10	*Small false start* Christie's, New York, November 7, 1989	3,700,000

TOP 10

MOST EXPENSIVE PAINTINGS BY ANDY WARHOL

	Work/sale	Price ($)
1	Shot Red Marilyn Sotheby's, New York, May 3, 1989	3,700,000
2	Marilyn Monroe, twenty times Sotheby's, New York, November 10, 1988	3,600,000
3	Marilyn X 100 Sotheby's, New York, November 17, 1992	3,400,000
4	Shot Red Marilyn Sotheby's, New York, November 2, 1994	3,300,000
5	Big torn Campbell's soup can Christie's, New York, May 7, 1997	3,200,000
6	Liz Christie's, New York, November 7, 1989	2,050,000
7	Triple Elvis Sotheby's, New York, November 8, 1989	2,000,000
8	210 Coca-Cola bottles Christie's, New York, May 5, 1992	1,900,000
9	Ladies and Gentlemen, 1975 Binoche et Godeau, Paris, November 30, 1989 (F.FR9,799,080)	1,607,420
10=	Race Riot Christie's, New York, November 7, 1989	1,600,000
=	The Last Supper Sotheby's, New York, November 8, 1989	1,600,000

TOP 10

MOST EXPENSIVE PAINTINGS BY JACKSON POLLOCK

	Work/sale	Price ($)
1	Number 8, 1950 Sotheby's, New York, May 2, 1989	10,500,000
2	Frieze Christie's, New York, November 9, 1988	5,200,000
3	Search Sotheby's, New York, May 2, 1988	4,400,000
4	Number 19, 1949 Sotheby's, New York, May 2, 1989	3,600,000
5	Number 31, 1949 Christie's, New York, May 3, 1988	3,200,000
6	Number 26, 1950 Sotheby's, New York, May 4, 1987	2,500,000
7	Number 13 Christie's, New York, November 7, 1990	2,800,000
8=	Number 20 Sotheby's, New York, May 8, 1990	2,200,000
=	Number 19 Christie's, New York, May 4, 1993	2,200,000
=	Something of the past Christie's, New York, May 7, 1996	2,200,000

HENRY MOORE
All 10 of the highest prices for his sculptures have been achieved at auctions in New York.

TOP 10 MOST EXPENSIVE SCULPTURES BY HENRY MOORE
(Prices in $)
❶ Working Model for UNESCO Reclining Figure (3,700,000) ❷ Reclining Figure, Angles (2,400,000) ❸ Draped reclining woman (2,350,000) ❹ Reclining connected forms (2,200,000) ❺= Working model for three way piece no.3 vertebrae (2,000,000), Reclining figure, bone skirt (2,000,000) ❼= Reclining figure (1,850,000), Festival reclining figure (1,850,000) ❾ Reclining figure – Festival (1,750,000) ❿ Reclining figure – Festival (1,600,000)

MUSIC

T O P   1 0

BESTSELLING SINGLE OF EACH YEAR OF THE 1970s IN THE US

Year	Title	Artist
1970	Bridge Over Troubled Water	Simon and Garfunkel
1971	Joy to the World	Three Dog Night
1972	The First Time Ever I Saw Your Face	Roberta Flack
1973	Tie a Yellow Ribbon Round the Old Oak Tree	Dawn featuring Tony Orlando
1974	The Way We Were	Barbra Streisand
1975	Love will Keep Us Together	Captain & Tennille
1976	Silly Love Songs	Wings
1977	Tonight's the Night (Gonna Be Alright)	Rod Stewart
1978	Shadow Dancing	Andy Gibb
1979	My Sharona	Knack

Source: Billboard

T O P   1 0

BESTSELLING SINGLE OF EACH YEAR OF THE 1980s IN THE US

Year	Title	Artist
1980	Call Me	Blondie
1981	Bette Davis Eyes	Kim Carnes
1982	Physical	Olivia Newton-John
1983	Every Breath You Take	Police
1984	When Doves Cry	TAFKA (Prince)
1985	Careless Whisper	George Michael
1986	That's What Friends are For	Dionne Warwick & Friends
1987	Walk Like an Egyptian	Bangles
1988	Faith	George Michael
1989	Look Away	Chicago

Source: Billboard

T O P   1 0

BESTSELLING ALBUM OF EACH YEAR OF THE 1970s IN THE US

Year	Title	Artist
1970	Bridge over Troubled Water	Simon and Garfunkel
1971	Jesus Christ Superstar	Various Artists
1972	Harvest	Neil Young
1973	The World is a Ghetto	War
1974	Goodbye Yellow Brick Road	Elton John
1975	Greatest Hits	Elton John
1976	Frampton Comes Alive!	Peter Frampton
1977	Rumours	Fleetwood Mac
1978	Saturday Night Fever	The Bee Gees
1979	52nd Street	Billy Joel

Source: Billboard

TOP 10

JUKEBOX SINGLES OF ALL TIME IN THE US

	Artist/song	Year
1	Patsy Cline, *Crazy*	1962
2	Bob Seger, *Old Time Rock 'n' Roll*	1979
3	Elvis Presley, *Hound Dog/Don't Be Cruel*	1956
4	Bobby Darin, *Mack The Knife*	1959
5	Steppenwolf, *Born To Be Wild*	1968
6	Frank Sinatra, *New York, New York*	1980
7	Bill Haley and His Comets, *Rock Around The Clock*	1955
8	Marvin Gaye, *I Heard It Through The Grapevine*	1968
9	Otis Redding, *(Sittin' on) The Dock of the Bay*	1968
10	The Doors, *Light My Fire*	1967

This list was last compiled in 1996 by the Amusement and Music Operators Association, whose members service and operate over 250,000 jukeboxes in the US, and is based on the estimated popularity of jukebox singles from 1950 to the present day. Garth Brook's Friends In Low Places is the highest new entry into the Top 40 (at No. 25.)

Source: Amusement and Music Operators Association

TOP 10 GROUPS OF THE 1960s IN THE US

❶ The Beatles ❷ The Supremes
❸ Four Seasons ❹ The Beach Boys
❺ The Rolling Stones ❻ Miracles
❼ The Temptations ❽ Tommy James and The Shondells ❾ Dave Clark Five
❿ Herman's Hermits

THE BEACH BOYS

TOP 10

SINGLES OF THE 1950s IN THE US

	Title/artist	Year
1	*Hound Dog/Don't Be Cruel*, Elvis Presley	1956
2	*The Chipmunk Song*, Chipmunks	1958
3	*Love Letters in the Sand*, Pat Boone	1957
4	*Rock Around the Clock*, Bill Haley and His Comets	1955
5	*Tom Dooley*, Kingston Trio	1958
6	*Love Me Tender*, Elvis Presley	1956
7	*Tennessee Waltz*, Patti Page	1951
8	*Volare (Nel Blu Dipintu Di Blu)*, Domenico Modugno	1958
9	*Jailhouse Rock*, Elvis Presley	1957
10	*All Shook Up*, Elvis Presley	1957

TOP 10

GROUPS OF THE 70s IN THE US

1	The Bee Gees
2	The Carpenters
3	Chicago
4	The Jackson Five
5	Three Dog Night
6	Gladys Knight and The Pips
7	Dawn
8	Earth, Wind and Fire
9	The Eagles
10	Fleetwood Mac

TOP 10

SINGLES OF THE 1960s IN THE US

	Title/artist	Year
1	*I Want to Hold Your Hand*, The Beatles	1964
2	*It's Now or Never*, Elvis Presley	1960
3	*Hey Jude*, The Beatles	1968
4	*The Ballad of the Green Berets*, S/Sgt. Barry Sadler	1966
5	*Love is Blue*, Paul Mauriat	1968
6	*I'm a Believer*, The Monkees	1966
7	*Can't Buy Me Love*, The Beatles	1964
8	*She Loves You*, The Beatles	1964
9	*Sugar Sugar*, Archies	1969
10	*The Twist*, Chubby Checker	1960

TOP 10

BESTSELLING ALBUM OF EACH YEAR OF THE 1980s IN THE US

Year	Title	Artist
1980	*The Wall*	Pink Floyd
1981	*Hi Infidelity*	REO Speedwagon
1982	*Asia*	Asia
1983	*Thriller*	Michael Jackson
1984	*Thriller*	Michael Jackson
1985	*Born in the USA*	Bruce Springsteen
1986	*Whitney Houston*	Whitney Houston
1987	*Slippery When Wet*	Bon Jovi
1988	*Faith*	George Michael
1989	*Don't Be Cruel*	Bobby Brown

Source: Billboard

CHART HITS

LOUIS ARMSTRONG

ARTISTS WITH THE MOST WEEKS ON THE US ALBUM CHARTS

	Artist	Total no. of weeks
1	Frank Sinatra	2,238
2	Johnny Mathis	2,222
3	Beatles	1,955
4	Elvis Presley	1,858
5	Barbra Streisand	1,702
6	Rolling Stones	1,598
7	Mitch Miller	1,347
8	Elton John	1,337
9	Pink Floyd	1,309
10	Kingston Trio	1,262

Source: The Popular Music Database

SINGLES WITH THE MOST WEEKS ON THE US SINGLES CHARTS

	Artist/title/year	Weeks
1	Jewel, *Foolish Games/You Were Meant for Me* (1996)	65
2	Los Del Rio, *Macarena (Bayside Boys Mix)* (1996)	60
3 =	Everything But the Girl, *Missing* (1996)	55
=	Duncan Sheik, *Barely Breathing* (1996)	55
5	The Four Seasons, *December 1963 (Oh, What a Night)* (1976)*	54
6	Blues Traveler, *Run Around* (1995)	49
7	Dishwalla, *Counting Blue Cars* (1996)	48
8	Tony Rich Project, *Nobody Knows* (1996)	47
9	Gin Blossoms, *Follow You Down/ Til I Hear It from You* (1996)	46
10 =	Tag Team, *Whoomp! (There It Is)* (1993)	45
=	Real McCoy, *Another Night* (1994)	45
=	Crystal Waters, *100% Pure Love* (1994)	45

* *Re-charted in 1994*

Source: The Popular Music Database

SINGLES OF ALL TIME WORLDWIDE

	Artist/title	Sales exceed
1	Elton John, *Candle in the Wind 1997*	35,000,000
2	Bing Crosby, *White Christmas*	30,000,000
3	Bill Haley and His Comets, *Rock Around the Clock*	17,000,000
4	Beatles, *I Want to Hold Your Hand*	12,000,000
5 =	Elvis Presley, *It's Now or Never*	10,000,000
=	Whitney Houston, *I Will Always Love You*	10,000,000
7 =	Elvis Presley, *Hound Dog/ Don't Be Cruel*	9,000,000
=	Paul Anka, *Diana*	9,000,000
9 =	Beatles, *Hey Jude*	8,000,000
=	Monkees, *I'm a Believer*	8,000,000
=	Bryan Adams, *(Everything I Do) I Do it for You*	8,000,000

ALBUMS OF ALL TIME WORLDWIDE

	Artist/title	Est. sales
1	Michael Jackson, *Thriller*	40,000,000
2	Pink Floyd, *Dark Side of the Moon*	28,000,000
3	Meat Loaf, *Bat Out of Hell*	27,000,000
4	Soundtrack, *The Bodyguard*	26,000,000
5	Soundtrack, *Saturday Night Fever*	25,000,000
6 =	Beatles, *Sgt. Pepper's Lonely Hearts Club Band*	24,000,000
=	Eagles, *Their Greatest Hits 1971–1975*	24,000,000
8	Mariah Carey, *Music Box*	23,000,000
9 =	Carole King, *Tapestry*	22,000,000
=	Simon and Garfunkel, *Bridge Over Troubled Water*	22,000,000
=	Soundtrack, *Grease*	22,000,000
=	Michael Jackson, *Dangerous*	22,000,000

TOP 10

SINGLES OF ALL TIME IN THE US

	Artist/title	Est. US sales
1	Elton John, *Candle in the Wind 1997*	11,000,000
2=	USA for Africa, *We are the World*	4,000,000
=	Whitney Houston, *I Will Always Love You*	4,000,000
=	Tag Team, *Whoomp! (There It Is)*	4,000,000
5=	Elvis Presley, *Hound Dog*	3,000,000
=	Bryan Adams, *Every Thing I Do (I Do it for You)*	3,000,000
=	Los Del Rio, *Macarena*	3,000,000
=	Puff Daddy and Faith Evans (featuring 112), *I'll Be Missing You*	3,000,000
=	LeAnn Rimes, *How Do I Live*	3,000,000
10	Madonna, *Vogue*	2,000,000

Source: RIAA

THE 10

ALBUMS WITH THE MOST WEEKS ON THE US ALBUM CHARTS

	Artist/title	Weeks
1	Pink Floyd, *The Dark Side of the Moon*	741
2	Johnny Mathis, *Johnny's Greatest Hits*	490
3	Original Cast, *My Fair Lady*	480
4	Original Cast, *Highlights from The Phantom of the Opera*	331
5	Soundtrack, *Oklahoma!*	305
6	Carole King, *Tapestry*	302
7	Johnny Mathis, *Heavenly*	295
8	Enigma, *MCMXC AD*	282
9	Metallica, *Metallica*	281
10=	Soundtrack, *The King and I*	277
=	Tennessee Ernie Ford, *Hymns*	277

Source: The Popular Music Database

THE 10

ARTISTS WITH THE MOST CONSECUTIVE TOP 10 SINGLES IN THE US

	Artist/years	Total
1	Elvis Presley (1956–62)	30
2	Beatles (1964–76)	20
3=	Michael Jackson (1979–88)	17
=	Madonna (1984–89)	17
=	Janet Jackson (1989–97)	17
6	Pat Boone (1956–58)	14
7=	Whitney Houston (1985–91)	13
=	Phil Collins (1984–90)	13
=	Lionel Richie (1981–87)	13
10	Mariah Carey (1990–94)	11

Source: Record Research

THE 10

ARTISTS WITH THE MOST CONSECUTIVE TOP 10 US ALBUMS

	Artist	Period	Albums
1	Rolling Stones	Nov 1964–July 1980	26
2	Johnny Mathis	Sep 1957–Dec 1960	14
3	Frank Sinatra	Feb 1958–Mar 1962	12
4=	Beatles	June 1965–Mar 1970	11
=	Elton John	Nov 1971–Nov 1976	11
=	Van Halen	Apr 1979–Nov 1996	11
7=	Led Zeppelin	Feb 1969–Dec 1982	10
=	Chicago	Feb 1970–Oct 1977	10
=	Bruce Springsteen	Sep 1975–Mar 1995	10
10=	Barbra Streisand	Apr 1963–Nov 1966	9
=	Paul McCartney/Wings	May 1970–Apr 1978	9

Source: The Popular Music Database

THE 10 ARTISTS WITH THE MOST WEEKS IN THE US SINGLES CHARTS
(Total no. of weeks)

❶ Elvis Presley (1,586) ❷ Elton John (956) ❸ Stevie Wonder (770)
❹ Rod Stewart (724) ❺ James Brown (706) ❻ Pat Boone (697)
❼ Madonna (673) ❽ Michael Jackson (661) ❾ Beatles (629)
❿ Fats Domino (604)
Source: The Popular Music Database

STEVIE WONDER
A recording artist since the age of 13, Stevie Wonder's hit singles include Living in the City *and* I Just Called to Say I Love You.

RECORD FIRSTS

BILL HALEY AND HIS COMETS
This group personifies the birth of the rock era. Its Rock Around the Clock *was the first single ever by a US group to reach No. 1 in the UK, and the first UK record to sell a million copies.*

THE 10

FIRST MILLION-SELLING SINGLES IN THE US

	Artist/title	Certification date
1	Perry Como, *Catch a Falling Star*	March 14, 1958
2	Laurie London, *He's Got the Whole World in his Hands*	July 18, 1958
3	Elvis Presley, *Hard Headed Woman*	August 11, 1958
4	Perez Prado, *Patricia*	August 18, 1958
5	Kingston Trio, *Tom Dooley*	January 21, 1959
6	Lawrence Welk, *Calcutta*	February 14, 1961
7	Jimmy Dean, *Big Bad John*	December 14, 1961
8	The Tokens, *The Lion Sleeps Tonight*	January 19, 1962
9	Elvis Presley, *Can't Help Falling in Love*	March 30, 1962
10	Ray Charles, *I Can't Stop Loving You*	July 19, 1962

Source: RIAA

THE 10

FIRST MILLION-SELLING ALBUMS IN THE US

	Artist/title	Certification date
1	Soundtrack, *Oklahoma*	Aug 18, 1958
2	Tennessee Ernie Ford, *Hymns*	Feb 20, 1959
3	Johnny Mathis, *Johnny's Greatest Hits*	June 1, 1959
4=	Mitch Miller, *Sing Along with Mitch*	Nov 16, 1959
=	Original Cast, *The Music Man*	Nov 16, 1959
6	Soundtrack, *South Pacific*	Dec 18, 1959
7	Henry Mancini, *Peter Gunn*	Dec 31, 1959
8	Mario Lanza, *The Student Prince*	Jan 19, 1960
9	Pat Boone, *Pat's Great Hits*	Feb 12, 1960
10=	Elvis Presley, *Elvis*	Feb 17, 1960
=	Various Artists, *Honoring 30 Great Artists – 60 Years of Music*	Feb 17, 1960

Source: RIAA

THE 10

FIRST US TOP 10 SINGLES CHART

	Artist	Title
1	Tommy Dorsey	*I'll Never Smile Again*
2	Jimmy Dorsey	*The Breeze and I*
3	Glenn Miller	*Imagination*
4	Kay Kyser	*Playmates*
5	Glenn Miller	*Fools Rush In*
6	Charlie Barnet	*Where Was I*
7	Glenn Miller	*Pennsylvania 6-5000*
8	Tommy Dorsey	*Imagination*
9	Bing Crosby	*Sierra Sue*
10	Mitchell Ayres	*Make-Believe Island*

This was the first singles Top 10 compiled by *Billboard* magazine, for its issue dated July 20, 1940. Since the 7-inch 45-rpm single was still almost a decade in the future, all these would have been 10-inch 78-rpm discs. Note the almost total domination of big-name bands more than a half century ago – and spare a thought for Mitchell Ayres, who crept in at the bottom of this very first chart, and then never had a hit again.

Source: Billboard

THE 10

FIRST FEMALE SINGERS TO HAVE A NO. 1 HIT IN THE US DURING THE ROCK ERA

	Artist/title	Date at No. 1
1	Joan Weber, *Let Me Go Lover*	Jan 1, 1955
2	Georgia Gibbs, *Dance with Henry (Wallflower)*	May 14, 1955
3	Kay Starr, *Rock and Roll Waltz*	Feb 18, 1956
4	Gogi Grant, *The Wayward Wind*	June 16, 1956
5	Debbie Reynolds, *Tammy*	Aug 19, 1957
6	Connie Francis, *Everybody's Somebody's Fool*	June 27, 1960
7	Brenda Lee, *I'm Sorry*	July 18, 1960
8	Shelley Fabares, *Johnny Angel*	April 7, 1962
9	Little Eva, *The Loco-motion*	Aug 25, 1962
10	Little Peggy March, *I Will Follow Him*	April 27, 1963

Source: The Popular Music Database

THE 10

FIRST BRITISH SOLO ARTISTS TO HAVE A NO. 1 HIT IN THE US

	Artist	Title	Date at No. 1
1	Mr. Acker Bilk	*Stranger on the Shore*	May 26, 1962
2	Petula Clark	*Downtown*	Jan 23, 1965
3	Donovan	*Sunshine Superman*	Sept 3, 1966
4	Lulu	*To Sir with Love*	Oct 21, 1967
5	George Harrison	*My Sweet Lord*	Dec 26, 1970
6	Rod Stewart	*Maggie May*	Oct 2, 1971
7	Gilbert O'Sullivan	*Alone Again Naturally*	Jul 29, 1972
8	Elton John	*Crocodile Rock*	Feb 3, 1973
9	Ringo Starr	*Photograph*	Nov 24, 1973
10	Eric Clapton	*I Shot the Sheriff*	Sep 14, 1974

The majority of British acts that topped the US chart in the 1960s were groups. Prior to the rock era, the first number was Vera Lynn's *Auf Wiedersehen (Sweetheart)* in 1952.

Source: The Popular Music Database

THE 10

FIRST AMERICAN SOLO ARTISTS TO HAVE A NO. 1 HIT IN THE UK

	Artist	Title	Date at No. 1
1	Al Martino	*Here in my Heart*	Nov 14, 1952
2	Jo Stafford	*You Belong to Me*	Jan 16, 1953
3	Kay Starr	*Comes A-Long A-Love*	Jan 23, 1953
4	Eddie Fisher	*Outside of Heaven*	Jan 30, 1953
5	Perry Como	*Don't Let the Stars Get in your Eyes*	Feb 6, 1953
6	Guy Mitchell	*She Wears Red Feathers*	Mar 13, 1953
7	Frankie Laine	*I Believe*	Apr 24, 1953
8	Doris Day	*Secret Love*	Apr 16, 1954
9	Johnnie Ray	*Such a Night*	Apr 30, 1954
10	Kitty Kallen	*Little Things Mean a Lot*	Sep 10, 1954

Clearly, in the 1950s, it was a great deal easier for American solo artists to top the UK survey than it was for British artists to compete in the US market.

Source: The Popular Music Database

THE 10

FIRST BRITISH GROUPS TO HAVE A NO. 1 HIT IN THE US

	Artist/title	Date at No. 1
1	The Tornados, *Telstar*	Dec 22, 1962
2	The Beatles, *I Want to Hold Your Hand*	Feb 1, 1964
3	The Animals, *House of the Rising Sun*	Sept 5, 1964
4	Manfred Mann, *Do Wah Diddy Diddy*	Oct 17, 1964
5	Freddie and the Dreamers, *I'm Telling You Now*	Apr 10, 1965
6	Wayne Fontana and the Mindbenders, *The Game of Love*	Apr 24, 1965
7	Herman's Hermits, *Mrs. Brown You've Got a Lovely Daughter*	May 1, 1965
8	The Rolling Stones, *(I Can't Get No) Satisfaction*	Jul 10, 1965
9	The Dave Clark Five, *Over and Over*	Dec 25, 1965
10	The Troggs, *Wild Thing*	Jul 30, 1966

Source: The Popular Music Database

TORNADOS
Telstar sold over five million copies and was the first single by a UK group to reach No. 1 in the US.

THE 10

FIRST AMERICAN GROUPS TO HAVE A NO. 1 HIT IN THE UK

	Artist/title	Date at No. 1
1	Bill Haley and His Comets, *Rock Around the Clock*	Nov 25, 1955
2	Dream Weavers, *It's Almost Tomorrow*	Mar 16, 1956
3	Teenagers featuring Frankie Lymon, *Why Do Fools Fall in Love?*	Jul 20, 1956
4	Buddy Holly and the Crickets, *That'll Be the Day*	Nov 1, 1957
5	The Platters, *Smoke Gets in Your Eyes*	Mar 20, 1959
6	The Marcels, *Blue Moon*	May 4, 1961
7	The Highwaymen, *Michael*	Oct 12, 1961
8	B. Bumble and the Stingers, *Nut Rocker*	May 17, 1962
9	The Supremes, *Baby Love*	Nov 19, 1964
10	The Byrds, *Mr. Tambourine Man*	Jul 22, 1965

Source: The Popular Music Database

CHART TOPPERS

THE 10

ALBUMS WITH THE MOST WEEKS AT NO.1 IN THE US CHARTS*

	Artist/album/release year	Weeks at No.1
1	Michael Jackson, *Thriller* (1982)	37
2=	Harry Belafonte, *Calypso* (1956)	31
=	Fleetwood Mac, *Rumours* (1977)	31
4=	Soundtrack, *Saturday Night Fever* (1978)	24
=	Prince, *Purple Rain* (Soundtrack) (1984)	24
6	MC Hammer, *Please Hammer Don't Hurt 'Em* (1990)	21
7=	Whitney Houston, *The Bodyguard* (Soundtrack) (1992)	20
=	Elvis Presley, *Blue Hawaii* (Soundtrack) (1962)	20
9=	Monkees, *More of the Monkees* (1967)	18
=	Soundtrack, *Dirty Dancing* (1988)	18
=	Garth Brooks, *Ropin' the Wind* (1991)	18

* *Based on Billboard charts, up to December 31, 1997*

Some sources identify the soundtrack album of *West Side Story* (1962) as the longest No. 1 resident of the Billboard chart, but its 57-week stay was in a chart exclusively for stereo albums – then a relatively new phenomenon. The *South Pacific* soundtrack album (1958) similarly enjoyed 31 weeks on this special chart. Not all of the albums from the general chart had continuous No.1 runs: in some cases, their chart-topping sojourns were punctuated by briefer stays by other records. Five of the Top 10 are movie soundtracks, suggesting that a successful movie tie-in is often an aid to sales longevity.

THE 10

ALBUMS WITH THE MOST CONSECUTIVE WEEKS AT NO.1 IN THE US

	Artist/title	Dates at No.1	No. of weeks
1 =	Bee Gees, *Saturday Night Fever*	Jan 21–Jul 1, 1978	24
=	Prince/Soundtrack, *Purple Rain*	Aug 4, 1984– Jan 12, 1985	24
3	Elvis Presley/ Soundtrack, *Blue Hawaii*	Dec 11, 1961– Apr 28, 1962	20
4 =	Harry Belafonte, *Calypso*	Jan 12–May 20, 1956	19
=	Fleetwood Mac, *Rumours*	Jun 23–Nov 26, 1977	19
6 =	Monkees, *More of the Monkees*	Feb 11–May 27, 1967	18
=	Michael Jackson, *Thriller*	Feb 26–Jun 18, 1983	18
=	Michael Jackson, *Thriller*	Dec 24, 1983– Apr 14, 1984	18
=	MC Hammer, *Please Hammer Don't Hurt 'Em*	Jul 7–Nov 3, 1990	18
10=	Doris Day/Soundtrack, *Love Me or Leave Me*	Aug 6, 1955– Jan 21, 1956	17
=	Billy Ray Cyrus, *Some Gave All*	Jun 13–Oct 3, 1992	17

Source: The Popular Music Database

TOP 10

ALBUMS OF ALL TIME IN THE US

	Artist/title	Sales
1	Michael Jackson, *Thriller*	25,000,000
2	Eagles, *Their Greatest Hits 1971–1975*	24,000,000
3	Pink Floyd, *The Wall*	22,000,000
4	Billy Joel, *Greatest Hits Volumes I and II*	18,000,000
5=	Fleetwood Mac, *Rumours*	17,000,000
=	Led Zeppelin, *Led Zeppelin IV*	17,000,000
7=	Boston, *Boston*	16,000,000
=	AC/DC, *Back In Black*	16,000,000
9=	Hootie and the Blowfish, *Cracked Rear View*	15,000,000
=	Alanis Morissette, *Jagged Little Pill*	15,000,000
=	Bruce Springsteen, *Born in the USA*	15,000,000
=	Whitney Houston/Soundtrack, *The Bodyguard*	15,000,000

Source: RIAA

THE 10

LONGEST GAPS BETWEEN NO.1 HIT SINGLES IN THE US

	Artist	Period	Gap years	months
1	Elton John	Nov 11, 1975–Oct 11, 1997	21	11
2	Beach Boys	Dec 10, 1966–Nov 5, 1988	21	11
3	Paul Anka	July 13, 1959–Aug 24, 1974	15	1
4	George Harrison	June 30, 1973–Jan 16, 1988	14	7
5	Neil Sedaka	Aug 11, 1962–Feb 1, 1975	12	6
6	Four Seasons	July 18, 1964–Mar 13, 1976	11	8
7	Herb Alpert	June 22, 1968–Oct 20, 1979	11	4
8	Frank Sinatra	July 9, 1955–July 2, 1966	11	0
9	Stevie Wonder	Aug 10, 1963–Jan 27, 1973	10	5
10	Dean Martin	Jan 7, 1956–Aug 15, 1964	8	7

Source: The Popular Music Database

THE 10

OLDEST ARTISTS TO HAVE A NO.1 SINGLE IN THE US*

	Artist/title	Age[#] yrs	mths
1	Louis Armstrong, *Hello Dolly!*	63	10
2	Lawrence Welk, *Calcutta*	57	11
3	Morris Stoloff, *Moonglow and Theme from Picnic*	57	10
4	Frank Sinatra,† *Somethin' Stupid*	51	4
5	Elton John, *(1997) Candle in the Wind*	50	6
6	Lorne Greene, *Ringo*	49	9
7	Dean Martin, *Everybody Loves Somebody*	47	2
8	Bill Medley,★ *(I've Had) The Time of My Life*	47	2
9	Sammy Davis, Jr., *The Candy Man*	46	6
10	Tina Turner, *What's Love Got to Do with It*	45	9

* *To December 31, 1997*

\# *During first week of No.1 US single*

† *Duet with Nancy Sinatra*

★ *Duet with Jennifer Warnes*

Source: The Popular Music Database

THE 10

YOUNGEST ARTISTS TO HAVE A NO.1 SINGLE IN THE US*

	Artist/year/title	Age[#] yrs	mths
1	Jimmy Boyd (1952), *I Saw Mommy Kissing Santa Claus*	12	11
2	Stevie Wonder (1963), *Fingertips*	13	1
3	Donny Osmond (1971), *Go Away Little Girl*	13	7
4	Michael Jackson (1972), *Ben*	13	11
5	Laurie London (1958), *He's Got the Whole World in His Hands*	14	2
6	Little Peggy March (1963), *I Will Follow Him*	15	0
7	Brenda Lee (1960), *I'm Sorry*	15	5
8	Paul Anka (1957), *Diana*	16	0
9	Tiffany (1987), *I Think We're Alone Now*	16	10
10	Lesley Gore (1963), *It's My Party*	17	0

* *To December 31, 1997*

\# *During first week of debut No.1 US single*

If group members were eligible for the list, all three Hanson brothers would be in the Top 10. Isaac was 16 years and 6 months, Taylor 14 years and 2 months, and Zachary 11 years and 7 months when Mmmbop topped the charts in 1997.

Source: The Popular Music Database

ELVIS PRESLEY
No artist has matched his record number of weeks at the top of the UK as well as the US singles chart.

THE 10

ARTISTS WITH THE MOST NO.1 SINGLES IN THE US*

	Artist	No.1 singles
1	The Beatles	20
2	Elvis Presley	18
3	Michael Jackson	13
4=	The Supremes	12
=	Mariah Carey	12[#]
6=	Whitney Houston	11
=	Madonna	11
8	Stevie Wonder	10
9=	Paul McCartney/Wings	9
=	Bee Gees	9
=	Elton John	9

* *Up to December 31, 1997*

\# *Includes a duet with Boyz II Men*

Source: The Popular Music Database

THE 10

ARTISTS WITH THE MOST WEEKS AT NO.1 IN THE US

	Artist	Weeks at No.1		Artist	Weeks at No.1
1	Elvis Presley	80	6	Elton John	32
2	Beatles	59	7	Whitney Houston	31
3	Mariah Carey	57*	8	Paul McCartney/Wings	30
4	Boyz II Men	50*	9	Madonna	28
5	Michael Jackson	37	10	Bee Gees	27

* *Boyz II Men and Mariah Carey share a 16-week run with a duet.*

Source: The Popular Music Database

STAR SINGLES & ALBUMS

TOP 10

ROLLING STONES SINGLES IN THE US

	Single	Year
1	(I Can't Get No) Satisfaction	1965
2	Miss You	1978
3	Honky Tonk Women	1969
4	Get Off of My Cloud	1965
5	Ruby Tuesday	1967
6	Angie	1973
7	Brown Sugar	1971
8	Paint It Black	1966
9	19th Nervous Breakdown	1966
10	Jumpin' Jack Flash	1968

Source: MRIB

THE ROLLING STONES

TOP 10

ELVIS PRESLEY SINGLES IN THE US

	Single	Year
1	Don't Be Cruel/Hound Dog	1956
2	It's Now or Never	1960
3	Love Me Tender	1956
4	Heartbreak Hotel	1956
5	Jailhouse Rock	1957
6	All Shook Up	1957
7	(Let Me Be Your) Teddy Bear	1957
8	Are You Lonesome Tonight?	1960
9	Don't	1958
10	Too Much	1957

Elvis had dozens of million-selling singles, scattered throughout his career, but most of his absolute monsters were during his 1950s heyday when he was the spearhead of Rock 'n' Roll music. The inspired coupling of *Don't Be Cruel* and *Hound Dog*, which held the No. 1 spot for almost a quarter of 1956, sold some 6,000,000 copies in the US alone. *It's Now or Never*, the biggest of his post-Army successes, sold in the region of 5,000,000.

Source: MRIB

TOP 10

BOB DYLAN SINGLES IN THE US

	Single	Year
1	Like a Rolling Stone	1965
2	Rainy Day Women, Nos. 12 and 35	1966
3	Positively 4th Street	1965
4	Lay Lady Lay	1969
5	Knockin' on Heaven's Door	1973
6	I Want You	1966
7	Just Like a Woman	1966
8	Gotta Serve Somebody	1979
9	Hurricane	1976
10	Subterranean Homesick Blues	1965

Source: MRIB

TOP 10

FRANK SINATRA SINGLES IN THE US*

	Single	Year
1	Oh! What It Seemed To Be	1946
2	Five Minutes More	1946
3	Somethin' Stupid – with Nancy Sinatra	1967
4	Learnin' The Blues	1955
5	Strangers In The Night	1966
6	Mam'selle	1947
7	All or Nothing At All – with Harry James and his Orchestra	1943
8	All the Way	1957
9	Young-At-Heart	1954
10	You'll Never Know	1943

* Based on Billboard chart performance
Source: Music Data Canada

TOP 10

WHITNEY HOUSTON SINGLES IN THE US

	Single	Year
1	I Will Always Love You	1992
2	Exhale (Shoop Shoop)	1995
3	I Wanna Dance with Somebody (Who Loves Me)	1987
4	I Believe in You and Me	1996
5	The Greatest Love of All	1986
6	How Will I Know	1986
7	I'm Your Baby Tonight	1990
8	All the Man that I Need	1991
9	Saving All My Love for You	1985
10	Where Do Broken Hearts Go	1988

Source: MRIB

TOP 10

MADONNA SINGLES IN THE US

	Single	Year
1	*Vogue*	1990
2	*Justify My Love*	1990
3	*Like a Prayer*	1989
4	*Like a Virgin*	1984
5	*Crazy for You*	1985
6	*This Used to be My Playground*	1992
7	*Take a Bow*	1994
8	*I'll Remember*	1994
9	*Express Yourself*	1989
10	*Secret*	1994

Source: The Popular Music Database

TOP 10

MADONNA ALBUMS IN THE US

	Album	Year
1	*Like a Virgin*	1984
2	*True Blue*	1986
3	*The Immaculate Collection*	1990
4	*Madonna*	1983
5	*Like a Prayer*	1989
6	*Erotica*	1992
7	*Bedtime Stories*	1994
8	*Something to Remember*	1995
9	*I'm Breathless*	1990
10	*You Can Dance*	1987

Source: The Popular Music Database

TOP 10

MICHAEL JACKSON SINGLES IN THE US

	Single	Year
1	*Billie Jean*	1983
2	*Rock with You*	1980
3	*Beat It*	1983
4	*Don't Stop 'Til You Get Enough*	1979
5	*Say Say Say**	1983
6	*You are Not Alone*	1995
7	*Rock with You*	1979
8	*Thriller*	1984
9	*Scream#*	1995
10	*Black Or White*	1990

* *With Paul McCartney*
\# *With Janet Jackson*

Source: The Popular Music Database

TOP 10

GARTH BROOKS ALBUMS IN THE US

	Album	Year
1	*No Fences*	1990
2	*Ropin' the Wind*	1991
3	*The Hits*	1994
4	*Garth Brooks*	1990
5	*In Pieces*	1993
6	*The Chase*	1992
7	*Sevens*	1997
8	*Fresh Horses*	1995
9	*The Garth Brooks Collection*	1997
10	*Beyond the Season*	1992

Source: The Popular Music Database

TOP 10

TAFKA (PRINCE) ALBUMS IN THE US

	Album	Year
1	*Purple Rain*	1984
2	*1999*	1982
3	*Around the World in a Day*	1985
4	*Batman*	1989
5	*Diamonds and Pearls*	1991
6	*(Symbol)*	1992
7	*The Hits I*	1993
8	*The Hits II*	1993
9	*Sign "O" the Times*	1987
10	*The Hits/B Sides*	1993

Source: The Popular Music Database

TOP 10

BRUCE SPRINGSTEEN ALBUMS IN THE US

	Album	Year
1	*Born in the USA*	1984
2	*Bruce Springsteen and the E Street Band Live/1975–85*	1986
3	*Born to Run*	1975
4	*The River*	1980
5	*Tunnel of Love*	1987
6	*Greatest Hits*	1995
7	*Darkness on the Edge of Town*	1978
8	*Greetings from Asbury Park, N. J.*	1975
9	*Nebraska*	1982
10	*The Wild, the Innocent and the E Street Shuffle*	1975

Source: The Popular Music Database

TOP 10

BILLY JOEL ALBUMS IN THE US

	Album	Year			Album	Year
1	*Greatest Hits Volumes I and II*	1985		6	*Storm Front*	1989
2	*The Stranger*	1977		7	*River of Dreams*	1993
3	*An Innocent Man*	1983		8	*Piano Man*	1974
4	*52nd Street*	1978		9	*The Bridge*	1986
5	*Glass Houses*	1980		10	*The Nylon Curtain*	1982

Source: The Popular Music Database

THE BEATLES

McCARTNEY AND HARRISON
Frank Sinatra described George Harrison's much-covered Something *(1969) as the greatest love song of the past 50 years.*

THE 10

MOST VALUABLE BEATLES ALBUMS IN THE US

	Title/label	Est. value ($)
1	*Introducing the Beatles*, Vee Jay SR 1062 (oval Vee Jay logo)	20,000
2	*Hear the Beatles Tell All*, Vee Jay PRO 202	15,000
3	*A Hard Day's Night*, United Artists UAS 6366	12,000
4=	*Introducing the Beatles*, Vee Jay SR 1062 (mono)	10,000
=	*Introducing the Beatles*, Vee Jay LP 1062 (stereo)	10,000
=	*The Beatles and Frank Ifield On Stage*, Vee Jay SR 1085 (stereo)	10,000
7=	*The Beatles Again*, Apple SO-385	8,000
=	*Yesterday and Today*, Capitol ST-2553	8,000
9=	*Yesterday and Today*, Capitol ST-2553 (trunk cover)	4,000
=	*Yesterday and Today*, Capitol T-2553 (mono)	4,000
=	*Introducing the Beatles*, Vee Jay SR 1062 (back cover blank)	4,000
=	*The Beatles and Frank Ifield On Stage*, Vee Jay LP 1085 (mono)	4,000

Source: Goldmine *British Invasion Record Price Guide*, Tim Neely and Dave Thompson *(Krause Publications, 1997)*

THE 10

MOST VALUABLE BEATLES SINGLES IN THE US

	Title/label	Est. value ($)
1=	*My Bonnie/The Saints**, Decca 31382 (black label)	10,000
=	*Ask Me Why/Anna*, Vee Jay Spec. DJ No. 8	10,000
3	*Can't Buy Me Love/You Can't Do That*, Capitol 5150	4,000
4	*My Bonnie/The Saints**, Decca 31382 (pink label)	3,000
5=	*Can't Buy Me Love/You Can't Do That*, Capitol 5150	2,000
=	*Please Please Me/Ask Me Why*, Vee Jay 498 (Beatles spelled correctly – No. listed as VJ498)	2,000
7=	*Please Please Me/Ask Me Why*, Vee Jay 498 (name misspelled "The Beattles")	1,600
=	*Please Please Me/Ask Me Why*, Vee Jay 498 (Beatles spelled correctly – No. listed as #498)	1,600
9	*We Can Work It Out/Day Tripper*, Capitol 5555	1,500
10	*Please Please Me/Ask Me Why*, Vee Jay 498 (white label promotional copy)	1,100

* Credited to Tony Sheridan and the Beat Brothers

Source: Goldmine *British Invasion Record Price Guide, Tim Neely and Dave Thompson (Krause Publications, 1997)*

BEATLEMANIA
The Beatles' first tour of the US in 1964 took the country by storm. In April of that year, they unprecedentedly held all five top slots on the Billboard chart.

THE 10
BEATLES ALBUMS THAT STAYED LONGEST ON THE US CHARTS

	Title	Weeks
1	Sgt. Pepper's Lonely Hearts Club Band	175
2	The Beatles 1967–1970	169
3	The Beatles 1962–1966	164
4	The Beatles	155
5	Abbey Road	129
6	Magical Mystery Tour	91
7	Revolver	77
8=	Meet The Beatles!	71
=	Beatles '65	71
10	Rubber Soul	59

Source: The Popular Music Database

TOP 10
BEATLES CHART SINGLES IN THE US

	Title	Week of entry
1	A Hard Day's Night	Jan 18, 1964
2	She Loves You	Jan 25, 1964
3	Please Please Me	Feb 1, 1964
4	I Saw Her Standing There	Feb 8, 1964
5	My Bonnie	Feb 15, 1964
6	From Me To You	Mar 7, 1964
7	Twist and Shout	Mar 14, 1964
8	Roll Over Beethoven	Mar 21, 1964
9=	All My Loving	Mar 28, 1964
=	Can't Buy Me Love	Mar 28, 1964
=	Do You Want to Know A Secret	Mar 28, 1964

Source: The Popular Music Database

TOP 10
BEATLES ALBUMS IN THE US

	Title	Est. sales
1=	Sgt. Pepper's Lonely Hearts Club Band	9,000,000
=	Abbey Road	9,000,000
3	The Beatles	8,000,000
4=	The Beatles 1967–1970	6,000,000
=	The Beatles Anthology Volume 1	6,000,000
6=	Meet The Beatles!	5,000,000
=	Magical Mystery Tour	5,000,000
=	The Beatles 1962–1966	5,000,000
9=	Rubber Soul	4,000,000
=	Live at the BBC	4,000,000

Source: RIAA

THE 10
BEATLES SINGLES THAT STAYED LONGEST ON THE US CHARTS

	Title	Weeks
1	Hey Jude	19
2=	Come Together/Something	16
=	Got to Get You into My Life	16
4=	I Want to Hold Your Hand	15
=	She Loves You	15
=	Twist and Shout	15
7=	Love Me Do	14
=	Let It Be	14
9=	Please Please Me	13
=	A Hard Day's Night	13
=	Help!	13

Source : The Popular Music Database

MUSICAL HERITAGE
In the eight years from 1962 to 1970, the Beatles established themselves as a musical legend.

THE 10
FIRST BEATLES SINGLES IN THE US

	Title/label	Release date
1	My Bonnie/The Saints (with Tony Sheridan), Decca	Apr 1962
2	Please Please Me/Ask Me Why, Vee Jay	Feb 1963
3	From Me To You/Thank You Girl, Vee Jay	May 1963
4	She Loves You/I'll Get You, Swan	Sep 1963
5	I Want to Hold Your Hand/I Saw Her Standing There, Capitol	Dec 1963
6	Please Please Me/From Me To You, Vee Jay	Jan 1964
7	My Bonnie/The Saints (with Tony Sheridan), MGM	Feb 1964
8	Twist and Shout/There's a Place, Tollie	Mar 1964
9	Can't Buy Me Love/You Can't Do That, Capitol	Mar 1964
10	Do You Want to Know a Secret/Thank You Girl, Vee Jay	Mar 1964

Source: MRIB

SINGLES & ALBUMS

T O P   1 0

COUNTRY SINGLES IN THE US

	Artist	Title
1	LeAnn Rimes	*How Do I Live*
2	Kenny Rogers and Dolly Parton	*Islands in the Stream*
3	Oak Ridge Boys	*Elvira*
4	Billy Ray Cyrus	*Achy Breaky Heart*
5	Charlie Daniels Band	*The Devil Went Down to Georgia*
6	Willie Nelson	*Always On My Mind*
7	Tim McGraw with Faith Hill	*It's Your Love*
8	C. W. McCall	*Convoy*
9	Johnny Cash	*A Boy Named Sue*
10	Lynn Anderson	*Rose Garden*

Source: The Popular Music Database

T O P   1 0

HEAVY METAL ALBUMS IN THE US

	Artist/title	Approx. sales
1=	AC/DC, *Back in Black*	16,000,000
=	Boston, *Boston*	16,000,000
3	Meat Loaf, *Bat Out of Hell*	13,000,000
4	Bon Jovi, *Slippery When Wet*	12,000,000
5=	Def Leppard, *Hysteria*	10,000,000
=	Metallica, *Metallica*	10,000,000
=	Van Halen, *Van Halen*	10,000,000
=	ZZ Top, *Eliminator*	10,000,000
9=	Def Leppard, *Pyromania*	9,000,000
=	Aerosmith, *Aerosmith's Greatest Hits*	9,000,000

Source: RIAA

T O P   1 0

HEAVY METAL SINGLES IN THE US

	Artist	Title
1	Survivor	*Eye of the Tiger*
2	REO Speedwagon	*Keep On Loving You*
3	Joan Jett and the Blackhearts,	*I Love Rock 'n' Roll*
4	Bon Jovi	*Always*
5	Meat Loaf	*I'd Do Anything for Love (But I Won't Do That)*
6	Jon Bon Jovi	*Blaze of Glory*
7	Guns 'N Roses	*Sweet Child O' Mine*
8	Van Halen	*Jump*
9	Bachman Turner Overdrive	*You Ain't Seen Nothing Yet/Free Wheelin'*
10	Motley Crue	*Dr. Feelgood*

Source: The Popular Music Database

T O P   1 0

COUNTRY ALBUMS IN THE US

	Artist/title	Approx. sales
1	Garth Brooks, *No Fences*	13,000,000
2	Kenny Rogers, *Greatest Hits*	12,000,000
3	Garth Brooks, *Ropin' the Wind*	11,000,000
4	Shania Twain, *The Woman in Me*	10,000,000
5=	Garth Brooks, *The Hits*	9,000,000
=	Billy Ray Cyrus, *Some Gave All*	9,000,000
7	Patsy Cline, *Greatest Hits*	8,000,000
8=	Garth Brooks, *Garth Brooks*	7,000,000
=	Garth Brooks, *In Pieces*	7,000,000
10=	Garth Brooks, *The Chase*	6,000,000
=	Alan Jackson, *A Lot About Livin', (And a Little 'Bout Love)*	6,000,000

Source: RIAA

T O P   1 0

RAP SINGLES IN THE US

	Artist/title	Approx. sales
1	Tag Team, *Whoomp! (There It Is)*	4,000,000
2	Puff Daddy and Faith Evans (featuring 112), *I'll Be Missing You*	3,000,000
3=	2Pac, *How Do U Want It*	2,000,000
=	Bone Thugs-N-Harmony, *Tha Crossroads*	2,000,000
=	Coolio featuring L. V., *Gangsta's Paradise*	2,000,000
=	Duice, *Dazzey Duks*	2,000,000
=	Naughty by Nature, *O.P.P.*	2,000,000
=	Sir Mix-a-Lot, *Baby Got Back*	2,000,000
=	Tone Loc, *Wild Thing*	2,000,000
=	Kris Kross, *Jump*	2,000,000

Source: RIAA

T O P   1 0

GREATEST HITS ALBUMS IN THE US

	Artist/title	Approx. sales
1	Eagles, *Their Greatest Hits 1971–1975*	24,000,000
2	Billy Joel, *Greatest Hits Volumes I and II*	18,000,000
3	Elton John, *Greatest Hits*	13,000,000
4	Kenny Rogers, *Greatest Hits*	12,000,000
5	James Taylor, *James Taylor's Greatest Hits*	11,000,000
6	Doobie Brothers, *Best Of The Doobies*	10,000,000
7=	Aerosmith, *Aerosmith's Greatest Hits*	9,000,000
=	Garth Brooks, *The Hits*	9,000,000
=	Eagles, *Greatest Hits, Volume II*	9,000,000
=	Journey, *Greatest Hits*	9,000,000

Source: RIAA

TOP 10
FOREIGN-LANGUAGE SINGLES IN THE US

	Artist	Title
1	Los Del Rio	*Macarena (Bayside Boys Mix)*
2	Domenico Modugno	*Volare (Nel Blu Dipintu Di Blu)*
3	Singing Nun	*Dominique*
4	Kyu Sakamoto	*Sukiyaki*
5	Los Lobos	*La Bamba*
6	Falco	*Rock Me Amadeus*
7	Nena	*99 Luftballons*
8	Ritchie Valens	*La Bamba*
9	Lolita	*Sailor*
10	Emilio Pericoli	*Al Di La*

Source: MRIB

TOP 10
INSTRUMENTAL SINGLES IN THE US

	Artist	Title
1	Meco	*Star Wars Theme/ Cantina Band*
2	Paul Mauriat	*Love is Blue*
3	Percy Faith	*Theme from A Summer Place*
4	Herb Alpert	*Rise*
5	Champs	*Tequila*
6	Perez Prado	*Cherry Pink and Apple Blossom White*
7	Acker Bilk	*Stranger on the Shore*
8	Tornados	*Telstar*
9	Perez Prado	*Patricia*
10	Bert Kaempfert	*Wonderland By Night*

Source: The Popular Music Database

TOP 10
SOUNDTRACK ALBUMS IN THE US

	Title	Sales
1	*The Bodyguard*	16,000,000
2	*Purple Rain*	13,000,000
3=	*Saturday Night Fever*	11,000,000
=	*Dirty Dancing*	11,000,000
5	*The Lion King*	10,000,000
6	*Titanic*	9,000,000
7=	*Grease*	8,000,000
=	*Footloose*	8,000,000
9=	*Top Gun*	7,000,000
=	*Waiting to Exhale*	7,000,000

Source: RIAA

TOP 10
CHART-TOPPING ONE-HIT WONDERS IN THE US

	Artist	Title
1	USA For Africa	*We are the World*
2	Bobby McFerrin	*Don't Worry Be Happy*
3	M	*Pop Muzik*
4	Zager and Evans	*In the Year 2525 (Exordium and Terminus)*
5	Jan Hammer	*Miami Vice*
6	Elegants	*Little Star*
7	Hollywood Argyles	*Alley-Oop*
8	Laurie London	*He's Got the Whole World in His Hands*
9	Morris Stoloff	*Moonglow*
10	Silhouettes	*Get a Job*

Source: The Popular Music Database

BOYZ II MEN
Boyz II Men, a Philadelphia R&B vocal quartet, are Motown's biggest-selling act of the 1990s by far, scoring three platinum singles within a period of 18 months.

THE 10
SINGLES THAT STAYED LONGEST AT NO. 1 IN THE US*

	Artist/title/year	Weeks at No.1
1	Maria Carey and Boyz II Men, *One Sweet Day* (1995)	16
2=	Whitney Houston, *I Will Always Love You* (1992)	14
=	Boyz II Men, *I'll Make Love To You* (1994)	14
=	Los Del Rios, *Macarena (Bayside Boys Mix)* (1995)	14
=	Elton John, *Candle in the Wind 1997/Something About the Way You Look Tonight* (1997)	14
6	Boyz II Men, *End of the Road* (1992)	13
7=	Elvis Presley, *Don't Be Cruel/Hound Dog* (1956)	11
=	All-4-One, *I Swear* (1994)	11
=	Toni Braxton, *Un-break My Heart* (1996)	11
10=	Perez Prado, *Cherry Pink and Apple Blossom White* (1955)	10
=	Debby Boone, *You Light Up My Life* (1977)	10
=	Olivia Newton-John, *Physical* (1981)	10

* Based on Billboard charts

Source: The Popular Music Database

SNAP FACTS

- Country music exploded into the mainstream at the end of 1992, with almost half of the national album chart taken up by country artists.
- Boyz II Men debut single *End of the Road* topped the charts on both sides of the Atlantic. In the US, it enjoyed an unprecedented 13 weeks at No.1.
- In July 1988, for the first time in the history of the album charts, heavy metal stars – Van Halen, Def Leppard, and Guns 'N Roses – held the top three positions.

GOLD & PLATINUM DISCS

THE 10

MALE ARTISTS WITH THE MOST PLATINUM ALBUMS IN THE US

	Artist	Platinum albums
1	Billy Joel	69
2	Garth Brooks	68
3	Michael Jackson	51
4	Bruce Springsteen	48
5	Elton John	47
6	Kenny Rogers	45
7	Elvis Presley	42
8	Kenny G	37
9	Neil Diamond	35
10	George Strait	34

The award of a platinum album, made by the Recording Industry Association of America (RIAA), the trade association of record companies in the US, confirms a minimum sale of 1,000,000 copies of an album. For each further 1,000,000 copies sold, another platinum album is awarded.

Source: The Popular Music Database

THE 10

FEMALE ARTISTS WITH THE MOST PLATINUM ALBUMS IN THE US

	Artist	Platinum albums
1	Barbra Streisand	47
2	Madonna	46
3	Whitney Houston	42
4	Mariah Carey	41
5	Celine Dion	24
6	Linda Ronstadt	23
7	Reba McEntire	22
8	Janet Jackson	19
9=	Gloria Estefan	18
=	Sade	18

Source: The Popular Music Database

ALBUM SALES TAKE OFF

Prior to 1948, records were 78-rpm, restricting the length of recordings to four minutes. In that year, Columbia Records broke through this barrier with the launch of its 12-inch microgroove disc of nonbreakable vinyl, played at 33⅓ revolutions per minute and offering 23 minutes per side. The company's range of "Long Players" was released on September 18. By June 18, 1949, Columbia was able to announce sales of 3.5 million LPs in its first year. Now that the new format was an obvious success, Capital and Decca began producing albums. Decca's cast recording of *Oklahoma* became the first-ever multimillion selling LP. It was to take a further 40 years, until 1989, before sales of compact discs overtook those of vinyl LPs.

YEARS AGO • YEARS AGO • YEARS AGO • YEARS AGO
50

THE 10

ARTISTS WITH THE MOST GOLD AND PLATINUM ALBUMS COMBINED IN THE US

	Artist	Platinum/gold albums
1	Elvis Presley	181
2	The Beatles	131
3	Elton John	110
4	Led Zeppelin	95
5	Barbra Streisand	93
6	Billy Joel	89
7	Michael Jackson	82
8	Madonna	80
9	Pink Floyd	79
10	Garth Brooks	78

Source: The Popular Music Database

THE 10

FEMALE SINGERS WITH THE MOST GOLD SINGLES IN THE US

	Artist	Gold singles
1	Janet Jackson*	18
2	Madonna	17
3	Aretha Franklin	15
4=	Mariah Carey*	13
=	Donna Summer*	13
6	Olivia Newton-John*	11
7	Whitney Houston	9
8	Barbra Streisand*	8
9=	Paula Abdul	5
=	Toni Braxton	5
=	Celine Dion	5
=	Roberta Flack*	5

* *Denotes a gold single as part of a duet*

Source: The Popular Music Database

• The first gold record awarded for sales of a million singles went to bandleader Glenn Miller for *Chattanooga Choo Choo*. It was presented to him during a live broadcast on February 10, 1942.

SNAP FACT

T H E   1 0

GROUPS WITH THE MOST GOLD SINGLES IN THE US

	Artist	Gold singles
1	The Beatles	22
2	Creedence Clearwater Revival	13
3	The Bee Gees	11
4	Boyz II Men*	10
5=	Earth Wind & Fire	8
=	Kool & the Gang	8
7=	Three Dog Night	7
=	TLC	7
9=	Captain & Tennille	6
=	Dr. Hook	6
=	The Monkees	6
=	New Kids On The Block	6
=	Salt-n-Pepa	6
=	The Spinners	6

* Denotes a gold single as part of a duet.
Duos are not included as groups

Source: The Popular Music Database

T H E   1 0

MALE SINGERS WITH THE MOST GOLD SINGLES IN THE US

	Artist	Gold singles
1	Elvis Presley	49
2	Elton John*	16
3	Michael Jackson*	15
4	Paul McCartney*	12
5	Prince	11
6=	Al Green	8
=	George Michael	8
8=	Bobby Brown	7
=	R. Kelly	7
=	L. L. Cool J.	7

* Denotes a gold single as part of a duet.

Source: The Popular Music Database

T H E   1 0

FEMALE ARTISTS WITH THE MOST GOLD ALBUMS

	Artist	Gold albums
1	Barbra Streisand	33
2=	Linda Ronstadt	15
=	Madonna	15
4=	Olivia Newton-John	13
=	Reba McEntire	13
6=	Anne Murray	11
=	Donna Summer	11
=	Aretha Franklin	11
=	Amy Grant	11
=	Natalie Cole	11
=	Gloria Estefan*	11

* Includes hits with Miami Sound Machine

Source: The Popular Music Database

T H E   1 0

GROUPS WITH THE MOST GOLD ALBUMS IN THE US

	Group	Gold albums
1	Rolling Stones	37
2	Beatles	29
3	KISS	22
4 =	Rush	21
=	Alabama	21
6 =	Chicago	20
=	Aerosmith	20
8 =	Beach Boys	17
=	Jefferson Airplane/Starship	17
10=	AC/DC	16
=	Santana	16
=	Pink Floyd	16
=	Doors	16

The RIAA introduced its gold certificate for albums in 1958. The criteria changed with inflation, and gold awards are now made in recognition of half a million dollars' worth of an album's sales.

Source: The Popular Music Database

ELTON JOHN
Britain's most successful solo artist ever in the US, Elton had his first US Top 10 hit in 1970 and followed it with numerous No.1s and bestselling albums.

TOP 10 MALE ARTISTS WITH THE MOST GOLD ALBUMS IN THE US
(Gold albums)

❶ Elvis Presley (59) ❷ Neil Diamond (32)
❸ Elton John (31) ❹ Kenny Rogers (27)
❺ Bob Dylan (25) ❻= Frank Sinatra (22),
George Strait (22) ❽ Willie Nelson (21)
❾ Paul McCartney/Wings (20) ❿= TAFKA
(Prince) (19), Rod Stewart (19)
Source: The Popular Music Database

T H E   1 0

GROUPS WITH THE MOST PLATINUM ALBUMS IN THE US

	Group	Platinum albums
1=	Beatles	80
=	Led Zeppelin	80
3	Pink Floyd	62
4	Eagles	60
5	Aerosmith	49
6	Van Halen	47
7	Fleetwood Mac	45
8	AC/DC	42
9	Alabama	41
10	U2	40

Source: The Popular Music Database

MOVIE MUSIC

SAMMY CAHN
In the 33 years from 1942 to 1975, prolific lyricist Sammy Cahn (1913–93) was nominated for 26 "Best Song" Oscars, winning on four occasions.

TOP 10 ARTISTS WITH MOST "BEST SONG" OSCAR NOMINATIONS
(Nominations)

❶ Sammy Cahn (26) ❷ Johnny Mercer (18)
❸= Paul Francis Webster (16), Alan and Marilyn Bergman (16)
❺ James Van Heusen (14) ❻= Henry Warren (11), Henry Mancini (11), Ned Washington (11) ❾= Alan Menken (10), Sammy Fain (10), Leo Robin (10), Jule Styne (10)

T O P   1 0
ELVIS PRESLEY MOVIE SONGS IN THE US

	Song	Movie	Year
1	*Love Me Tender*	*Love Me Tender*	1956
2	*Jailhouse Rock*	*Jailhouse Rock*	1957
3	*Teddy Bear*	*Loving You*	1957
4	*Return to Sender*	*Girls! Girls! Girls!*	1962
5	*Can't Help Falling in Love*	*Blue Hawaii*	1961
6	*Hard Headed Woman*	*King Creole*	1958
7	*Bossa Nova Baby*	*Fun in Acapulco*	1963
8	*One Broken Heart for Sale*	*It Happened at the World's Fair*	1963
9	*Follow that Dream*	*Follow that Dream*	1962
10	*I'm Yours*	*Tickle Me*	1965

Elvis' movie singles from 1963–69, which actually formed the bulk of his releases during this period, ironically sold much less well than those from the 1950s, when his recording career was at its peak, or from the 1970s, when he was concentrating on live performance. The title song from his first movie, *Love Me Tender*, though a multimillion seller in the US, was a much smaller hit elsewhere in the world, not even figuring in his UK Top 10.

Source: MRIB

T O P   1 0
"BEST SONG" OSCAR-WINNING SINGLES IN THE US

	Artist	Title	Year
1	Debby Boone	*You Light Up My Life*	1977
2	Joe Cocker and Jennifer Warnes	*Up Where We Belong*	1982
3	Barbra Streisand	*Love Theme* from *A Star is Born (Evergreen)*	1976
4	Celine Dion	*My Heart Will Go On*	1997
5	Stevie Wonder	*I Just Called to Say I Love You*	1984
6	Christopher Cross	*Arthur's Theme (Best That You Can Do)*	1981
7	Barbra Streisand	*The Way We Were*	1973
8	Peabo Bryson and Regina Belle	*A Whole New World*	1992
9	B.J. Thomas	*Raindrops Keep Falling on My Head*	1969
10	Bill Medley and Jennifer Warnes	*(I've Had) The Time of My Life*	1987

Source: The Popular Music Database

T O P   1 0
JAMES BOND MOVIE THEMES IN THE US

	Artist	Title	Year
1	Duran Duran	*A View to a Kill*	1985
2	Carly Simon	*Nobody Does It Better* (from *The Spy Who Loved Me*)	1977
3	Paul McCartney and Wings	*Live and Let Die*	1973
4	Sheena Easton	*For Your Eyes Only*	1981
5	Shirley Bassey	*Goldfinger*	1965
6	Tom Jones	*Thunderball*	1966
7	Rita Coolidge	*All Time High* (from *Octopussy*)	1983
8	Nancy Sinatra	*You Only Live Twice*	1967
9	Shirley Bassey	*Diamonds are Forever*	1972
10	John Barry	*Goldfinger*	1965

STEVE McQUEEN
The Windmills of Your Mind *from his* The Thomas Crown Affair *won the 1968 "Best Song" Oscar.*

THE 10

"BEST SONG" OSCAR WINNERS OF THE 1940s

Year	Song	Movie
1940	When You Wish upon a Star	Pinocchio
1941	The Last Time I Saw Paris	Lady Be Good
1942	White Christmas	Holiday Inn
1943	You'll Never Know	Hello, Frisco, Hello
1944	Swinging on a Star	Going My Way
1945	It Might as Well be Spring	State Fair
1946	On the Atchison, Topeka and Santa Fe	The Harvey Girls
1947	Zip-A-Dee-Doo-Dah	Song of the South
1948	Buttons and Bows	The Paleface
1949	Baby, It's Cold Outside	Neptune's Daughter

The first "Best Song" Oscar was won in 1934 by *The Continental* from the movie *The Gay Divorcée.*

THE 10 "BEST SONG" OSCAR WINNERS OF THE 1960s
(Movie)
1960 *Never on Sunday (Never on Sunday)*
1961 *Moon River (Breakfast at Tiffany's)*
1962 *Days of Wine and Roses (Days of Wine and Roses)* **1963** *Call Me Irresponsible (Papa's Delicate Condition)* **1964** *Chim Chim Cheree (Mary Poppins)* **1965** *The Shadow of Your Smile (The Sandpiper)* **1966** *Born Free (Born Free)* **1967** *Talk to the Animals (Dr. Doolittle)* **1968** *The Windmills of Your Mind (The Thomas Crown Affair)* **1969** *Raindrops Keep Fallin' on My Head (Butch Cassidy and the Sundance Kid)*

**AUDREY HEPBURN IN
*BREAKFAST AT TIFFANY'S***

THE 10

"BEST SONG" OSCAR WINNERS OF THE 1950s

Year	Song	Movie	Year	Song	Movie
1950	Mona Lisa	Captain Carey	1955	Love is a Many-splendored Thing	Love is a Many-splendored Thing
1951	In the Cool, Cool, Cool of the Evening	Here Comes the Groom	1956	Whatever Will Be, Will Be (Que Sera, Sera)	The Man Who Knew too Much
1952	High Noon (Do Not Forsake Me, Oh My Darling)	High Noon	1957	All the Way	The Joker is Wild
1953	Secret Love	Calamity Jane	1958	Gigi	Gigi
1954	Three Coins in the Fountain	Three Coins in the Fountain	1959	High Hopes	A Hole in the Head

THE 10

"BEST SONG" OSCAR WINNERS OF THE 1970s

Year	Song	Movie
1970	For All We Know	Lovers and Other Strangers
1971	Theme from "Shaft"	Shaft
1972	The Morning After	The Poseidon Adventure
1973	The Way We Were	The Way We Were
1974	We May Never Love Like This Again	The Towering Inferno
1975	I'm Easy	Nashville
1976	Evergreen	A Star is Born
1977	You Light up My Life	You Light up My Life
1978	Last Dance	Thank God it's Friday
1979	It Goes Like it Goes	Norma Rae

The Way We Were and *Evergreen* were both sung by Barbra Streisand, who became the first artist since Frank Sinatra to win two Oscar song awards in the same decade.

THE 10

"BEST SONG" OSCAR WINNERS OF THE 1980s

Year	Song	Movie
1980	Fame	Fame
1981	Up Where We Belong	An Officer and a Gentleman
1982	Arthur's Theme (Best that You Can Do)	Arthur
1983	Flashdance	Flashdance
1984	I Just Called to Say I Love You	The Woman in Red
1985	Say You, Say Me	White Nights
1986	Take My Breath Away	Top Gun
1987	(I've Had) The Time of My Life	Dirty Dancing
1988	Let the River Run	Working Girl
1989	Under the Sea	The Little Mermaid

MUSIC AWARDS

TOP 10

COUNTRIES WITH THE MOST WINS AT THE EUROVISION SONG CONTEST

	Country	Years	Wins
1	Ireland	1970, 1980, 1987, 1992, 1993, 1994, 1996	7
2=	France	1958, 1960, 1962, 1969*, 1977	5
=	Luxembourg	1961, 1965, 1972, 1973, 1983	5
=	UK	1967, 1969*, 1976, 1981, 1997	5
5	Netherlands	1957, 1959, 1969*, 1975	4
6=	Sweden	1974, 1984, 1991	3
=	Israel	1978, 1979, 1998	3
8=	Italy	1964, 1990	2
=	Spain	1968, 1969*	2
=	Switzerland	1956, 1988	2

* All four countries tied as winners in 1969

The Eurovision Song Contest has been an annual event since its 25 May 1956 debut. Johnny Logan completed a hat-trick for Ireland (even though he is Australian by birth). Having won as a performer in 1980 and 1987, he wrote the Irish entry *Why Me?* for the 1992 winner, Linda Martin.

TOP 10

ARTISTS WITH THE MOST GRAMMY AWARDS

	Artist	Awards
1	Sir George Solti	31
2	Quincy Jones	26
3	Vladimir Horowitz	25
4=	Pierre Boulez	20
=	Henry Mancini	20
6	Stevie Wonder	19
7=	Leonard Bernstein	16
=	John Williams	16
=	Paul Simon	16
10=	Aretha Franklin	15
=	Itzhak Perlman	15

Source: NARAS

TOP 10

NON-CLASSICAL ARTISTS WITH THE MOST GRAMMY AWARDS

	Artist	Awards
1	Quincy Jones	26
2	Henry Mancini	20
3	Stevie Wonder	19
4=	Paul Simon	16
=	John Williams	16
6	Aretha Franklin	15
7=	Chet Atkins	14
=	David Foster	14
9=	Ella Fitzgerald	13
=	Michael Jackson	13
=	Paul McCartney	13

Source: NARAS

THE 10

LATEST INDUCTEES INTO THE COUNTRY MUSIC HALL OF FAME

	Artist	Awards
1	Harlan Howard	1997
=	Cindy Walker	1997
=	Brenda Lee	1997
4=	Patsy Montana	1996
=	Buck Owens	1996

	Artist	Awards
=	Ray Price	1996
7=	Roger Miller	1995
=	Jo Walker-Meador	1995
9	Merle Haggard	1994
10	Willie Nelson	1993

Source: Country Music Association

THE 10

FIRST GRAMMY RECORDS OF THE YEAR

Year	Record	Artist
1958	*Nel Blu Dipinto di Blu (Volare)*	Domenico Modugno
1959	*Mack the Knife*	Bobby Darin
1960	*Theme From a Summer Place*	Percy Faith
1961	*Moon River*	Henry Mancini
1962	*I Left My Heart in San Francisco*	Tony Bennett
1963	*The Days of Wine and Roses*	Henry Mancini
1964	*The Girl from Ipanema*	Stan Getz & Astrud Gilberto
1965	*A Taste of Honey*	Herb Alpert & the Tijuana Brass
1966	*Strangers in the Night*	Frank Sinatra
1967	*Up Up and Away*	5th Dimension

Source: NARAS

THE 10

LATEST GRAMMY RECORDS OF THE YEAR

Year	Record	Artist
1998	*Sunny Come Home*	Shawn Colvin
1997	*Change the World*	Eric Clapton
1996	*Kiss from a Rose*	Seal
1995	*All I Wanna Do*	Sheryl Crow
1994	*I Will Always Love You*	Whitney Houston
1993	*Tears in Heaven*	Eric Clapton
1992	*Unforgettable*	Natalie Cole with Nat "King" Cole
1991	*Another Day in Paradise*	Phil Collins
1990	*The Wind Beneath My Wings*	Bette Midler
1989	*Don't Worry Be Happy*	Bobby McFerrin

Source: NARAS

TOP 10
ARTISTS WITH THE MOST GRAMMY AWARDS IN A YEAR

	Artist	Year	Grammys
1	Michael Jackson	1984	7
2=	Roger Miller	1966	6
=	Quincy Jones	1991	6
=	Eric Clapton	1993	6
5=	Henry Mancini	1962	5
=	Roger Miller	1965	5
=	Simon & Garfunkel	1971	5
=	Stevie Wonder	1977	5
=	Bee Gees	1979	5
=	Christopher Cross	1981	5
=	Quincy Jones	1982	5
=	Toto	1983	5

Source: The Popular Music Database

THE 10
LATEST RECIPIENTS OF THE SONGWRITERS HALL OF FAME SAMMY CAHN LIFETIME ACHIEVEMENT AWARD

	Recipient	Year
1	Berry Gordy	1998
2	Vic Damone	1997
3	Frankie Laine	1996
4	Steve Lawrence and Eydie Gorme	1995
5	Lena Horne	1994
6	Ray Charles	1993
7	Nat "King" Cole	1992
8	Gene Autry	1991
9	B. B. King	1990
10	Quincy Jones	1989

Source: National Academy of Popular Music

THE 10
LATEST WINNERS OF THE ASCAP SONGWRITER OF THE YEAR (POP CATEGORY)

	Artist	Year
1	Glen Ballard	1997
2	Melissa Etheridge/ Hootie and the Blowfish	1996
3	Robert John "Mutt" Lange	1995
4	Elton John and Bernie Taupin	1994
5	Diane Warren	1993
6	Jimmy Jam and Terry Lewis	1992
7	Diane Warren	1991
8	Diane Warren	1990
9	Debbie Gibson/Bruce Springsteen	1989
10	Jimmy Jam and Terry Lewis	1988

Source: ASCAP

TOP 10
COUNTRY MUSIC AWARD WINNERS

	Artist	Awards
1	Vince Gill	16
2=	George Strait	11
=	Garth Brooks	11
4	Roy Clark	10
5=	Alabama	9
=	Chet Atkins	9
=	Judds	9
8=	Loretta Lynn	8
=	Ronnie Milsap	8
=	Willie Nelson	8
=	Dolly Parton	8
=	Ricky Skaggs	8
=	Brooks and Dunn	8

The Country Music Awards are the most prestigious Country awards, held as an annual ceremony since 1967. Veteran Country instrumentalist Roy Clark netted the Instrumentalist of the Year award for seven consecutive years between 1974 and 1980.

Source: Country Music Association

THE 10
FIRST RECIPIENTS OF THE GRAMMYS' LIFETIME ACHIEVEMENT AWARD

Year	Artist
1962	Bing Crosby, vocalist
1965	Frank Sinatra, vocalist
1966	Duke Ellington, jazz musician
1967	Ella Fitzgerald, jazz vocalist
1968	Irving Berlin, composer
1971	Elvis Presley, vocalist
1972	Louis Armstrong*, jazz musician
1972	Mahalia Jackson*, gospel vocalist
1984	Chuck Berry, composer/performer
1984	Charlie Parker*, jazz musician

* *Presented posthumously*

The Lifetime Achievement Award is the most prestigious of Grammy Awards. An ebony and gold plaque, it is not awarded annually but is presented as and when appropriate to artists who have made "creative contributions of outstanding significance to the field of recordings."

Source: NARAS

TOP 10
AMERICAN MUSIC AWARDS WINNERS

	Artist	Total awards
1	Whitney Houston	21
2=	Kenny Rogers*	19
=	Alabama	19
4	Michael Jackson	18
5	Lionel Richie#	15
6	Willie Nelson†	14
7	Reba McEntire	12
8	Stevie Wonder	11
9=	Garth Brooks	10
=	Randy Travis	10

* *Two awards shared with Dolly Parton*
\# *Two awards shared with Diana Ross*
† *Two awards shared with Waylon Jennings*

The only "populist" music awards in the United States based on voting by the American public, the AMAs have been held annually since their February 19, 1974 inaugural ceremony, which took place at the Aquarius Theater, Hollywood.

Source: The Popular Music Database

CLASSICAL & OPERA

WOLFGANG AMADEUS MOZART
Considered by many the greatest musical genius of all time, Mozart died at the age of just 35 after a lifetime devoted to composing and performing.

T O P 1 0
MOST PROLIFIC* CLASSICAL COMPOSERS#

	Composer/nationality	Hours
1	Joseph Haydn (1732–1809), Austrian	340
2	George Handel (1685–1759), German/English	303
3	Wolfgang Amadeus Mozart (1756–91), Austrian	202
4	Johann Sebastian Bach (1685–1750), German	175
5	Franz Schubert (1797–1828), German	134
6	Ludwig van Beethoven (1770–1827), German	120
7	Henry Purcell (1659–95), English	116
8	Giuseppe Verdi (1813–1901), Italian	87
9	Antonín Dvořák (1841–1904), Czechoslovakian	79
10 =	Franz Liszt (1811–86), Hungarian	76
=	Peter Tchaikovsky (1840–93), Russian	76

* Refers to number of hours of music composed

 # Based on a survey conducted by Classical Music *magazine*

T O P 1 0
LARGEST OPERA HOUSES IN THE WORLD

	Opera house	Location	Seating	Capacity standing	Total
1	The Metropolitan Opera	New York, NY	3,800	265	4,065
2	Cincinnati Opera	Cincinnati, OH	3,630	–	3,630
3	Lyric Opera of Chicago	Chicago, IL	3,563	–	3,563
4	San Francisco Opera	San Francisco, CA	3,176	300	3,476
5	The Dallas Opera	Dallas, TX	3,420	–	3,420
6	Canadian Opera Company	Toronto, Canada	3,167	–	3,167
7	Los Angeles Music Center Opera	Los Angeles, CA	3,098	–	3,098
8	San Diego Opera	San Diego, CA	2,992	84	3,076
9	Seattle Opera	Seattle, WA	3,017	–	3,017
10	L'Opéra de Montréal	Montreal, Canada	2,874	–	2,874

T O P 1 0
OPERAS MOST FREQUENTLY PERFORMED AT THE METROPOLITAN OPERA HOUSE, NEW YORK*

	Opera	Composer	Performances
1	*La Bohème*	Giacomo Puccini	1,047
2	*Aïda*	Giuseppi Verdi	1,012
3	*Carmen*	Georges Bizet	869
4	*La Traviata*	Giuseppi Verdi	818
5	*Tosca*	Giacomo Puccini	795
6	*Madama Butterfly*	Giacomo Puccini	740
7	*Rigoletto*	Giuseppi Verdi	724
8	*Faust*	Charles Gounod	706
9	*Pagliacci*	Ruggero Leoncavallo	677
10	*Cavalleria Rusticana*	Pietro Mascagni	637

* As of the end of the 1997–98 season

DEATH OF THE WALTZ KING

The most remarkable member of an extraordinary musical dynasty died in 1899. Born in 1825, Johann Strauss, Jr., had earned the nickname "the Waltz King" for his output of over 400 waltzes, including the most famous of all, *The Blue Danube* (1867). He was one of three brothers, all of whom composed waltzes. Ironically, their father, Johann Strauss, Sr., (1804-49), had forbidden any of his children to take up music, insisting they pursue careers in business. He was known as "the Father of the Waltz," although his output of 152 waltzes was puny in comparison with his most famous son. His grandson, the third Johann, carried on the family waltz tradition until his death in 1939.

YEARS AGO • YEARS AGO
100
YEARS AGO • YEARS AGO

T O P 1 0

CLASSICAL ALBUMS OF ALL TIME IN THE US

	Title	Artist	Year
1	*The Three Tenors In Concert*	Carreras, Domingo, Pavarotti	1994
2	*Chant*	Benedictine Monks of Santo Domingo De Silos	1994
3	*In Concert*	Carreras, Domingo, Pavarotti	1990
4	*Tchaikovsky: Piano Concerto No. 1*	Van Cliburn	1958
5	*Fantasia* soundtrack (50th anniversary ed.)	Philadelphia Orchestra	1990
6	*Perhaps Love*	Placido Domingo	1981
7	*Amadeus*	Neville Marriner	1984
8	*O Holy Night*	Luciano Pavarotti	1983
9	*1812 Overture/ Capriccio Italien*	Antal Dorati/Minneapolis Symphony Orchestra	1959
10	*Switched-on Bach*	Walter Carlos	1969

T H E 1 0

LATEST WINNERS OF THE "BEST CLASSICAL ALBUM" GRAMMY AWARD

Year	Composer/title	Artist
1998	Danielpour, Kirchner, Rouse, *Premières – Cello Concertos*	Yo–Yo Ma, David Zinman, Philadelphia Orchestra
1997	Corigliano, *Of Rage and Remembrance*	Leonard Slatkin, National Symphony Orchestra
1996	Claude Debussy, *La Mer*	Pierre Boulez, Cleveland Orchestra
1995	Béla Bartók, *Concerto for Orchestra; Four Orchestral Pieces, Op. 12*	Pierre Boulez, Chicago Symphony Orchestra
1994	Béla Bartók, *The Wooden Prince*	Pierre Boulez, Chicago Symphony Orchestra and Chorus
1993	Gustav Mahler, *Symphony No. 9*	Leonard Bernstein, Berlin Philharmonic Orchestra
1992	Leonard Bernstein, *Candide*	Leonard Bernstein, London Symphony Orchestra
1991	Charles Ives, *Symphony No. 2 (And Three Short Works)*	Leonard Bernstein, New York Philharmonic Orchestra
1990	Béla Bartók, *Six String Quartets*	Emerson String Quartet
1989	Giuseppi Verdi, *Requiem and Operatic Choruses*	Robert Shaw Atlanta Symphony Orchestra

Source: NARAS

T H E 1 0

LATEST WINNERS OF THE "BEST OPERA RECORDING" GRAMMY AWARD

Year	Composer/title	Principal soloists/orchestra
1998	Richard Wagner, *Die Meistersinger von Nürnberg*	Sir Georg Solti, Ben Heppner, Herbert Lippert, Karita Mattila, Alan Opie, Rene Pape, Jose van Dam, Iris Vermillion, Chicago Symphony Chorus, Chicago Symphony Orchestra
1997	Benjamin Britten, *Peter Grimes*	Philip Langridge, Alan Opie, Janice Watson, Opera London, London Symphony Chorus, City of London Sinfonia
1996	Hector Berlioz, *Les Troyens*	Charles Dutoit, Orchestre Symphonique de Montréal
1995	Carlisle Floyd, *Susannah*	Jerry Hadley, Samuel Ramey, Cheryl Studer, Kenn Chester
1994	George Handel, *Semele*	Kathleen Battle, Marilyn Horne, Samuel Ramey, Sylvia McNair, Michael Chance
1993	Richard Strauss, *Die Frau ohne Schatten*	Placido Domingo, Jose Van Dam, Hildegard Behrens
1992	Richard Wagner, *Götterdämmerung*	Hildegard Behrens, Ekkehard Wlashiha
1991	Richard Wagner, *Das Rheingold*	James Morris, Kurt Moll, Christa Ludwig
1990	Richard Wagner, *Die Walküre*	Gary Lakes, Jessye Norman, Kurt Moll
1989	Richard Wagner, *Lohengrin*	Placido Domingo, Jessye Norman, Eva Randova

Source: NARAS

STAGE, SCREEN & BROADCASTING

TOP 10

LONGEST-RUNNING NONMUSICALS ON BROADWAY

	Show	Performances
1	Oh! Calcutta! (1976–89)	5,959
2	Life with Father (1939–47)	3,224
3	Tobacco Road (1933–41)	3,182
4	Abie's Irish Rose (1922–27)	2,327
5	Deathtrap (1978–82)	1,792
6	Gemini (1977–81)	1,788
7	Harvey (1944–49)	1,775
8	Born Yesterday (1946–49)	1,642
9	Mary, Mary (1961–64)	1,572
10	Voice of the Turtle (1943–48)	1,558

Source: Theatre World

TOP 10

LONGEST-RUNNING THRILLERS ON BROADWAY

	Thriller	Performances
1	Deathtrap (1978–82)	1,793
2	Arsenic and Old Lace (1941–44)	1,444
3	Angel Street (1941–44)	1,295
4	Sleuth (1970–73)	1,222
5	Dracula (1977–80)	925
6	Witness for the Prosecution (1954–56)	644
7	Dial M for Murder (1952–54)	552
8	Sherlock Holmes (1975–76)	479
9	An Inspector Calls (1994–95)	454
10	Ten Little Indians (1944–45)	424

Source: Theatre World

TOP 10

LONGEST-RUNNING COMEDIES ON BROADWAY

	Comedy	Performances
1	Life with Father (1939–47)	3,224
2	Abie's Irish Rose (1922–27)	2,327
3	Gemini (1977–81)	1,788
4	Harvey (1944–49)	1,775
5	Born Yesterday (1946–49)	1,642
6	Mary, Mary (1961–64)	1,572
7	Voice of the Turtle (1943–48)	1,558
8	Barefoot in the Park (1963–67)	1,532
9	Same Time Next Year (1975–78)	1,444
10	Brighton Beach Memoirs (1983–86)	1,299

Source: Theatre World

TOP 10

LONGEST-RUNNING MUSICALS ON BROADWAY

	Show	Performances
1	Cats (1982–)	6,463*
2	A Chorus Line (1975–90)	6,137
3	Les Misérables (1987–)	4,545*
4	The Phantom of the Opera (1988–)	4,263*
5	42nd Street (1980–89)	3,486
6	Grease (1972–80)	3,388
7	Fiddler on the Roof (1964–72)	3,242
8	Miss Saigon (1991–)	2,910*
9	Hello Dolly! (1964–71)	2,844
10	My Fair Lady (1956–62)	2,717

* Still running; total as of March 31, 1998

Off Broadway, the musical show *The Fantasticks*, by Tom Jones and Harvey Schmidt, has been performed 15,653 times.

Source: Playbill

LONGEST-RUNNING MUSICALS IN THE UK
(Dates/no. of performances)

❶ *Cats* (1981– /7,242*) ❷ *Starlight Express* (1984– /5,846*) ❸ *Les Misérables* (1985– /5,109*) ❹ *The Phantom of the Opera* (1986– /4,763*) ❺ *Oliver!* (1960–69/4,125) ❻ *Miss Saigon* (1989– /3,737*) ❼ *Jesus Christ, Superstar* (1972–80/3,357) ❽ *Evita* (1978–86/2,900) ❾ *The Sound of Music* (1961–67/2,386) ❿ *Salad Days* (1954–60/2,283)

* *Still running; total as of March 31, 1998*

TOP 10

LONGEST-RUNNING SHOWS IN THE UK

	Show	Performances
1	The Mousetrap (1952–)	18,872*
2	Cats (1981–)	7,242*
3	No Sex, Please – We're British (1971–81; 1982–86; 1986–87)	6,761
4	Starlight Express (1984–)	5,846*
5	Les Misérables (1985–)	5,109*
6	The Phantom of the Opera (1986–)	4,763*
7	Oliver! (1960–69)	4,125
8	Oh! Calcutta! (1970–74; 1974–80)	3,918
9	Miss Saigon (1989–)	3,737*
10	Jesus Christ, Superstar (1972–80)	3,357

* Still running; total as of March 31, 1998

TOP 10

LONGEST-RUNNING NONMUSICALS IN THE UK

	Show	Performances
1	The Mousetrap (1952–)	18,872
2	No Sex, Please – We're British (1971–81; 1982–86; 1986–87)	6,761
3	Oh! Calcutta! (1970–74; 1974–80)	3,918
4	Run for Your Wife (1983–91)	2,638
5	There's a Girl in My Soup (1966–69; 1969–72)	2,547
6	Pyjama Tops (1969–75)	2,498
7	Sleuth (1970; 1972; 1973–75)	2,359
8	Worm's Eye View (1945–51)	2,245
9	Boeing Boeing (1962–65; 1965–67)	2,035
10	Blithe Spirit (1941–42; 1942; 1942–46)	1,997

* Still running; total as of March 31, 1998

ANDREW LLOYD WEBBER
In a 30-year career, originally in partnership with lyricist Tim Rice, Andrew Lloyd Webber has composed the music for and produced some of the most successful shows in theater history.

TOP 10

LONGEST-RUNNING SHOWS ON BROADWAY

	Show	Performances
1	Cats (1982–)	6,463*#
2	A Chorus Line (1975–90)	6,137
3	Oh! Calcutta! (1976–89)	5,959
4	Les Misérables (1987–)	4,545*
5	The Phantom of the Opera (1988–)	4,263*
6	42nd Street (1980–89)	3,486
7	Grease (1972–80)	3,388
8	Fiddler on the Roof (1964–72)	3,242
9	Life with Father (1939–47)	3,224
10	Tobacco Road (1933–41)	3,182

* Still running; total as of March 31, 1998

Cats became the longest running show of all time on June 19, 1997, when it notched up its 6,138th performance.

Source: Playbill

TOP 10

LONGEST-RUNNING COMEDIES IN THE UK

	Show	Performances
1	No Sex, Please – We're British (1971–81; 1982–86; 1986–87)	6,761
2	Run for Your Wife (1983–91)	2,638
3	There's a Girl in My Soup (1966–69; 1969–72)	2,547
4	Pyjama Tops (1969–75)	2,498
5	Worm's Eye View (1945–51)	2,245
6	Boeing Boeing (1962–65; 1965–67)	2,035
7	Blithe Spirit (1941–42; 1942; 1942–46)	1,997
8	Dirty Linen (1976–80)	1,667
9	Reluctant Heroes (1950–54)	1,610
10	Seagulls over Sorrento (1950–54; 1954)	1,551

No Sex Please – We're British is the longest-running comedy in the world. It opened on June 3, 1971 and, after transfers, finally closed on September 5, 1987.

ALL THE WORLD'S A STAGE

THE 10

LATEST TONY AWARDS FOR A DIRECTOR

1997	Anthony Page, *A Doll's House*
1996	Gerald Gutierrez, *A Delicate Balance*
1995	Gerald Gutierrez, *The Heiress*
1994	Stephen Daldry, *An Inspector Calls*
1993	George C. Wolfe, *Angels in America Part I: Millennium Approaches*
1992	Patrick Mason, *Dancing at Lughnasa*
1991	Jerry Zaks, *Six Degrees of Separation*
1990	Frank Galati, *The Grapes of Wrath*
1989	Jerry Zaks, *Lend me a Tenor*
1988	John Dexter, *M. Butterfly*

THE 10

LATEST TONY AWARDS FOR A PLAY

1997	*The Last Night of Ballyhoo*
1996	*Master Class*
1995	*Love! Valour! Compassion!*
1994	*Angels in America Part II: Perestroika*
1993	*Angels in America Part I: Millennium Approaches*
1992	*Dancing at Lughnasa*
1991	*Lost in Yonkers*
1990	*The Grapes of Wrath*
1989	*The Heidi Chronicles*
1988	*M. Butterfly*

The Tony Awards, established in 1947 by the American Theater Wing, honor outstanding Broadway plays and musicals, actors and actresses, music, costume, and other contributions. They are named for the actress and director Antoinette Perry (1888–1946), who headed the American Theater Wing during the Second World War.

THE 10

LATEST TONY AWARDS FOR AN ACTOR

1997	Christopher Plummer, *Barrymore*
1996	George Grizzard, *A Delicate Balance*
1995	Ralph Fiennes, *Hamlet*
1994	Stephen Spinella, *Angels in America Part II: Perestroika*
1993	Ron Leibman, *Angels in America Part I: Millennium Approaches*
1992	Judd Hirsch, *Conversations with my Father*
1991	Nigel Hawthorne, *Shadowlands*
1990	Robert Morse, *Tru*
1989	Philip Bosco, *Lend me a Tenor*
1988	Ron Silver, *Speed-the-Plow*

THE 10

LATEST TONY AWARDS FOR AN ACTRESS

1997	Janet McTeer, *A Doll's House*
1996	Zoe Caldwell, *Master Class*
1995	Cherry Jones, *The Heiress*
1994	Diana Rigg, *Medea*
1993	Madeline Kahn, *The Sisters Rosensweig*
1992	Glenn Close, *Death and the Maiden*
1991	Mercedes Ruehl, *Lost in Yonkers*
1990	Maggie Smith, *Lettice and Lovage*
1989	Pauline Collins, *Shirley Valentine*
1988	Joan Allen, *Burn This*

THE 10

LATEST TONY AWARDS FOR A MUSICAL

1998	*The Lion King*
1997	*Titanic*
1996	*Rent*
1995	*Sunset Boulevard*
1994	*Passion*
1993	*Kiss of the Spider Woman*
1992	*Crazy for You*
1991	*The Will Rogers' Follies*
1990	*City of Angels*
1989	*Jerome Robbins' Broadway*

THE 10

LATEST PULITZER DRAMA AWARDS

1998	Paula Vogel, *How I Learned to Drive*
1997	no award
1996	Jonathan Larson, *Rent*
1995	Horton Foote, *The Young Man from Atlanta*
1994	Edward Albee, *Three Tall Women*
1993	Tony Kushner, *Angels in America: Millennium Approaches*
1992	Robert Schenkkan, *The Kentucky Cycle*
1991	Neil Simon, *Lost in Yonkers*
1990	August Wilson, *The Piano Lesson*
1989	Wendy Wasserstein, *The Heidi Chronicles*
1988	Alfred Uhry, *Driving Miss Daisy*

THE RECONSTRUCTED GLOBE THEATRE ON THE SOUTH BANK OF THE RIVER THAMES, LONDON

TOP 10

OLDEST LONDON THEATERS

	Theater	Date opened
1	Theatre Royal, Drury Lane	May 7, 1663
2	Sadler's Wells, Rosebery Avenue	June 3, 1683
3	The Haymarket (Theatre Royal), Haymarket	December 29, 1720
4	Royal Opera House, Covent Garden	December 7, 1732
5	The Adelphi (originally Sans Pareil), Strand	November 27, 1806
6	The Old Vic (originally Royal Coburg), Waterloo Road	May 11, 1818
7	The Vaudeville, Strand	April 16, 1870
8	The Criterion, Piccadilly Circus	March 21, 1874
9	The Savoy, Strand	October 10, 1881
10	The Comedy, Panton Street	October 15, 1881

These are London's 10 oldest theaters still operating on their original sites, although most of them have been rebuilt.

TOP 10

LARGEST BROADWAY HOUSES

	Theater	Seating capacity
1	Gershwin Theater	1,933
2	Ford Center for the Performing Arts	1,839
3	New Amsterdam Theater	1,771
4	Broadway Theater	1,752
5	Palace Theater	1,740
6	Minskoff Theater	1,685
7	St. James Theater	1,623
8	Majestic Theater	1,607
9	Marquis Theater	1,595
10	Shubert Theater	1,513

Source: Stubs

TOP 10

MOST DEMANDING SHAKESPEAREAN ROLES

	Role	Play	Lines
1	Hamlet	*Hamlet*	1,422
2	Falstaff	*Henry IV, Parts I* and *II*	1,178
3	Richard III	*Richard III*	1,124
4	Iago	*Othello*	1,097
5	Henry V	*Henry V*	1,025
6	Othello	*Othello*	860
7	Vincentio	*Measure for Measure*	820
8	Coriolanus	*Coriolanus*	809
9	Timon	*Timon of Athens*	795
10	Antony	*Antony and Cleopatra*	766

Hamlet's role is made up of 11,610 words – over 36 percent of the total number of lines spoken in the play, but if multiple plays are considered he is beaten by Falstaff who, as well as appearing in *Henry IV, Parts I* and *II*, also appears in *The Merry Wives of Windsor*, in which he has 436 lines.

SNAP FACTS

- Shakespeare used a total vocabulary of 29,066 different words (the average person's vocabulary is about 8,000).

- Shakespeare was the first to use certain words that are now common, including "hurry," "bump," "eyeball," and "anchovy."

- He used the word "America" just once, in *The Comedy of Errors*.

TOP 10

THEATER-GOING COUNTRIES IN THE WORLD

	Country	Annual theater attendance per 1,000 population
1	Cuba	2,559
2	Mongolia	1,700
3	Vietnam	1,000
4	UK	720
5	Iceland	658
6	Bulgaria	650
7	Luxembourg	613
8	Albania	590
9	Romania	578
10	Netherlands	575
	US	170

MOVIE HITS & MISSES

In earlier editions of *The Top 10 of Everything*, the rentals earned by the US and Canadian distributors were used to measure the relative success of the movies of various artists. However, while this remains a valid way of comparing the success of movies over long periods, movies have become an international medium, and today many Hollywood movies earn more outside the US than within it: this is true of most of the James Bond movies, for example. Movie lists are therefore now based on total worldwide box-office income. When compared with rental-based lists, this revision means that the ranking of certain movies of particular stars or genres that achieved greater global than domestic success will appear to have gained ground.

THEN & NOW

TOP 10 MOVIES

1987		1997
Fatal Attraction	**1**	Titanic
Beverly Hills Cop II	**2**	The Lost World: Jurassic Park
The Living Daylights	**3**	Men in Black
The Untouchables	**4**	Air Force One
Dirty Dancing	**5**	Liar Liar
Three Men and a Baby	**6**	Tomorrow Never Dies
Good Morning, Vietnam	**7**	My Best Friend's Wedding
Moonstruck	**8**	The Fifth Element
The Secret of My Success	**9**	Hercules
Stakeout	**10**	Batman and Robin

TOP 10

BIGGEST MOVIE FLOPS OF ALL TIME

	Movie/year	Estimated loss ($)
1	Cutthroat Island (1995)	81,000,000
2	The Adventures of Baron Munchausen (1988)	48,100,000
3	Ishtar (1987)	47,300,000
4	Hudson Hawk (1991)	47,000,000
5	Inchon (1981)	44,100,000

	Movie/year	Estimated loss ($)
6	The Cotton Club (1984)	38,100,000
7	Santa Claus – The Movie (1985)	37,000,000
8	Heaven's Gate (1980)	34,200,000
9	Billy Bathgate (1991)	33,000,000
10	Pirates (1986)	30,300,000

Since the figures shown here are based upon North American rental earnings balanced against the movies' original production cost, some in the list may eventually recoup a proportion of their losses via overseas earnings, video, and TV revenue, while for others, such as *Inchon* and *Pirates*, time has run out.

TOP 10

HIGHEST GROSSING MOVIES OF ALL TIME IN THE US

	Movie	US release	US gross ($)
1	Titanic	1997	565,700,000
2	Star Wars	1977	461,000,000
3	E.T.: The Extra-Terrestrial	1982	399,800,000
4	Jurassic Park	1993	357,100,000
5	Forrest Gump	1994	329,700,000
6	The Lion King	1994	312,900,000
7	Return of the Jedi	1983	309,100,000
8	Independence Day	1996	306,200,000
9	The Empire Strikes Back	1980	290,200,000
10	Home Alone	1990	285,800,000

Inevitably, bearing inflation in mind, the top-grossing movies of all time are releases from the 1990s, although it is also true that US movie-theater admissions have risen sharply in recent years. From the nadir of the late 1960s to the late 1970s, today's movies are both more widely viewed (even excluding video) than those of 15 to 25 years ago, and gross considerably more at the box office.

JURASSIC PARK
After a four-year run, its status as highest grossing movie of all time worldwide was finally eclipsed by 1997's mega-blockbuster Titanic.

STAR WARS
Although made over 20 years ago, Star Wars remains one of the biggest earning movies – second highest in the US, and fourth worldwide. With the follow-ups The Empire Strikes Back *and* Return of the Jedi, *it is also first among sequels.*

TOP 10 MOVIE SEQUELS OF ALL TIME

❶ *Star Wars / The Empire Strikes Back / Return of the Jedi* ❷ *Jurassic Park / The Lost World: Jurassic Park* ❸ *Batman / Batman Returns / Batman Forever / Batman and Robin* ❹ *Raiders of the Lost Ark / Indiana Jones and the Temple of Doom / Indiana Jones and the Last Crusade* ❺ *Star Trek I–VI / Generations / First Contact* ❻ *Home Alone 1–2* ❼ *Back to the Future I–III* ❽ *Die Hard 1–2 / Die Hard: With a Vengeance* ❾ *Jaws I–IV* ❿ *Rocky I–V*

TOP 10

MOST EXPENSIVE MOVIES EVER MADE

	Movie*/year	Estimated cost ($)
1	*Titanic* (1997)	200,000,000
2	*Waterworld* (1995)	175,000,000
3	*Dante's Peak* (1997)	116,000,000
4=	*Batman and Robin* (1997)	110,000,000
=	*Tomorrow Never Dies* (1997)	110,000,000
=	*True Lies* (1994)	110,000,000
=	*Speed 2: Cruise Control* (1997)	110,000,000
8	*Inchon* (US/Korea), (1981)	102,000,000
9=	*Batman Forever* (1995)	100,000,000
=	*War and Peace* (USSR, 1967)	100,000,000

* All US-made unless otherwise stated

This is the first time that all those in the list exceed $100,000,000, with half the entrants being movies released in 1997.

TOP 10

HIGHEST GROSSING MOVIES OF ALL TIME

	Movie/year	Gross income ($) US	World total
1	*Titanic* (1997)	565,700,000	1,619,700,000
2	*Jurassic Park* (1993)	357,100,000	920,100,000
3	*Independence Day* (1996)	306,200,000	811,200,000
4	*Star Wars* (1977/97)	461,000,000	780,100,000
5	*The Lion King* (1994)	312,900,000	766,900,000
6	*E.T.: The Extra-Terrestrial* (1982)	399,800,000	704,800,000
7	*Forrest Gump* (1994)	329,700,000	679,700,000
8	*Lost World: Jurassic Park* (1997)	229,100,000	614,100,000
9	*Men in Black* (1997)	250,100,000	586,100,000
10	*The Empire Strikes Back* (1980/97)	290,200,000	533,900,000

TOP 10

MOVIE OPENINGS OF ALL TIME IN THE US

	Movie	Release	Opening weekend gross ($)
1	*The Lost World: Jurassic Park**	May 23, 1997	92,729,064
2	*Mission: Impossible**	May 22, 1996	56,811,602
3	*Batman Forever*	Jun 16, 1995	52,784,433
4	*Men in Black*	Jul 2, 1997	51,068,455
5	*Independence Day*	Jul 3, 1996	50,228,264
6	*Jurassic Park*	Jun 11, 1993	50,159,460
7	*Batman Returns*	Jun 19, 1992	45,687,711
8	*Batman and Robin*	Jun 20, 1996	42,872,606
9	*Batman*	Jun 22, 1989	42,705,884
10	*Twister*	May 10, 1996	41,059,405

* Estimate based on four-day holiday weekend

A movie may start its run relatively quietly, then gather momentum; for example, *Titanic* earned $28,638,131 on its opening weekend, which would not even rank it in the top 20, but it has gone on to become the highest-earning movie of all time.

YESTERDAY'S STARS & DIRECTORS

TOP 10
MARILYN MONROE MOVIES

	Movie	Year
1	Some Like It Hot	1959
2	How to Marry a Millionaire	1953
3	The Seven Year Itch	1955
4	Gentlemen Prefer Blondes	1953
5	There's No Business like Show Business	1954
6	Bus Stop	1956
7	The Misfits	1961
8	River of No Return	1954
9	All About Eve	1950
10	Let's Make Love	1960

INGRID BERGMAN
In a career spanning 44 years, the Swedish-born actress (1915–82) appeared in 40 films, including such acclaimed classics as Casablanca.

TOP 10 INGRID BERGMAN MOVIES
(Year)

❶ *Murder on the Orient Express** (1974)
❷ *Cactus Flower* (1969) ❸ *The Bells of St. Mary's* (1945) ❹ *For Whom the Bell Tolls* (1943) ❺ *Spellbound* (1945) ❻ *Notorious* (1946) ❼ *Casablanca* (1942) ❽ *The Yellow Rolls Royce* (1964) ❾ *The Inn of the Sixth Happiness* (1958) ❿ *Anastasia*# (1956)
* *Academy Award for "Best Supporting Actress"*
# *Academy Award for "Best Actress"*

TOP 10
MOVIES DIRECTED BY BILLY WILDER

	Movie	Year			Movie	Year
1	Irma La Douce	1963		6=	The Lost Weekend	1945
2	Some Like It Hot	1959		=	The Emperor Waltz	1948
3	The Front Page	1974		8	Sabrina	1954
4	The Apartment	1960		9	Witness for the Prosecution	1957
5	The Seven Year Itch	1955		10	Stalag 17	1953

TOP 10
PETER SELLERS MOVIES

	Movie	Year
1	The Revenge of the Pink Panther	1978
2	The Return of the Pink Panther	1974
3	The Pink Panther Strikes Again	1976
4	Murder by Death	1976
5	Being There	1979
6	Casino Royale	1967
7	What's New Pussycat?	1965
8	A Shot in the Dark	1964
9	The Pink Panther	1963
10=	Dr. Strangelove	1963
=	The Fiendish Plot of Dr. Fu Manchu	1980

TOP 10
MOVIES DIRECTED BY JOHN HUSTON

	Movie	Year
1	Annie	1982
2	The Bible	1966
3	Prizzi's Honor	1985
4	The Man Who Would Be King	1975
5	Casino Royale	1967
6	The Life and Times of Judge Roy Bean	1972
7	Moby Dick	1956
8	Night of the Iguana	1964
9	Moulin Rouge	1952
10=	Heaven Knows, Mr. Allison	1957
=	Victory	1981

TOP 10

JOHN WAYNE MOVIES

	Movie	Year
1	How the West Was Won	1962
2	The Longest Day	1962
3	True Grit*	1969
4	The Green Berets	1968
5	The Alamo	1960
6=	The Cowboys	1972
=	Big Jake	1971
8	Rooster Cogburn	1975
9	Hatari!	1962
10	The Greatest Story Ever Told	1965

* Academy Award for "Best Actor"

John Wayne (born Marion Michael Morrison) was one of Hollywood's most prolific actors, making more than 150 movies during a career that spanned 48 years. He is remembered mainly for his tough-guy roles as a soldier or cowboy – often with a Scottish name, such as his title roles in *Big Jim McLain* (1952), *McLintock* (1963), and *McQ* (1974). Occasionally he found himself miscast; for example, as Genghis Khan in *The Conqueror* (1955), and in the 10th film on this list, where he appeared, mercifully briefly, as the Roman centurion who gazes at the crucified Jesus and, in a Western drawl, recites his single memorable line, "Truly, this man was the son of God."

TOP 10

AUDREY HEPBURN MOVIES

	Movie	Year
1	My Fair Lady	1964
2	Always	1989
3	Wait until Dark	1967
4	Charade	1963
5	War and Peace	1956
6	The Nun's Story	1959
7	Bloodline	1979
8	How to Steal a Million	1966
9	Breakfast at Tiffany's	1961
10=	Sabrina	1954
=	Robin and Marian	1976

Audrey Hepburn (born Edda van Heemstra Hepburn-Ruston May 4, 1929, Brussels, Belgium; died January 20, 1993) had a British father and a Dutch mother. She began as a dancer and stage actress and appeared in minor parts before achieving acclaim and a "Best Actress" Oscar for *Roman Holiday* (1954). After 1967 her roles were few, and her last years were devoted to charity work with UNICEF.

TOP 10

HUMPHREY BOGART MOVIES

	Movie	Year
1	The Caine Mutiny	1954
2	Casablanca	1942
3	The African Queen*	1951
4=	Sabrina	1954
=	The Left Hand of God	1955
6	To Have and Have Not	1945
7=	Key Largo	1948
=	The Barefoot Contessa	1954
9=	Dark Passage	1947
=	The Big Sleep	1946

* Academy Award for "Best Actor"

TOP 10

MOVIES DIRECTED BY ALFRED HITCHCOCK

	Movie	Year
1	Psycho	1960
2	Rear Window	1954
3	North by Northwest	1959
4	Family Plot	1976
5	Torn Curtain	1966
6	Frenzy	1972
7	Vertigo	1958
8	The Man Who Knew Too Much	1956
9	The Birds	1963
10	Spellbound	1945

ALFRED HITCHCOCK
British director of more than 50 movies, Hitchcock (1899–1980) is considered the "master of suspense," often filming plots in which ordinary people become tangled in sinister events.

MOVIES OF THE DECADES

ALMOST A VICTORY
The colossal success of Independence Day, *in which the Earth's conquest by aliens is averted, makes it a close rival to the 1990s' top two money earners.*

TOP 10

MOVIES OF THE 1990s

	Movie	Year
1	Titanic*	1997
2	Jurassic Park	1993
3	Independence Day	1996
4	The Lion King	1994
5	Forrest Gump*	1994
6	The Lost World: Jurassic Park	1997
7	Men in Black	1997
8	Home Alone	1990
9	Ghost	1990
10	Terminator 2: Judgment Day	1991

* *Academy Award for "Best Picture"*

Each of the Top 10 movies of the present decade has earned more than $500,000,000 around the world, a total of more than $7 billion among them.

TOP 10

MOVIES OF THE 1980s

	Movie	Year
1	E.T.: the Extra-Terrestrial	1982
2	Indiana Jones and the Last Crusade	1989
3	Batman	1989
4	Rain Man	1988
5	Return of the Jedi	1983
6	Raiders of the Lost Ark	1981
7	The Empire Strikes Back	1980
8	Who Framed Roger Rabbit?	1988
9	Back to the Future	1985
10	Top Gun	1986

The 1980s was clearly the decade of the adventure movie, with George Lucas and Steven Spielberg continuing to assert their control of Hollywood, carving up the Top 10 between them, with Lucas as producer of 5 and 7 and Spielberg director of 1, 2, 6, 8, and 9. The 10 highest-earning movies scooped in more than $4 billion among them at the global box office.

TOP 10

MOVIES OF THE 1970s

	Movie	Year
1	Star Wars	1977/97
2	Jaws	1975
3	Close Encounters of the Third Kind	1977/80
4	Moonraker	1979
5	The Spy Who Loved Me	1977
6	The Exorcist	1973
7	The Sting*	1973
8	Grease	1978
9	The Godfather*	1972
10	Saturday Night Fever	1977

* *Academy Award for "Best Picture"*

In the 1970s the arrival of the two prodigies, Steven Spielberg and George Lucas, set the scene for the high adventure blockbusters whose domination has continued ever since. Lucas wrote and directed *Star Wars*, formerly the highest-earning film of all time. Spielberg directed *Jaws* and wrote and directed *Close Encounters of the Third Kind*.

TOP 10

MOVIES OF THE 1960s

	Movie	Year
1	101 Dalmatians	1961
2	The Jungle Book	1967
3	The Sound of Music*	1965
4	Thunderball	1965
5	Goldfinger	1964
6	Doctor Zhivago	1965
7	You Only Live Twice	1967
8	The Graduate	1968
9	Mary Poppins	1964
10	Butch Cassidy and the Sundance Kid	1969

* Academy Award for "Best Picture"

Many of the top-earning movies of the 1960s were musicals, with *The Sound of Music* producing the then fastest-selling album ever, while *Mary Poppins* and those featuring the music from *The Jungle Book* and *Doctor Zhivago* were all No. 1 albums.

TOP 10

MOVIES OF THE 1950s

	Movie	Year
1	Lady and the Tramp	1955
2	Peter Pan	1953
3	Ben-Hur *	1959
4	The Ten Commandments	1956
5	Sleeping Beauty	1959
6	Around the World in 80 Days*	1956
7=	The Robe	1953
=	The Greatest Show on Earth*	1952
9	The Bridge on the River Kwai*	1957
10	Peyton Place	1957

* Academy Award for "Best Picture"

While the popularity of animated movies continued with *Lady and the Tramp*, *Peter Pan*, and *Sleeping Beauty*, the 1950s was outstanding as the decade of the "big" picture in terms of cast and scale and also in terms of the magnitude of the subjects they tackled, such as the biblical epic.

TOP 10

MOVIES OF THE 1940s

	Movie	Year
1	Bambi	1942
2	Pinocchio	1940
3	Fantasia	1940
4	Cinderella	1949
5	Song of the South	1946
6	The Best Years of Our Lives*	1946
7	The Bells of St. Mary's	1945
8	Duel in the Sun	1946
9	Mom and Dad	1944
10	Samson and Delilah	1949

* Academy Award for "Best Picture"

With the top four movies of the decade classic Disney cartoons, the drab 1940s may truly be regarded as the "golden age" of the colorful animated movie.

TOP 10

MOVIES OF THE 1930s

	Movie	Year
1	Gone with the Wind*	1939
2	Snow White and the Seven Dwarfs	1937
3	The Wizard of Oz	1939
4	The Woman in Red	1935
5	King Kong	1933
6	San Francisco	1936
7=	Hell's Angels	1930
=	Lost Horizon	1937
=	Mr. Smith Goes to Washington	1939
10	Maytime	1937

* Academy Award for "Best Picture"

Gone with the Wind and *Snow White and the Seven Dwarfs* have generated more income than any other prewar film. However, if the income of *Gone with the Wind* were adjusted to allow for inflation in the period since its release, it could be regarded as the most successful film ever.

THE WONDERFUL WIZARD OF OZ
Although held to an honorable third place by blockbusters Gone with the Wind *and* Snow White and the Seven Dwarfs, The Wizard of Oz *was one of the most popular movies of the 1930s.*

164 MOVIE GENRES

INTERVIEW WITH THE VAMPIRE

(Year)
❶ *Interview with the Vampire* (1994)
❷ *Bram Stoker's Dracula* (1992)
❸ *Love at First Bite* (1979) ❹ *The Lost Boys*
(1987) ❺ *Dracula* (1979) ❻ *Fright Night*
(1985) ❼ *Vampire in Brooklyn* (1995)
❽ *Buffy the Vampire Slayer* (1992)
❾ *Dracula: Dead and Loving It* (1995)
❿ *Transylvania 6-5000* (1985)

TOP 10

COP MOVIES

	Movie	Year
1	Die Hard with a Vengeance	1995
2	The Fugitive	1993
3	Basic Instinct	1992
4	Seven	1995
5	Lethal Weapon 3	1993
6	Beverly Hills Cop	1984
7	Beverly Hills Cop II	1987
8	Speed	1994
9	Lethal Weapon 2	1989
10	Kindergarten Cop	1990

Although movies in which one of the central characters is a policeman have never been among the most successful movies of all time, many have earned respectable amounts at the box office. Both within and outside the Top 10, they are divided between those with a comic slant, such as the two *Beverly Hills Cop* films, and darker police thrillers, such as *Basic Instinct*. Movies featuring FBI and CIA agents have been excluded from the reckoning, hence eliminating blockbusters such as *Mission: Impossible* and *The Silence of the Lambs*.

TOP 10

WAR MOVIES

	Movie	Year
1	Platoon	1986
2	Good Morning, Vietnam	1987
3	Apocalypse Now	1979
4	M*A*S*H	1970
5	Patton	1970
6	The Deer Hunter	1978
7	Full Metal Jacket	1987
8	Midway	1976
9	The Dirty Dozen	1967
10	A Bridge Too Far	1977

This list excludes movies with military, rather than war, themes, such as *A Few Good Men* (1992), *The Hunt for Red October* (1990), *Crimson Tide* (1995), and *An Officer and a Gentleman* (1982), which would have been in the top five; and *Top Gun* (1986), which would top the list, just beating *Rambo: First Blood 2* (1985), a post-Vietnam action film.

TOP 10

COMEDY MOVIES

	Movie	Year
1	Forrest Gump	1994
2	Home Alone	1990
3	Ghost	1990
4	Pretty Woman	1990
5	Mrs. Doubtfire	1993
6	Flintstones	1995
7	Who Framed Roger Rabbit	1988
8	The Mask	1994
9	Beverly Hills Cop	1984
10	Liar, Liar	1997

TOP 10

GHOST MOVIES

	Movie	Year		Movie	Year
1	Ghost	1990	6	Scrooged	1988
2	Ghostbusters	1984	7	The Frighteners	1996
3	Casper	1995	8	Ghost Dad	1990
4	Ghostbusters II	1989	9	The Sixth Man	1997
5	Beetlejuice	1988	10	High Spirits	1988

TOP 10
JAMES BOND MOVIES

	Movie/year	Bond actor
1	*Goldeneye* (1995)	Pierce Brosnan
2	*Tomorrow Never Dies* (1997)	Pierce Brosnan
3	*Moonraker* (1979)	Roger Moore
4	*Never Say Never Again* (1983)	Sean Connery
5	*For Your Eyes Only* (1981)	Roger Moore
6	*The Living Daylights* (1987)	Timothy Dalton
7	*The Spy Who Loved Me* (1977)	Roger Moore
8	*Octopussy* (1983)	Roger Moore
9	*Licence to Kill* (1990)	Timothy Dalton
10	*A View to a Kill* (1985)	Roger Moore

TOP 10
ANIMATED MOVIES

	Movie	Year
1	*The Lion King*	1994
2	*Aladdin*	1992
3	*Toy Story*	1995
4	*Beauty and the Beast*	1991
5	*Who Framed Roger Rabbit**	1988
6	*Pocahontas*	1995
7	*The Hunchback of Notre Dame*	1996
8	*Casper**	1995
9	*Hercules*	1997
10	*Bambi*	1942

* *Part animated, part live action*

TOP 10
DISASTER MOVIES

	Movie	Year
1	*Titanic*	1997
2	*Twister*	1996
3	*Die Hard with a Vengeance*	1995
4	*Apollo 13*	1995
5	*Outbreak*	1995
6	*Dante's Peak*	1997
7	*Daylight*	1996
8	*Die Hard*	1988
9	*Volcano*	1997
10	*Die Hard 2*	1990

TOP 10
MOVIES FEATURING DINOSAURS

	Movie	Year
1	*Jurassic Park*	1993
2	*The Lost World: Jurassic Park*	1997
3	*Fantasia**	1940
4	*The Land Before Time**	1988
5	*Baby...Secret of the Lost Legend*	1985
6	*One of Our Dinosaurs is Missing*	1975
7	*Journey to the Center of the Earth*	1959
8	*We're Back: A Dinosaur's Story**	1993
9	*King Kong*	1933
10	*At the Earth's Core*	1976

* *Animated*

TOP 10
BIBLE MOVIES

	Movie	Year
1	*Ben Hur*	1959
2	*The Ten Commandments*	1956
3	*The Robe*	1953
4	*Jesus Christ Superstar*	1973
5	*Quo Vadis*	1951
6	*Samson and Delilah*	1949
7	*Jesus*	1979
8	*The Greatest Story Ever Told*	1965
9	*King of Kings*	1961
10	*Solomon and Sheba*	1959

TOP 10
SCIENCE-FICTION MOVIES

	Movie	Year
1	*Jurassic Park*	1993
2	*Independence Day*	1996
3	*Star Wars*	1977
4	*E.T.: The Extra-Terrestrial*	1982
5	*The Lost World: Jurassic Park*	1997
6	*Men in Black*	1997
7	*The Empire Strikes Back*	1980
8	*Terminator 2: Judgment Day*	1991
9	*Return of the Jedi*	1983
10	*Batman*	1989

The first seven movies in this list also feature in the all-time Top 10 world movies, and all 10 are among the 23 most successful movies ever, having earned over $400,000,000 each from worldwide box office income. Three other movies in this genre have each earned more than $300,000,000 globally: *Back to the Future* (1985), *Batman Forever* (1995), and *Close Encounters of the Third Kind* (1977/80).

TOP 10 WESTERN MOVIES
(Year)

❶ *Dances with Wolves* (1990) ❷ *Maverick* (1994) ❸ *Unforgiven* (1992) ❹ *Butch Cassidy and the Sundance Kid* (1969) ❺ *Jeremiah Johnson* (1972) ❻ *How the West Was Won* (1962) ❼ *Young Guns* (1988) ❽ *Young Guns II* (1990) ❾ *Pale Rider* (1985) ❿= *Bronco Billy* (1980), *Little Big Man* (1970)

OSCAR WINNERS – MOVIES

HIGHEST-EARNING "BEST PICTURE" OSCAR WINNERS

	Film	Year
1	*Titanic*	1997
2	*Forrest Gump*	1994
3	*Dances With Wolves*	1990
4	*Rain Man*	1988
5	*Schindler's List*	1993
6	*The English Patient*	1996
7	*Braveheart*	1995
8	*Gone With the Wind*	1939
9	*The Sound of Music*	1965
10	*The Sting*	1973

STUDIOS WITH THE MOST "BEST PICTURE" OSCARS

	Studio	Awards
1	United Artists	13
2	Columbia	12
3	Paramount	11
4	MGM	9
5	Twentieth Century Fox	7
6	Warner Bros	6
7	Universal	5
8	Orion	4
9	RKO	2
10	Miramax	1

"BEST PICTURE" OSCAR WINNERS OF THE 1930s

1930	*All Quiet on the Western Front*
1931	*Cimarron*
1932	*Grand Hotel*
1933	*Cavalcade*
1934	*It Happened One Night* *
1935	*Mutiny on the Bounty*
1936	*The Great Ziegfeld*
1937	*The Life of Emile Zola*
1938	*You Can't Take It with You*
1939	*Gone with the Wind*

* *Winner of Oscars for "Best Director," "Best Actor," "Best Actress," and "Best Screenplay"*

MOVIES NOMINATED FOR THE MOST OSCARS*

	Movie	Year	Awards	Nominations
1=	*All About Eve*	1950	6	14
=	*Titanic*	1997	11	14
3=	*Gone With the Wind*	1939	8#	13
=	*From Here to Eternity*	1953	8	13
=	*Mary Poppins*	1964	5	13
=	*Who's Afraid of Virginia Woolf*	1966	5	13
=	*Forrest Gump*	1994	6	13
8=	*Mrs. Miniver*	1942	6	12
=	*The Song of Bernadette*	1943	4	12
=	*Johnny Belinda*	1948	1	12
=	*A Streetcar Named Desire*	1951	4	12
=	*On the Waterfront*	1954	8	12
=	*Ben-Hur*	1959	11	12
=	*Becket*	1964	1	12
=	*My Fair Lady*	1964	8	12
=	*Reds*	1981	3	12
=	*Dances With Wolves*	1990	7	12
=	*Schindler's List*	1993	7	12
=	*The English Patient*	1996	9	12

* *Oscar® is a Registered Trademark*

Plus two special awards

MOVIES TO WIN THE MOST OSCARS

	Movie	Year	Nominations	Awards
1=	*Ben-Hur*	1959	12	11
=	*Titanic*	1997	14	11
3	*West Side Story*	1961	11	10
4=	*Gigi*	1958	9	9
=	*The Last Emperor*	1987	9	9
=	*The English Patient*	1996	12	9
7=	*Gone With the Wind*	1939	13	8*
=	*From Here to Eternity*	1953	13	8
=	*On the Waterfront*	1954	12	8
=	*My Fair Lady*	1964	12	8
=	*Cabaret*	1972	10	8
=	*Gandhi*	1982	11	8
=	*Amadeus*	1984	11	8

* *Plus two special awards*

Nine other movies have won seven Oscars each: *Going My Way* (1944), *The Best Years of Our Lives* (1946), *The Bridge on the River Kwai* (1957), *Lawrence of Arabia* (1962), *Patton* (1970), *The Sting* (1973), *Out of Africa* (1985), *Dances with Wolves* (1991), and *Schindler's List* (1993), each of the last two movies being nominated for 12 Awards. *Titanic* (1997) matched the 14 nominations of *All About Eve* (1950), but outshone it by winning 11, compared with the latter's six.

GOLDEN IDOL
*Standing 13½-in
(34-cm) high,
the gold-plated
"Oscar" was
reputedly named
for his resemblance
to a film librarian's
Uncle Oscar.*

THE 10
"BEST PICTURE" OSCAR WINNERS OF THE 1940s

1940	*Rebecca*
1941	*How Green Was My Valley*
1942	*Mrs. Miniver*
1943	*Casablanca*
1944	*Going My Way*
1945	*The Lost Weekend*
1946	*The Best Years of Our Lives*
1947	*Gentleman's Agreement*
1948	*Hamlet*
1949	*All the King's Men*

Several of the "Best Picture" winners are now regarded as movie classics. Many critics number *Casablanca* among the greatest movies of all time. *Mrs. Miniver* (which won a total of six Oscars) and *The Best Years of Our Lives* (seven Oscars) were both directed by William Wyler and reflected the concerns of wartime and post-war life, respectively. *How Green Was My Valley* and *Going My Way* each won five Oscars. *Rebecca* and *Hamlet* both starred Laurence Olivier, who also directed the latter, winning not only the "Best Picture" award but also "Best Actor."

THE 10
"BEST PICTURE" OSCAR WINNERS OF THE 1950s

1950	*All About Eve*
1951	*An American in Paris*
1952	*The Greatest Show on Earth*
1953	*From Here to Eternity*
1954	*On the Waterfront*
1955	*Marty*
1956	*Around the World in 80 Days*
1957	*The Bridge on the River Kwai*
1958	*Gigi*
1959	*Ben-Hur*

The first "Best Picture" Oscar winning movie of the 1950s, *All about Eve*, received the most nominations (14), while the last, *Ben-Hur*, won the most (11).

THE 10
"BEST PICTURE" OSCAR WINNERS OF THE 1980s

1980	*Ordinary People*
1981	*Chariots of Fire*
1982	*Gandhi*
1983	*Terms of Endearment*
1984	*Amadeus*
1985	*Out of Africa*
1986	*Platoon*
1987	*The Last Emperor*
1988	*Rain Man*
1989	*Driving Miss Daisy*

The winners of "Best Picture" Oscars during the 1990s are: 1990 *Dances With Wolves*; 1991 *The Silence of the Lambs* – which also won Oscars for "Best Director," "Best Actor," "Best Actress," and "Best Screenplay"; 1992 *Unforgiven*; 1993 *Schindler's List* – which won a total of seven Awards; 1994 *Forrest Gump*, which also won Oscars in a total of five other categories; 1995 *Braveheart*; 1996 *The English Patient*; and 1997 *Titanic*.

THE 10
"BEST PICTURE" OSCAR WINNERS OF THE 1960s

1960	*The Apartment*
1961	*West Side Story*
1962	*Lawrence of Arabia*
1963	*Tom Jones*
1964	*My Fair Lady*
1965	*The Sound of Music*
1966	*A Man for All Seasons*
1967	*In the Heat of the Night*
1968	*Oliver!*
1969	*Midnight Cowboy*

The Apartment (1960) was the last black-and-white movie to receive a "Best Picture" Oscar until Steven Spielberg's *Schindler's List* in 1993, which won seven Oscars.

THE 10
"BEST PICTURE" OSCAR WINNERS OF THE 1970s

1970	*Patton*
1971	*The French Connection*
1972	*The Godfather*
1973	*The Sting*
1974	*The Godfather, Part II*
1975	*One Flew over the Cuckoo's Nest* *
1976	*Rocky*
1977	*Annie Hall*
1978	*The Deer Hunter*
1979	*Kramer vs. Kramer*

* *Winner of Oscars for "Best Director,"
"Best Actor," "Best Actress," and
"Best Screenplay"*

OSCAR WINNERS – STARS

TOP 10

"BEST ACTOR IN A SUPPORTING ROLE" OSCAR WINNERS OF THE 1980s

Year	Actor	Movie
1980	Timothy Hutton	Ordinary People
1981	John Gielgud	Arthur
1982	Louis Gossett, Jr.	An Officer and a Gentleman
1983	Jack Nicholson	Terms of Endearment
1984	Haing S. Ngor	The Killing Fields
1985	Don Ameche	Cocoon
1986	Michael Caine	Hannah and Her Sisters
1987	Sean Connery	The Untouchables
1988	Kevin Kline	A Fish Called Wanda
1989	Denzel Washington	Glory

TOP 10

"BEST ACTRESS IN A SUPPORTING ROLE" OSCAR WINNERS OF THE 1980s

Year	Actress	Movie
1980	Mary Steenburgen	Melvin and Howard
1981	Maureen Stapleton	Reds
1982	Jessica Lange	Tootsie
1983	Linda Hunt	The Year of Living Dangerously
1984	Peggy Ashcroft	A Passage to India
1985	Anjelica Huston	Prizzi's Honor
1986	Dianne Wiest	Hannah and Her Sisters
1987	Olympia Dukakis	Moonstruck
1988	Geena Davis	The Accidental Tourist
1989	Brenda Fricker	My Left Foot

The same movie has received three nominations for "Best Supporting Actress" only once – Diane Cilento, Dame Edith Evans, and Joyce Redman for *Tom Jones.*

TOP 10 "BEST ACTOR" OSCAR WINNERS OF THE 1980s
(Movie/year)
❶ Robert De Niro (*Raging Bull*, 1980)
❷ Henry Fonda (*On Golden Pond*, 1981)
❸ Ben Kingsley (*Gandhi**, 1982) ❹ Robert Duvall (*Tender Mercies*, 1983) ❺ F. Murray Abraham (*Amadeus**, 1984) ❻ William Hurt (*Kiss of the Spider Woman*, 1985) ❼ Paul Newman (*The Color of Money*, 1986) ❽ Michael Douglas (*Wall Street*, 1987) ❾ Dustin Hoffman (*Rain Man**, 1988) ❿ Daniel Day-Lewis (*My Left Foot*, 1989)
* *Academy Award for "Best Picture"*

RAIN MAN
Dustin Hoffman researched autism for a year before his Oscar-winning performance as Raymond Babbitt in Rain Man.

TOP 10

YOUNGEST OSCAR WINNERS

	Actor/actress	Award/movie (where specified)	Award year	Age*
1	Shirley Temple	Special Award – outstanding contribution during 1934	1934	6
2	Margaret O'Brien	Special Award (*Meet Me in St. Louis*, etc.)	1944	8
3	Vincent Winter	Special Award (*The Little Kidnappers*)	1954	8
4	Ivan Jandl	Special Award (*The Search*)	1948	9
5	Jon Whiteley	Special Award (*The Little Kidnappers*)	1954	10
6	Tatum O'Neal	Best Supporting Actress (*Paper Moon*)	1973	10
7	Anna Paquin	Best Supporting Actress (*The Piano*)	1993	11
8	Claude Jarman Jr.	Special Award (*The Yearling*)	1946	12
9	Bobby Driscoll	Special Award (*The Window*)	1949	13
10	Hayley Mills	Special Award (*Pollyanna*)	1960	13

* *At the time of the Award ceremony, those of apparently identical age have been ranked according to their precise age in days at the time of the ceremony.*

TOP 10

"BEST ACTOR" OSCAR WINNERS OF THE 1930s

Year	Actor	Movie	Year	Actor	Movie
1930	George Arliss	Disraeli	1935	Victor McLaglen	The Informer
1931	Lionel Barrymore	A Free Soul	1936	Paul Muni	The Story of Louis Pasteur
1932	Wallace Beery	The Champ	1937	Spencer Tracy	Captains Courageous
1933	Charles Laughton	The Private Life of Henry VIII	1938	Spencer Tracy	Boys' Town
1934	Clark Gable	It Happened One Night	1939	Robert Donat	Goodbye, Mr. Chips

TOP 10
OLDEST OSCAR-WINNING ACTORS

	Actor/actress	Award/movie	Year	Age*
1	Jessica Tandy	"Best Actress" (*Driving Miss Daisy*)	1989	80
2	George Burns	"Best Supporting Actor" (*The Sunshine Boys*)	1975	80
3	Melvyn Douglas	"Best Supporting Actor" (*Being There*)	1979	79
4	John Gielgud	"Best Supporting Actor" (*Arthur*)	1981	77
5	Don Ameche	"Best Supporting Actor" (*Cocoon*)	1985	77
6	Peggy Ashcroft	"Best Supporting Actress" (*A Passage to India*)	1984	77
7	Henry Fonda	"Best Actor" (*On Golden Pond*)	1981	76
8	Katharine Hepburn	"Best Actress" (*On Golden Pond*)	1981	74
9	Edmund Gwenn	"Best Supporting Actor" (*Miracle on 34th Street*)	1947	72
10	Ruth Gordon	"Best Supporting Actress" (*Rosemary's Baby*)	1968	72

* At the time of the Award ceremony, those of apparently identical age have been ranked according to their precise age in days at the time of the ceremony.

Among those senior citizens who received nominations but did not win Oscars is Ralph Richardson, who was nominated as "Best Supporting Actor" for his role in *Greystoke: The Legend of Tarzan* (1984) at the age of 82. Eva Le Gallienne was the same age when she was nominated as "Best Supporting Actress" for her part in *Resurrection* (1980). Outside the four acting categories, the oldest director to be nominated for a "Best Director" Oscar was John Huston, 79 at the time of his nomination for *Prizzi's Honor* (1985), and the oldest winner was George Cukor for *My Fair Lady* (1964), when he was 65.

TOP 10 "BEST ACTRESS" OSCAR WINNERS OF THE 1980s
(Movie/year)

❶ Sissy Spacek (*Coal Miner's Daughter*, 1980) ❷ Katharine Hepburn (*On Golden Pond*, 1981) ❸ Meryl Streep (*Sophie's Choice*, 1982) ❹ Shirley MacLaine (*Terms of Endearment**, 1983) ❺ Sally Field (*Places in the Heart*, 1984) ❻ Geraldine Page (*The Trip to Bountiful*, 1985) ❼ Marlee Matlin (*Children of a Lesser God*, 1986) ❽ Cher (*Moonstruck*, 1987) ❾ Jodie Foster (*The Accused*, 1988) ❿ Jessica Tandy (*Driving Miss Daisy**, 1989)
* Academy Award for "Best Picture"

TOP 10
"BEST ACTRESS" OSCAR WINNERS OF THE 1930s

Year	Actress	Movie
1930	Norma Shearer	*The Divorcee*
1931	Marie Dressler	*Min and Bill*
1932	Helen Hayes	*The Sin of Madelon Claudet*
1933	Katharine Hepburn	*Morning Glory*
1934	Claudette Colbert	*It Happened One Night**#
1935	Bette Davis	*Dangerous*
1936	Luise Rainer	*The Great Ziegfeld**
1937	Luise Rainer	*The Good Earth*
1938	Bette Davis	*Jezebel*
1939	Vivien Leigh	*Gone With the Wind**

* *Academy Award for "Best Picture"*

\# *Academy Award for "Best Director," "Best Actor," and "Best Screenplay."*

PLAYING MISS DAISY
Jessica Tandy was aged 80 years 9 months when she won an Oscar for Driving Miss Daisy.

AND THE WINNER IS . . .

THE 10

LATEST GOLDEN GLOBE AWARDS FOR "BEST MOTION PICTURE – MUSICAL OR COMEDY"

Year	Movie
1997	As Good As It Gets
1996	Evita
1995	Babe
1994	The Lion King
1993	Mrs. Doubtfire
1992	The Player
1991	Beauty and the Beast
1990	Green Card
1989	Driving Miss Daisy
1988	Working Girl

THE 10

LATEST GOLDEN GLOBE AWARDS FOR "BEST MOTION PICTURE – DRAMA"

Year	Movie
1997	Titanic
1996	The English Patient
1995	Sense and Sensibility
1994	Forrest Gump
1993	Schindler's List
1992	Scent of a Woman
1991	Bugsy
1990	Dances with Wolves
1989	Born on the Fourth of July
1988	Rain Man

THE 10

FIRST GOLDEN GLOBE AWARDS FOR "BEST PICTURE"

Year	Movie
1943	The Song of Bernadette
1944	Going My Way*
1945	The Lost Weekend*
1946	The Best Years of Our Lives*
1947	Gentleman's Agreement*
1948	Treasure of Sierra Madre and Johnny Belinda#
1949	All the King's Men*
1950	Sunset Boulevard
1951	A Place in the Sun
1952	The Greatest Show on Earth*

* Also won "Best Picture" Academy Award

\# Joint winners

The Golden Globe Awards are presented annually by the Hollywood Foreign Press Association, a group of US journalists who report on the entertainment industry. Although the Golden Globe categories differ in some respects from those of the Academy Awards ("Oscars"), they are often seen as a prediction of the Oscars.

- The Cannes Film Festival was conceived in 1938 by two French journalists – as they traveled by train to the Venice Film Festival.

- Before a "Best Film" category was established, the Disney cartoon *Dumbo* was among the movies honored at Cannes.

- No awards were presented at the 1968 Cannes Festival, which was disrupted by student protests.

SNAP FACTS

THE 10

LATEST GOLDEN GLOBE AWARDS FOR "BEST PERFORMANCE BY AN ACTOR IN A MOTION PICTURE – DRAMA"

Year	Actor/movie
1997	Peter Fonda in Ulee's Gold
1996	Geoffrey Rush in Shine
1995	Nicolas Cage in Leaving Las Vegas
1994	Tom Hanks in Forrest Gump
1993	Tom Hanks in Philadelphia
1992	Al Pacino in Scent of a Woman
1991	Nick Nolte in The Prince of Tides
1990	Jeremy Irons in Reversal of Fortune
1989	Tom Cruise in Born on the Fourth of July
1988	Dustin Hoffman in Rain Man

THE 10

LATEST GOLDEN GLOBE AWARDS FOR "BEST PERFORMANCE BY AN ACTRESS IN A MOTION PICTURE – DRAMA"

Year	Actress/movie
1997	Judi Dench in Mrs. Brown
1996	Brenda Blethyn in Secrets and Lies
1995	Sharon Stone in Casino
1994	Jessica Lange in Blue Sky
1993	Holly Hunter in The Piano
1992	Emma Thompson in Howard's End
1991	Jodie Foster in The Silence of the Lambs
1990	Kathy Bates in Misery
1989	Michele Pfeiffer in The Fabulous Baker Boys
1988*	Jodie Foster in The Accused and Shirley MacLaine in Madame Sousatzka

* Prize shared

THE 10

LATEST GOLDEN GLOBE AWARDS FOR "BEST PERFORMANCE BY AN ACTOR IN A MOTION PICTURE – MUSICAL OR COMEDY"

Year	Actor/movie
1997	Jack Nicholson in *As Good as it Gets*
1996	Tom Cruise in *Jerry Maguire*
1995	John Travolta in *Get Shorty*
1994	Hugh Grant in *Four Weddings and a Funeral*
1993	Robin Williams in *Mrs. Doubtfire*
1992	Tim Robbins in *The Player*
1991	Robin Williams in *The Fisher King*
1990	Gerard Depardieu in *Green Card*
1989	Morgan Freeman in *Driving Miss Daisy*
1988	Tom Hanks in *Big*

While the similarity of identity between the Golden Globes and Oscars is notable among the drama awards and those movies' leading actors and actresses, the "Musical or Comedy" awards tend to be presented to movies that have received popular and commercial success, but seldom also receive the critical accolade of an Academy Award. During the past 10 years, more than half the Golden Globe awards in this category went to the stars of movies that earned in excess of $100,000,000 apiece.

THE 10

LATEST GOLDEN GLOBE AWARDS FOR "BEST PERFORMANCE BY AN ACTRESS IN A MOTION PICTURE – MUSICAL OR COMEDY"

Year	Actress/movie
1997	Helen Hunt in *As Good as it Gets*
1996	Madonna in *Evita*
1995	Nicole Kidman in *To Die For*
1994	Jamie Lee Curtis in *True Lies*
1993	Angela Bassett in *What's Love Got To Do With It*
1992	Miranda Richardson in *Enchanted April*
1991	Bette Midler in *For the Boys*
1990	Julia Roberts in *Pretty Woman*
1989	Jessica Tandy in *Driving Miss Daisy*
1988	Melanie Griffith in *Working Girl*

Although romantic comedies feature predominantly among the winners, a number of the successful actresses in this category received their awards for roles in movies that are either traditional musicals or have a high musical content.

THE 10

FIRST RECIPIENTS OF THE AMERICAN FILM INSTITUTE LIFETIME ACHIEVEMENT AWARDS

Year	Recipient	Year	Recipient
1973	John Ford	1978	Henry Fonda
1974	James Cagney	1979	Alfred Hitchcock
1975	Orson Welles	1980	James Stewart
1976	William Wyler	1981	Fred Astaire
1977	Bette Davis	1982	Frank Capra

This award is bestowed on individuals whose "talent has in a fundamental way advanced the film art; whose accomplishment has been acknowledged by scholars, critics, professional peers, and the general public; and whose work has withstood the test of time."

THE 10

LATEST RECIPIENTS OF THE AMERICAN FILM INSTITUTE LIFETIME ACHIEVEMENT AWARDS

Year	Recipient	Year	Recipient
1998	Robert Wise	1993	Elizabeth Taylor
1997	Martin Scorsese	1992	Sidney Poitier
1996	Clint Eastwood	1991	Kirk Douglas
1995	Steven Spielberg	1990	David Lean
1994	Jack Nicholson	1989	Gregory Peck

THE 10

FIRST WINNERS OF THE CANNES BEST FILM AWARDS

Year	Director/movie	Country of origin
1949	Carol Reed, *The Third Man*	UK
1951*	Vittoria De Sica, *Miracle in Milan*	Italy
	and Alf Sjoberg, *Miss Julie*	Sweden
1952*	Orson Welles, *Othello*	Morocco
	and Renato Castellani, *Two Cents Worth of Hope*	Italy
1953	Henri-Georges Clouzot, *Wages of Fear*	France
1954	Teinosuke Kinugasa, *Gates of Hell*	Japan
1955	Delbert Mann, *Marty*	US
1956	Louis Malle and Jacques-Yves Cousteau, *World of Silence*	France
1957	William Wyler, *Friendly Persuasion*	US
1958	Mikhail Kalatozov, *The Cranes Are Flying*	USSR
1959	Marcel Camus, *Orfeu Negro*	France

* *Prize shared*

MOVIE STARS – ACTORS

T O P 1 0

CLINT EASTWOOD MOVIES

1	In the Line of Fire	1993
2	The Bridges of Madison County	1995
3	Unforgiven*	1992
4	A Perfect World	1993
5	Every Which Way But Loose	1978
6	Absolute Power	1997
7	Any Which Way You Can	1980
8	Sudden Impact	1983
9	The Enforcer	1976
10	Firefox	1982

* Academy Award for "Best Director"

T O P 1 0

ROBERT DE NIRO MOVIES

1	Heat	1995
2	The Untouchables	1987
3	Cape Fear	1991
4	Sleepers	1996
5	Backdraft	1991
6	The Godfather, Part II*	1974
7	Casino	1995
8	Mary Shelley's Frankenstein	1994
9	Awakenings	1990
10	Goodfellas	1990

* Academy Award for "Best Supporting Actor"

T O P 1 0

JOHN TRAVOLTA MOVIES

1	Grease	1978
2	Look Who's Talking	1989
3	Saturday Night Fever*	1977
4	Face/Off	1997
5	Pulp Fiction	1994
6	Phenomenon	1996
7	Broken Arrow	1996
8	Staying Alive	1983
9	Get Shorty	1995
10	Michael	1996

* Academy Award for "Best Actor"

TOP 10 MEL GIBSON MOVIES

❶ *Lethal Weapon 3* (1992) ❷ *Ransom* (1996) ❸ *Lethal Weapon 2* (1989) ❹ *Braveheart** (1995) ❺ *Maverick* (1994) ❻ *Conspiracy Theory* (1887) ❼ *Forever Young* (1992) ❽ *Bird on a Wire* (1990) ❾ *Lethal Weapon* (1987) ❿ *Tequila Sunrise* (1988)

* Academy Award for "Best Director" and "Best Picture"

T O P 1 0

HARRISON FORD MOVIES

1	Star Wars	1977
2	Indiana Jones and the Last Crusade	1989
3	Return of the Jedi	1983
4	Raiders of the Lost Ark	1981
5	The Empire Strikes Back	1980
6	The Fugitive	1993
7	Indiana Jones and the Temple of Doom	1984
8	Air Force One	1997
9	Presumed Innocent	1990
10	Clear and Present Danger	1994

Uniquely in Hollywood history, every single one of Harrison Ford's Top 10 films has earned more than $200,000,000 at the world box office – in fact, the cumulative earnings of his Top 10 films alone is in excess of $3.5 billion.

T O P 1 0

TOM CRUISE MOVIES

1	Mission: Impossible	1996
2	Rain Man	1988
3	Top Gun	1986
4	Jerry Maguire	1996
5	The Firm	1993
6	A Few Good Men	1992
7	Interview with the Vampire	1994
8	Days of Thunder	1990
9	Cocktail	1988
10	Born on the Fourth of July	1989

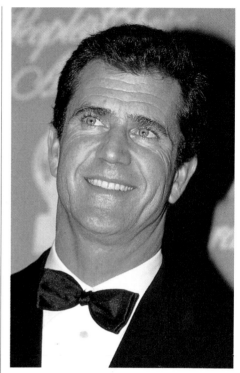

MEL GIBSON

T O P 1 0

DANNY DEVITO MOVIES

1	Batman Returns	1992
2	Get Shorty	1995
3	Romancing the Stone	1984
4	One Flew Over the Cuckoo's Nest	1975
5	Twins	1988
6	Terms of Endearment	1983
7	Mars Attacks!	1996
8	Junior	1994
9	The War of the Roses*	1989
10	Ruthless People	1986

* Also director

Danny DeVito had a relatively minor role in *One Flew Over the Cuckoo's Nest*. If this is discounted from the reckoning, his 10th most successful movie becomes *L.A. Confidential* (1997). He provided the voices of Whiskers in *Last Action Hero* (1993), Rocks in *Look Who's Talking Now* (1993), and Swackhammer in *Space Jam* (1996), and directed, appeared in, and narrated *Matilda* (1996), which just fails to make his personal Top 10.

MOVIE STARS – ACTORS

TOP 10

TOM HANKS MOVIES

1	*Forrest Gump**	1994
2	*Apollo 13*	1995
3	*Sleepless in Seattle*	1993
4	*Philadelphia**	1993
5	*Big*	1988
6	*A League of Their Own*	1992
7	*Turner & Hooch*	1989
8	*Splash!*	1984
9	*Dragnet*	1987
10	*Joe Versus the Volcano*	1990

* Academy Award for "Best Actor"

TOP 10

SYLVESTER STALLONE MOVIES

1	*Rambo: First Blood Part Two*	1985
2	*Cliffhanger*	1993
3	*The Specialist*	1994
4	*Daylight*	1996
5	*Rocky IV*	1985
6	*Rocky III*	1982
7	*Rocky*	1976
8	*Judge Dredd*	1995
9	*Daylight*	1996
10	*Assassins*	1995

TOP 10

ARNOLD SCHWARZENEGGER MOVIES

1	*Terminator 2: Judgment Day*	1991
2	*True Lies*	1994
3	*Total Recall*	1990
4	*Eraser*	1996
5	*Twins*	1988
6	*Kindergarten Cop*	1990
7	*Jingle All the Way*	1996
8	*Last Action Hero*	1993
9	*Junior*	1994
10	*The Terminator*	1984

TOP 10

ROBIN WILLIAMS MOVIES

1	*Mrs. Doubtfire*	1993	6	*Good Will Hunting**	1997
2	*Hook*	1991	7	*Nine Months*	1995
3	*Jumanji*	1995	8	*Good Morning, Vietnam*	1987
4	*Dead Poets Society*	1989	9	*Jack*	1996
5	*The Birdcage*	1996	10	*Flubber*	1997

* Academy Award for "Best Supporting Actor"

Robin Williams' voice appears as that of the genie in the 1992 animated blockbuster *Aladdin*. If this were included, its earnings would easily place it at the head of the list. His voice also appears in *Ferngully: The Last Rainforest* (1992).

TOP 10

JIM CARREY MOVIES

1	*Batman Forever*	1995
2	*The Mask*	1994
3	*Liar Liar*	1997
4	*Dumb & Dumber*	1994
5	*Ace Ventura: When Nature Calls*	1995
6	*The Cable Guy*	1996
7	*Ace Ventura: Pet Detective*	1994
8	*Peggy Sue Got Married*	1986
9	*The Dead Pool*	1988
10	*Pink Cadillac*	1989

TOP 10

GENE HACKMAN MOVIES

1	*The Firm*	1993
2	*The Birdcage*	1996
3	*Unforgiven**	1992
4	*Crimson Tide*	1995
5	*Superman*	1978
6	*Get Shorty*	1995
7	*Superman II*	1980
8	*The Poseidon Adventure*	1972
9	*Young Frankenstein*	1974
10	*Absolute Power*	1997

* Academy Award for "Best Supporting Actor"

TOP 10

BRUCE WILLIS MOVIES

1	*Die Hard: With a Vengeance*	1995
2	*The Fifth Element*	1997
3	*Die Hard 2*	1990
4	*Pulp Fiction*	1994
5	*Twelve Monkeys*	1995
6	*Death Becomes Her*	1992
7	*Die Hard*	1988
8	*The Jackal*	1997
9	*The Last Boy Scout*	1991
10	*Last Man Standing*	1996

TOP 10

JACK NICHOLSON MOVIES

1	*Batman*	1989
2	*A Few Good Men*	1992
3	*As Good As It Gets*#	1997
4	*Terms of Endearment**	1983
5	*Wolf*	1994
6	*One Flew Over the Cuckoo's Nest*#	1975
7	*Mars Attacks!*	1996
8	*The Witches of Eastwick*	1987
9	*The Shining*	1980
10	*Broadcast News*	1987

* Academy Award for "Best Supporting Actor"
 # Academy Award for "Best Actor"

MOVIE STARS – ACTRESSES

TOP 10

NICOLE KIDMAN MOVIES

1	*Batman Forever*	1995
2	*Days of Thunder*	1990
3	*The Peacemaker*	1997
4	*Far and Away*	1992
5	*Malice*	1993
6	*My Life*	1993
7	*To Die For*	1995
8	*Billy Bathgate*	1991
9	*Dead Calm*	1989
10	*Portrait of a Lady*	1996

TOP 10 WHOOPI GOLDBERG MOVIES

❶ *Ghost** (1990) ❷ *Sister Act* (1992)
❸ *The Color Purple* (1985) ❹ *Star Trek: Generations* (1994) ❺ *Made in America* (1993) ❻ *In & Out* (1997) ❼ *Sister Act 2: Back in the Habit* (1993) ❽ *The Little Rascals* (1994) ❾ *Eddie* (1996) ❿ *Soapdish* (1991)
Academy Award for "Best Supporting Actress"

WHOOPI GOLDBERG

TOP 10

SHARON STONE MOVIES

1	*Basic Instinct*	1992
2	*Total Recall*	1990
3	*The Specialist*	1995
4	*Last Action Hero*	1993
5	*Sliver*	1993
6	*Casino**	1995
7	*Diabolique*	1996
8	*Police Academy 4: Citizens on Patrol*	1987
9	*Intersection*	1994
10	*Action Jackson*	1988

* *Academy Award for "Best Actress"*

Sharon Stone's part in *Last Action Hero* amounted to no more than a brief cameo. If discounted, *Above the Law* (1988) would occupy 10th place.

TOP 10

BETTE MIDLER MOVIES

1	*The First Wives Club*	1996
2	*Get Shorty*	1995
3	*Ruthless People*	1986
4	*Down and Out in Beverly Hills*	1986
5	*Beaches**	1988
6	*Outrageous Fortune*	1987
7	*The Rose*	1979
8	*Big Business*	1988
9	*Hocus Pocus*	1993
10	*Hawaii*	1966

* *Also producer*

Bette Midler's role in *Get Shorty* is no more than a cameo, and that in *Hawaii*, her first movie part, is as an extra. If excluded, *Stella* (1990) and *For the Boys* (1991), which she also produced and for which she received an Academy Award nomination for "Best Actress," would join the list. Her voice appears as that of the character Georgette in the animated movie *Oliver and Company* (1988). If included, based on its earnings, it would be in third position.

TOP 10

JULIA ROBERTS MOVIES

1	*Pretty Woman*	1990
2	*My Best Friend's Wedding*	1997
3	*The Pelican Brief*	1993
4	*Sleeping with the Enemy*	1991
5	*Conspiracy Theory*	1997
6	*Hook*	1991
7	*Steel Magnolias*	1989
8	*Flatliners*	1990
9	*Something to Talk About*	1995
10	*Everyone Says I Love You*	1996

Julia Roberts also appeared in a cameo role as herself in *The Player* (1992), which, along with *Dying Young* (1991), *I Love Trouble* (1994), and *Michael Collins* (1996), just fail to make her personal Top 10.

TOP 10

DEMI MOORE MOVIES

1	*Ghost*	1990
2	*Indecent Proposal*	1993
3	*A Few Good Men*	1992
4	*Disclosure*	1995
5	*Striptease*	1996
6	*G.I. Jane*	1997
7	*The Juror*	1996
8	*About Last Night*	1986
9	*St. Elmo's Fire*	1985
10	*Young Doctors in Love*	1982

Demi Moore provided the voice of Esmeralda in the animated movie *The Hunchback of Notre Dame* (1996). If included in her Top 10, it would be in second place. Although uncredited, her voice also appears in *Beavis and Butt-head Do America* (1996).

T O P   1 0

EMMA THOMPSON MOVIES

1=	*Sense and Sensibility**	1995
=	*Junior*	1994
3	*Dead Again*	1991
4	*Howards End*#	1992
5	*In the Name of the Father*	1993
6	*The Remains of the Day*	1993
7	*Much Ado About Nothing*	1993
8	*Henry V*	1989
9=	*Impromptu*	1991
=	*Peter's Friends*	1992

* *Academy Award for "Best Adapted Screenplay"*

Academy Award for "Best Actress"

SIGOURNEY WEAVER

TOP 10 SIGOURNEY WEAVER MOVIES

❶ *Ghostbusters* (1984) ❷ *Ghostbusters II* (1989) ❸ *Aliens* (1986) ❹ *Alien* (1979) ❺ *Working Girl* (1988) ❻ *Dave* (1993) ❼= *Alien: Resurrection* (1997), *Alien³* (1992) ❾ *Copycat* (1995) ❿ *Gorillas in the Mist* (1988)

T O P   1 0

GOLDIE HAWN MOVIES

1	*The First Wives Club*	1996
2	*Death Becomes Her*	1992
3	*Bird on a Wire*	1990
4	*Private Benjamin*	1980
5	*Housesitter*	1992
6	*Foul Play*	1978
7	*Shampoo*	1975
8	*Seems Like Old Times*	1980
9	*Best Friends*	1982
10	*Everyone Says I Love You*	1996

T O P   1 0

GLENN CLOSE MOVIES

1	*Fatal Attraction*	1987
2	*101 Dalmatians*	1996
3	*Hook*	1991
4	*Air Force One*	1997
5	*Mars Attacks!*	1996
6	*The Big Chill*	1983
7	*The Natural*	1984
8	*The Paper*	1994
9	*Dangerous Liaisons*	1988
10	*The World According to Garp*	1982

Glenn Close appeared as herself in *In & Out* (1997), and provided the voice for Andie McDowell who played the female lead in *Greystoke: The Legend of Tarzan, Lord of the Apes* (1984), both of which would merit places in her personal Top 10 movies.

T O P   1 0

JODIE FOSTER MOVIES

1	*The Silence of the Lambs**	1990
2	*Maverick*	1994
3	*Sommersby*	1993
4	*Nell*	1994
5	*The Accused**	1988
6	*Taxi Driver*	1976
7	*Freaky Friday*	1976
8	*Little Man Tate*	1991
9	*Home for the Holidays*#	1995
10	*Alice Doesn't Live Here Any More*	1975

* *Academy Award for "Best Actress"*

Directed only

MERYL STREEP MOVIES

1	*The Bridges of Madison County*	1995
2	*Kramer vs. Kramer**	1979
3	*Out of Africa*	1985
4	*Death Becomes Her*	1992
5	*The Deer Hunter*	1978
6	*Manhattan*	1979
7	*Postcards from the Edge*	1990
8	*Silkwood*	1983
9	*Sophie's Choice*#	1982
10	*Julia*	1982

* *Academy Award for "Best Supporting Actress"*

Academy Award for "Best Actress"

It is perhaps surprising that *Sophie's Choice*, the movie for which Meryl Streep won an Oscar, scores so far down this list, while one of her most celebrated movies, *The French Lieutenant's Woman* (1981), does not make her personal Top 10 at all.

SNAP FACTS

- In 1915, Mary Pickford, the most prolific actress of all time (in the period 1908–42 she made at least 238 movies), was one of the first to be identified as a major box-office draw.

- Surveys of the most commercially important actresses during the past 65 years place Doris Day as the all-time leader.

- During the 1990s, Julia Roberts has been the most consistently nominated actress in audience appeal listings, followed by such stars as Sandra Bullock, Demi Moore, Jodie Foster, and Whoopi Goldberg.

THE STUDIOS

TOP 10

UNITED ARTISTS MOVIES OF ALL TIME*

1	*Moonraker*	1979
2	*The Spy Who Loved Me*	1977
3	*Thunderball*	1965
4	*Live and Let Die*	1973
5	*Goldfinger*	1964
6	*Rocky*	1976
7	*Diamonds Are Forever*	1971
8	*One Flew Over the Cuckoo's Nest*	1975
9	*You Only Live Twice*	1967
10	*The Man with the Golden Gun*	1974

* *Excluding movies made since MGM takeover*

United Artists was formed in 1919 by actors, including Charlie Chaplin and Douglas Fairbanks, and director D. W. Griffith to provide an independent means of producing and distributing their movies. It never actually owned a studio, but rented production facilities. After many vicissitudes, and a successful run in the 1970s with the consistently successful James Bond movies, it merged with MGM in 1981.

TOP 10

PARAMOUNT MOVIES OF ALL TIME

1	*Titanic*	1997
2	*Forrest Gump*	1994
3	*Terminator 2: Judgment Day*	1991
4	*Ghost*	1990
5	*Indiana Jones and the Last Crusade*	1989
6	*Mission: Impossible*	1996
7	*Raiders of the Lost Ark*	1981
8	*Top Gun*	1986
9	*Grease*	1978
10	*Indiana Jones and the Temple of Doom*	1984

Paramount owes its origins in 1912 to Adolph Zukor's Famous Players Film Company. Following a series of company mergers and name changes in the 1920s, Paramount Pictures eventually emerged and became one of the most commercially successful Hollywood studios. With stars such as the Marx Brothers, Mae West, and Bing Crosby and Bob Hope, and directors including Cecil B. De Mille, Paramount entered a golden age in the 1930s and 1940s.

TOP 10

WALT DISNEY/BUENA VISTA MOVIES OF ALL TIME

1	*The Lion King*	1994
2	*Aladdin*	1992
3	*Pretty Woman*	1990
4	*Toy Story*	1995
5	*Beauty and the Beast*	1991
6	*Who Framed Roger Rabbit?*	1988
7	*Pocahontas*	1995
8	*The Rock*	1996
9	*The Hunchback of Notre Dame*	1996
10	*101 Dalmatians*	1996

In 1923, having started his business in Kansas City, Walt Disney moved to California where he experienced modest success with his animated movies until the advent of sound made a notable commercial success of *Steamboat Willie* (1928), Mickey Mouse's first starring vehicle. Distribution deals with major studios enabled the Disney Studio to capitalize on such blockbusters as *Snow White and the Seven Dwarfs* (1937), which became the second highest-earning movie of the 1940s.

TOP 10

MGM MOVIES OF ALL TIME

1	*Rain Man*	1988
2	*GoldenEye*	1995
3	*Tomorrow Never Dies*	1997
4	*Rocky IV*	1985
5	*Stargate*	1994
6	*Gone With the Wind*	1939
7	*The Birdcage*	1996
8	*Rocky III*	1982
9	*Poltergeist*	1982
10	*Get Shorty*	1995

Founded in 1924, Metro Goldwyn Mayer's pre-eminence was firmly established in the 1930s and 1940s with the success of movies such as *The Wizard of Oz* (1939) and contracts with numerous notable stars including Greta Garbo, Joan Crawford, Spencer Tracy, and Clark Gable.

STUDIO TOUR
Previously inaccessible to the movie-going public, Universal's decision to open its studios to organized tours has made them one of the world's foremost tourist attractions.

WARNER BROS MOVIES
OF ALL TIME

1	*Twister*	1996
2	*Batman*	1989
3	*The Bodyguard*	1992
4	*Robin Hood: Prince of Thieves*	1991
5	*The Fugitive*	1993
6	*Batman Forever*	1995
7	*Lethal Weapon 3*	1992
8	*Batman Returns*	1992
9	*Eraser*	1996
10	*Batman and Robin*	1997

20TH CENTURY FOX MOVIES
OF ALL TIME

1	*Independence Day*	1996
2	*Star Wars*	1977
3	*The Empire Strikes Back*	1980
4	*Home Alone*	1990
5	*Return of the Jedi*	1983
6	*Mrs. Doubtfire*	1993
7	*True Lies*	1994
8	*Die Hard: With a Vengeance*	1995
9	*Speed*	1994
10	*Home Alone 2: Lost in New York*	1992

COLUMBIA/TRI-STAR/SONY
MOVIES OF ALL TIME

1	*Men in Black*	1997
2	*Terminator 2: Judgment Day*	1991
3	*Basic Instinct*	1992
4	*Hook*	1991
5	*Close Encounters of the Third Kind*	1977/80
6	*Look Who's Talking*	1989
7	*Air Force One*	1997
8	*Ghostbusters*	1984
9	*Jerry Maguire*	1997
10	*The Fifth Element*	1997

It was the coming of sound that launched the newly formed Warner Brothers into its important place in movie history, with *The Jazz Singer* (1927) its best-known early sound production. In the 1970s, following a series of takeovers, Warner Bros. embarked on an era of notable success that began with *The Exorcist* in 1973 and continued with a number of movies starring Clint Eastwood.

William Fox founded a movie production company in 1912. With the coming of sound he pioneered its use, especially through the medium of Fox Movietone newsreels. The company was merged with 20th Century Pictures in 1935, and under the control of Darryl F. Zanuck and Joseph M. Schenck achieved some of its greatest successes in the 1940s.

Founded in 1924 by Harry Cohn and his brother Jack, Columbia's first major success came in 1934 with Frank Capra's *It Happened One Night*. In the 1950s Columbia's award-winning and successful movies included *The Bridge on the River Kwai* (1957), *On the Waterfront* (1954), and *From Here to Eternity* (1953).

MCA/UNIVERSAL MOVIES
OF ALL TIME

1	*Jurassic Park*	1993
2	*E.T.: the Extra-Terrestrial*	1982
3	*The Lost World: Jurassic Park*	1997
4	*Jaws*	1975
5	*The Flintstones*	1994
6	*Back to the Future*	1985
7	*Apollo 13*	1995
8	*Schindler's List*	1993
9	*Liar Liar*	1997
10	*Casper*	1995

SNAP FACTS

- William Fox, the colorful founder of 20th Century Fox, was forced to sell out to a syndicate of bankers in 1930. He later went bankrupt and served time in a Pennsylvania penitentiary for bribing a judge.

- Jack L. Warner, the most powerful of the four Warner Brothers, began his career singing to entertain the audience during intermissions in the family nickledeon in Newcastle, Pennsylvania.

- In the first Disney sound animation, *Steamboat Willie* (1928), Walt Disney himself recorded the squeaky voice of Mickey Mouse.

Universal Pictures was founded in 1912 by Carl Laemmle, who soon developed it into the world's largest movie studio. However, despite a handful of worthy and successful productions such as *All Quiet on the Western Front* (1930), Universal went through a financially precarious period in the 1930s. In 1962 it was sold to MCA, which developed its strengths as a TV production company and inaugurated the organized studio tours.

OUT-TAKES

MOVIE-GOING COUNTRIES

	Country	Annual attendance per inhabitant
1	Lebanon	35.3
2	China	12.3
3	Georgia	5.6
4	India	5.0
5	Iceland	4.5
6=	Australia	3.9
=	New Zealand	3.9
=	US	3.9
9	Monaco	3.7
10	Canada	2.8

It is not the country with the most movie theaters or the highest total number of visits to the movies per year that records the highest rate of movie-going per person, since the inhabitants of Lebanon record an annual average of more that 35 visits a year. This compares with an average of just 3.9 visits a year in the US.

Source: UNESCO

MOVIE-PRODUCING COUNTRIES

	Country	Average no. of films produced per annum (1991–96)
1	India	851
2	US	569
3	Japan	252
4	Russia	192
5	France	143
6	China	137
7	Italy	107
8	South Korea	80
9	Turkey	71
10	UK	65

Source: Screen Digest

YEARS WITH THE MOST THEATER VISITS IN THE US, 1946–97

	Year	No. of movies released	Admissions
1	1946	400	4,067,300,000
2	1947	426	3,664,400,000
3	1948	444	3,422,700,000
4	1949	490	3,168,500,000
5	1950	483	3,017,500,000
6	1951	433	2,840,100,000
7	1952	389	2,777,700,000
8	1953	404	2,630,600,000
9	1954	369	2,270,400,000
10	1955	319	2,072,300,000

From 1956, admissions continued to decline until 1963, when there was a slight increase. In 1971, the totals reached an all time low of 820,300,000. Since 1991, admissions have increased each year, reaching 1,387,700,000 in 1997.

Source: Motion Picture Association of America, Inc.

MOVIE GIANT
India's insatiable demand for movies has resulted in its movie output outstripping even that of Hollywood.

MOVIE-VIEWING COUNTRIES

	Country	Total annual attendance
1	China	14,428,400,000
2	India	4,297,500,000
3	US	981,900,000
4	Russia	140,100,000
5	Japan	130,700,000
6	France	130,100,000
7	Germany	124,500,000
8	UK	114,600,000
9	Lebanon	99,200,000
10	Australia	69,000,000

Source: UNESCO

MOVIES WITH THE MOST EXTRAS

	Movie/country/year	Extras
1	*Gandhi,* UK, 1982	300,000
2	*Kolberg,* Germany, 1945	187,000
3	*Monster Wang-magwi,* South Korea, 1967	157,000
4	*War and Peace,* USSR, 1967	120,000
5	*Ilya Muromets,* USSR, 1956	106,000
6	*Tonko,* Japan, 1988	100,000
7	*The War of Independence,* Romania, 1912	80,000
8	*Around the World in 80 Days,* US, 1956	68,894
9=	*Intolerance,* US, 1916	60,000
=	*Dny Zrady,* Czechoslovakia, 1972	60,000

RUBY SLIPPERS FROM *THE WIZARD OF OZ*

TOP 10

LONGEST MOVIES EVER SCREENED

	Title	Country	Year	Duration hrs	mins
1	*The Longest and Most Meaningless Movie in the World*	UK	1970	48	0
2	*The Burning of the Red Lotus Temple*	China	1928–31	27	0
3	****	US	1967	25	0
4	*Heimat*	West Germany	1984	15	40
5	*Berlin Alexanderplatz*	West Germany/Italy	1980	15	21
6	*The Journey*	Sweden	1987	14	33
7	*The Old Testament*	Italy	1922	13	0
8	*Comment Yukong déplace les montagnes*	France	1976	12	43
9	*Out 1: Noli me Tangere*	France	1971	12	40
10	*Ningen No Joken (The Human Condition)*	Japan	1958–60	9	29

TOP 10

MOST EXPENSIVE ITEMS OF MOVIE MEMORABILIA EVER SOLD AT AUCTION

	Item/sale	Price ($)*
1	Clark Gable's Oscar for *It Happened One Night*, Christie's, Los Angeles, December 15, 1996	607,500
2	Vivien Leigh's Oscar for *Gone with the Wind*, Sotheby's, New York, December 15, 1993	562,500
3	Poster for *The Mummy*, 1932, Sotheby's, New York, March 1, 1997	453,500
4	James Bond's Aston Martin DB5 from *Goldfinger*, Sotheby's, New York, June 28, 1986	275,000
5	Clark Gable's personal script for *Gone with the Wind*, Christie's, Los Angeles, December 15, 1996	244,500
6	"Rosebud" sled from *Citizen Kane*, Christie's, Los Angeles, December 15, 1996	233,500
7	Herman J. Mankiewicz's scripts for *Citizen Kane* and *The American*, Christie's, New York, June 21, 1989	231,000
8	Judy Garland's ruby slippers from *The Wizard of Oz*, Christie's, New York, June 21, 1988	165,000
9	Piano from the Paris scene in *Casablanca*, Sotheby's, New York, December 16, 1988	154,000
10	Charlie Chaplin's hat and cane, Christie's, London, December 11, 1987 (resold at Christie's, London, December 17, 1993, for $86,900)	130,350

* $/£ conversion at rate then prevailing

TOP 10

COUNTRIES WITH THE MOST MOVIE SCREENS PER MILLION

	Country	Movie screens per million
1	Belarus	414.9
2	Ukraine	295.0
3	Sweden	137.8
4	US	105.9
5	Latvia	101.7
6	Uzbekistan	99.0
7	Norway	91.5
8	Iceland	86.3
9	France	80.0
10	Czech Republic	79.3

TOP 10

COUNTRIES WITH THE MOST MOVIE THEATERS

	Country	No. of theaters
1	US	23,662
2	Ukraine	14,960
3	India	8,975
4	China	4,639
5	France	4,365
6	Italy	3,816
7	Germany	3,814
8	Belarus	3,780
9	Uzbekistan	2,365
10	Spain	2,090

Source: UNESCO

ON THE RADIO

GOING FOR A SPIN
The universal appeal of popular music of all types means that radio stations that play it dominate the world's airwaves.

TOP 10

NPR AUDIOCASSETTES

1	*Father Cares: The Last of Jonestown*	**6**	*Cape Cod: The Grand Tour*
2	*Kim Williams: A Missoula Sampler*	**7**	*Brain Trauma*
3	*Ross Perot at the National Press Club*	**8**	*Computers and Education*
4	*John Ciardi: Speaking of Words*	**9**	*Hiroshima Bomb: A Historical Perspective*
5	*Ghetto Life 101*	**10**	*Anne Frank Commemorative*

Although precise figures are unavailable, these are believed to be NPR's bestselling audio cassettes since the early 1970s.

Source: National Public Radio

TOP 10

RADIO-OWNING COUNTRIES

	Country	Radios per 1,000 population
1	US	2,093
2	UK	1,433
3	Australia	1,304
4	Canada	1,053
5	Denmark	1,034
6	South Korea	1,024
7	Monaco	1,019
8	Finland	1,008
9	New Zealand	997
10	Germany	944

The top eight countries in this list have at least one radio per person. In addition, many small island communities in the world have very high numbers of radios for their small populations, to enable them to maintain regular contact with the outside world. In Bermuda there are 1,285 per 1,000 population (or 1.3 per person), in Gibraltar 1,300 per 1,000 population, and in Guam there are 1,407 radios per 1,000 population. The world record, however, is still held by the US, with over two radios per inhabitant.

Source: UNESCO

TOP 10

RADIO FORMATS IN THE US

	Format	Percentage share*
1	News/talk	16.5
2	Adult Contemporary	14.4
3	Country	10.3
4	Top 40	8.2
5	Urban	7.7
6	Album Rock	6.8
7	Spanish	6.2
8	Oldies	5.9
9	Classic Rock	4.7
10	Modern Rock	4.2

* *Of all radio listening during an average week, 6 am to midnight, fall 1996, for listeners age 12 and over*

TOP 10

LONGEST-RUNNING PROGRAMS ON NATIONAL PUBLIC RADIO

	Program	First broadcast
1	*All Things Considered*	1971
2	*Weekend All Things Considered*	1974
3	*Fresh Air with Terry Gross*	1977
4	*Piano Jazz with Marian McPartland*	1978
5	*Morning Edition*	1979
6	*Weekend Edition/ Saturday with Scott Simon*	1985
7	*Performance Today*	1987
8	*Weekend Edition/ Sunday with Liane Hansen*	1987
9	*Car Talk*	1987
10	*Talk of the Nation*	1991

Source: National Public Radio

TOP 10
US RADIO STATIONS WITH THE GREATEST AUDIENCE SHARE

	Station	City	Format	Percentage share
1	WJIZ-FM	Albany, GA	Black Hits	30.3
2	KMON-FM	Great Falls, MT	Country	26.4
3	WZWW-FM	State College, PA	Adult Contemporary	26.0
4	WFRY-FM	Watertown, NY	Country	25.9
5	KJMZ-FM	Lawton, OK	Black Hits	25.8
6	KEAN-FM	Abilene, TX	Country	24.9
7	WXBQ-FM	Johnson City-Kingsport,TN-VA	Country	24.6
8	WIVK-FM	Knoxville, TN	Country	24.2
9	KCTR-FM	Billings, MT	Country	24.1
10	WTHI-FM	Terre Haute, IN	Country	23.8

Source: Duncan's American Radio, spring 1997 Arbitron data

TOP 10
MOST LISTENED-TO RADIO STATIONS IN THE US

	Station	City	Format	AQH*
1	WQHT-FM	New York	Top 40/Urban	167,400
2	WLTW-FM	New York	Soft Adult /Contemporary	161,300
3	WCBS-FM	New York	Oldies	127,000
4	WKTU-FM	New York	Urban Hits	126,800
5	KLVE-FM	Los Angeles	Hispanic Adult Contemporary	124,500
6	WSKQ-FM	New York	Hispanic Hits	114,500
7	WRKS-FM	New York	Black Adult Contemporary	110,300
8	WXRK-FM	New York	Howard Stern/New Rock	105,800
9	WOR	New York	Talk	102,700
10	KFI	Los Angeles	Talk	99,200

* Average Quarter Hour statistic based on number of listeners age 12 and over, listening between Monday and Sunday 6:00 am to midnight, from spring 1997 Arbitron data

Source: Duncan's American Radio

TOP 10
GEORGE FOSTER PEABODY AWARDS FOR BROADCASTING WON BY NATIONAL PUBLIC RADIO*

Year	Program
1996	*Remorse: The 14 Stories of Eric Morse*
1995	*Wynton Marsalis: Making The Music/Marsalis On Music*
1994	*Tobacco Stories* and *Wade in the Water: African American Sacred Music Traditions* (NPR/Smithsonian Institution)
1993	*Health Reform Coverage 1993*
1992	*Prisoners in Bosnia*
1991	*The Coverage of the Judge Clarence Thomas Confirmation*
1990	*Manicu's Story: The War in Mozambique*
1989	*Scott Simon's Radio Essays on Weekend Edition Saturday*
1988	*Cowboys on Everest*
1983	*The Sunday Show* and *Taylor Made Piano: A Jazz History*

* Includes only programs made or co-produced by NPR

Source: Peabody Awards

TOP 10
STATES WITH THE MOST NATIONAL PUBLIC RADIO MEMBER STATIONS

	State	NPR stations
1	New York	39
2	California	34
3	Ohio	26
4	Wisconsin	24
5	Michigan	22
6	Alaska	20
7	Texas	18
8	Florida	17
9	Colorado	16
10=	Illinois	15
=	Minnesota	15
=	North Carolina	15

Source: National Public Radio

TOP TELEVISION

TELEVISION
In the second half of the 20th century, TV has evolved as the dominant worldwide medium.

T O P   1 0
BASIC CABLE CHANNELS IN THE US

	Channel	Subscribers*
1	C-SPAN	71,100,000
2	The Discovery Channel	69,354,000
3	TNN	68,960,000
4	USA Network	68,205,000
5	ESPN	67,036,000
6	Nickelodeon	66,769,000
7	TNT	66,474,000
8	A&E	64,600,000
9	MTV	64,180,000
10	Lifetime	62,657,000

With 60,100,000 subscribers, CNN, which was rated number two the previous year, has dropped out of the Top 10, mainly due to the emergence of CNBC, which has 61,227,000 subscribers.

Source: Cablevision

TOP 10 TALK SHOWS OF THE 1996–97 SEASON
(Rating)

❶ *Oprah Winfrey Show* (8.2) ❷ *Montel Williams Show* (4.4) ❸ *Live with Regis and Kathie Lee* (4.2) ❹= *Jenny Jones Show* (4.1), *Sally Jessy Raphael* (4.1) ❻ *Maury Povich Show* (3.9) ❼ *Ricki Lake* (3.6) ❽ *Siskel and Ebert* (3.0) ❾ *Jerry Springer* (2.8) ❿ *Leeza* (2.4)
Source: Nielsen Media Research

T O P   1 0
MOST WATCHED SYNDICATED SHOWS OF 1997

	Program	Rating		Program	Rating
1	*Wheel of Fortune*	11.8	**6**	*National Geographic on Assignment*	7.6
2=	*Home Improvement*	9.7	**7**	*Buena Vista I*	7.4
=	*Jeopardy*	9.7	**8**	*ESPN NFL Regular Season*	6.6
4	*Oprah Winfrey Show*	8.2	**9**	*The Simpsons*	6.5
5	*Seinfeld*	7.8	**10**	*Entertainment Tonight*	6.2

Source: Nielsen Media Research

T O P   1 0
TV AUDIENCES OF ALL TIME IN THE US

	Program	Date	Households total	Viewing percentage
1	*M*A*S*H* Special	Feb 28, 1983	50,150,000	60.2
2	*Dallas*	Nov 21, 1980	41,470,000	53.3
3	*Roots* Part 8	Jan 30, 1977	36,380,000	51.1
4	Super Bowl XVI	Jan 24, 1982	40,020,000	49.1
5	Super Bowl XVII	Jan 30, 1983	40,480,000	48.6
6	XVII Winter Olympics	Feb 23, 1994	45,690,000	48.5
7	Super Bowl XX	Jan 26, 1986	41,490,000	48.3
8	*Gone With the Wind* Pt.1	Nov 7, 1976	33,960,000	47.7
9	*Gone With the Wind* Pt.2	Nov 8, 1976	33,750,000	47.4
10	Super Bowl XII	Jan 15, 1978	34,410,000	47.2

As more and more households acquire television sets (there are currently 94,000,000 "TV households" in the US), the most recently screened programs naturally tend to be watched by larger audiences, which distorts the historical picture. By listing the Top 10 according to percentage of households viewing, we get a clearer picture of who watches what.

T O P   1 0
MOST WATCHED COMEDY/VARIETY SHOWS OF ALL TIME

	Program	Air date	Rating
1	*M*A*S*H* Special	Feb 28, 1983	60.2
2	*Bob Hope Christmas Show*	Jan 15, 1970	46.6
3	*Cheers*	May 20, 1993	45.5
4	*Ed Sullivan*	Feb 9, 1964	45.3
5	*Bob Hope Christmas Show*	Jan 14, 1971	45.0
6	*The Beverly Hillbillies*	Jan 8, 1964	44.0
7	*Ed Sullivan*	Feb 16, 1964	43.8
8	*Academy Awards*	Apr 7, 1970	43.4
9	*The Beverly Hillbillies*	Jan 15, 1964	42.8
10	*The Beverly Hillbillies*	Feb 26, 1964	42.4

Source: Nielsen Media Research

T O P   1 0

TV-WATCHING COUNTRIES IN THE WORLD

	Country	Average daily viewing time (minutes)
1	US	239
2 =	Italy	216
=	Turkey	216
4	UK	215
5	Spain	214
6	Hungary	213
7	Japan	205
8	Greece	202
9	Canada	192
10	Argentina	191

Source: Screen Digest/Eurodata TV

T H E   1 0

FIRST COUNTRIES TO HAVE TELEVISION*

	Country	Year
1	UK	1936
2	US	1939
3	USSR	1939
4	France	1948
5	Brazil	1950
6	Cuba	1950
7	Mexico	1950
8	Argentina	1951
9	Denmark	1951
10	Netherlands	1951

* *High-definition regular public broadcasting service*

T O P   1 0

TV-OWNING COUNTRIES IN THE WORLD

	Country	TVs in use
1	China	250,000,000
2	US	215,000,000
3	Japan	85,500,000
4	Russia	56,000,000
5	India	47,000,000
6	Germany	46,000,000
7	Brazil	35,000,000
8	France	34,250,000
9	UK	26,000,000
10	Italy	25,500,000

Source: UNESCO

T O P   1 0

MOST WATCHED PROGRAMS ON PBS TELEVISION*

	Program	Date	Average audience
1	The Civil War	Sep 1990	8.8
2	Life On Earth	Jan 1982	7.9
3	The Living Planet: A Portrait of the Earth	Feb 1985	7.8
4	The American Experience: The Kennedys	Sep 1992	7.0
5	Nature: Kingdom of the Ice Bear	Feb 1986	6.9
6	Cosmos	Sep 1980	6.5
7 =	Planet Earth	Jan 1986	6.3
=	Lewis and Clark: The Journey of the Corps of Discovery	Nov 1997	6.3
9	Baseball	Sep 1994	5.5
10	The Dinosaurs!	Nov 1992	5.3

* *As of April 1998*

Source: PBS Research Department

T O P   1 0

DAYTIME SOAP OPERAS IN THE US, 1996–97

	Program	Rating			Program	Rating
1	The Young and the Restless	7.2		6	As the World Turns	4.5
2	Days of Our Lives	5.9		7	One Life to Live	4.1
3	The Bold and the Beautiful	5.1		8	Guiding Light	3.8
4	General Hospital	4.8		9	Another World	3.2
5	All My Children	4.7		10	Sunset Beach	1.8

Source: Nielsen Media Research

T H E N   &   N O W

TOP 10 MOST WATCHED TV PROGRAMS

1987 Program	Rating		Rating	1997 Program
Bill Cosby Show	32.3	1	21.2	E.R.
A Different World	28.5	2	20.5	Seinfeld
Cheers	26.4	3	17.0	Suddenly Susan
Night Court	25.3	4	16.8	Friends
Growing Pains	24.3	5	16.8	The Naked Truth
60 Minutes	23.1	6	16.5	Fired Up
Who's the Boss?	22.8	7	16.2	NFL Monday Night Football
Murder, She Wrote	22.0	8	14.1	The Single Guy
Golden Girls	21.5	9	14.0	Home Improvement
L.A. Law	20.0	10	13.6	Touched By An Angel

Source: Nielsen Media Research

TOP VIDEO

THEN & NOW

TOP 10 COUNTRIES WITH THE MOST VIDEO RECORDERS

1987 Country	VCRs		1997 VCRs	Country
US	52,565,000	**1**	86,825,000	US
Japan	22,771,000	**2**	40,000,000	China
UK	11,830,000	**3**	34,309,000	Japan
Germany	11,531,000	**4**	26,328,000	Germany
France	6,935,000	**5**	18,848,000	UK
Canada	5,926,000	**6**	15,488,000	Brazil
Australia	3,787,000	**7**	15,483,000	France
Spain	3,619,000	**8**	13,161,000	Italy
Brazil	3,200,000	**9**	10,315,000	Russia
Italy	2,843,000	**10**	8,540,000	Mexico

Source: Screen Digest

- The terms "video recording" and "videotape" were first used in the early 1950s – but only among TV professionals.
- The first domestic videocassette recorders were sold in 1974, but the cost of both machines and tapes was prohibitively expensive.
- The VHS (Video Home System) was launched in 1976 in the US and 1978 in Europe.
- The abbreviation VCR (VideoCassette Recorder) was first used in the UK and US in 1971.
- By 1980, there were an estimated 7,687,000 homes with video recorders; by 1996, the global figure was put at 400,976,000 – a more than 50-fold increase.

SNAP FACTS

TOP 10

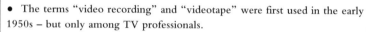
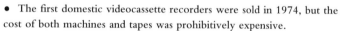

MOVIE RENTALS ON VIDEO, 1997

	Movie	Label	1997 Release	Video earnings ($)*
1	Liar Liar	Universal	Sep 30	47,270,000
2	Jerry Maguire	Columbia TriStar	May 29	44,080,000
3	Jungle 2 Jungle	Buena Vista/Disney	Jul 29	41,060,000
4	Ransom	Buena Vista/Touchstone	May 13	40,490,000
5	Michael	Warner	Jun 10	39,300,000
6	Scream	Buena Vista/Dimension	Jun 24	37,900,000
7	Courage Under Fire	Fox Video	Mar 4	35,550,000
8	101 Dalmatians	Buena Vista/Disney	Apr 15	34,700,000
9	Kingpin	MGM	Jan 7	34,100,000
10	Sleepers	Warner	Apr 1	33,570,000

* Spent by US consumers renting the title during its first four months of release
Source: Video Store magazine

TOP 10

BEST-SELLING SPORTS VIDEOS OF 1997 IN THE US

	Video	Sport
1	NFL Super Bowl 31	Football
2	Stanley Cup Championship 1997	Hockey
3	NBA Championship Finals 1997	Basketball
4	Michael Jordan	Basketball
5	Hockey All Time Allstars	Hockey
6	NBA at 50	Basketball
7	1997 World Series	Baseball
8	Son, Hero, and Champion: Tiger Woods	Golf
9	101 Sport Bloopers	Various
10	Highlights of the 1997 Masters	Golf

Source: Videoscan, Inc.

TOP 10

VIDEO RENTAL CATEGORIES IN THE US, 1997

	Genre	Annual revenue ($)
1	Comedy	689,100,000
2	Action	445,900,000
3	Drama	432,400,000
4	Family	229,400,000
5	Suspense	208,000,000
6	Romance	130,400,000
7	Horror	105,600,000
8	Thriller	92,100,000
9	Science fiction	54,100,000
10	Animated	51,100,000

Source: Video Store magazine

T O P 1 0

COUNTRIES WITH THE MOST VIDEO RENTAL OUTLETS

	Country	Estimated number of rental outlets
1	US	27,944
2	Pakistan	25,000
3	China	20,000
4	South Korea	19,000
5	Romania	15,000
6=	Bulgaria	10,000
=	India	10,000
=	Japan	10,000
=	Poland	10,000
10	Brazil	9,710

Source: Screen Digest

T O P 1 0

DVD SALES IN THE US, 1997

	Title	Label
1	Twister	WHV
2	Goldeneye	MGM
3	Batman and Robin	WHV
4	Eraser	WHV
5	Blade Runner (Director's Cut)	WHV
6	The Fugitive	WHV
7	The Rock	Disney
8	Terminator 2	Live
9	Total Recall	Live
10	Stargate	Live

Source: Videoscan, Inc.

T O P 1 0

MOVIE SALES ON VIDEO, 1997

	Film	Label
1	Men In Black	Columbia
2	Bambi	Disney
3	Space Jam	Warner
4	101 Dalmatians	Disney
5	The Hunchback of Notre Dame	Disney
6	Jurassic Park: The Lost World	Universal
7	Sleeping Beauty	Disney
8	Star Wars Trilogy	Fox Video
9	Jerry Maguire	Columbia
10	Enchanted Christmas	Disney

Source: Videoscan, Inc.

T O P 1 0

BEST-SELLING MUSIC VIDEOS OF ALL TIME IN THE US*

	Title	Artist
1	Hangin' Tough Live	New Kids On The Block
2	Hangin' Tough	New Kids On The Block
3	Step by Step	New Kids On The Block
4	Live Shit: Binge and Purge	Metallica
5	Moonwalker	Michael Jackson
6	Lord of the Dance	Michael Flatley
7	In Concert	Jose Carreras, Placido Domingo, Luciano Pavarotti
8	Live at the Acropolis	Yanni
9	Garth Brooks	Garth Brooks
10	Justify My Love	Madonna

* Excluding children's videos

In a diverse list, the three New Kids' titles are now joined by Metallica as the only music video releases to sell over 1,000,000 units each in the US.

Source: The Popular Music Database

T O P 1 0

COUNTRIES WITH THE MOST VIDEO RENTAL OUTLETS PER 1,000,000 POPULATION

	Country	Outlets per 1,000,000 pop.		Country	Outlets per 1,000,000 pop.
1	Bulgaria	1,186.5	6	Ireland	311.0
2	Iceland	697.1	7	Canada	267.2
3	Romania	663.5	8	Poland	258.8
4	South Korea	415.6	9	Sri Lanka	231.6
5	Denmark	323.9	10	Hungary	200.2
	US	*102.9*			

Source: Screen Digest

T O P 1 0

BEST-SELLING CHILDREN'S VIDEOS OF 1997 IN THE US

	Video	Label		Video	Label
1	Enchanted Christmas	Disney	6	Casper, a Spirited Beginning	Fox
2	Annabelle's Wish	Hallmark	7	The Land Before Time V	Universal
3	Pooh's Grand Adventure	Disney	8	Dr. Seuss: How the Grinch Stole Christmas	MGM
4	The Land Before Time IV: Journey	Universal	9	Barney's Colors/Shapes	Lyons
5	Honey, We Shrunk Ourselves	Disney	10	Rugrats: a Rugrat Vacation	Paramount

Source: Videoscan, Inc.

THE COMMERCIAL WORLD

TOP 10

CORPORATIONS IN THE US

	Corporation	Revenue $ (1997)
1	General Motors	178,174,000,000
2	Ford Motor Co.	153,627,000,000
3	Exxon Corporation	122,379,000,000
4	Wal-Mart Stores	119,299,000,000
5	General Electric	90,840,000,000
6	IBM	78,508,000,000
7	Chrysler	61,147,000,000
8	Mobil	59,978,000,000
9	Philip Morris	56,114,000,000
10	AT&T	53,261,000,000

Source: Fortune 500

TOP 10

TYPES OF JOBS IN THE US 100 YEARS AGO

	Job sector	Employees
1	Farmers and farm managers	5,763,000
2	Farm laborers and foremen	5,125,000
3	Operatives and kindred workers (miners, etc)	3,720,000
4	Laborers (except farm and mine)	3,620,000
5	Craftsmen and foremen	3,062,000
6	Private household workers	1,579,000
7	Salesworkers	1,307,000
8	Professional and technical workers	1,234,000
9	Service workers (except private household)	1,047,000
10	Clerical workers	877,000
	Total labor force	29,030,000

Source: US Bureau of the Census

SNAP FACT

The 1900 US Census provides a snapshot of the occupations of a century ago, enumerating professions that today have relatively few members, among them: 596,000 carpenters; 280,000 laundresses; 220,000 blacksmiths; 134,000 tailors; 102,000 shoemakers; 42,000 porters; 37,000 stonecutters; 25,000 millers; 8,000 bootblacks; 7,000 furriers.

TOP 10

ITEMS OF CONSUMER EXPENDITURE IN THE US

		Average per capita expenditure, 1995 ($)
1	Housing	10,458
2	Transportation	6,014
3	Food	4,505
4	Personal insurance and pensions	2,964
5	Utilities	2,191
6	Health care	1,732
7	Apparel and services	1,704
8	Entertainment	1,612
9	Household furnishings and equipment	1,401
10	Education	471
	Total (including items not in Top 10)	32,264

Source: US Bureau of Labor Statistics

TOP 10

DUTY-FREE SHOPS IN THE WORLD

1	London Heathrow Airport (UK)
2	Honolulu Airport (Hawaii)
3	Silja Ferries (Finland)
4	Hong Kong Airport (China)
5	Singapore Changi Airport (Singapore)
6	Amsterdam Schiphol Airport (Netherlands)
7	Paris Charles De Gaulle Airport (France)
8	Viking Line Ferries (Finland)
9	Frankfurt Airport (Germany)
10	Manila Airport (Philippines)

In 1996 total global duty- and tax-free sales were worth $21,000,000. Sales of several of those outlets featured in the Top 10 are confidential, but industry insiders have ranked them and place them in the range of more than $250,000,000 at the bottom of the list to over $500,000,000 at the top.

TOP 10

OCCUPATIONS IN THE US

	Job sector*	Employees#
1	Sales workers (retail and personal services)	6,747,000
2	Food service	5,967,000
3	Construction trades	5,568,000
4	Teachers (except college and university)	5,095,000
5	Mechanics and repairers	4,743,000
6	Sales supervisors and proprietors	4,635,000
7	Management-related	4,614,000
8	Motor vehicle operators	3,963,000
9	Secretaries, stenographers, and typists	3,627,000
10	Cleaning and building services	3,159,000
	US Total (including occupations not in Top 10):	130,150,000

* Excluding general and miscellaneous group categories

\# As of March 1998

Source: US Bureau of Labor Statistics

PORT TO PORT
Although service industries have become increasingly significant in recent years, the import and export of goods remain the driving forces of international trade.

TOP 10

COUNTRIES WITH THE MOST WORKERS

	Country	Labor force
1	China	709,000,000
2	India	398,000,000
3	US	133,000,000
4	Indonesia	89,000,000
5	Russia	77,000,000
6	Brazil	71,000,000
7	Japan	66,000,000
8	Bangladesh	60,000,000
9	Pakistan	46,000,000
10	Nigeria	44,000,000

As defined by the International Labor Organization, the "labor force" includes people between the ages of 15 and 64.

Source: World Bank

TOP 10

RETAILERS IN THE US

	Retailer	Sales $ (1997)
1	Wal-Mart Stores	119,299,000,000
2	Sears Roebuck and Co.	41,296,000,000
3	KMart Corp.	32,183,000,000
4	J.C. Penney Co., Inc.	30,546,000,000
5	Dayton Hudson	27,757,000,000
6	The Kroger Co.	26,567,300,000
7	Home Depot	24,146,000,000
8	Safeway Stores	22,483,800,000
9	Costco	21,874,000,000
10	American Stores Co.	19,138,900,000

Sears Roebuck, once No. 1 in this list, was established in Chicago in 1892, originally exclusively as a mail order company, by Richard Warren Sears, a former railroad worker turned watch salesman, and Alvah C. Roebuck, a watchmaker.

Source: Fortune 500

PATENTS & INVENTIONS

TOP 10

COUNTRIES THAT REGISTER THE MOST TRADEMARKS

	Country	Trademarks registered (1995)
1	Japan	144,911
2	China	91,866
3	US	85,557
4	Spain	69,642
5	France	60,712
6	Argentina	37,743
7	UK	33,400
8	Mexico	29,954
9	South Korea	29,807
10	Brazil	25,330

This list includes all trademarks (product names that are thereby legally protected) and service marks (which apply to company and other names applied to services rather than products) that were actually registered in 1995. More applications are filed than granted, since many are rejected, for being too similar to ones that already exist, for example.

Source: World Intellectual Property Organization

POLAROID CAMERA INVENTED BY EDWIN H. LAND

TOP 10

MOST PROLIFIC PATENTEES IN THE US

	Patentee	No. of patents*
1	Thomas A. Edison	1,093
2	Francis H. Richards	619
3	Edwin Herbert Land	533
4=	Marvin Camras	500
=	Jerome H. Lemelson	500
6	Elihu Thomson	444
7	Charles E. Scribner	374
8	Philo Taylor Farnsworth	300
9	Lee de Forest	300
10	Luther Childs Crowell	293

* Minimum number credited to each inventor

THE 10

FIRST TRADEMARKS ISSUED IN THE US

	Issued to	Product
1	Averill Chemical-Paint Company	Liquid paint
2	J. B. Baldy and Co	Mustard
3	Ellis Branson	Retail coal
4	Tracy Coit	Fish
5	William Lanfair Ellis and Co	Oyster packing
6	Evans, Clow, Dalzell and Co	Wrought-iron pipe
7	W. E. Garrett and Sons	Snuff
8	William G. Hamilton	Car wheel
9	John K. Hogg	Soap
10	Abraham P. Olzendam	Woolen hose

All of these trademarks were registered on the same day, October 25, 1870, and are distinguished in the ranking only by the trademark numbers assigned to them.

THE 10

FIRST PATENTS IN THE UK

	Patentee	Patent	Date
1	Nicholas Hillyard	Engraving and printing the king's head on documents	May 5, 1617
2	John Gason	Locks, mills, and other river and canal improvements	July 1, 1617
3	John Miller and John Jasper Wolfen	Oil for suits of armor	November 3, 1617
4	Robert Crumpe	Tunnels and pumps	January 9, 1618
5	Aaron Rathburne and Roger Burges	Making maps of English cities	March 11, 1618
6	John Gilbert	River dredger	July 16, 1618
7	Clement Dawbeney	Water-powered engine for making nails	December 11, 1618
8	Thomas Murray	Sword blades	January 11, 1619
9	Thomas Wildgoose and David Ramsey	Plows, pumps, and ship stabilizing devices	January 17, 1619
10	Abram Baker	Smalt (glass) manufacture	February 16, 1619

TOP 10

ORGANIZATIONS RECEIVING PATENTS IN THE US, 1994

	Issued to	No. of patents
1	IBM	1,298
2	US Government	1,251
3	Canon Kabushiki Kaisha	1,096
4	Hitachi Ltd	976
5=	General Electric Company	970
=	Mitsubishi Denki Kabushiki Kaisha	970
7	Toshiba Corporation	968
8	NEC Corporation	897
9	Eastman Kodak Company	888
10	Motorola, Inc.	837

The 1,298 patents received by IBM were the most ever granted to a nonfederal organization in one year and ensured that IBM overtook the US Government, which had topped the list the previous year.

TOP 10

COUNTRIES THAT REGISTER THE MOST PATENTS

	Country	Patents registered (1995)
1	Japan	101,676
2	US	101,419
3	Germany	56,633
4	France	55,681
5	UK	48,350
6	Italy	29,896
7	Russia	25,633
8	Netherlands	23,444
9	Sweden	20,816
10	Switzerland	20,345

EDISON LIGHT BULB
Thomas Alva Edison (1847–1931) is the most prolific inventor of all time. His filament light bulb dates from 1879.

THE 10

FIRST PATENTS IN THE US

	Patentee	Patent	Date
1	Samuel Hopkins	Making pot and pearl ash	July 31, 1790
2	Joseph S. Sampson	Candle making	August 6, 1790
3	Oliver Evans	Flour and meal making	December 18, 1790
4=	Francis Bailey	Punches for type	January 29, 1791
=	Aaron Putnam	Improvement in distilling	January 29, 1791
6	John Stone	Driving piles	March 10, 1791
7=	Samuel Mullikin	Threshing machine	March 11, 1791
=	Samuel Mullikin	Breaking hemp	March 11, 1791
=	Samuel Mullikin	Polishing marble	March 11, 1791
=	Samuel Mullikin	Raising nap on cloth	March 11, 1791

THE 10

FIRST WOMEN PATENTEES IN THE US

	Patentee	Patent	Date
1	Mary Kies	Straw weaving with silk or thread	May 5, 1809
2	Mary Brush	Corset	July 21, 1815
3	Sophia Usher	Carbonated liquid	September 11, 1819
4	Julia Planton	Foot stove	November 4, 1822
5	Lucy Burnap	Weaving grass hats	February 16, 1823
6	Diana H. Tuttle	Accelerating spinning-wheel heads	May 17, 1824
7	Catharine Elliot	Manufacturing moccasins	January 26, 1825
8	Phoebe Collier	Sawing wheel fellies (rims)	May 20, 1826
9	Elizabeth H. Buckley	Sheet-iron shovel	February 28, 1828
10	Henrietta Cooper	Whitening leghorn straw	November 12, 1828

PAPER CLIP PIONEER

Norwegian inventor Johan Vaaler devised the paper clip in 1899. Because Norway had no patent law in force at the time, he had to travel to Germany, where he patented the clip in 1900. His US Patent was granted the following year in 1901. Although there were some earlier claimants (such as that of Matthew Schooley, who applied for a paper clip patent in the US in 1896, and the "gem" clip, which is similar to the type still in use, and was being sold in 1899), today Vaaler is still widely considered to be the originator of the paper clip as we know it. To commemorate his achievement a giant paper clip measuring 23 ft/7 m and weighing 1,328 lb/602 kg was unveiled near Oslo in 1989.

100 YEARS AGO

COMMUNICATION MATTERS

MOST POPULAR COMMEMORATIVE STAMPS OF 1997

	Subject	No. of stamps saved
1	Bugs Bunny	45,300,000
2	Classic American Aircraft	35,600,000
3	World of Dinosaurs	35,300,000
4	Endangered Species	28,800,000
5	Classic American Dolls	24,400,000
6	Humphrey Bogart	18,100,000
7	Legendary Football Coaches	17,800,000
8	Songwriters	11,600,000
9	Lunar New Year	8,400,000
10	Pacific '97 – Franklin	6,550,000

Source: United States Postal Service

COUNTRIES WITH THE MOST POST OFFICES

	Country	Post offices*
1	India	280,181
2	China	113,622
3	Russia	44,669
4	US	38,212
5	Turkey	24,860
6	Japan	24,625
7	UK	19,128
8	France	17,069
9	Ukraine	16,421
10	Germany	16,172

* 1996 or latest year available

COUNTRIES WITH THE MOST TELEPHONES PER PERSON

	Country	Telephones per 100 inhabitants
1	Sweden	68.41
2	Switzerland	64.40
3	US	63.66
4	Denmark	62.03
5	Luxembourg	57.56
6	Norway	56.49
7	Iceland	56.46
8	France	55.91
9	Germany	55.76
10	Finland	55.75

Source: Siemens AG

FIRST COUNTRIES AND CITIES TO ISSUE POSTAGE STAMPS

	Country/city	Stamps issued
1	Great Britain	1840
2	New York City	1842
3	Zurich, Switzerland	1843
4	Brazil	1843
5	Geneva, Switzerland	1843

	Country/city	Stamps issued
6	Basle, Switzerland	1845
7	US	1847
8	Mauritius	1847
9	Bermuda	1848
10	France	1849

TOP 10 COUNTRIES WITH THE HIGHEST RATIO OF WIRELESS MOBILE PHONE USERS

(Subscribers per 1,000)

❶ Norway (296.1) ❷ Finland (292.4)
❸ Sweden (281.4) ❹ Denmark (248.6)
❺ Australia (245.5) ❻ US (161.9)
❼ Singapore (147.5) ❽ Japan (143.2)
❾ New Zealand (131.3)
❿ UK (122.5)
World (23.4)
Source: Siemens AG

MOBILE PHONE

COUNTRIES SENDING THE MOST LETTERS PER PERSON

	Country	Average*
1	Vatican	9,545
2	US	689
3	Liechtenstein	573
4	Norway	525
5	Sweden	503
6	Netherlands	420
7	France	416
8	Finland	379
9	Canada	360
10	Denmark	335

* Number of letters mailed per person in 1996, or latest year available

The remarkable anomaly of the Vatican, it may be surmised, is a statistical oddity resulting from the large numbers of official missives and tourist mail dispatched from the Holy See, and does not represent personal letter-writing on a massive scale by its small resident population – an average of 26 letters a day per inhabitant, all passing through the Holy See's 31 mailboxes.

TOP 10

COUNTRIES SENDING AND RECEIVING THE MOST LETTERS (INTERNATIONAL)

	Country	Items of mail handled per annum*
1	US	1,658,350,000
2	UK	1,343,230,603
3	Germany	1,060,000,000
4	France	847,932,677
5	Saudi Arabia	626,146,000
6	Belgium	446,502,826
7	Nigeria	444,874,000
8	Japan	413,745,000
9	Australia	412,205,582
10	Italy	347,299,000

* *1996 or latest year available*

Source: Universal Postal Union

COLLECTING THE MAIL
Domestic and international postal services have been developed during the past 150 years. Despite the recent burgeoning of alternative electronic methods, traditional or "snail mail" remains an important means of communication.

TOP 10

COUNTRIES SENDING AND RECEIVING THE MOST LETTERS (DOMESTIC)

	Country	Items of mail handled per annum*
1	US	182,660,700,000
2	Japan	24,971,279,000
3	France	23,913,644,000
4	UK	17,296,000,000
5	Germany	16,638,000,000
6	India	13,462,073,000
7	Canada	10,714,615,000
8	China	7,722,465,000
9	Italy	6,236,985,000
10	Russia	6,079,300,000

* *1996 or latest year available*

Source: Universal Postal Union

TOP 10

COUNTRIES WITH THE MOST INTERNET USERS

	Country	Percentage of population	Internet users*		Country	Percentage of population	Internet users*
1	US	23	62,000,000	6	Sweden	22	1,900,000
2	Japan	7	8,840,000	7	India	0.16	1,500,000
3	Canada	27	8,000,000	8	Norway	32	1,400,000
4	UK	10	6,000,000	9	Taiwan	6	1,260,000
5	Germany	7	5,800,000	10	Australia	7	1,210,000
					World total	1.9	112,750,000

* *Estimates from various surveys, March 1998*

TOP 10

OLDEST POST OFFICES IN THE US

	City/post office address	Opened
1	Galena, IL, 110 Green Street	Nov 1, 1858
2	Memphis, TN, 1 N. Front Street	June 1, 1887
3	Brooklyn, NY, 271 Cadman Plaza East	Feb 1, 1892
4	Hoboken, NJ, 89 River Street	Jan 1, 1893
5	Port Townsend, WA, 1322 Washington Street	June 1, 1893
6	Atchison, KS, 621 Kansas Avenue	June 1, 1894
7	Mankato, MN, 401 S. Second Street	June 1, 1895
8	Pueblo, CO, 421 N. Main Street	Jan 1, 1898
9	Omaha, NE, 4730 S. 24th Street	June 1, 1898
10	Carrollton, KY, 520 Highland Avenue	June 1, 1901

Source: United States Postal Service

THE BIRTH OF RADIO TELEGRAPHY

Guglielmo Marconi (1874–1937) began his studies of radio transmission in his native Italy in the early 1890s, but soon moved his operations to England, where he established the Wireless Telegraph Company. There, on March 27, 1899, he succeeded in transmitting the first international radio signals, from a station at South Foreland, Kent, to one at Wimereux, near Boulogne, France, about 32 miles/51 km away. By 1901 Marconi had developed his system to such an extent that on December 12 he was able to transmit the first transatlantic radio signal (the letter "S" in Morse code) from Poldhu, Cornwall, to St. Johns, Newfoundland.

YEARS AGO · 100 · YEARS AGO · YEARS AGO

FUEL & POWER

T O P 1 0

ENERGY CONSUMERS IN THE WORLD

	Country	Energy consumption 1996*					
		Oil	Gas	Coal	Nuclear	Hydro	Total
1	US	918.2	627.4	568.8	202.1	31.7	2,348.3
2	China	190.1	17.5	734.1	4.1	17.5	963.4
3	Russia	141.1	349.4	131.2	31.0	14.6	667.2
4	Japan	297.5	65.6	97.3	84.7	8.2	553.3
5	Germany	151.5	82.9	98.0	46.0	2.0	380.3
6	India	86.8	21.5	154.7	2.3	6.6	271.8
7	France	100.3	32.0	19.2	113.3	6.6	271.4
8	UK	92.3	84.5	49.5	27.0	0.3	253.6
9	Canada	87.6	73.2	25.5	26.3	33.4	246.0
10	South Korea	111.8	13.4	34.8	21.1	0.4	181.6
	World total	*3,651.7*	*2,173.3*	*2,487.9*	*685.0*	*240.4*	*9,238.4*

* *Millions of tons of oil equivalent*

Source: BP Statistical Review of World Energy 1997

T O P 1 0

OIL CONSUMERS IN THE WORLD

	Country	Consumption 1996 (tons)			Country	Consumption 1996 (tons)
1	US	918,200,000		6	South Korea	111,800,000
2	Japan	297,500,000		7	Italy	103,700,000
3	China	190,100,000		8	France	100,300,000
4	Germany	151,500,000		9	UK	91,600,000
5	Russia	141,100,000		10	Canada	84,300,000

Source: BP Statistical Review of World Energy 1997

ATOMIC WORDS

While we may think of nuclear energy as a modern concept, it is a century since the words "neutron" and "radium" first appeared in print. Neutron (related to the word "neutral") was first suggested as a name in a scientific paper, although applied to a different concept, since the existence of the particle that is now called a neutron was not discovered until 33 years later. Radium (from "radius," a ray) was described and named in *Chemical News* of January 6, 1899, after the research of the previous year by Pierre and Marie Curie first implied the existence of the element. They shared the Nobel Physics Prize in 1903 and in 1911 Marie Curie was awarded the Chemistry Prize for her discoveries of radium and polonium.

100 YEARS AGO • YEARS AGO • YEARS AGO

T O P 1 0

HYDROELECTRIC ENERGY CONSUMERS IN THE WORLD

	Country	Consumption 1996 (tons of oil equivalent)
1	Canada	33,400,000
2	US	31,700,000
3	Brazil	25,000,000
4	China	17,500,000
5	Russia	14,600,000
6	Norway	9,800,000
7	Japan	8,200,000
8 =	France	6,600,000
=	India	6,600,000
10	Venezuela	5,070,000
	World total	*240,400,000*

Tons of oil equivalent is the amount of oil that would be required to produce the same amount of energy. 1,000,000 tons of oil is equivalent to approximately 13,000,000,000 kilowatt hours of electricity.

Source: BP Statistical Review of World Energy 1997

T O P 1 0

NATURAL GAS CONSUMERS IN THE WORLD

	Country	Consumption 1996	
		billion m³	billion ft³
1	US	632.4	22,333.0
2	Russia	352.2	12,437.8
3	UK	85.2	3,008.8
4	Germany	83.6	2,952.3
5	Ukraine	78.2	2,761.6
6	Canada	73.7	2,602.7
7	Japan	66.1	2,334.3
8	Italy	52.1	1,839.9
9	Uzbekistan	44.4	1,568.0
10	Netherlands	41.7	1,472.6
	World total	*2,190.6*	*77,360.2*

Source: BP Statistical Review of World Energy 1997

NORTH SEA OIL
A high proportion of the oil consumed by Norway and the UK has been extracted by North Sea production platforms since 1972.

T O P 1 0

ELECTRICITY PRODUCERS IN THE WORLD

	Country	Production kW/hr
1	US	3,145,892,000,000
2	Russia	956,587,000,000
3	Japan	906,705,000,000
4	China	839,453,000,000
5	Canada	527,316,000,000
6	Germany	525,721,000,000
7	France	471,448,000,000
8	India	356,519,000,000
9	UK	323,029,000,000
10	Brazil	251,484,000,000

The Top 10 electricity-consuming countries are virtually synonymous with these producers, since relatively little electricity is transmitted across international borders. Electricity production has burgeoned phenomenally in the postwar era.

T O P 1 0

COUNTRIES WITH THE LARGEST CRUDE OIL RESERVES

	Country	Reserves (tons)		Country	Reserves (tons)
1	Saudi Arabia	39,463,000,000	6	Venezuela	10,251,000,000
2	Iraq	16,645,000,000	7	Mexico	7,716,000,000
3	Kuwait	14,661,000,000	8	Russia	7,385,000,000
4	United Arab Emirates	13,889,000,000	9	Libya	4,299,000,000
5	Iran	13,999,000,000	10	US	4,079,000,000
				World total	*155,316,000,000*

Source: BP Statistical Review of World Energy 1997

T O P 1 0

COUNTRIES PRODUCING THE MOST ELECTRICITY FROM NUCLEAR SOURCES

	Country	Nuclear power stations in operation	Nuclear percent of total	Output (megawatt-hours)
1	US	110	21.9	100,685
2	France	57	77.4	59,948
3	Japan	53	34.0	42,369
4	Germany	20	30.3	22,282
5	Russia	29	13.1	19,843
6	Canada	21	16.0	14,902
7	Ukraine	16	43.8	13,765
8	UK	35	26.0	12,928
9	Sweden	12	52.4	10,040
10	South Korea	11	35.8	9,120
	World total	*442*	*—*	*350,964*

Source: International Atomic Energy Agency

T O P 1 0

COAL CONSUMERS IN THE WORLD

	Country	Consumption 1997 (tons of oil equivalent)
1	China	734,100,000
2	US	568,800,000
3	India	154,700,000
4	Russia	131,200,000
5	Germany	98,999,000
6	Japan	97,300,000
7	South Africa	90,100,000
8	Poland	79,400,000
9	UK	49,500,000
10	Australia	47,300,000

Source: BP Statistical Review of World Energy 1997

SAVE THE PLANET

TOP 10

STATES WITH THE HIGHEST RECYCLING RATES

	State	Percentage of waste recycled
1	New Jersey	45
2=	Maine	40
=	Wisconsin	40
4=	Washington	39
=	New York	39
6	Florida	38
7	Arkansas	36
8	Vermont	35
9	Oregon	34
10	Massachusetts	33

Source: National Solid Waste Management Association

TOP 10

STATES WITH THE HIGHEST BUDGET FOR RECYCLING

	State	Budget 1996-97($)
1	Wisconsin	45,200,000
2	Florida	25,000,000
3	Minnesota	18–20,000,000
4	Illinois	12,200,000
5	South Carolina	5,500,000
6	Massachusetts	4,800,000
7	Indiana	4,400,000
8	Nebraska	4,000,000
9	Ohio	3,500,000
10	Hawaii	2,900,000

Source: National Solid Waste Management Association

TOP 10

ITEMS OF DOMESTIC GARBAGE IN THE US

	Item	Tons
1	Yard trimmings	29,750,000
2	Corrugated boxes	28,800,000
3	Food waste	14,000,000
4	Newspapers	13,100,000
5	Miscellaneous durables	12,000,000
6	Wood packaging	10,600,000
7	Furniture and furnishings	7,200,000
8	Other commercial printing	7,100,000
9	Office type papers	6,800,000
10	Paper folding cartons	5,300,000

Source: Environmental Protection Agency

TOP 10

ENVIRONMENTAL CONCERNS

	Issue	Percentage of people concerned
1=	Air pollution	49
=	Exhaust fumes from cars/trucks	49
3	Too much traffic	48
4	Pollution of rivers/streams/water	46
5	Pollution of seas/waste disposal at sea	44
6	Litter in streets/countryside	42
7	Pollution of beaches/coastline	41
8=	Nuclear waste	39
=	Toxic/chemical waste/toxic dumping	39
10	Destruction of rainforests/deforestation	36

MORI, the market research organization, carried out a survey in the UK of 1,874 adults in 1997, asking them which environment and conservation issues concerned them most. Pollution is clearly the Number 1 concern, including air pollution, rivers, sea, beaches, industrial pollution, and especially pollution caused by traffic. When considering the environment, most people think about issues close to home; global issues such as deforestation, global warming, and destruction of the ozone layer come much farther down the list.

Source: MORI

• The Fresh Kills Landfill site on Staten Island, New York, opened in 1948, is the world's largest. It covers 3,000 acres and receives up to 14,000 tons of garbage a day. It is scheduled to close by the year 2002.

Fresh Kills' closest rival is Puente Hills, Whittier, Los Angeles, which takes an average of 13,000 tons of LA's garbage every day.

HOUSEHOLD WASTE
Disposable packaging is increasingly designed to be fully recyclable.

TOP 10

CARBON DIOXIDE EMITTERS IN THE WORLD

	Country	CO_2 emissions (tons per head p.a.)
1	United Arab Emirates	33.93
2	US	21.41
3	Singapore	21.00
4	Norway	18.57
5	Australia	17.77
6	Canada	16.16
7	Saudi Arabia	15.34
8=	Kazakhstan	14.54
=	Trinidad and Tobago	14.54
10	Russia	13.33

CO_2 emissions derive from three principal sources – fossil fuel burning, cement manufacturing, and gas flaring. Since World War II, increasing industrialization in many countries has resulted in huge increases in carbon output, a trend that most countries are now actively attempting to reverse. The US remains the worst offender in total, with 5,683,727 tons of CO_2 released in 1995.

Source: Carbon Dioxide Information Analysis Center

TOP 10

SULFUR DIOXIDE EMITTERS IN THE WORLD

	Country	Annual SO_2 emissions per head		
		kg	lb	oz
1	Czech Republic	149.4	329	6
2	Former Yugoslavia	138.2	304	11
3	Bulgaria	116.8	257	8
4	Canada	104.0	229	4
5	Hungary	81.4	179	7
6=	Romania	79.2	174	10
=	US	79.2	174	10
8	Poland	71.1	156	12
9	Slovakia	70.0	154	5
10	Belarus	57.5	126	12

Source: World Resources Institute

TOP 10

DEFORESTING COUNTRIES IN THE WORLD

	Country	Average annual forest loss 1990-95 (sq miles)
1	Brazil	9,861
2	Indonesia	4,185
3	Dem. Rep. of Congo	2,857
4	Bolivia	2,243
5	Mexico	1,961
6	Venezuela	1,942
7	Malaysia	1,544
8	Myanmar	1,494
9	Sudan	1,363
10	Thailand	1,270

While Brazil tops the list of countries with the highest amount of forest loss, the actual rate of deforestation is only 0.5 percent per year. Other countries are losing a much higher proportion of their total forest cover as the following list shows:

	Country	Annual rate of forest loss (percent)
1	Lebanon	7.8
2	Jamaica	7.2
3	Afghanistan	6.8
4	Comoros	5.6
5	Philippines	3.5
6	Haiti	3.4
7	El Salvador	3.3
8=	Costa Rica	3.0
=	Sierra Leone	3.0
10	Pakistan	2.9

Source: Food and Agriculture Organization of the United Nations

THE BIRTH OF "BIOSPHERE"

In an issue of the journal *International Geography* published in 1899, Scottish geographer and meteorologist Hugh Robert Mill (1861–1950) introduced the word "biosphere." He divided the globe into four parts: the lithosphere (Earth), hydrosphere (oceans), atmosphere, and biosphere – defined as the portion that is occupied by living things – a narrow band of earth, sea, and sky in which life is possible. This concept has been developed by environmentalists, and the name was applied to the Biosphere, a structure erected in Arizona to conduct experiments in global warming and other environmental changes that may threaten life on Earth.

100 YEARS AGO • YEARS AGO • YEARS AGO •

THE WORLD'S RICHEST

TOP 10 HIGHEST-EARNING ACTORS IN THE WORLD

	1987 Actor	Income ($)		1997 Actor	Income ($)
1	William H. Cosby Jr.	57,000,000	1	Jerry Seinfeld	66,000,000
2	Eddie Murphy	27,000,000	2=	Harrison Ford	47,000,000
3	Sylvester Stallone	21,000,000	=	Tim Allen	47,000,000
4	Arnold Schwarzenegger	18,000,000	4	Mel Gibson	42,000,000
5=	Tom Selleck	11,000,000	5	John Travolta	39,000,000
=	Jack Nicholson	11,000,000	6	Roseanne	34,000,000
7=	Paul Hogan	10,000,000	7	Eddie Murphy	24,000,000
=	Steve Martin	10,000,000	8	Robin Williams	23,000,000
9	Michael J. Fox	9,000,000	9	Arnold Schwarzenegger	22,000,000
10	Bruce Willis	8,000,000	10	Michael Douglas	21,000,000

Based on *Forbes* magazine's survey of top entertainers' income, in 1987 William H. Cosby, Jr., was No. 1 in the list of all entertainers (including pop stars, professional athletes, and others). The comparative survey for 1997 calculated Cosby's income as $18,000,000. Meanwhile, during the past decade, actors with the audience magnetism of Arnold Schwarzenegger and Harrison Ford have been able to command $20,000,000 or more per movie, while percentage earnings can add further sums, although their actual estimated income fluctuates according to whether they have appeared in a recent successful movie.

Source: Forbes magazine

RICHEST RULERS IN THE WORLD*

	Ruler	Country/ in power since	Estimated wealth ($)
1	Sultan Hassanal Bolkiah	Brunei, 1967	38,000,000,000
2	King Fahd Bin Abdulaziz Alsaud	Saudi Arabia, 1982	20,000,000,000
3	President Suharto	Indonesia, 1967	16,000,000,000
4	Sheikh Jaber Al-Ahmed Al-Jaber Al-Sabah	Kuwait, 1977	15,000,000,000
5	Sheikh Zayed Bin Sultan Al Nahyan	United Arab Emirates, 1966	10,000,000,000
6	President Saddam Hussein	Iraq, 1979	5,000,000,000
7	Queen Beatrix	Netherlands, 1980	4,700,000,000#
8	Prime Minister Rafik al-Hariri	Lebanon, 1992	3,000,000,000
9	King Bhumibol Adulyadej	Thailand, 1946	1,800,000,000
10	President Fidel Castro	Cuba, 1959	1,400,000,000

* *As of July 28, 1997*

\# *Jointly with her mother, the former Queen Juliana*

According to analysts at *Forbes* magazine, Queen Elizabeth II's personal fortune is $350,000,000. She also has further property, art treasures, and jewelry worth a total of $16,000,000,000, but is considered their custodian, holding them in trust for the nation.

Source: Forbes magazine

HIGHEST-EARNING SINGERS IN THE WORLD

	Singer(s)	1996–97 income ($)
1	The Beatles	98,000,000
2	The Rolling Stones	68,000,000
3	Celine Dion	65,000,000
4	David Bowie	63,000,000
5	Sting	57,000,000
6=	Garth Brooks	55,000,000
=	Michael Jackson	55,000,000
8	Kiss	48,000,000
9=	Gloria Estefan	47,000,000
=	The Spice Girls	47,000,000

Even though the Beatles no longer exist as a group, they continue to earn huge revenue from their recordings. The Rolling Stones typify the huge income generated by major rock tours: their Voodoo Lounge tour made $300,000,000, while Microsoft paid $4,000,000 to use their song *Start Me Up* to promote Windows95. The Spice Girls are newcomers to this highly volatile list.

Source: Forbes magazine

CITIES WITH THE MOST *FORBES* 400 MEMBERS

	City	Members
1	New York, New York	38
2	San Francisco, California	27
3	Los Angeles, California	12
4=	Boston, Massachusetts	9
=	Fort Worth, Texas	9
6=	Beverly Hills, California	8
=	Chicago, Illinois	8
=	Dallas, Texas	8
9=	Atlanta, Georgia	5
=	Greenwich, Connecticut	5

TOP 10

COMPUTER FORTUNES IN THE US

	Name	Company	Wealth ($)
1	Bill Gates	Microsoft	38,660,000,000
2	Paul Allen	Microsoft	14,770,000,000
3	Steve Ballmer	Microsoft	8,210,000,000
4	Larry Ellison	Oracle	8,200,000,000
5	Gordon Moore	Intel	7,970,000,000
6	Michael Dell	Dell	4,660,000,000
7	William Hewlett	Hewlett-Packard	4,200,000,000
8	Ted Waitt	Gateway	2,830,000,000
9	David Duffield	Peoplesoft	1,730,000,000
10	Charles B. Wang	Computer Associates	1,200,000,000

The 10 individuals in this Top 10 list, together with Robert Galvin of Motorola ($1,100,000,000), represent the elite group of American computer billionaires, although the industry has also produced innumerable multimillionaires.

Source: Forbes magazine

TOP 10

CLOTHING FORTUNES IN THE US

	Name	Company	Wealth ($)
1	Philip Hampson Knight	Nike	5,400,000,000
2	Peter E. Haas Sr.	Levi Strauss	2,400,000,000
3	Ralph Lauren	Ralph Lauren	1,800,000,000
4	Leslie Herbert Wexner	The Limited	1,600,000,000
5	Richard N. Goldman	Levi Strauss	1,300,000,000
6	Jim Jannard	Oakley Sunglasses	1,000,000,000
7	Peter E. Haas Jr.	Levi Strauss	970,000,000
8	Sidney Kimmel	Jones Apparel	960,000,000
9 =	Frances Koshland Geballe	Levi Strauss	900,000,000
=	Evelyn Danzig Haas	Levi Strauss	900,000,000

Heirs of jeans pioneer Levi Strauss (1830–1902) make up half this Top 10 list, with other more distant members of the family just outside, along with major shareholders in contemporary fashion companies such as Reebok and The Gap.

Source: Forbes magazine

TOP 10

HIGHEST-EARNING ENTERTAINERS IN THE WORLD*

	Entertainer	Profession	1996–97 income ($)
1	Steven Spielberg	Film producer/director	313,000,000
2	George Lucas	Film producer/director	241,000,000
3	Oprah Winfrey	TV host/producer	201,000,000
4	Michael Crichton	Novelist/screenwriter	102,000,000
5	David Copperfield	Illusionist	85,000,000
6	Stephen King	Novelist/screenwriter	84,000,000
7	John Grisham	Novelist/screenwriter	66,000,000
8	Siegfried and Roy	Illusionists	58,000,000
9 =	Michael Flatley	Dancer	54,000,000
=	Ron Howard and Brian Grazer	Film director/film producer partnership	54,000,000

* Other than actors and pop stars

Source: Forbes magazine

TOP 10

FOOD AND CANDY FORTUNES IN THE US

	Name	Company	Wealth ($)
1 =	Forrest Edward Mars, Sr.	Mars	3,300,000,000
=	Forrest Edward Mars, Jr.	Mars	3,300,000,000
=	John Franklyn Mars	Mars	3,300,000,000
=	Jacqueline Mars Vogel	Mars	3,300,000,000
5	Mary Alice Dorrance Malone	Campbell Soup	2,800,000,000
6 =	Bennett Dorrance	Campbell Soup	2,600,000,000
=	William Wrigley	Wrigley gum	2,600,000,000
8	Joan Beverly Kroc	McDonalds	2,100,000,000
9	Dorrance Hill Hamilton	Campbell Soup	1,800,000,000
10	Hope Hill Van Beuren	Campbell Soup	1,600,000,000

Source: Forbes magazine

SNAP FACTS

- The first reference to a millionaire in print appears in British author and Prime Minister Benjamin Disraeli's novel *Vivian Grey* (1826).

- $1,000,000 in $1 bills would weigh one ton. Placed in a pile it would be 360 ft/110 m high – as tall as 60 average adults standing on top of each other.

DIAMONDS & GOLD

TOP 10

GOLD-PRODUCING COUNTRIES

	Country	Production 1996 (tons)
1	South Africa	545.0
2	US	363.0
3	Australia	318.3
4	Canada	180.7
5	China	159.4
6	Russia	143.3
7	Indonesia	101.5
8	Uzbekistan	78.3
9	Peru	71.4
10	Brazil	70.8

TOP 10

COUNTRIES MAKING GOLD JEWELRY

	Country	Gold used in 1996 (tons)
1	Italy	483.9
2	India	471.6
3	China	202.8
4	Saudi Arabia and Yemen	175.6
5	US	168.0
6	Turkey	155.1
7	Indonesia	145.5
8	Taiwan	100.3
9	Malaysia	87.6
10	Hong Kong	87.1

TOP 10

LARGEST UNCUT DIAMONDS

	Diamond	Carats
1	Cullinan	3,106.00

Measuring approximately 4 x 2¹/2 x 2 in/10 x 6.5 x 5 cm , and weighing 1 lb 6 oz/621 gm, the Cullinan was unearthed in 1905. Bought by the Transvaal Government for the equivalent of about $750,000, it was presented to King Edward VII. The King decided to have it cut, and the most important of the separate gems are now among the British Crown Jewels.

2	Braganza	1,680.00

All traces of this enormous stone have been lost.

3	Excelsior	995.20

Cut by the celebrated Amsterdam firm of Asscher in 1903, the Excelsior produced 21 superb stones, which were sold mainly through Tiffany's of New York.

4	Star of Sierra Leone	968.80

Found in Sierra Leone on St. Valentine's Day, 1972, the uncut diamond weighed 8 oz/225 g and measured 2¹/2 x 1¹/2 in/6.5 x 4 cm.

5	Zale Corporation "Golden Giant"	890.00

Its origin is so shrouded in mystery that it is not even known which country it came from.

	Diamond	Carats
6	Great Mogul	787.50

When found in 1650 in the Gani Mine, India, this diamond was presented to Shah Jehan, the builder of the Taj Mahal. After Nadir Shah conquered Delhi in 1739, it entered the Persian treasury and apparently vanished from history.

7	Woyie River	770.00

Found in 1945 beside the river in Sierra Leone, whose name it now bears, it was cut into 30 stones. The largest of these, known as Victory and weighing 31.35 carats, was auctioned in 1984 at Christie's, New York, for $880,000.

8	Presidente Vargas	726.60

Discovered in the Antonio River, Brazil, in 1938, it was named after the then president.

9	Jonker	726.00

Jacobus Jonker found this massive diamond in 1934, after it had been exposed by a heavy storm. Acquired by Harry Winston, it was exhibited in the American Museum of Natural History and attracted enormous crowds.

10	Reitz	650.80

Like the Excelsior, the Reitz was found in the Jagersfontein Mine in South Africa in 1895.

TOP 10

DIAMOND-PRODUCING COUNTRIES

	Country	Production per annum (carats)
1	Australia	41,000,000
2	Dem. Rep. of Congo	16,500,000
3	Botswana	14,700,000
4	Russia	11,500,000
5	South Africa	9,800,000
6	Brazil	2,000,000
7	Namibia	1,100,000
8 =	Angola	1,000,000
=	China	1,000,000
10	Ghana	700,000
	World total	*100,850,000*

TOP 10

LARGEST POLISHED GEM DIAMONDS

	Diamond/last known whereabouts or owner	Carats
1	Golden Jubilee (King of Thailand)	545.67
2	Great Star of Africa/Cullinan I (British Crown Jewels)	530.20
3	Incomparable/Zale (sold in New York, 1988)	407.48
4	Second Star of Africa/Cullinan II (British Crown Jewels)	317.40
5	Centenary (De Beers)	273.85
6	Jubilee (Paul-Louis Weiller)	245.35
7	De Beers (sold in Geneva, 1982)	234.50
8	Red Cross (sold in Geneva, 1973)	205.07
9	Black Star of Africa (unknown)	202.00
10	Anon (unknown)	200.87

WORKING IN A GOLD MINE
South African gold mines have long been the world's No. 1 source of gold, producing almost a quarter of the world's total annual output of almost 2,535 tons.

T O P 1 0

COUNTRIES HOLDING GOLD RESERVES

	Country	Gold reserves, 1998 (troy ounces)	(tons)
1	US	261,710,000	8,973
2	Germany	95,180,000	3,263
3	Switzerland	83,280,000	2,855
4	France	81,890,000	2,808
5	Italy	66,670,000	2,285
6	Netherlands	27,070,000	927
7	Japan	24,230,000	830
8	UK	18,420,000	631
9	Portugal	16,070,000	550
10	Spain	15,630,000	536

Gold and precious stones have been measured in troy, or fine, ounces since medieval times. A troy ounce is equivalent to 31.103 gm, and a ton of gold is 29,167 ounces. Gold has a density of 19.3 gm per cm^3, so another way of looking at, say, the US's gold reserves is to consider that it would occupy the volume of a cube with sides 25 ft/7.5 m long.

Source: International Monetary Fund

T O P 1 0

MOST EXPENSIVE SINGLE DIAMONDS SOLD AT AUCTION

	Diamond	Sale	Price ($)
1	Pear-shaped 100.10-carat "D" Flawless	Sotheby's, Geneva, May 17, 1995	16,548,750 (SF19,958,500)
2	The Mouawad Splendor, pear-shaped 11-sided 101.84-carat diamond	Sotheby's, Geneva, November 14, 1990	12,760,000 (SF15,950,000)
3	Rectangular-cut 100.36-carat diamond	Sotheby's, Geneva, November 17, 1993	11,882,333 (SF17,823,500)
4	Fancy blue emerald-cut diamond ring, 20.17 carats	Sotheby's, New York, October 18, 1994	9,902,500
5	Unnamed pear-shaped 85.91-carat pendant	Sotheby's, New York, April 19, 1988	9,130,000
6	Rectangular-cut fancy deep-blue diamond ring, 13.49 carats	Christie's, New York, April 13, 1995	7,482,500
7	Rectangular-cut 52.59-carat diamond ring	Christie's, New York, April 20, 1988	7,480,000
8	Fancy pink rectangular-cut diamond, 19.66 carats	Christie's, Geneva, November 17, 1994	7,421,318 (SF9,573,500)
9	The Jeddah Bride, rectangular-cut 80.02-carat diamond	Sotheby's, New York, October 24, 1991	7,150,000
10	The Agra Diamond, fancy light pink cushion-shaped 32.24-carat diamond	Christie's, London, June 20, 1990	6,959,700 (£4,070,000)

TOP 10 GOLD MANUFACTURERS IN THE WORLD
(Tons of gold used in fabrication, 1996)

❶ India (501.3) ❷ Italy (495.8) ❸ US (270.6)
❹ China (218.1) ❺ Japan (206.7) ❻ Saudi Arabia and Yemen (178.9) ❼ Turkey (173.7) ❽ Indonesia (145.5)
❾ Taiwan (109.1) ❿ Hong Kong (92.5)

THE WEALTH OF NATIONS

THE 10
RICHEST COUNTRIES IN THE WORLD

	Country	GDP per capita ($)
1=	Liechtenstein	42,416
=	Switzerland	42,416
3	Japan	41,718
4	Luxembourg	35,109
5	Norway	33,734
6	Denmark	33,191
7	Germany	29,632
8	Austria	29,006
9	Belgium	26,582
10	Monaco	26,470
	US	*26,037*
	UK	*18,913*

GDP (Gross Domestic Product) is the total value of all the goods and services that are produced annually within a country. (Gross National Product, GNP, also includes income from overseas.)

Source: United Nations

THE 10
COUNTRIES WITH THE FASTEST-GROWING ECONOMIES

	Country	Average annual growth in GNP per capita 1970–95 (%)
1	South Korea	10.0
2	Botswana	7.3
3	China	6.9
4	Malta	6.1
5=	Cape Verde	5.7
=	Singapore	5.7
7=	Bhutan	5.5
=	Cyprus	5.5
9=	St. Kitts and Nevis	5.2
=	Thailand	5.2
	UK	*1.8*
	US	*1.7*

Source: World Bank

THE 10
POOREST COUNTRIES IN THE WORLD

	Country	GDP per capita ($)
1	Sudan	36
2	São Tome and Principe	49
3	Mozambique	77
4=	Eritrea	96
=	Ethiopia	96
6	Dem. Rep. of Congo	117
7	Somalia	119
8	Tajikistan	122
9	Cambodia	130
10	Guinea-Bissau	131

Source: United Nations

THE 10
COUNTRIES WITH THE FASTEST-SHRINKING ECONOMIES

	Country	Average annual growth in GNP per capita 1970–95 (%)
1	Qatar	-5.9
2	Nicaragua	-5.3
3	Libya	-4.8
4	Dem. Rep. of Congo	-4.0
5	Kuwait	-3.5
6	Liberia	-3.0
7	Gabon	-2.8
8	Saudi Arabia	-2.9
9=	Guyana	-2.6
=	Niger	-2.6
=	Zambia	-2.6

These are countries where over the last 25 years people have on average become poorer each year. For example, at the top of the list, in Qatar people's incomes have dropped by 5.9 percent per year.

Source: World Bank

THE 10
COUNTRIES MOST IN DEBT

	Country	Total external debt ($)
1	Mexico	165,743,000,000
2	Brazil	159,139,000,000
3	Russia	120,461,000,000
4	China	118,090,000,000
5	Indonesia	107,831,000,000
6	India	93,766,000,000
7	Argentina	89,747,000,000
8	Turkey	73,592,000,000
9	Thailand	56,789,000,000
10	Poland	42,291,000,000

The World Bank's annual debt calculations estimated the total indebtedness (including "official" debt, which is guaranteed by governments, and "private" debt, which is not) of low and middle income countries at $2,177,000,000,000 in 1996, nearly double the figure for 1986, when total debt was estimated to be $1,132,400,000,000.

Source: World Bank

THE 10
POOREST STATES IN THE US

	State	Average income per head ($)
1	Mississippi	17,471
2	West Virginia	18,444
3	New Mexico	18,770
4	Arkansas	18,928
5	Montana	19,047
6	Utah	19,156
7	Oklahoma	19,350
8	Kentucky	19,678
9	South Carolina	19,755
10	Louisiana	19,824

In 1996 the national average income was $24,231. Historically, the Southern States have tended to be the poorest, with the average annual income in Mississippi less than half that of the District of Columbia.

Source: US Bureau of Economic Analysis

TOP 10

BILLS AND COINS IN CIRCULATION IN THE US*

	Unit	Value in circulation ($)
1	$100 bill	291,581,249,700
2	$20 bill	87,953,394,480
3	$50 bill	48,240,047,000
4	$10 bill	14,201,043,010
5	$1 bill	8,718,482,681
6	$5 bill	7,845,149,655
7	$2 bill	1,128,405,494
8	quarter	271,170,000
9	dime	178,581,000
10	nickel	42,086,000

* As of December 31, 1997

As well as the denominations in the Top 10, there are 288,192 $500 bills (value $144,096,000), 167,289 $1,000 bills ($167,289,000), 351 $5,000 bills ($1,755,000), and 345 $10,000 bills ($3,450,000), along with 13,123,260,000 cents ($13,123,260,000) in circulation.

Sources: Bureau of Engraving & Printing (bills)/US Mint (coins)

TOP 10

NOTES AND COINS IN CIRCULATION IN THE UK

	Unit	Value in circulation (£)
1	£20 note	9,559,000,000
2	£10 note	5,915,000,000
3	£50 note	3,273,000,000
4	£1 coin	1,142,000,000
5	£5 note	1,047,000,000
6	20p coin	337,400,000
7	50p coin	290,500,000
8	5p coin	160,800,000
9	10p coin	146,400,000
10	2p coin	92,180,000

The total value of bills in circulation as of December 1997 was £22,011,000,000 – the equivalent of a pile of £5 notes 273 miles/ 440 km high – and the total number of new bills issued in 1997 was a staggering 1,316,000,000. In addition to the bills and coins that appear in this list there are also 56,000,000 £1 notes that are still legal tender in Scotland, and 7,496,000,000 1p coins (worth £74,960,000).

TOP 10

COUNTRIES WITH THE HIGHEST INFLATION

	Country	Annual inflation rate (%)
1	Dem. Rep. of Congo	658.8
2	Venezuela	99.9
3=	Turkey	80.3
=	Ukraine	80.3
5	Belarus	52.7
6	Guinea Bissau	50.7
7	Russia	47.6
8	Mongolia	45.8
9	Mozambique	45.0
10	Zambia	43.9
	US	*2.9*
	UK	*2.4*
	Canada	*1.6*
	World	*7.5*

Source: International Monetary Fund

TOP 10

COUNTRIES IN WHICH IT IS EASIEST TO BE A MILLIONAIRE

	Country/ currency unit	Value of 1,000,000 units ($)
1	Ukraine, Karbovanets	5.52
2	Turkey, Lira	11.44
3	Dem. Rep. of Congo	19.90
4	Angola, Kwanza	31.25
5	Guinea-Bissau, Peso	55.07
6	Belarus, Rouble	57.82
7	Mozambique, Metical	89.16
8	Vietnam, Dông	90.14
9	Russia, Rouble	185.10
10	Afghanistan, Afghani	209.11

With an exchange rate running at an average of 428,287.55 Ukrainian Karbovanets to the dollar, total assets of just $5.62 will qualify a person as a Ukrainian millionaire.

TOP 10

COUNTRIES WITH MOST CURRENCY IN CIRCULATION 100 YEARS AGO

	Country	Currency in circulation 100 years ago ($) gold	silver	paper	Total
1	France	863,300,000	727,500,000	557,750,000	2,148,550,000
2	US	683,850,000	421,950,000	1,008,800,000	2,114,600,000
3	Germany	591,700,000	218,250,000	344,350,000	1,154,300,000
4	India	48,500,000	824,500,000	58,200,000	931,200,000
5	Russia	189,150,000	67,900,000	596,550,000	853,600,000
6	UK	494,700,000	106,700,000	189,150,000	790,550,000
7	China	–	727,500,000	–	727,500,000
8	Austria	38,800,000	92,150,000	368,600,000	499,550,000
9	Italy	106,700,000	53,350,000	276,450,000	436,500,000
10	Spain	92,150,000	116,400,000	145,500,000	354,050,000

It is interesting to consider that there are now individuals in these countries who, on paper at least, own more than the entire country's money supply in the late 1890s. Today there is in excess of $1,000,000,000,000 in circulation in the US.

FOOD FOR THOUGHT

FOOD AND DRINK ITEMS CONSUMED IN THE US

	Item	Annual consumption (lb)
1	Vegetables	398.3
2	Fruits	279.5
3	Eggs	238.0
4	Flour & cereals	198.5
5	Meat	193.6
6	Caloric sweeteners	147.6
7	Beverages	52.2
8	Frozen dairy products	30.0
9	Cheese	26.8
10	Milk	24.7

Source: United States Department of Agriculture

CALORIE-CONSUMING COUNTRIES IN THE WORLD

	Country	Average daily per capita consumption
1	Cyprus	3,708
2	Denmark	3,704
3	Portugal	3,639
4	Ireland	3,638
5	US	3,603
6	Turkey	3,593
7	France	3,588
8	Greece	3,561
9	Belgium/Luxembourg	3,530
10	Italy	3,458
	World average	*2,712*

The calorie requirement of the average man is 2,700 and of a woman 2,500. Inactive people need less, and those engaged in heavy labor need more.

Source: Food and Agriculture Organization of the United Nations

TOP 10 CHEESE-PRODUCING COUNTRIES IN THE WORLD
(Tons per annum)

❶ US (3,826,123) ❷ France (1,754,714)
❸ Germany (1,565,778) ❹ Italy (1,013,023)
❺ Netherlands (749,656) ❻ Russia (525,671) ❼ Argentina (446,436)
❽ UK (390,218) ❾ Poland (387,099)
❿ Egypt (384,431)

Source: Food and Agriculture Organization of the United Nations

MUSSELS

BUTTER-PRODUCING COUNTRIES IN THE WORLD

	Country	Tons per annum*
1	India	1,433,047
2	US	642,372
3	Germany	535,931
4	France	500,449
5	Russia	462,406
6	Pakistan	410,803
7	New Zealand	292,480
8	Poland	178,574
9	Ireland	156,969
10	Australia	148,742

* Including ghee

Source: Food and Agriculture Organization of the United Nations

THE CREATION OF THE CROISSANT

In 1899 William Morrow Chambers published *Bohemian Paris of Today*, which contained the first known reference in English to a croissant. The croissant has an interesting history. In 1683, when the Austrian capital Vienna was besieged by Turks, the city's bakers heard the invaders tunneling beneath the walls at night and so thwarted the attack. As a result, they were given the privilege of making rolls in a crescent shape, like the emblem on the Turkish flag. Known as *kipfels*, they became popular in the Austro-Hungarian Empire. When Austrian princess Marie Antoinette married the French dauphin in 1770, her bakers brought *kipfels* to France, where they became known as croissants.

YEARS AGO · 100 · YEARS AGO · YEARS AGO

TOP 10

MEAT-EATING COUNTRIES IN THE WORLD

	Country	Consumption per capita per annum	
		lb	oz
1	US	261	0
2	New Zealand	259	4
3	Australia	239	4
4	Cyprus	235	14
5	Uruguay	230	6
6	Austria	229	4
7	Saint Lucia	222	7
8	Denmark	219	5
9	Spain	211	3
10	Canada	210	15

Figures from the Meat and Livestock Commission show a huge range of meat consumption in countries around the world, ranging from the Number 1 meat consumer, the US, at 261 lb per person per year, to very poor countries such as India, where it is estimated that meat consumption may be as little as 7½ lb per person per year. In general, meat is an expensive food, and in poor countries is saved for special occasions; therefore, the richer the country, the more likely it is to have a high meat consumption. However, in recent years, health scares relating to meat, "healthy eating" concerns in many Western countries, and the rise in the number of vegetarians have all contributed to deliberate declines in consumption.

TOP 10

FAST FOOD CHAINS IN THE US

	Chain	Annual sales ($)
1	McDonald's	16,369,600,000
2	Burger King	7,484,645,000
3	Pizza Hut	4,917,000,000
4	Taco Bell	4,419,122,000
5	Wendy's	4,284,046,000
6	KFC	3,900,000,000
7	Hardee's	2,988,653,000
8	Subway	2,700,000,000
9	Dairy Queen	2,602,883,000
10	Domino	2,300,000,000

Source: Restaurants & Institutions Magazine from Technomics

TOP 10

SUGAR-CONSUMING COUNTRIES IN THE WORLD

	Country	lb per capita per annum
1	Swaziland	145.06
2	Belize	127.21
3	Israel	125.69
4	Réunion	120.17
5	Costa Rica	114.35
6	New Zealand	109.70
7	Barbados	108.60
8	Brazil	105.23
9	Trinidad and Tobago	102.47
10	Malaysia	101.88
	US	*64.77*

Source: Food and Agriculture Organization of the United Nations

TOP 10 FISH-CONSUMING COUNTRIES IN THE WORLD

(Average consumption per capita per annum)

❶ Japan (147 lb 8 oz/66.9 kg) ❷ Norway (99 lb 3 oz/45.0 kg)
❸ Portugal (94 lb 13 oz/43.0 kg) ❹= Spain (66 lb 2 oz/30.0 kg),
Sweden (66 lb 2 oz/30.0 kg) ❻ Belgium (41 lb 14 oz/19.0 kg)
❼= Germany (30 lb 14 oz/14.0 kg), Italy (30 lb 14 oz/14.0 kg),
Netherlands (30 lb 14 oz/14.0 kg), Poland (30 lb 14 oz/14.0 kg)

CANDY IS DANDY

TOP 10

COCOA-CONSUMING COUNTRIES IN THE WORLD

	Country	Total cocoa consumption (tons)
1	US	599,800
2	Germany	269,700
3	UK	202,800
4	France	172,500
5	Russian Federation	158,600
6	Japan	124,200
7	Brazil	122,000
8	Italy	94,100
9	Belgium/Luxembourg	68,500
10	Spain	66,400

Cocoa is the principal ingredient of chocolate, and its consumption is therefore closely linked to the production of chocolate in each consuming country. Like coffee, the consumption of chocolate tends to occur mainly in the Western world and in relatively affluent countries. Since some of these Top 10 consuming nations also have large populations, the figures for cocoa consumption per capita present a somewhat different picture, being dominated by those countries with a long-established tradition of manufacturing high-quality chocolate products:

TOP 10

CANDY-CONSUMING COUNTRIES IN THE WORLD

	Country	Consumption per capita (per annum)					
		chocolate kg	lb	other candy kg	lb	total kg	lb
1	Denmark	7	15	10	22	17	37
2	Ireland	8	18	6	13	14	31
3=	UK	8	18	5	11	13	29
=	Switzerland	10	22	3	7	13	29
=	Germany	7	16	6	13	13	29
6=	Austria	8	17	3	7	11	24
=	Belgium/Luxembourg	6	13	5	11	11	24
=	Netherlands	5	11	6	13	11	24
=	Australia	5	11	6	13	11	24
10	US	5	11	5	11	10	22

TOP 10

CONFECTIONERY MANUFACTURERS IN THE US

	Brand	Market share (%)	Sales ($)*
1	Hershey	25.09	245,374,812
2	M&M/Mars	18.57	181,573,178
3	Wrigley	10.83	105,870,543
4	Adams	8.01	78,347,762
5	Lifesavers	7.05	68,939,206
6	Nestlé	6.12	59,800,013
7	Sunmark	5.19	50,765,532
8	Sathers	2.84	27,793,564
9	Tootsie Roll Industries	1.85	18,043,473
10	Ferrero US	1.60	15,611,205

Based on a 12-week survey

Source: American Wholesale Marketers Association

TOP 10

GUM BRANDS IN THE US

	Brand	Market share (%)	Sales ($)
1	Trident	8.95	9,440,932
2	Winterfresh	8.08	8,528,386
3	Doublemint	6.92	7,299,687
4	Big Red	5.88	6,201,538
5	Bubblicious	4.83	5,095,131
6	Wrigley Spearmint	4.65	4,902,331
7	Carefree	4.59	4,846,881
8	Juicy Fruit	4.50	4,747,796
9	Bubble Yum	4.36	4,605,000
10	Extra Spearmint	3.80	4,013,989

Source: American Wholesale Marketers Association

	Country	Consumption per capita		
		kg	lb	oz
1	Belgium/ Luxembourg	5.900	13	0
2	Iceland	4.444	9	13
3	Switzerland	3.491	7	11
4	UK	3.145	6	15
5	Denmark	3.122	6	14
6	Austria	3.071	6	12
7	Germany	2.997	6	10
8	Norway	2.771	6	2
9	Malta	2.711	6	0
10	France	2.692	5	15

TOP 10

CONFECTIONERY BRANDS IN THE US

	Brand	Sales ($)*
1	Snickers Original	21,541,170
2	Reeses Peanut Butter Cups	17,504,498
3	M&M's Peanut	14,326,132
4	M&M's Plain	13,798,195
5	Trident	9,440,932
6	Kit Kat	9,143,782
7	Winterfresh	8,528,386
8	Butterfinger Bar	8,426,695
9	Tic Tac	8,417,657
10	Hershey Almond	8,063,595

Based on a 12-week survey

Source: American Wholesale Marketers Assoc.

TOP 10

ICE CREAM BRANDS IN THE US

	Brand	Sales 1997 ($)
1	Private Label	857,100,000
2	Breyers	394,200,000
3	Dreyer's/Edy's Grand Ice Cream	317,600,000
4	Blue Bell Creameries	172,900,000
5	Häagen-Dazs	149,900,000
6	Ben & Jerry's	111,800,000
7	Healthy Choice	109,500,000
8	Dreyer's/Edy's Grand Lite	82,500,000
9	Turkey Hill Dairy	74,800,000
10	Friendly	48,000,000

Source: Information Resources

TOP 10

ICE CREAM FLAVORS IN THE US

	Flavor	Annual sales 1997 (gallons)
1	Vanilla	125,592.5
2	Neapolitan	35,236.7
3	Assorted	28,473.7
4	Chocolate	27,962.8
5	Butter Pecan	21,090.7
6	Cookies & Cream	20,529.1
7	French Vanilla	16,344.1
8	Chocolate Chip	15,730.0
9	Mint Chocolate Chip	13,196.5
10	Rocky Road	12,792.4

Source: International Dairy Foods Association

TOP 10

CHOCOLATE BRANDS IN THE US

	Brand	Sales ($)*
1	Snickers Original	21,541,710
2	Reeses Peanut Butter Cups	17,504,498
3	M&M's Peanut	14,326,132
4	M&M's Plain	13,798,195
5	Kit Kat	9,143,782
6	Butterfinger Bar	8,426,695
7	Hershey Almond	8,063,595
8	Hershey Milk	7,213,409
9	Milky Way Original	6,612,771
10	Twix Caramel	5,663,605

Based on a 12-week survey

Source: American Wholesale Marketers Assoc.

TOP 10

ICE CREAM-CONSUMING COUNTRIES IN THE WORLD

	Country	Production per capita pints
1	US	56.17
2	Finland	45.80
3	Denmark	41.74
4	Australia	39.20
5	Canada	35.08
6	Sweden	34.64
7	Norway	33.75
8	Belgium/Luxembourg	30.28
9	UK	26.37
10	New Zealand	26.27

Global statistics for ice cream consumption are hard to come by, but this list presents recent and reliable International Ice Cream Association estimates for per capita production of ice cream and related products (frozen yogurt, sherbert, water ices, etc.). Since only small amounts of such products are exported, consumption figures can be assumed to be similar.

Source: International Dairy Foods Association

JELL-O SOLD FOR $450

Jell-O, one of the most popular desserts in the US, was first patented in 1842 by Peter Cooper of New York, but it was not until 1897 that cough medicine manufacturer Pearl B. Wait started manufacturing the product, for which his wife Mary had coined the name. However, it proved to be unsuccessful, and in 1899 Wait sold the company for only $450 to his neighbor Francis Woodward, the manufacturer of a cereal drink called Grain-O. Unfortunately for Wait, Jell-O's popularity then began to steadily increase, and by 1902 Woodward was selling $250,000 worth. By 1906 he was selling in excess of $1 million.

YEARS AGO • YEARS AGO • YEARS AGO • 100

ALCOHOLIC BEVERAGES

THEN & NOW

THE TOP 10 WINE-DRINKING COUNTRIES IN THE WORLD

Country	1987 Gallons per capita per annum		1997 Gallons per capita per annum	Country
France	19.84	**1**	16.01	Portugal
Italy	17.44	**2**	15.85	France
Portugal	16.99	**3**	15.32	Luxembourg
Luxembourg	15.45	**4**	14.53	Italy
Argentina	15.35	**5**	11.44	Switzerland
Switzerland	13.08	**6**	11.17	Argentina
Spain	12.15	**7**	8.98	Greece
Chile	9.03	**8**	8.45	Uruguay
Austria	8.96	**9**	8.32	Austria
Greece	8.40	**10**	8.00	Spain
US	2.40		1.93	US

The US still does not make it into the Top 10 or even Top 20 wine-drinking countries in the world, but consumption of wine has become more popular over the last 25 years. Between 1970 and 1997 wine consumption increased by over 350 percent. In contrast, in France, one of the world's top wine-drinking and wine-producing countries, people have been drinking less. Wine consumption per person per year peaked at 33.63 gallons in 1963, and has dropped steadily over the last 35 years to 15.85 gallons today.

TOP 10

MOST EXPENSIVE BOTTLES OF WINE EVER SOLD AT AUCTION

	Wine	Price ($)
1	Château Lafite 1787, Christie's, London, December 5, 1985 (£105,000)	140,700
2	Château d'Yquem 1784, Christie's, London, December 4, 1986 (£39,600)	58,608
3	Château Mouton-Rothschild 1945 (jeroboam) Christie's, Geneva, May 14, 1995 (SF68,200)	56,229
4	Château Lafite Rothschild 1832 (double magnum) International Wine Auctions, London, April 9, 1988 (£24,000)	40,320
5	Château Pétrus 1945 (jeroboam), Sotheby's, New York, September 16, 1995	37,375
6	Château Mouton Rothschild 1986 (Nebuchadnezzar - equivalent to 20 bottles) Sotheby's, New York, April 22, 1995	36,800
7	Château Lafite 1806 Sotheby's, Geneva, November 13, 1988 (SF57,200)	36,456
8=	Château Mouton Rothschild 1985 (Nebuchadnezzar) Sotheby's, Los Angeles, October 12, 1996	33,350
=	Château Mouton Rothschild 1989 (Nebuchadnezzar) Sotheby's, Los Angeles, October 12, 1996	33,350
10	Cheval-blanc 1947 (Imperial – equivalent to eight bottles) Christie's, London, December 1, 1994 (£21,450)	33,248

TOP 10

ALCOHOL-CONSUMING COUNTRIES IN THE WORLD

	Country	Annual consumption per capita (100% alcohol) gallons
1	Luxembourg	3.12
2	Portugal	2.96
3	France	2.93
4	Czech Republic	2.67
5	Denmark	2.64
6=	Austria	2.59
=	Germany	2.59
8	Hungary	2.51
9=	Spain	2.46
=	Switzerland	2.46
	US	1.74

TOP 10

CHAMPAGNE IMPORTERS IN THE WORLD

	Country	Bottles imported (1997)		Country	Bottles imported (1997)
1	UK	22,262,972	6	Italy	6,685,582
2	Germany	19,457,909	7	Japan	2,508,842
3	US	15,496,393	8	Netherlands	2,259,330
4	Belgium	7,948,022	9	Spain	1,244,250
5	Switzerland	6,841,842	10	Australia	1,231,596

TOP 10

BREWERIES IN THE US

	Brewery	Total sales 1997 (barrels)*		Brewery	Total sales 1997 (barrels)*
1	Anheuser-Busch	91,800,000	6	Genesee	1,700,000
2	Miller Brewing Company	41,800,000	7=	Boston Beer	1,100,000
3	Coors	20,400,000	=	Latrobe	1,100,000
4	Stroh	15,300,000	9=	Labatts	500,000
5	S&P Industries	5,300,000	=	Minnesota Brewing	500,000

* Wholesale sales; a barrel contains 31.5 US gallons
Source: Beverage Marketing Corporation

TOP 10

SPIRIT-DRINKING COUNTRIES IN THE WORLD

	Country	Annual consumption per capita (pure alcohol) quarts
1	Russia	5.60
2 =	Romania	4.23
=	Slovak Republic	4.23
4	Cyprus	3.59
5	Poland	3.49
6 =	China	3.17
=	Hungary	3.17
8	Greece	2.85
9	Bulgaria	2.64
10 =	France	2.54
=	Spain	2.54

TOP 10

CONSUMERS OF SCOTCH WHISKY IN THE WORLD

	Country	Annual sales (quarts)
1	France	38,717,048
2	US	35,642,086
3	Spain	24,885,002
4	South Korea	12,088,511
5	Japan	11,528,466
6	Germany	10,831,052
7	Thailand	9,510,192
8	Greece	8,305,568
9	Italy	7,026,975
10	Taiwan	2,768,523

Source: The Scotch Whisky Association

TOP 10

BEER-DRINKING COUNTRIES IN THE WORLD

	Country	Annual consumption per capita quarts
1	Czech Republic	169.07
2	Ireland	150.58
3	Germany	142.12
4	Denmark	124.27
5	Austria	122.58
6	Luxembourg	115.18
7	UK	108.10
8	Belgium	107.78
9	Australia	100.81
10	New Zealand	99.22

Despite its position as the world's leading producer of beer, the US is ranked in 13th position. Many people in Africa drink a lot of beer, but as bottled beer is often very expensive, they tend to consume home-made beers sold in local markets, which are hence excluded from national statistics.

SOFT DRINKS

NONALCOHOLIC DRINKS IN THE US

	Brand	Market share percentage
1	Coca-Cola Classic	20.8
2	Pepsi-Cola	14.5
3	Diet Coke	8.5
4	Mountain Dew	6.3
5	Sprite	6.2
6	Dr. Pepper	5.9
7	Diet Pepsi	5.5
8	7-Up	2.3
9	Caffeine Free Diet Coke	1.8
10	Caffeine Free Diet Pepsi	1.0

Source: Beverage Digest

CONSUMERS OF COCA-COLA AROUND THE WORLD

	Country	Daily consumption (servings)
1	China	1,244,000,000
2	India	960,000,000
3	US	272,000,000
4	Indonesia	203,000,000
5	Brazil	163,000,000
6	Russia	148,000,000
7	Japan	126,000,000
8	Mexico	94,000,000
9	Germany	82,000,000
10	Philippines	71,000,000

After heading this list for 10 years, the US has plummeted dramatically to third place as the two most populous countries, China and India, have adopted the world's bestselling nonalcoholic drink in a big way.

Source: Coca-Cola

BRANDS OF BOTTLED WATER IN THE US

	Brand	Sales ($)
1	Poland Spring	297,900,000
2	Arrowhead	265,700,000
3	Evian	185,000,000
4	Sparkletts	183,900,000
5	Hinckley-Schmitt	123,100,000
6	Zephyrhills	111,800,000
7	Ozarka	106,300,000
8	Deer Park	97,200,000
9	Alpine Spring	95,000,000
10	Crystal (Suntory)	86,000,000

Source: Beverage Marketing Corporation

TEA-DRINKING COUNTRIES

	Country	Consumption per capita p.a. lb	oz	cups*
1	Irish Republic	7	0	1,395
2	Kuwait	5	14	1,170
3	UK	5	7	1,082
4	Qatar	4	7	880
5	Turkey	4	4	849
6	Syria	3	3	634
7	Bahrain	3	0	603
8	Sri Lanka	2	14	568
9=	New Zealand	2	11	541
=	Morocco	2	11	541
	US	0	12	150

* *Based on 200 cups per pound*

Despite the UK's traditional passion for tea, during the recent years its consumption has consistently lagged behind that of Ireland. In the same period, Qatar's tea consumption has dropped from its former world record of 8 lb 12 oz (1,750 cups) per head. Within Europe, consumption varies enormously from the current world-leading Irish figure down to just 3 oz (50 cups) in Italy, while in the rest of the world, Thailand's 0.4 oz (four cups) is one of the lowest.

Source: International Tea Committee

COKE IN BOTTLES

The first Coca-Cola was served in Jacob's Pharmacy, a drugstore in Atlanta, Georgia, on May 8, 1886, the creation of pharmacist Dr. John Styth Pemberton (1831–88). Although it was an instant success, attempts at bottling it proved short-lived, and in its early years it was generally sold from soda fountains. Benjamin F. Thomas and Joseph B. Whitehead of Chattanooga, Tennessee, acquired bottling rights, incorporating the Coca-Cola Bottling Company on December 9, 1899 and selling the drink at five cents a bottle. Within 20 years there were more than 1,000 bottling plants across the US, part of a major franchising operation that has since spread worldwide.

100 YEARS AGO

TOP 10

COFFEE-DRINKING COUNTRIES

	Country	Consumption per capita p.a. lb	oz	cups*
1	Finland	23	4	1,581
2	Denmark	21	14	1,488
3	Netherlands	21	11	1,475
4	Norway	21	9	1,466
5	Sweden	19	6	1,318
6	Austria	17	5	1,177
7	Switzerland	17	4	1,173
8	Germany	15	13	1,075
9	Belgium/Luxembourg	14	10	995
10	France	12	8	850
	US	*10*	*4*	*697*

* *Based on 68 cups per pound*

Levels of coffee consumption have remained quite similar in most countries in the 1990s, with the exception of Belgium/Luxembourg, where annual coffee consumption has doubled since 1991.

Source: International Coffee Organization

TOP 10

SOFT DRINK COMPANIES IN THE US

	Company	1997 sales (gallons)
1	Coca-Cola Company	6,473,000,000
2	PepsiCo, Inc.	4,500,200,000
3	Dr. Pepper/7-Up	2,088,100,000
4	Cott Corporation	414,100,000
5	National Beverage	275,400,000
6	Royal Crown	216,200,000
7	Monarch	119,100,000
8	Double Cola Company	55,600,000
9	Big Red	34,500,000
10	Seagrams Mixers	31,500,000

Source: Beverage Marketing Corporation

TAKING TEA
The world divides between countries with a tradition of tea-drinking and those where it is rarely consumed.

TOP 10

MILK-DRINKING COUNTRIES IN THE WORLD

	Country*	Consumption per capita p.a. quarts
1	Ireland	164.42
2	Finland	162.10
3	Iceland	160.83
4	Norway	158.61
5	Ukraine	141.91
6	Luxembourg	137.48
7	UK	134.31
8	Sweden	132.61
9	Australia	117.72
10	US	110.85

* *Those reporting to the International Dairy Federation only*

Source: National Dairy Council

TRANSPORTATION & TOURISM

THE 10

COUNTRIES PRODUCING THE MOST MOTOR VEHICLES

	Country	Cars	Commercial vehicles	Total
1	US	6,083,227	5,715,678	11,798,905
2	Japan	7,863,763	2,482,023	10,345,786
3	Germany	4,539,583	303,326	4,842,909
4	France	3,147,622	442,965	3,590,587
5	South Korea	2,264,709	548,005	2,812,714
6	Spain	2,213,102	199,207	2,412,309
7	Canada	1,279,312	1,117,731	2,397,043
8	UK	1,686,134	238,263	1,924,397
9	Brazil	1,466,900	345,700	1,812,600
10	Italy	1,317,995	227,370	1,545,365
	World	*37,318,281*	*14,194,882*	*51,513,163*

Source: American Automobile Manufacturers Association

TOP 10

VEHICLE-OWNING COUNTRIES IN THE WORLD

	Country	Cars	Commercial vehicles	Total
1	US	134,981,000	65,465,000	200,446,000
2	Japan	44,680,000	22,173,463	66,853,463
3	Germany	40,499,442	3,061,874	43,561,316
4	Italy	30,000,000	2,806,500	32,806,500
5	France	25,100,000	5,195,000	30,295,000
6	UK	24,306,781	3,635,176	27,941,957
7	Russia	13,638,600	9,856,000	23,494,600
8	Spain	14,212,259	3,071,621	17,283,880
9	Canada	13,182,996	3,484,616	16,667,612
10	Brazil	12,000,000	3,160,689	15,160,689
	World	*477,010,289*	*169,748,819*	*646,759,108*

Almost three-quarters of the world's vehicles are registered in the Top 10 countries. Of these, some 233,810,745 are in Europe, and 232,607,90 in North and Central America.

Source: American Automobile Manufacturers Association

COUNTRIES WITH THE LONGEST ROAD SYSTEMS

	Country	Length km	miles
1	US	6,261,154	3,890,500
2	India	2,009,600	1,248,707
3	Brazil	1,939,000	1,204,839
4	France	1,512,700	939,948
5	Japan	1,144,360	711,072
6	China	1,117,000	694,072
7	Canada	1,021,000	634,420
8	Russia	948,000	589,060
9	Australia	895,030	556,146
10	Germany	639,800	397,553

BEST-SELLING CARS OF ALL TIME

	Model	Year first produced	Estimated no. made
1	Volkswagen Beetle	1937*	21,220,000
2	Toyota Corolla	1963	20,000,000
3	Ford Model T	1908	16,536,075
4	Volkswagen Golf/Rabbit	1974	14,800,000
5	Lada Riva	1970	13,500,000
6	Ford Escort/Orion	1967	12,000,000
7	Nissan Sunny/Pulsar	1966	10,200,000
8	Mazda 323	1977	9,500,000
9	Renault 4	1961	8,100,000
10	Honda Civic	1972	8,000,000

* Still produced in Mexico and Brazil

Estimates of manufacturers' output of their best-selling models vary from the vague to the unusually precise 16,536,075 of the Model T Ford, with 15,007,033 produced in the US, and the rest in Canada and the UK, between 1908 and 1927.

FIRST COUNTRIES TO MAKE SEAT BELTS COMPULSORY

	Country	Introduced		Country	Introduced
1	Czechoslovakia	Jan 1969	7	Puerto Rico	Jan 1974
2	Ivory Coast	Jan 1970	8	Spain	Oct 1974
3	Japan	Dec 1971	9	Sweden	Jan 1975
4	Australia	Jan 1972	10=	Netherlands	Jun 1975
5=	Brazil	Jun 1972	=	Belgium	Jun 1975
=	New Zealand	Jun 1972	=	Luxembourg	Jun 1975

Seat belts, long in use in aircraft, were not designed for use in private cars until the 1950s. Ford was the first manufacturer in the US to fit anchorage-points, and belts were first fitted as standard equipment in Swedish Volvos from 1959. They were optional extras in most cars until the 1970s, when they were fitted to all models.

TOP 10 BEST-SELLING CARS IN THE US

	1987 Model	Sales		1997 Sales	Model
	Escort	392,360	1	397,156	Camry
	Taurus	354,971	2	384,609	Accord
	Accord	334,876	3	357,162	Taurus
	Cavalier	307,028	4	315,546	Civic
	Celebrity	306,480	5	302,161	Cavalier
	Excel	263,610	6	283,898	Escort
	Ciera	244,607	7	250,810	Saturn
	Sentra	241,763	8	228,451	Lumina
	Tempo	219,296	9	218,461	Corolla
	Corsica/Beretta	214,074	10	204,078	Grand Am

Source: Ward's

PRODUCTION LINE
By applying mass-production methods to its Model T, Ford established a world record for sales that was unbroken for over 50 years.

LAND SPEED RECORDS

THRUST SCC

LATEST HOLDERS OF THE LAND SPEED RECORD

	Driver/car	Location	Date	Max speed km/h	mph
1	Andy Green (UK), *ThrustSSC*	Black Rock Desert	Oct 15, 1997	1,227.99	763.04
2	Richard Noble (UK), *Thrust 2*	Black Rock Desert	Oct 4, 1983	1,013.47	633.47
3	Gary Gabelich (US), *The Blue Flame*	Bonneville Salt Flats	Oct 23, 1970	995.85	622.41
4	Craig Breedlove (US), *Spirit of America – Sonic 1*	Bonneville Salt Flats	Nov 15, 1965	960.96	600.60
5	Art Arfons (US), *Green Monster*	Bonneville Salt Flats	Nov 7, 1965	922.48	576.55
6	Craig Breedlove (US), *Spirit of America – Sonic 1*	Bonneville Salt Flats	Nov 2, 1965	888.76	555.48
7	Art Arfons (US), *Green Monster*	Bonneville Salt Flats	Oct 27, 1964	958.73	536.71
8	Craig Breedlove (US), *Spirit of America*	Bonneville Salt Flats	Oct 15, 1964	842.04	526.28
9	Craig Breedlove (US), *Spirit of America*	Bonneville Salt Flats	Oct 13, 1964	749.95	468.72
10	Art Arfons (US), *Spirit of America*	Bonneville Salt Flats	Oct 5, 1964	694.43	434.02

On September 16, 1947, British driver John Cobb achieved a speed of 394.20 mph/ 630.72 km/h in his Railton Mobil Special, at Bonneville Salt Flats. His record stood for 16 years until 1963, since when it has been successively broken. In the 50 years since Cobb gained the land speed record, the record speed has almost doubled.

FASTEST PRODUCTION CARS IN THE WORLD

	Model*	Max speed# km/h	mph
1	Lamborghini Diablo Roadster	335	208
2	Ferrari F50	325	202
3	Lister Storm GTL	322	200
4	Aston Martin V8 Vantage	298	185
5	Porsche 911 Turbo 4	291	181
6	Chrysler Viper GTS	285	177
7=	Marcos 4.6 Spyder†	274	170
=	TVR Cerbera	274	170
=	Lotus Esprit V8-GT	274	170
10	Maserati Ghibli Cup	272	169

* *Fastest of each manufacturer*

\# *May vary according to specification changes to meet national legal requirements*

† *Other models are capable of the same speed*

FIRST AMERICAN HOLDERS OF THE LAND SPEED RECORD*

	Driver/date	Max speed km/h	mph
1	William Vanderbilt, Aug 5, 1902	121.72	76.08
2	Henry Ford#, Jan 12, 1904	146.19	91.37
3	Fred Marriott#, Jan 23, 1906	194.51	121.57
4	Barney Oldfield#, Mar 16, 1910	210.03	131.27
5	Bob Burman#, Apr 23, 1911	226.19	141.37
6	Ralph de Palma#, Feb 17, 1919	239.79	149.87
7	Tommy Milton#, Apr 27, 1920	249.64	156.03
8	Ray Keech, Apr 22, 1928	332.08	207.55
9	Craig Breedlove#, Aug 5, 1963	651.92	407.45
10	Tom Green, Oct 2, 1964	661.12	413.20

* *Excluding those who subsequently broke their own records*

\# *Record not recognized in Europe*

T H E   1 0

LATEST HOLDERS OF THE MOTORCYCLE SPEED RECORD

Rider/ motorcycle/year	Max speed km/h	mph
1 Dave Campos, Twin 91 cu in/1,491 cc Ruxton Harley-Davidson *Easyriders*, 1990	518.45	322.15
2 Donald A. Vesco, Twin 1,016 cc Kawasaki *Lightning Bolt*, 1978	512.73	318.60
3 Donald A. Vesco, 1,496 cc Yamaha *Silver Bird*, 1975	487.50	302.93
4 Calvin Rayborn, 1,480 cc Harley-Davidson, 1970	426.40	264.96
5 Calvin Rayborn, 1,480 cc Harley-Davidson, 1970	410.37	254.99
6 Donald A. Vesco, 700 cc Yamaha, 1970	405.25	251.82
7 Robert Leppan, 1298 cc Triumph, 1966	395.27	245.62
8 William A. Johnson, 667 cc Triumph, 1962	361.40	224.57
9 Wilhelm Herz, 499 cc NSU, 1956	338.08	210.08
10 Russell Wright, 998 cc Vincent HRD, 1955	297.64	184.95

All the records listed here were achieved at the Bonneville Salt Flats, with the exception of No.10, which was attained at Christchurch, New Zealand.

THE FIRST TO TOP 100 KM PER HOUR

All the early attempts to establish and break the world land speed record were undertaken in Europe under the auspices of the Automobile Club de France. The first few years were dominated by the rivalry between the Frenchman Comte Gaston de Chasseloup-Laubat and the Belgian Camille Jenatzy, each of whom alternately held the record on three occasions. It was Jenatzy who first broke the psychologically significant 62 mph (100 km/h) barrier. He did so over a 2-km course at Achères in France, on April 29, 1899, in his electrically powered vehicle, *La Jamais Contente* ("The Never Satisfied"), achieving a speed of 65.79 mph (105.87 km/h).

100 YEARS AGO · YEARS AGO · YEARS AGO

T H E   1 0

FIRST HOLDERS OF THE MOTORCYCLE SPEED RECORD

Rider	Motorcycle	Location	Year	Max speed km/h	mph
1 Ernest Walker	994 cc Indian	Daytona Beach, FL	1920	167.67	104.19
2 Claude F. Temple	996 cc British Azani	Brooklands, UK	1923	174.58	108.48
3 Herbert Le Vack	867 cc Brough Superior	Arpajon, France	1924	191.59	118.05
4 Claude F. Temple	996 cc OEC Temple	Arpajon, France	1926	191.59	119.05
5 Oliver M. Baldwin	996 cc Zenith JAP	Arpajon, France	1928	200.56	124.62
6 Herbert Le Vack	995 cc Brough	Arpajon, France	1929	207.33	128.33
7 Joseph S. Wright	994 cc OEC Temple	Arpajon, France	1930	220.99	137.32
8 Ernst Henne	735 cc BMW	Ingolstadt, Germany	1930	221.54	137.66
9 Joseph S. Wright	995 cc OEC Temple JAP	Cork, Ireland	1930	242.50	150.68
10 Ernst Henne	735 cc BMW	Tat, Hungary	1932	244.40	151.86

THE 10 FIRST HOLDERS OF THE LAND SPEED RECORD
(Car/date/speed)

❶ Gaston de Chasseloup-Laubat (Jeantaud, Dec 18, 1898, 39.24 mph/62.78 km/h) ❷ Camile Jenatzy (Jenatzy, Jan 17, 1899, 41.420 mph/66.27 km/h) ❸ Gaston de Chasseloup-Laubat (Jeantaud, Jan 17, 1899, 43.69 mph/69.90 km/h) ❹ Camile Jenatzy (Jenatzy, Jan 27, 1899, 49.92 mph/79.37 km/h) ❺ Gaston de Chasseloup-Laubat (Jeantaud, Mar 4, 1899, 57.60 mph/92.16 km/h) ❻ Camile Jenatzy (Jenatzy, Apr 29, 1899, 65.79 mph/105.87 km/h) ❼ Leon Serpollet (Serpollet, Apr 13, 1902, 75.06 mph/120.09 km/h) ❽ William Vanderbilt (Mors, Aug 5, 1902, 76.08 mph/121.72 km/h) ❾ Henri Fournier (Mors, Nov 5, 1902, 76.60 mph/122.56 km/h) ❿ M. Augières (Mors, Nov 17, 1902, 77.13 mph/123.40 km/h)

ELECTRIC POWER
In 1899, in his electrically powered car La Jamais Contente, *the Belgian driver Jenatzy was the first to reach a speed of over 100km/h.*

RAILROADS

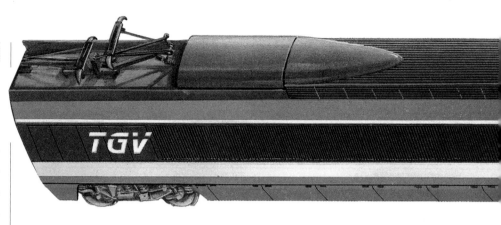

FIRST COUNTRIES WITH RAILROADS

	Country	First railroad established
1	UK	September 27, 1825
2	France	November 7, 1829
3	US	May 24, 1830
4	Ireland	December 17, 1834
5	Belgium	May 5, 1835
6	Germany	December 7, 1835
7	Canada	July 21, 1836
8	Russia	October 30, 1837
9	Austria	January 6, 1838
10	Netherlands	September 24, 1839

Although there were earlier horse-drawn railroads, the Stockton and Darlington Railway in the north of England inaugurated the world's first steam service. In their early years, some of the countries listed here offered only limited services over short distances, but their opening dates mark the generally accepted beginning of each country's steam railroad system.

GOING UNDERGROUND
London's Metropolitan Railway, the world's first underground service, opened on January 10, 1863. The wide-gauge track (7 ft/2.134 m) seen here at Bellmouth, Praed Street, was used in its early years.

LONGEST UNDERGROUND RAILROAD SYSTEMS IN THE WORLD*

	Location	Opened	Stations	Total track length km	miles
1	London, UK	1863	270	401	251
2	New York, NY	1904	469	398	249
3	Paris, France#	1900	432	323	202
4	Tokyo, Japan†	1927	250	289	181
5	Moscow, Russia	1935	150	244	153
6	Mexico City, Mexico	1969	154	178	112
7	Chicago, IL	1943	145	173	108
8	Copenhagen, Denmark	1934	79	170	106
9	Berlin, Germany	1902	135	167	104
10	Seoul, South Korea	1974	130	165	103

* Including systems that are only partly underground

\# Metro + RER

† Through-running extensions raise total to 391 miles/683 km, with 502 stations

OLDEST UNDERGROUND RAILROAD SYSTEMS IN THE WORLD

	City	Opened
1	London	1863
2=	Budapest	1896
=	Glasgow	1896
4	Boston	1897
5	Paris	1900
6	Berlin	1902
7	New York	1904
8	Philadelphia	1907
9	Hamburg	1912
10	Buenos Aires	1913

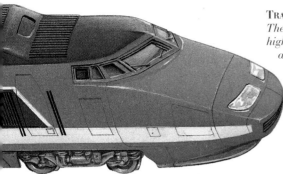

TRAIN À GRANDE VITESSE
The French TGV (Train à Grande Vitesse, or high-speed train) began service between Paris and Lyons in 1981. Its former world record scheduled speed is now exceeded by even faster "bullet trains" in service in Japan.

TOP 10
LONGEST RAIL SYSTEMS IN THE WORLD

	Location	Total rail length km	miles
1	US	240,000	149,129
2	Russia	154,000	95,691
3	Canada	70,176	43,605
4	India	62,462	38,812
5	China	58,399	36,287
6	Germany	43,966	27,319
7	Australia	38,563	23,962
8	Argentina	37,910	23,556
9	France	33,891	21,059
10	Brazil	27,418	17,037

Although remaining at the head of this list, US rail mileage has declined considerably since its 1916 peak of 254,000 miles/408,773 km The total of all world systems is today considered to be about 746,476 miles/1,201,337 km.

TOP 10
BUSIEST AMTRAK RAIL STATIONS IN THE US

	Station	Boardings (1997)		Station	Boardings (1997)
1	New York-Penn	5,623,219	6	Baltimore-Penn	798,893
2	Washington-Union	2,989,024	7	Boston-South	740,647
3	Philadelphia-30th St.	2,872,930	8	San Diego	702,884
4	Chicago-Union	2,084,621	9	Sacramento	560,120
5	Los Angeles-Union	1,009,381	10	Bakersfield	527,817

Source: Amtrak

TOP 10
FASTEST RAIL TRIPS IN THE WORLD*

	Journey	Train	Distance miles	Speed mph
1	Hiroshima–Kokura, Japan	Nozomi 503/508	119.3	162.7
2	Lille–Roissy, France	TGV 538/9	126.4	158.0
3	Madrid–Seville, Spain	AVE 9616/9617	292.4	129.9
4	Würzburg–Fulda, Germany	ICE	57.9	124.1
5	London–York, UK	Scottish Pullman	188.5	112.0
6	Hässleholm–Alvesta, Sweden	X2000	60.9	104.4
7	Rome–Florence, Italy	10 Pendolini	162.2	102.5
8	Baltimore–Wilmington, US	Metroliner 110	68.4	97.7
9	Salo–Karjaa, Finland	S220 132	33.0	94.3
10	Toronto–Dorval, Canada	Metropolis	322.8	87.6

* *Fastest journey for each country; all those in the Top 10 have other similarly or equally fast services*

The fastest international journeys are those between Paris, France, and Mons, Belgium, on 4 Thalys, a trip of 174.98 miles/281.6 km at an average speed of 131.23 mph/211.2 km/h.

TOP 10
BUSIEST RAIL SYSTEMS IN THE WORLD

	Country	Passenger/ km per annum	miles per annum*
1	Japan	396,332,000,000	246,269,000,000
2	China	354,700,000,000	219,965,000,000
3	India	319,400,000,000	198,500,000,000
4	Russia	191,900,000,000	119,200,000,000
5	Ukraine	75,900,000,000	47,200,000,000
6	France	58,380,000,000	36,276,000,000
7	Germany	58,003,000,000	36,041,000,000
8	Egypt	47,992,000,000	29,821,000,000
9	Italy	47,100,000,000	29,270,000,000
10	South Korea	30,216,000,000	18,775,000,000
	US	21,144,000,000	13,138,000,000

* *Number of passengers multiplied by distance carried*

WATER TRANSPORTATION

TOP 10

BUSIEST PORTS IN THE WORLD

	Port	Location	Goods handled p.a. (tons)
1	Rotterdam	Netherlands	385,809,000
2	Singapore	Singapore	319,670,000
3	Chiba	Japan	191,471,000
4	Kobe	Japan	188,495,000
5	Hong Kong	China	162,260,000
6	Houston	US	156,528,000
7	Shanghai	China	153,883,000
8	Nagoya	Japan	151,347,000
9	Yokohama	Japan	141,427,000
10	Antwerp	Belgium	120,703,000

The only other world port handling more than 100,000,000 tons is Kawasaki, Japan (115,853,000 tons per annum).

TOP 10

LARGEST OIL TANKERS IN THE WORLD

	Tanker	Year built	Country of origin	Gross tonnage*	Deadweight tonnage#
1	*Jahre Viking*	1979	Japan	260,851	564,763
2	*Sea Giant*	1979	France	261,862	555,051
3	*Kapetan Giannis*	1977	Japan	247,160	516,895
4	*Kapetan Michalis*	1977	Japan	247,160	516,423
5	*Sea World*	1978	Sweden	237,768	491,120
6	*Nissei Maru*	1975	Japan	238,517	484,276
7	*Stena King*	1978	Taiwan	218,593	457,927
8	*Stena Queen*	1977	Taiwan	218,593	457,841
9	*Kapetan Panagiotis*	1977	Japan	218,447	457,062
10	*Kapetan Giorgis*	1976	Japan	218,447	456,368

* The weight of the ship when empty

 # The total weight of the vessel, including its cargo, crew, passengers, and supplies

Source: Lloyds Register of Shipping, MIPG/PPMS

TOP 10

LONGEST SHIP CANALS IN THE WORLD

	Canal/location/opened	Length km	miles
1	St. Lawrence Seaway, Canada/US, 1959	304	189
2	Main-Danube, Germany, 1992	171	106
3	Suez, Egypt, 1869	162	101
4=	Albert, Belgium, 1939	129	80
=	Moscow-Volga, Russia, 1937	129	80
6	Kiel, Germany, 1895	99	62
7	Trollhätte, Sweden, 1916	87	54
8	Alphonse XIII, Spain, 1926	85	53
9	Panama, Panama, 1914	82	51
10	Houston, US, 1914	81	50

TOP 10

LONGEST CRUISE SHIPS IN THE WORLD

	Ship/year built/country of origin	Length m	ft in
1	*Norway* (formerly *France*), 1961, France	315.53	1,035 2
2	*United States**, 1952, US	301.76	990 0
3=	*Disney Magic*, 1998, Italy	294.00	964 7
=	*Disney Wonder*, 1998, Italy	294.00	964 7
5	*Queen Elizabeth 2*, 1969, UK	293.53	963 0
6	*Grand Princess*, 1998, Italy	285.00	935 0
7	*Enchantment of the Seas*, 1997, Finland	279.60	917 4
8	*Grandeur of the Seas*, 1996, Finland	279.10	915 8
9	*Vision of the Seas*, 1998, France	279.00	915 4
10	*Rhapsody of the Seas*, 1997, France	278.94	915 2

* Currently undergoing conversion to cruise ship

Source: Lloyds Register of Shipping, MIPG/PPMS

SUPERCRUISER

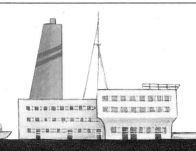

T O P 1 0

SHIPPING COUNTRIES IN THE WORLD

	Country	Ships	Total gross tonnage
1	Panama	6,188	91,128,000,000
2	Liberia	1,697	60,058,000,000
3	Bahamas	1,221	25,523,000,000
4	Greece	1,641	25,288,000,000
5	Cyprus	1,650	23,653,000,000
6	Malta	1,378	22,984,000,000
7	Norway	715	19,780,000,000
8	Singapore	1,656	18,875,000,000
9	Japan	9,310	18,516,000,000
10	China	3,175	16,339,000,000
	US	5,260	11,789,000,000

Source: Lloyds Register of Shipping, FMIPG/PPMS

T O P 1 0

COUNTRIES WITH THE LONGEST INLAND WATERWAYS*

	Country	km	miles
1	China	110,600	68,724
2	Russia	101,000	62,758
3	Brazil	50,000	31,069
4	US#	41,009	25,482
5	Indonesia	21,579	13,409
6	Vietnam	17,702	11,000
7	India	16,180	10,054
8	Dem. Rep. of Congo	15,000	9,321
9	France	14,932	9,278
10	Colombia	14,300	8,886

* Canals and navigable rivers
# Excluding the Great Lakes

T O P 1 0

LARGEST CRUISE SHIPS IN THE WORLD

	Ship	Built year	country	Passenger capacity	Gross tonnage
1	Grand Princess	1998	Italy	3,300	104,000
2	Carnival Triumph	1998	Italy	3,300	101,672
3	Carnival Destiny	1996	Italy	3,336	101,353
4 =	Disney Wonder	1998	Italy	2,500	85,000
=	Disney Magic	1998	Italy	2,500	85,000
6	Rhapsody of the Seas	1997	France	2,416	78,491
7 =	Dawn Princess	1997	Italy	1,950	77,441
=	Sun Princess	1995	Italy	2,272	77,441
9 =	Galaxy	1996	Germany	1,896	76,522
=	Mercury	1997	Germany	1,896	76,522

While the day of the passenger liner may be over, that of the cruise liner has dawned, with ever-larger vessels joining the world's cruise line fleets in the 1990s. By 2002, this list will be completely altered again as an additional four vessels of more than 100,000 tons are completed. Three identical ships currently under construction in Finland will head the new millennium's Top 10, with a massive leap to a size of 142,000 tons each, and passenger capacities of some 4,000.

Source: Lloyds Register of Shipping, MIPG/PPMS

THE WORLD'S BIGGEST LINER

The *Great Eastern*, launched in 1858 and scrapped in 1887, was the largest ship in the world until 1899, when the *Oceanic* was launched. Built by Harland and Wolff of Belfast, who were later to build the ill-fated *Titanic*, it was operated by the White Star company. The *Oceanic* measured 704 ft/215 m long and 68 ft/21 m wide and had a displacement of 17,551 tons. Sailing between the UK and New York, the liner, which carried 1,710 passengers, was considered the most luxurious afloat. At the outbreak of the First World War, she was converted into a cruiser, but within weeks, on September 8, 1914, was wrecked in fog off Foula, Shetland Islands, although the crew was rescued.

YEARS AGO 100 YEARS AGO

PIONEERS OF FLIGHT

MONTGOLFIER BALLOON
Although designed and built by the Mongolfiers, the first-ever balloon flight was made by two other men.

FIRST ROCKET AND JET AIRCRAFT

	Aircraft/country	First flight
1	Heinkel He 176*, Germany	Jun 20, 1939
2	Heinkel He 178, Germany	Aug 27, 1939
3	DFS 194*, Germany	Aug 1940#
4	Caproni-Campini N-1, Italy	Aug 28, 1940
5	Heinkel He 280V-1, Germany	Apr 2, 1941
6	Gloster E.28/39, UK	May 15, 1941
7	Messerschmitt Me 163 Komet*, Germany	Aug 13, 1941
8	Messerschmitt Me 262V-3, Germany	Jul 18, 1942
9	Bell XP-59A Airacomet, US	Oct 1, 1942
10	Gloster Meteor F Mk 1, UK	Mar 5, 1943

* *Rocket-powered*
\# *Precise date unknown*

FIRST MANNED BALLOON FLIGHTS*

	Balloonists/incident	Date
1	The Montgolfier Brothers	June 5, 1783

The Montgolfier Brothers, Joseph and Etienne, tested their first unmanned hot-air balloon in the French town of Annonay on June 5, 1783. On November 21, 1783, François Laurent, Marquis d'Arlandes, and Jean François Pilâtre de Rozier took off from the Bois de Boulogne, Paris, in a Montgolfier hot-air balloon. This first-ever manned flight covered a distance of about 5½ miles/ 9 km in 23 minutes, landing safely near Gentilly.

2	Jacques Alexandre César Charles and Nicholas-Louis Robert	December 1, 1783

Watched by a crowd of 400,000, Jacques Alexandre César Charles and Nicholas-Louis Robert made the first-ever flight in a hydrogen balloon. They took off from the Tuileries, Paris, and traveled about 27 miles/43 km north to Nesle in a time of about two hours. Charles then took off again alone, thus becoming the first solo flier.

3	Pilâtre de Rozier	January 19, 1784

La Flesselle, a gigantic 131-ft/ 40-m high Montgolfier hot-air balloon named after its sponsor, the local governor, ascended from Lyons piloted by Pilâtre de Rozier with Joseph Montgolfier, Prince Charles de Ligne, and the Comtes de La Porte d'Anglefort, de Dampierre, and de Laurencin – as well as the first aerial stowaway, a young man called Fontaine, who jumped in as it was taking off.

4	Chevalier Paolo Andreani, Augustino and Carlo Giuseppi Gerli	February 25, 1784

The Chevalier Paolo Andreani and the brothers Augustino and Carlo Giuseppi Gerli (the builders of the balloon) made the first-ever flight outside France, at Moncuco near Milan, Italy.

5	Jean-Pierre François Blanchard	March 2, 1784

Jean-Pierre François Blanchard made his first flight in a hydrogen balloon from the Champ de Mars, Paris, after experimental hops during the preceding months.

6	Mr. Rosseau	April 14, 1784

Mr. Rosseau and an unnamed 10-year-old drummer boy flew from Navan to Ratoath in Ireland, the first ascent in the British Isles.

7	Guyton de Morveau	April 25, 1784

Guyton de Morveau, a French chemist, and L'Abbé Bertrand flew at Dijon.

8	Bremond and Hughes Bernard Maret	May 8, 1784

Bremond and Hughes Bernard Maret flew at Marseilles.

9	Brun and Comte Xavier de Maistre	May 12, 1784

A 20-year-old ballooning pioneer named Brun ascended at Chambéry with the Comte Xavier de Maistre, also only 20 years of age.

10	Adorne	May 15, 1784

Adorne accompanied by an unnamed passenger took off but crash-landed near Strasbourg.

* *Several of the balloonists listed also made subsequent flights, but in each instance only their first flights are included.*

BIÉRIOT TYPE XI
Considered one of the great achievements of the early years of flying, Louis Biériot crossed the English Channel on July 25, 1909, at a speed of just 38 mph/61 km/h.

THE WRIGHT STUFF
Although primitive to modern eyes, the Wright Brothers' biplane successfully broke endurance records during 1908, thus proving that manned flight was a practical reality.

FIRST FLIGHTS OF MORE THAN ONE HOUR

	Pilot	hr	min	sec	Date
		Duration			
1	Orville Wright	1	2	15.0	Sep 9, 1908
2	Orville Wright	1	5	52.0	Sep 10, 1908
3	Orville Wright	1	10	0.0	Sep 11, 1908
4	Orville Wright	1	15	20.0	Sep 12, 1908
5	Wilbur Wright	1	31	25.8	Sep 21, 1908
6	Wilbur Wright	1	7	24.8	Sep 28, 1908
7	Wilbur Wright*	1	4	26.0	Oct 6, 1908
8	Wilbur Wright	1	9	45.4	Oct 10, 1908
9	Wilbur Wright	1	54	53.4	Dec 18, 1908
10	Wilbur Wright	2	20	23.2	Dec 31, 1908

* First flight of more than one hour with a passenger (M.A. Fordyce)

Following Orville Wright's first flight in a heavier-than-air aircraft (at Kitty Hawk, N. Carolina, on December 17, 1903), he and his brother Wilbur so mastered flying that they dominated the air for the next few years. In 1908 Orville (at Fort Meyer, near Washington, DC) and Wilbur (at the Champ d'Auvours, a military base near Le Mans, France) made a total of 10 flights lasting more than an hour – the last of which, on the last day of the year, actually exceeded two hours and covered a distance of 77 miles/124 km.

FIRST TRANSATLANTIC FLIGHTS

	Aircraft	Crossing	Date
1	US Navy/Curtiss flying boat NC-4	Trepassy Harbor, Newfoundland to Lisbon, Portugal	May 16–27, 1919
2	Twin Rolls-Royce-engined covered Vickers Vimy bomber	St. John's, Newfoundland to Galway, Ireland	June 14–15, 1919
3	British R-34 airship	East Fortune, Scotland to Roosevelt Field, New York	July 2–6, 1919
4	Fairey IIID seaplane *Santa Cruz*	Lisbon, Portugal to Recife, Brazil	March 30–June 5, 1922
5	Two Douglas seaplanes, *Chicago* and *New Orleans*	Orkneys, Scotland to Labrador, Canada	August 2–31, 1924
6	*Los Angeles*, a renamed German-built ZR 3 airship	Fredrichshafen, Germany to Lakehurst, New Jersey	October 12–15, 1924
7	*Plus Ultra*, a Dornier Wal twin-engined flying boat	Huelva, Spain to Recife, Brazil	January 22–February 10, 1926
8	*Santa Maria*, a Savoia-Marchetti S.55 flying boat	Cagliari, Sardinia to Recife, Brazil	February 8–24, 1927
9	Dornier Wal flying boat	Lisbon, Portugal to Natal, Brazil	March 16–17, 1927
10	Savoia Marchetti flying boat	Genoa, Italy to Natal, Brazil	April 28–May 14, 1927

THE FIRST TO FLY

The last year of the 19th century was notable for some of the first experiments in human flight. In England, US-born Samuel Franklin Cody began developing kites capable of lifting a person (Cody went on to become the first to fly a powered aircraft in the UK). On September 30, 1899, at Market Harborough, UK, pioneer birdman Percy Pilcher's flying machine broke up while being towed into the air by horses. In the same year, in the US, the Wright Brothers embarked on experiments with large kites and gliders that were to lead to their success with powered flight. The year 1899 also marked the birth of US pilot Wiley Post, who in 1933 accomplished the first solo round-the-world flight.

YEARS AGO • YEARS AGO • 100 • YEARS AGO • YEARS AGO

AIR TRAVEL

BOEING 727-200
An enhanced version of the 727 airliner, in service since 1963, the Boeing 727-200 first flew in 1972.

T O P   1 0

COMPLAINTS AGAINST AIRLINES IN THE US

	Complaint	Total (1996)
1	Flight problems (cancellations, delays, etc.)	1,626
2	Customer service (cabin service, meals, etc.)	1,000
3	Baggage	881
4	Ticketing/boarding	857
5	Refunds	521
6	Oversales/bumping	353
7	Fares	180
8	Advertising	61
9	Tours	16
10	Smoking	13
	Total (including others not in Top 10)	5,778

The category of complaints that has undergone the most notable change is that of smoking. In 1988, 546 people complained, mostly about others smoking close by. After the ban on smoking introduced on all US domestic flights in 1992, every year there are a few complaints from individuals who object to the prohibition.

Source: US Department of Transportation

T H E   1 0

BUSIEST AIRPORTS IN THE WORLD

	Airport/location	Passengers per annum*
1	Chicago O'Hare, Chicago	66,468,000
2	Hartsfield Atlanta Int., Atlanta	53,630,000
3	Dallas/Fort Worth Int., Dallas/Fort Worth	52,601,000
4	London Heathrow, London	51,368,000
5	Los Angeles Int., Los Angeles	51,050,000
6	Frankfurt, Frankfurt, Germany	34,376,000
7	San Francisco Int., San Francisco	33,965,000
8	Miami Int., Miami	30,203,000
9	John F. Kennedy Int., New York	28,807,000
10	Charles De Gaulle, Paris	28,363,000

*   *International and domestic flights*

Source: International Civil Aviation Organization

T H E   1 0

BUSIEST AIRPORTS IN THE US

	Airport	Passengers per annum*
1	O'Hare International, Chicago	29,970,255
2	Hartsfield International, Atlanta	25,669,559
3	Dallas/Fort Worth International	25,435,330
4	Los Angeles International (LAX)	19,885,450
5	Stapleton, Denver	14,788,640
6	San Francisco International	14,451,569
7	Phoenix Sky Harbor International	12,451,569
8	Detroit Metropolitan	12,256,251
9	Las Vegas McCarran International	11,997,567
10	Newark International	11,863,730

*   *Domestic flights only*

Source: Federal Aviation Authority

T O P   1 0

AIRCRAFT IN THE WORLD*

	Aircraft	Approximate no. in service
1	Boeing B-737	2,430
2	Douglas DC-9/MD-80	1,890
3	Boeing B-727	1,460
4	Boeing B-747	940
5	Boeing B-757	630
6	Airbus A-300/A-310	620
7	Boeing B-767	570
8	Airbus A-320	500
9	Douglas DC-10	320
10	Fokker F100	260

*   *Turbo-jet airliners only; scheduled and non-scheduled carriers, excluding China and former Soviet territories*

Source: International Civil Aviation Organization

THE 10
INTERNATIONAL FLIGHT ROUTES WITH THE MOST AIR TRAFFIC

	City A	City B	Passengers per route A to B	B to A	Total passengers
1	Hong Kong	Taipei	2,055,000	2,045,000	4,100,000
2	Paris	London	1,842,000	1,711,000	3,553,000
3	London	New York	1,322,000	1,311,000	2,633,000
4	London	Dublin	1,269,000	1,268,000	2,537,000
5	Kuala Lumpur	Singapore	1,196,000	1,119,000	2,315,000
6	Honolulu	Tokyo	1,157,000	1,137,000	2,294,000
7	Amsterdam	London	1,107,000	1,101,000	2,208,000
8	Seoul	Tokyo	1,089,000	1,081,000	2,170,000
9	Bangkok	Hong Kong	993,000	910,000	1,903,000
10	Hong Kong	Tokyo	940,000	937,000	1,877,000

Source: International Civil Aviation Organization

TOP 10
AIRLINE-USING COUNTRIES IN THE WORLD

	Country	Passenger-miles flown per annum*
1	US	1,351,860,500,000
2	UK	241,502,100,000
3	Japan	205,904,000,000
4	Australia	106,364,900,000
5	France	106,027,500,000
6	China	101,706,100,000
7	Germany	98,465,000,000
8	Russia	96,686,000,000
9	Canada	78,077,500,000
10	Netherlands	76,788,100,000

* Total distance traveled multiplied by number of passengers carried
Source: International Civil Aviation Organization

TOP 10
AIRLINES IN THE WORLD

	Airline/country	Aircraft in service	Passenger-miles flown per annum*
1	United Airlines, US	579	284,293,900,000
2	American Airlines, US	649	262,160,700,000
3	Delta Airlines, US	539	216,927,100,000
4	Northwest Airlines, US	385	159,308,700,000
5	British Airways, UK	212	144,065,300,000
6	JAL, Japan	121	107,537,300,000
7	Lufthansa, Germany	269	97,581,100,000
8	US Airlines, US	487	95,885,400,000
9	Continental Airlines, US	307	90,515,900,000
10	Air France, France	137	78,444,600,000

* Total distance traveled by aircraft of these airlines multiplied by number of passengers carried

Source: International Civil Aviation Organization

THE 10
BUSIEST INTERNATIONAL AIRPORTS IN THE WORLD

	Airport/location	International passengers per annum*
1	London Heathrow, London, UK	44,262,000
2	Frankfurt, Frankfurt, Germany	27,546,000
3	Charles de Gaulle, Paris, France	25,690,000
4	Hong Kong Int., Hong Kong, China	25,248,000
5	Schiphol, Amsterdam, Netherlands	22,943,000
6	New Tokyo International (Narita), Tokyo, Japan	20,681,000
7	Singapore International, Singapore	20,203,000
8	London Gatwick, Gatwick, UK	19,417,000
9	John F. Kennedy Int., New York	15,898,000
10	Bangkok, Bangkok, Thailand	13,747,000

Other than New York's JFK, only five airports in the US handle more than 5,000,000 international passengers a year, namely Miami (13,071,000), Los Angeles (12,679,000), Chicago O'Hare (6,174,000), Honolulu (5,504,000), and San Francisco (5,238,000).

* International flights only

Source: International Civil Aviation Organization

CHICAGO O'HARE AIRPORT

WORLD TOURISM

TOP 10

TOURIST COUNTRIES

	Country	Percentage world total	Visits (1997) *
1	France	10.9	66,800,000
2	US	8.0	49,038,000
3	Spain	7.1	43,403,000
4	Italy	5.6	34,087,000
5	UK	4.2	25,960,000
6	China	3.9	23,770,000
7	Poland	3.2	19,514,000
8	Mexico	3.2	19,351,000
9	Canada	2.9	17,610,000
10	Czech Republic	2.8	17,400,000

* *International tourist arrivals, excluding one-day visitors*

Source: World Tourism Organization

THE LEANING TOWER OF PISA

TOP 10

MOST VISITED ZOOS IN THE US

	Zoo/location	Visitors
1	Busch Gardens Tampa Bay Zoo, Tampa, FL	4,000,000
2	San Diego Zoo, San Diego, CA	3,500,000
3=	Lincoln Park Zoo, Chicago, IL	3,000,000
=	National Zoological Park, Washington, DC	3,000,000
5	St. Louis Zoological Park, St. Louis, MO	2,569,757
6	Brookfield Zoo, Brookfield, IL	2,212,508
7	Bronx Zoo, Bronx, NY	2,062,812
8	San Diego Wild Animal Park, Escondido, CA	1,650,000
9	Denver Zoological Gardens, Denver, CO	1,560,000
10	Houston Zoological Gardens, Houston, TX	1,400,000

Source: American Zoo and Aquarium Association

TOP 10

COUNTRIES EARNING THE MOST FROM TOURISM

	Country	Percentage world total	Total ($) receipts (1997)
1	US	15.1	75,056,000,000
2	Italy	6.8	30,000,000,000
3	France	6.3	27,947,000,000
4	Spain	6.1	27,190,000,000
5	UK	4.6	20,569,000,000
6	Germany	3.7	16,418,000,000
7	Austria	2.8	12,393,000,000
8	China	2.4	12,074,000,000
9	Australia	2.1	9,324,000,000
10	Hong Kong	2.1	9,242,000,000
	Canada	*2.0*	*8,928,000,000*

TOP 10

MOST VISITED AQUARIUMS IN THE US

	Aquarium	Visitors
1	Living Seas, Lake Buena Vista, FL	6,000,000
2	SeaWorld of Florida, Orlando, FL	5,100,000
3	SeaWorld of California, San Diego, CA	3,900,000
4	Monterey Bay Aquarium, Monterey, CA	2,029,815
5	John G. Shedd Aquarium, Chicago, IL	1,802,385
6	National Aquarium in Baltimore, Baltimore, MD	1,656,000
7	SeaWorld of Texas, San Antonio, TX	1,655,000
8	SeaWorld of Ohio, Aurora, TX	1,500,000
9	Marine World, Vallejo, CA	1,100,000
10	Tennessee Aquarium, Chattanooga, TN	1,083,165

Source: American Zoo and Aquarium Association

TOP 10

FOREIGN DESTINATIONS OF TOURISTS FROM THE US

	Country	Visitors
1	Mexico	19,616,000
2	Canada	12,909,000
3	UK	2,869,000
4	France	1,860,000
5	Germany	1,642,000
6	The Bahamas	1,504,000
7	Italy	1,385,000
8	Jamaica	1,029,000
9	Japan	871,000
10	The Netherlands	772,000

Source: Tourism Industries, International Trade Administration

TOP 10

AMUSEMENT AND THEME PARKS IN THE WORLD

Park/location	Estimated visitors (1996)
1 Tokyo Disneyland, Tokyo, Japan	16,980,000
2 Disneyland, Anaheim, California	15,000,000
3 Magic Kingdom at Walt Disney World, Lake Buena Vista, Florida	13,803,000
4 Disneyland Paris, Marne-la-Vallée, France	11,700,000
5 EPCOT at Walt Disney World, Lake BuenaVista, Florida	11,235,000
6 Disney-MGM Studios Theme Park at Walt Disney World, Lake Buena Vista, Florida	9,975,000
7 Universal Studios Florida, Orlando, Florida	8,400,000
8 Everland*, Kyonggi-Do, South Korea	8,000,000
9 Blackpool Pleasure Beach, Blackpool, UK	7,500,000
10 Yokohama Hakkeijima Sea Paradise, Japan	6,926,000

Formerly known as Yong-In Farmland

Source: Amusement Business

TOP 10

OLDEST AMUSEMENT PARKS IN THE US

Park/location	Year founded
1 Lake Compounce Amusement Park, Bristol, CT	1846
2 Cedar Point, Sandusky, OH	1870
3 Idlewild Park, Ligonier, PA	1878
4 Sea Breeze Amusement Park, Rochester, NY	1879
5 Dorney Park, Allentown, PA	1884
6 Pullen Park, Raleigh, NC	1887
7 Beech Bend Park, Bowling Green, KY	1888
8 Geauga Lake, Aurora, OH	1888
9 Arnold's Park, Arnold's Park, IA	1889
10 Carousel Gardens – City Park, New Orleans, LA	1891

TOP 10

TOURIST-SPENDING COUNTRIES

Tourist country of origin	Percentage world total	Total expenditure ($) (1996)
1 Germany	13.4	50,815,000,000
2 US	12.9	48,739,000,000
3 Japan	9.8	37,040,000,000
4 UK	6.7	24,445,000,000
5 France	4.7	17,746,000,000
6 Italy	4.1	15,516,000,000
7 Austria	3.1	11,811,000,000
8 Netherlands	3.0	11,370,000,000
9 Canada	2.9	11,090,000,000
10 Russia	2.8	10,723,000,000

In 1996 (the latest year for which comparative statistics are available), the world spent $379,129,000,000 on tourism in a foreign country, with the Top 10 countries (the only ones in the world spending more than $10 billion each) accounting for 63.4 percent of the total.

Source: World Tourism Organization

TOP 10

OLDEST AMUSEMENT PARKS IN THE WORLD

Park/location	Year founded
1 Bakken, Klampenborg, Denmark	1583
2 The Prater, Vienna, Austria	1766
3 Blackgang Chine Cliff Top Theme Park, Ventnor, Isle of Wight, UK	1842
4 Tivoli, Copenhagen, Denmark	1843
5 Lake Compounce Amusement Park, Bristol, CT	1846
6 Hanayashiki, Tokyo, Japan	1853
7 Grand Pier, Teignmouth, UK	1865
8 Blackpool Central Pier, Blackpool, UK	1868
9 Cedar Point, Sandusky, OH	1870
10 Clacton Pier, Clacton, UK	1871

SPORTS & GAMES

THE 10

MOST SUCCESSFUL COACHES IN AN NFL CAREER

	Coach	Games won
1	Don Shula	347
2	George Halas	324
3	Tom Landry	270
4	Curly Lambeau	229
5	Chuck Noll	209
6	Chuck Knox	193
7	Paul Brown	170
8	Bud Grant	168
9	Dan Reeves*	156
10	Marv Levy*#	154

* *Still active 1997–98 season*

Announced retirement at end of 1997–98 season

Source: National Football League

THE 10

NFL PLAYERS WITH THE MOST CAREER TOUCHDOWNS

	Player	Touchdowns
1	Jerry Rice*	166
2	Marcus Allen*	145
3	Jim Brown	126
4	Walter Payton	125
5	Emmitt Smith*	119
6	John Riggins	116
7	Lenny Moore	113
8	Don Hutson	105
9	Steve Largent	101
10	Franco Harris	100

* *Still active 1997–98 season*

Source: National Football League

THE 10

MOST SUCCESSFUL NFL TEAMS

	Team	Super Bowl games wins	losses	Pts*
1	Dallas Cowboys	5	3	13
2	San Francisco 49ers	5	0	10
3	Pittsburgh Steelers	4	1	9
4	Washington Redskins	3	2	8
5=	Green Bay Packers	3	1	7
=	Oakland/ Los Angeles Raiders	3	1	7
7	Miami Dolphins	2	3	7
8	Denver Broncos	1	4	6
9	New York Giants	2	0	4
10=	Buffalo Bills	0	4	4
=	Minnesota Vikings	0	4	4

* *Based on two points for a Super Bowl win and one for a loss; wins take precedence over losses in determining ranking*

Source: National Football League

THE 10
LARGEST NFL STADIUMS

	Stadium/home team	Capacity
1	Pontiac Silverdrome, Detroit Lions	80,368
2	Rich Stadium, Buffalo Bills	80,091
3	Arrowhead Stadium, Kansas City Chiefs	79,101
4	Jack Cooke Stadium, Washington Redskins	78,600
5	Giants Stadium, New York Giants*	78,148
6	Mile High Stadium, Denver Broncos	76,078
7	Pro Player Stadium, Miami Dolphins	74,916
8	Houlihan's Stadium, Tampa Bay Buccaneers	74,301
9	Sun Devil Stadium, Arizona Cardinals	73,243
10	Alltell Stadium, Jacksonville Jaguars	73,000

* Seating reduced to 77,716 for New York Jets games

Source: National Football League

THE 10
NFL PLAYERS WITH THE MOST CAREER POINTS

	Player	Points
1	George Blanda	2,002
2	Nick Lowery	1,711
3	Jan Stenerud	1,699
4	Gary Anderson	1,681
5	Morten Andersen	1,641
6	Norm Johnson	1,558
7	Eddie Murray	1,532
8	Pat Leahy	1,470
9	Jim Turner	1,439
10	Matt Bahr	1,422

Source: National Football League

TOP 10 PLAYERS WITH THE MOST PASSING YARDS IN AN NFL CAREER
(Passing yards)

❶ Dan Marino (55,416) ❷ John Elway (48,669) ❸ Warren Moon (47,465) ❹ Fran Tarkenton (47,003) ❺ Dan Fouts (43,040) ❻ Joe Montana (40,551) ❼ Johnny Unitas (40,239) ❽ Dave Krieg (37,946) ❾ Boomer Esiason (37,920) ❿ Jim Kelly (35,467)

Source: National Football League

TOP 10
RUSHERS IN AN NFL CAREER

	Player	Total yards gained rushing
1	Walter Payton	16,726
2	Barry Sanders*	13,778
3	Eric Dickerson	13,259
4	Tony Dorsett	12,739
5	Marcus Allen*	12,243
6	Jim Brown	12,312
7	Franco Harris	12,120
8	Thurman Thomas*	11,405
9	John Riggins	11,352
10	O. J. Simpson	11,236

* Still active at end of 1997–98 season

Source: National Football League

DAN MARINO

TOP 10
POINT-SCORERS IN AN NFL SEASON

	Player	Team	Year	Points
1	Paul Hornung	Green Bay Packers	1960	176
2	Mark Moseley	Washington Redskins	1983	161
3	Gino Cappelletti	Boston Patriots	1964	155*
4	Emitt Smith	Dallas Cowboys	1995	150
5	Chip Lohmiller	Washington Redskins	1991	149
6	Gino Cappelletti	Boston Patriots	1961	147
7	Paul Hornung	Green Bay Packers	1961	146
8 =	Jim Turner	New York Jets	1968	145
=	John Kasay	Carolina Panthers	1996	145
10=	John Riggins	Washington Redskins	1983	144
=	Kevin Butler#	Chicago Bears	1985	144

* Including a two-point conversion   # The only rookie in this Top 10

ATHLETICS

NEW YORK MARATHON
*Run annually since 1970, it is
paralleled by earlier and more recent
marathons in many major cities.*

T O P   1 0

HIGHEST POLE VAULTS

	Athlete/country	Year	Height (m)
1	Sergey Bubka, (Ukraine)	1994	6.14
2	Okkert Brits (SA)	1995	6.03
3	Igor Trandenkov (Russia)	1996	6.01
4	Rodion Gataullin (USSR)	1989	6.00
5	Lawrence Johnson (US)	1996	5.98
6	Scott Huffman (US)	1994	5.97
7	Joe Dial (US)	1987	5.96
8=	Andrei Tiwontschik (Germany)	1996	5.95
=	Maxim Tarasov (Russia)	1997	5.95
10	Jean Galfione (France)	1994	5.94

If indoor world records are included, the
following would also make the Top 10:

Sergey Bubka (Ukraine)	*1993*	*6.15*
Rodion Gataullin (USSR)	*1989*	*6.02*

T O P   1 0

FASTEST WINNING TIMES FOR THE NEW YORK MARATHON

MEN

	Runner/country	Year	Time
1	Juma Ikangaa (Tanzania)	1989	2.08.01
2	Alberto Salazar (US)	1981	2.08.13
3	Steve Jones (UK)	1988	2.08.20
4	Rod Dixon (New Zealand)	1983	2.08.59
5	Geoff Smith (UK)	1983	2.09.08
6	Salvador Garcia (Mexico)	1991	2.09.28
7=	Alberto Salazar (US)	1982	2.09.29
=	Willie Mtolo (South Africa)	1992	2.09.29
9	Rodolfo Gomez (Mexico)	1982	2.09.33
10	Ken Martin (US)	1989	2.09.38

Source: New York Road Runners Club

WOMEN

	Runner/country	Year	Time
1	Lisa Ondieki (Australia)	1992	2.24.40
2	Allison Roe (New Zealand)	1981	2.25.29
3	Ingrid Kristiansen (Norway)	1989	2.25.30
4	Grete Waitz (Norway)	1980	2.25.41
5	Uta Pippig (Germany)	1993	2.26.24
6	Olga Markova (Russia)	1992	2.26.38
7	Grete Waitz (Norway)	1983	2.27.00
8	Grete Waitz (Norway)	1982	2.27.14
9	Liz McGolgan (UK)	1991	2.27.32
10	Grete Waitz (Norway)	1979	2.27.33

Source: New York Road Runners Club

CARL LEWIS
*A champion long-jumper
and one-time 100-meter
record-holder.*

T O P   1 0

LONGEST LONG JUMPS

	Athlete/country	Year	Distance
1	Mike Powell (US)	1991	8.95
2	Bob Beamon (US)	1968	8.90
3	Carl Lewis (US)	1991	8.87
4	Robert Emmiyan (USSR)	1987	8.86
5=	Larry Myricks (US)	1988	8.74
=	Eric Walder (US)	1994	8.74

	Athlete/country	Year	Distance
7	Ivan Pedrosa (Cuba)	1995	8.71
8	K. Streete-Thompson (US)	1994	8.63
9	James Beckford (Jamaica)	1997	8.62
10	Lutz Dombrowski (East Germany)	1990	8.54

OLYMPIC RINGS
A symbol of athletic achievement for more than 100 years

TOP 10
FASTEST MEN ON EARTH*

Athlete/country	Year	Time
1 Donovan Bailey (Canada)	1996	9.84
2 Leroy Burrell (US)	1994	9.85
3= Carl Lewis (US)	1991	9.86
= Frank Fredericks (Namibia)	1996	9.86
5 Linford Christie (UK)	1993	9.87
6 Ato Boldon (Trinidad)	1997	9.89
7 Maurice Green (US)	1997	9.90
8 Dennis Mitchell (US)	1996	9.91
9= Andre Cason (US)	1993	9.92
= Tim Montgomery (US)	1997	9.92
= Jon Drummond (US)	1997	9.92

* Based on fastest time for the 100 meters

TOP 10
FASTEST WOMEN ON EARTH*

Athlete/country	Year	Time
1 Florence Griffith-Joyner (US)	1988	10.61
2 Merlene Ottey (Jamaica)	1996	10.74
3 Evelyn Ashford (US)	1984	10.76
4 Irina Privalova (Russia)	1994	10.77
5 Dawn Sowell (US)	1989	10.78
6 Marlies Göhr (East Germany)	1983	10.81
7= Gail Devers (US)	1992	10.82
= Gwen Torrence (US)	1994	10.82
9= Marita Koch (East Germany)	1983	10.83
= Juliet Cuthbert (Jamaica)	1992	10.83

* Based on fastest time for the 100 meters

TOP 10
HIGHEST HIGH JUMPS

Athlete/country/year	Height (m)
1 Javier Sotomayor (Cuba), 1993	2.45
2 Patrik Sjöberg (Sweden), 1987	2.42
3 Igor Paklin (USSR), 1985	2.41
4= Rudolf Povarnitsyn (USSR), 1985	2.40
= Sorin Matei (Romania), 1990	2.40
= Charles Austin (US), 1991	2.40
7= Zhu Jianhua (China), 1984	2.39
= Hollis Conway (US), 1989	2.39
9= Gennadi Avdeyenko (USSR), 1987	2.38
= Sergey Malchenko (USSR), 1988	2.38
= Dragutin Topic (Yugoslavia), 1993	2.38
= Troy Kemp (Bahamas), 1995	2.38
= Artur Partyka (Poland), 1996	2.38

TOP 10
FASTEST TIMES FOR THE BOSTON MARATHON

MEN

Runner/country	Year	Time
1 Cosmas Ndeti (Kenya)	1994	2.07.15
2 Andres Espinosa (Mex)	1994	2.07.19
3 Rob de Castella (Aus)	1986	2.07.51
4 Jackson Kipngok (Kenya)	1994	2.08.08
5 Hwang Young-Jo (Korea)	1994	2.08.09
6 I. Hussein (Kenya)	1992	2.08.14
7 Gelindo Bordin (Italy)	1990	2.08.19
8 Arturo Barrios (Mex)	1994	2.08.28
9 Lorry Boay Akonay (Tanzania)	1994	2.08.35
10 I. Hussein (Kenya)	1998	2.08.43

Source: Boston Athletic Association

WOMEN

Runner/country	Year	Time
1 Uta Pippig (Germany)	1994	2.21.45
2 Joan Benoit (US)	1983	2.22.43
3 Valentina Yegorova (Russia)	1994	2.23.33
4 Olga Markova (CIS)*	1992	2.23.43
5 Wanda Panfil (Poland)	1991	2.24.18
6 Rosa Mota (Portugal)	1988	2.24.30
7 Ingrid Kristiansen (Norway)	1989	2.24.33
8 Ingrid Kristiansen (Norway)	1986	2.24.55
9 Uta Pippig (Germany)	1995	2.25.11
10 Elana Meyer (SA)	1994	2.25.15

* Commonwealth of Independent States
Source: Boston Athletic Association

THE 10
FIRST ATHLETES TO RUN A MILE IN UNDER FOUR MINUTES

Athlete/country	Time min:sec	Date
1 Roger Bannister (UK)	3:59.4	May 6, 1954
2 John Landy (Australia)	3:57.9	Jun 21, 1954
3 Laszlo Tabori (Hungary)	3:59.0	May 28, 1955
4= Chris Chataway (UK)	3:59.8	May 28, 1955
= Brian Hewson (UK)	3:59.8	May 28, 1955
6 Jim Bailey (Australia)	3:58.6	May 5, 1956
7 Gunnar Nielsen (Denmark)	3:59.1	Jun 1, 1956
8 Ron Delany (Ireland)	3:59.4	Jun 1, 1956
9 Derek Ibbotson (UK)	3:59.4	Aug 6, 1956
10 István Rózsavölgyi (Hungary)	3:59.0	Aug 26, 1956

BASKETBALL

TOP 10

FREE THROW PERCENTAGES

	Player	Attempts	Made	Per-cent
1	Mark Price	2,362	2,135	.904
2	Rick Barry	4,243	3,818	.900
3	Calvin Murphy	3,864	3,445	.892
4	Scott Skiles	1,741	1,548	.889
5	Larry Bird	4,471	3,960	.886
6	Bill Sharman	3,559	3,143	.883
7	Reggie Miller	5,037	4,416	.877
8	Ricky Pierce	3,871	3,389	.875
9	Kiki Vandeweghe	3,997	3,484	.872
10	Jeff Malone	3,383	2,947	.871

Source: NBA

SHAQUILLE O'NEAL

THE 10

NBA PLAYERS WITH THE MOST CAREER ASSISTS

	Player	Assists
1	John Stockton*	12,713
2	Magic Johnson	10,141
3	Oscar Robertson	9,887
4	Isiah Thomas	9,061
5	Mark Jackson*	7,538
6	Maurice Cheeks	7,392
7	Lenny Wilkens	7,211
8	Bob Cousy	6,995
9	Guy Rodgers	6,917
10	Nate Archibald	6,476

* Still active at end of 1997–98 season

Source: NBA

TOP 10

POINT-SCORERS IN AN NBA CAREER*

	Player	Total points
1	Kareem Abdul-Jabbar	38,387
2	Wilt Chamberlain	31,419
3	Michael Jordan#	29,277
4	Karl Malone#	27,782
5	Moses Malone	27,409
6	Elvin Hayes	27,313
7	Oscar Robertson	26,710
8	Dominique Wilkins	26,534
9	John Havlicek	26,395
10	Alex English	25,613

* Regular season games only

 # Still active at end of 1998 season

If points from the ABA were also considered, then Abdul-Jabbar would still be No. 1, with the same total. The greatest point-scorer in NBA history, his career spanned 20 seasons before he retired at the end of the 1989 season.

Source: NBA

THE 10

HIGHEST-EARNING PLAYERS IN THE NBA, 1996–97

	Player/team	Earnings ($)*
1	Michael Jordan, Chicago Bulls	30,140,000
2	Horace Grant, Orlando Magic	14,857,000
3	Reggie Miller, Indiana Pacers	11,250,000
4	Shaquille O'Neal, Los Angeles Lakers	10,714,000
5	Gary Payton, Seattle Supersonics	10,212,000
6	David Robinson, San Antonio Spurs	9,952,000
7	Juwan Howard, Washington Bullets	9,750,000
8	Hakeem Olajuwon, Houston Rockets	9,655,000
9	Alonzo Mourning, Miami Heat	9,380,000
10	Dennis Rodman, Chicago Bulls	9,000,000

* Salary only

TOP 10

POINTS SCORED IN THE WNBA

	Game	Score
1	Utah Starzz vs. Los Angeles Sparks	102–89
2	Cleveland Rockers vs. Utah Starzz	95–68
3	Sacramento Monarchs vs. Utah Starzz	93–78
4	Los Angeles Sparks vs. Sacramento Monarchs	93–73
5	Los Angeles Sparks vs. Utah Starzz	91–69
6	Cleveland Rockers vs. Los Angeles Sparks	89–85
7	Houston Comets vs. Sacramento Monarchs	89–61
8	Los Angeles Sparks vs. Sacramento Monarchs	88–77
9	Los Angeles Sparks vs. Cleveland Rockers	87–84
10	Charlotte Sting vs. New York Liberty	87–69

Source: STATS Inc.

THE 10
BIGGEST ARENAS IN THE NBA

	Arena/location	Home team	Capacity
1	Georgia Dome, Atlanta, Georgia	Atlanta Hawks	34,821
2	The Alamodome, San Antonio, Texas	San Antonio Spurs	34,215
3	Charlotte Coliseum, Charlotte, North Carolina	Charlotte Hornets	24,042
4	United Center, Chicago, Illinois	Chicago Bulls	21,711
5	The Rose Garden, Portland, Oregon	Portland Trailblazers	21,538
6	The Palace of Auburn Hills, Auburn Hills, Michigan	Detroit Pistons	21,454
7	Gund Arena, Cleveland, Ohio	Cleveland Cavaliers	20,562
8	CoreStates Center, Philadelphia, Pennsylvania	Philadelphia 76ers	20,444
9	SkyDome, Toronto	Toronto Raptors	20,125
10	Continental Airlines Arena (Meadowlands), East Rutherford, New Jersey	New Jersey Nets	20,049

Source: The Sporting News Official NBA Guide

THE 10
MOST SUCCESSFUL NBA COACHES

	Coach	Games won*		Coach	Games won*
1	Lenny Wilkens#	1,120	6	Jack Ramsay	864
2	Bill Fitch#	944	7	Don Nelson	851
3	Red Auerbach	938	8	Cotton Fitzsimmons	832
4	Dick Motta	936	9	Gene Shue	784
5	Pat Riley#	909	10	John MacLeod	707

* Regular season games only

Still active 1997–98 season

Lenny Wilkens reached his 1,000th win on March 1, 1996, when the Atlanta Hawks beat the Cleveland Cavaliers 74–68 at The Omni. Pat Riley, coach of the LA Lakers, the New York Knicks, and the Miami Heat between 1981 and 1998, acquired the best percentage record with 909 wins from 1,295 games, representing a 0.702 percent success rate.

Source: NBA

THE 10
MOST SUCCESSFUL DIVISION 1 NCAA TEAMS

	College	Division 1 wins		College	Division 1 wins
1	Kentucky	1,720	6	Temple	1,496
2	North Carolina	1,709	7	Syracuse	1,477
3	Kansas	1,665	8=	Oregon State	1,454
4	St. John's	1,554	=	Pennsylvania	1,454
5	Duke	1,548	10	Indiana	1,429

Source: NCAA/STATS Inc.

THE 10
PLAYERS TO HAVE PLAYED MOST GAMES IN THE NBA AND ABA

	Player	Games played
1	Robert Parish	1,611
2	Kareem Abdul-Jabbar	1,560
3	Moses Malone	1,455
4	Artis Gilmore	1,329
5	Buck Williams*	1,307
6	Elvin Hayes	1,303
7	Caldwell Jones	1,299
8	John Havlicek	1,270
9	Paul Silas	1,254
10	Julius Erving	1,243

* Still active at end of 1997–98 season

The ABA (American Basketball Association) was established as a rival to the NBA (National Basketball Association) in 1968 and survived until 1976. Because many of the sport's top players "defected," their figures are still included in this list.

Source: NBA

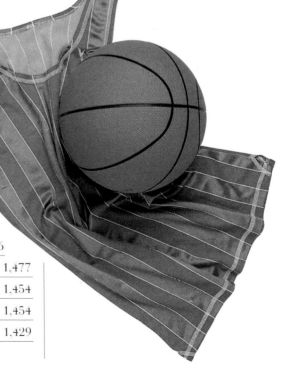

BASEBALL

THE 10

FIRST PITCHERS TO THROW PERFECT GAMES

	Player	Game	Date
1	Lee Richmond	Worcester *vs*. Cleveland	Jun 12, 1880
2	Monte Ward	Providence *vs*. Buffalo	Jun 17, 1880
3	Cy Young	Boston *vs*. Philadelphia	May 5, 1904
4	Addie Joss	Cleveland *vs*. Chicago	Oct 2, 1908
5	Charlie Robertson	Chicago *vs*. Detroit	Apr 30, 1922
6	Don Larsen*	New York *vs*. Brooklyn	Oct 8, 1956
7	Jim Bunning	Philadelphia *vs*. New York	Jun 21, 1964
8	Sandy Koufax	Los Angeles *vs*. Chicago	Sep 9, 1965
9	Catfish Hunter	Oakland *vs*. Minnesota	May 8, 1968
10	Len Barker	Cleveland *vs*. Toronto	May 15, 1981

* *Larsen's perfect game was, uniquely, in the World Series*

Fifteen pitchers have thrown perfect games; that is, they have pitched in all nine innings, dismissing 27 opposing batters, and without giving up a hit or walk. The last player to pitch a perfect game was David Wells, for New York Yankees against Minnesota, on May 17, 1998.

THE 10

FIRST PLAYERS TO HIT FOUR HOME RUNS IN ONE GAME

	Player	Club	Date
1	Bobby Lowe	Boston	May 30, 1884
2	Ed Delahanty	Philadelphia	Jul 13, 1896
3	Lou Gehrig	New York	Jun 3, 1932
4	Chuck Klein	Philadelphia	Jul 10, 1936
5	Pat Seerey	Chicago	Jul 18, 1948
6	Gil Hodges	Brooklyn	Aug 31, 1950
7	Joe Adcock	Milwaukee	Jul 31, 1954
8	Rocky Colavito	Cleveland	Jun 10, 1959
9	Willie Mays	San Francisco	Apr 30, 1961
10	Mike Schmidt	Philadelphia	Apr 17, 1976

The only other players to score four homers in one game are Bob Horner, who did so for Atlanta on July 6, 1986, and Mark Whitten, for St. Louis on September 7, 1993.

TOP 10

PITCHERS WITH THE MOST CAREER STRIKEOUTS

	Player	Strikeouts		Player	Strikeouts
1	Nolan Ryan	5,714	6	Gaylord Perry	3,534
2	Steve Carlton	4,136	7	Walter Johnson	3,508
3	Bert Blyleven	3,701	8	Phil Niekro	3,342
4	Tom Seaver	3,640	9	Ferguson Jenkins	3,192
5	Don Sutton	3,574	10	Bob Gibson	3,117

Source: Major League Baseball

TOP 10

TEAMS WITH THE MOST WORLD SERIES WINS

	Team*	Wins
1	New York Yankees	23
2 =	St. Louis Cardinals	9
=	Philadelphia/Kansas City/Oakland Athletics	9
4	Brooklyn/Los Angeles Dodgers	6
5 =	New York/San Francisco Giants	5
=	Boston Red Sox	5
=	Cincinnati Reds	5
=	Pittsburgh Pirates	5
9	Detroit Tigers	4
10 =	Boston/Milwaukee/Atlanta Braves	3
=	St. Louis/Baltimore Orioles	3
=	Washington Senators/Minnesota Twins	3

* *Teams separated by / indicate changes of franchise and are regarded as the same team for Major League record purposes*

Source: Major League Baseball

BASEBALL ANNIVERSARY

The National League dates from 1876 and the American League from 1901. Of the 28 current teams in the two Leagues, only six date back to 1876. One of these, the St. Louis Cardinals, was originally the St. Louis Browns. In 1899, when Cy Young, the pitcher who was to achieve the record for the most wins in baseball history, joined the team, the Browns also underwent a change of name. One of the team owners, Frank Robinson, introduced red stockings to the team uniform, and in his column in the *St. Louis Republic*, sports writer Willie McHale began calling the now colorfully attired Browns "the Cardinals." The nickname stuck and has been used ever since.

100 YEARS AGO · YEARS AGO · YEARS AGO

TOP 10

PLAYERS WITH THE HIGHEST CAREER BATTING AVERAGES

	Player	At bat	Hits	Av.*
1	Ty Cobb	11,434	4,189	.366
2	Rogers Hornsby	8,173	2,930	.358
3	Joe Jackson	4,981	1,772	.356
4	Ed Delahanty	7,505	2,597	.346
5	Tris Speaker	10,195	3,514	.345
6 =	Billy Hamilton	6,268	2,158	.344
=	Ted Williams	7,706	2,654	.344
8 =	Dan Brouthers	6,711	2,296	.342
=	Harry Heilmann	7,787	2,660	.342
=	Babe Ruth	8,399	2,873	.342

* Calculated by dividing the number of hits by the number of times a batter was "at bat"

Source: Major League Baseball

TOP 10

PLAYERS WHO PLAYED THE MOST GAMES IN A CAREER

	Player	Games
1	Pete Rose	3,562
2	Carl Yastrzemski	3,308
3	Hank Aaron	3,298
4	Ty Cobb	3,035
5	Stan Musial	3,026
6	Willie Mays	2,992
7	Dave Winfield	2,973
8	Eddie Murray*	3,026
9	Rusty Staub	2,951
10	Brooks Robinson	2,896

* Still active at end of 1996–97 season

Source: Major League Baseball

TOP 10

PITCHERS WITH THE MOST CAREER WINS

	Player	Wins
1	Cy Young	511
2	Walter Johnson	416
3 =	Christy Mathewson	373
=	Grover Alexander	373
5	Warren Spahn	363
6 =	Kid Nichols	361
=	Pud Galvin	361
8	Tim Keefe	342
9	Steve Carlton	329
10	John Clarkson	328

Cy (Denton True) Young (1867–1955) also holds the record for the most games pitched in a lifetime – a total of 906 between 1890 and 1911.

Source: Major League Baseball

TOP 10

PLAYERS WITH THE MOST RUNS IN A CAREER*

	Player	Runs
1	Ty Cobb	2,246
2 =	Babe Ruth	2,174
=	Hank Aaron	2,174
4	Pete Rose	2,165
5	Willie Mays	2,062
6	Stan Musial	1,949
7	Rickey Henderson#	1,913
8	Lou Gehrig	1,888
9	Tris Speaker	1,882
10	Mel Ott	1,859

* Regular season only, excluding World Series
# Still active in 1998 season

As well as his many other records, Ty (Tyrus Raymond) Cobb (1886–1961) is the only player ever to collect six hits in six at bats and hit three home runs in the same game, a feat he achieved on May 5, 1925.

Source: Major League Baseball

TOP 10

PLAYERS WITH MOST CONSECUTIVE GAMES PLAYED

	Player	Games		Player	Games
1	Cal Ripken Jr.*	2,477	6	Joe Sewell	1,103
2	Lou Gehrig	2,130	7	Stan Musial	895
3	Everett Scott	1,307	8	Eddie Yost	829
4	Steve Garvey	1,207	9	Gus Suhr	822
5	Billy Williams	1,117	10	Nellie Fox	798

* Still active during 1998 season

Source: Major League Baseball

THE 10

LOWEST EARNED RUN AVERAGES IN A CAREER

	Player	ERA		Player	ERA
1	Ed Walsh	1.82	6	Rube Waddell	2.16
2	Addie Joss	1.89	7	Walter Johnson	2.17
3	Three Finger Brown	2.06	8	Orval Overall	2.23
4	John Ward	2.10	9	Tommy Bond	2.25
5	Christy Mathewson	2.13	10	Ed Reulbach	2.28

Source: Major League Baseball

GOLF

TIGER WOODS

TOP 10 MONEY WINNERS
WORLDWIDE, 1997*
(Winnings)

❶ Tiger Woods, $2,082,381 ❷ David Duval, $1,885,308 ❸ Ernie Els (South Africa), $1,814,029 ❹ Greg Norman (Australia), $1,720,573 ❺ Davis Love III, $1,635,953 ❻ Jim Furyk, $1,619,460 ❼ Colin Montgomerie (Scotland), $1,609,300 ❽ Justin Leonard, $1,587,531 ❾ Scott Hoch, $1,418,272 ❿ Jumbo Ozaki (Japan), $1,362,433
* All US players unless otherwise stated

T O P   1 0

BEST WINNING SCORES
IN THE US MASTERS

	Player*	Year	Score
1	Tiger Woods	1997	270
2=	Jack Nicklaus	1965	271
=	Raymond Floyd	1976	271
4=	Ben Hogan	1953	274
=	Ben Crenshaw	1995	274
6=	Severiano Ballesteros (Spain)	1980	275
=	Fred Couples	1992	275
8=	Arnold Palmer	1964	276
=	Jack Nicklaus	1975	276
=	Tom Watson	1977	276
=	Nick Faldo (UK)	1996	276

* All US players unless otherwise stated

T O P   1 0

BEST FOUR-ROUND SCORES IN THE BRITISH OPEN

	Player	Country	Year	Venue	Score
1	Greg Norman	Australia	1993	Sandwich	267
2=	Tom Watson	US	1977	Turnberry	268
=	Nick Price	South Africa	1994	Turnberry	268
4=	Jack Nicklaus	US	1977	Turnberry	269
=	Nick Faldo	UK	1993	Sandwich	269
=	Jesper Parnevik	Sweden	1994	Turnberry	269
7=	Nick Faldo	UK	1990	St. Andrews	270
=	Bernhard Langer	Germany	1993	Sandwich	270
9=	Tom Watson	US	1980	Muirfield	271
=	Fuzzy Zoeller	US	1994	Turnberry	271
=	Tom Lehman	US	1996	Lytham	271

T O P   1 0

BEST WINNING TOTALS IN THE US OPEN

	Player*	Year	Venue	Score
1=	Jack Nicklaus	1980	Baltusrol	272
=	Lee Janzen	1993	Baltusrol	272
3	David Graham (Aus)	1981	Merion	273
4=	Jack Nicklaus	1967	Baltusrol	275
=	Lee Trevino	1968	Oak Hill	275
6=	Ben Hogan	1948	Riviera	276
=	Fuzzy Zoeller	1984	Winged Foot	276
=	Ernie Els (SA)	1997	Congressional	276
9=	Jerry Pate	1976	Atlanta	277
=	Scott Simpson	1987	Olympic Club	277

* All US players unless otherwise stated

THE GOLF TEE

On December 12, 1899, Dr. George F. Grant registered US Patent No. 638,920. His invention was the golf tee, the little piece of wood or plastic that tees the ball up at the start of each hole. Grant was an African-American Boston dentist and an avid golfer. Not wishing to get his hands dirty by shaping a mound of earth or sand, as all golfers, or their caddies, previously did, he came up with the invention of the tapered wooden tee peg, with a concave top to hold the ball in place. Although the majority of golfers use tees, which today are most commonly made of plastic, their use is not compulsory.

100 YEARS AGO

TOP 10

PLAYERS WITH THE MOST WINS ON THE US TOUR IN A CAREER

	Player*	Tour wins
1	Sam Snead	81
2	Jack Nicklaus	71
3	Ben Hogan	63
4	Arnold Palmer	60
5	Byron Nelson	52
6	Billy Casper	51
7 =	Walter Hagen	40
=	Cary Midlecoff	40
9	Gene Sarazen	38
10	Lloyd Mangrum	36

* All US players

For many years Sam Snead's total of wins was held to be 84, but the PGA Tour amended his figure in 1990 after discrepancies had been found in their previous lists. They deducted 11 wins from his total but added eight others, which should have been included, for a revised total of 81. The highest-placed current member of the regular Tour is Tom Watson, in joint 11th place with 32 wins. The highest placed non-US player is Gary Player (South Africa), with 22 wins. Sam Snead, despite being the most successful golfer on the US Tour, never won the US Open. After more than 25 attempts, his best finish was 2nd on four occasions. The most successful woman on the US Women's Tour is Kathy Whitworth with 88 Tour wins. Like Snead, she never won the US Open.

TOP 10

PLAYERS TO WIN THE MOST MAJORS IN A CAREER

	Player*	British Open	US Open	Masters	PGA	Total
1	Jack Nicklaus	3	4	6	5	18
2	Walter Hagen	4	2	0	5	11
3 =	Ben Hogan	1	4	2	2	9
=	Gary Player (SA)	3	1	3	2	9
5	Tom Watson	5	1	2	0	8
6 =	Harry Vardon (UK)	6	1	0	0	7
=	Gene Sarazen	1	2	1	3	7
=	Bobby Jones	3	4	0	0	7
=	Sam Snead	1	0	3	3	7
=	Arnold Palmer	2	1	4	0	7

* All US players unless otherwise stated

TOP 10

MONEY WINNERS OF ALL TIME*

	Player#	Career winnings ($)
1	Greg Norman (Australia)	11,936,443
2	Tom Kite	10,286,177
3	Fred Couples	8,885,487
4	Nick Price (Zimbabwe)	8,869,231
5	Mark O'Meara	8,656,374
6	Davis Love III	8,509,657
7	Payne Stewart	8,465,062
8	Tom Watson	8,307,277
9	Corey Pavin	8,130,356
10	Scott Hoch	7,930,700

* Through January 12, 1998

 # All US players unless otherwise stated

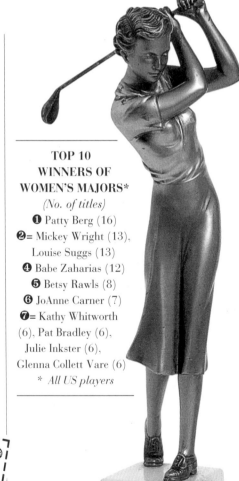

TOP 10 WINNERS OF WOMEN'S MAJORS*
(No. of titles)

❶ Patty Berg (16)
❷= Mickey Wright (13), Louise Suggs (13)
❹ Babe Zaharias (12)
❺ Betsy Rawls (8)
❻ JoAnne Carner (7)
❼= Kathy Whitworth (6), Pat Bradley (6), Julie Inkster (6), Glenna Collett Vare (6)
* All US players

● At the golf course at Richmond, Surrey, UK, on May 25, 1957, an actor holed in one from the eighth tee. Later on the same day a lawyer holed in one from the sixth tee. Both golfers were called Edward Chapman – a unique example of two holes in one on one day by two men with one name.

SNAP FACT

HORSE RACING

T O P   1 0
MONEY-WINNING NORTH AMERICAN JOCKEYS

	Jockey	Earnings ($)
1	Chris McCarron	214,139,278
2	Laffit Pincay Jr.	196,688,043
3	Pat Day	188,700,801
4	Angel Cordero Jr.	164,561,227
5	Eddie Delahoussaye	163,302,852
6	Gary Stevens	160,552,475
7	Jerry Bailey	153,662,886
8	Jorge Velasquez	125,524,557
9	Bill Shoemaker	123,375,524
10	Jose Santos	122,045,902

Sources: Daily Racing Form, The Jockey Club Information Systems, Inc., Equine Line, and Thoroughbred Racing Communications

T O P   1 0
US JOCKEYS WITH THE MOST WINS IN A CAREER

	Jockey	Years riding	Wins
1	Willie Shoemaker	42	8,833
2	Laffit Pincay Jr.	34	8,569
3	Angel Cordero Jr.	34	7,373
4	David Gall	41	7,185
5	Pat Day	25	7,106
6	Jorge Velasquez	34	6,796
7	Chris McCarron	24	6,558
8	Sandy Hawley	30	6,441
9	Larry Snyder	37	6,388
10	Carl Gambardella	39	6,349

Sources: Daily Racing Form, The Jockey Club Information Systems, Inc., Equine Line, and Thoroughbred Racing Communications

T H E   1 0
LATEST TRIPLE CROWN-WINNING HORSES*

	Horse	Year
1	Affirmed	1978
2	Seattle Slew	1977
3	Secretariat	1973
4	Citation	1948
5	Assault	1946
6	Count Fleet	1943
7	Whirlaway	1941
8	War Admiral	1937
9	Omaha	1935
10	Gallant Fox	1930

* Horses that have won the Kentucky Derby, the Preakness, and Belmont Stakes in the same season

T O P   1 0
JOCKEYS IN THE BREEDERS CUP

	Jockey	Years	Wins
1	Pat Day	1984–97	9
2	Mike Smith	1992–97	8
3 =	Eddie Delahoussaye	1984–93	7
=	Laffit Pincay Jr.	1985–93	7
=	Chris McCarron	1985–96	7
6 =	Pat Valenzuela	1986–92	6
=	Jerry Bailey	1991–96	6
=	Jose Santos	1986–97	6
9 =	Angel Cordero Jr.	1985–89	4
=	Craig Perret	1984–96	4
=	Gary Stevens	1990–96	4

T O P   1 0
FASTEST-WINNING TIMES OF THE KENTUCKY DERBY

	Horse	Year	Time min:sec
1	Secretariat	1973	1:59.2
2	Northern Dancer	1964	2:00.0
3	Spend A Buck	1985	2:00.2
4	Decidedly	1962	2:00.4
5	Proud Clarion	1967	2:00.6
6	Grindstone	1996	2:01.0
7 =	Lucky Debonair	1965	2:01.2
=	Affirmed	1978	2:01.2
=	Thunder Gulch	1995	2:01.2
10	Whirlaway	1941	2:01.4

Source: The Jockey Club

T O P   1 0
MONEY-WINNING HORSES DURING 1997

	Horse	Winnings ($)
1	Skip Away	4,089,000
2	Gentleman	2,125,300
3	Siphon	2,021,000
4	Chief Bearhart	2,011,259
5	Deputy Commander	1,849,440
6	Silver Charm	1,638,750
7	Touch Gold	1,522,313
8	Marlin	1,521,600
9	Free House	1,336,910
10	Favorite Trick	1,231,998

Source: The Jockey Club

Held at a different venue each year, the Breeders Cup is an end-of-season gathering with seven races run during the day, with the season's best thoroughbreds competing in each category. Staged in October or November, there is $10,000,000 in prize money with $3,000,000 going to the winner of the day's senior race, the Classic.

Source: The Jockey Club

- Bay horses have won the Kentucky Derby a record 55 times, chestnuts have won on 39 occasions, and black horses only four times.

- There have been just three maiden winners (horses that have not previously won a race) of the Kentucky Derby: Buchanan (1884), Sir Barton (1919), and Brokers Tip (1933).

- The greatest-ever attendance at the Kentucky Derby was the 100th event, in 1974, with 163,628. This event also had the largest field – 23 starters.

- Regret (1915), Genuine Risk (1980), and Winning Colors (1988) are the only fillies ever to have won the Kentucky Derby.

SNAP FACTS

TOP 10

JOCKEYS IN THE US DURING 1997

	Jockey	Winnings ($)
1	Jerry Bailey	18,320,743
2	Gary Stevens	15,861,224
3	Mike Smith	14,730,546
4	Pat Day	14,060,954
5	Alex Solis	13,517,376
6	Shane Sellers	13,042,441
7	Corey Nakatani	11,334,806
8	Chris McCarron	10,701,231
9	Kent Desormeaux	10,560,690
10	Jorge Chavez	9,093,180

Source: The Jockey Club

TOP 10

JOCKEYS OF ALL TIME IN THE UK

	Jockey	Champion Jockey titles	Best season total	Career Flat winners
1	Gordon Richards	26	269	4,870
2	Lester Piggott	11	191	4,493
3	Pat Eddery	11	209	4,000
4	Willie Carson	5	182	3,828
5	Doug Smith	5	173	3,111
6	Joe Mercer	1	164	2,810
7	Fred Archer	13	246	2,748
8	Edward Hide	0	137	2,593
9	George Fordham	14	166	2,587
10	Eph Smith	0	144	2,312

When Pat Eddery rode Silver Patriarch to victory in the St. Leger at Doncaster on September 13, 1997, he became only the third member of the elite "4,000 club" – jockeys who had won more than 4,000 races during their careers. This Top 10 consists of members of this elite group together with the runners-up at that time.

TOP 10

JOCKEYS IN ENGLISH CLASSICS

	Jockey	Years	1,000 Guineas	2,000 Guineas	Derby	Oaks	St. Leger	Wins
1	Lester Piggott	1954–92	2	5	9	6	8	30
2	Frank Buckle	1792–1827	6	5	5	9	2	27
3	Jem Robinson	1817–48	5	9	6	2	2	24
4	Fred Archer	1874–86	2	4	5	4	6	21
5=	Bill Scott	1821–46	0	3	4	3	9	19
=	Jack Watts	1883–97	4	2	4	4	5	19
7	Willie Carson	1972–94	2	4	4	4	3	17
8=	John Day	1826–41	5	4	0	5	2	16
=	George Fordham	1859–83	7	3	1	5	0	16
10	Joe Childs	1912–33	2	2	3	4	4	15

TOP 10

JOCKEYS IN THE US TRIPLE CROWN RACES*

	Jockey	Kentucky	Preakness	Belmont	Total
1	Eddie Arcaro	5	6	6	17
2	Bill Shoemaker	4	2	5	11
3=	Bill Hartack	5	3	1	9
=	Earle Sande	3	1	5	9
=	Pat Day	1	6	2	9
6	Jimmy McLaughlin	1	1	6	8
7=	Angel Cordero Jr.	3	2	1	6
=	Chris McCarron	2	3	1	6
=	Chas Kurtsinger	2	2	2	6
=	Ron Turcotte	2	2	2	6

* The US Triple Crown consists of the Kentucky Derby, Preakness Stakes, and Belmont Stakes.

TOP 10

HARNESS DRIVERS OF ALL TIME*

	Jockey	Wins	Earnings ($)		Jockey	Wins	Earnings ($)
1	John Campbell	7,591	155,576,651	6	Ronald Waples	6,399	66,685,462
2	Michel Lachance	7,999	100,574,725	7	Douglas Brown	6,957	66,275,181
3	William O'Donnell	5,364	90,555,622	8	Catello Manzi	7,626	64,838,626
4	Herve Filion	14,783	85,044,328	9	David Magee	7,833	54,939,716
5	Jack Moiseyev	7,130	69,394,236	10	Stephen Condren	4,571	51,325,182

* Up to and including races on January 11, 1998   Source: United States Trotting Association

MOTOR RACING

TOP 10 FASTEST GRAND PRIX RACES

| 1987 | | | | 1997 | |
Speed (mph)	Circuit	Grand Prix		Grand Prix	Circuit	Speed (mph)
146.28	Osterreichring	Austrian	1	Italian	Monza	147.91
146.21	Silverstone	British	2	German	Hockenheim	142.03
144.56	Monza	Italian	3	Austrian	A1 Ring	130.87
136.95	Hockenheim	German	4	Japanese	Suzuka	129.40
127.81	Spa-Francor champs	Belgian	5	British	Silverstone	128.53
121.29	Imola	San Marino	6	Australian	Albert Park	126.98
120.18	Mexico City	Mexican	7	Spanish	Jerez	126.67
119.83	Suzuka	Japanese	8	San Marino	Imola	126.27
117.17	Paul Ricard	French	9	Luxembourg	Nürburgring	124.68
116.96	Estoril	Portuguese	10	Belgian	Spa-Francor champs	122.31

DRIVERS WITH THE MOST GRAND PRIX WINS IN A CAREER

	Driver/country	Years	Wins
1	Alain Prost (France)	1981–93	51
2	Ayrton Senna (Brazil)	1985–93	41
3	Nigel Mansell (UK)	1985–94	31
4	Jackie Stewart (UK)	1965–73	27
5=	Jim Clark (UK)	1962–68	25
=	Niki Lauda (Austria)	1974–85	25
=	Michael Schumacher (Germany)	1992–97	25
8	Juan Manuel Fangio (Argentina)	1950–57	24
9	Nelson Piquet (Brazil)	1980–91	23
10	Damon Hill (UK)	1993–96	21

TOP 10 YOUNGEST FORMULA ONE WORLD CHAMPIONS OF ALL TIME
(Country/age)

❶ Emerson Fittipaldi (Brazil, 25 yrs 9 mths) ❷ Michael Schumacher (Germany, 25 yrs 10 mths) ❸ Jacques Villeneuve (Canada, 26 yrs 5 mths) ❹ Niki Lauda (Austria, 26 yrs 7 mths) ❺ Jim Clark (UK, 27 yrs 7 mths) ❻ Jochen Rindt (Austria, 28 yrs 6 mths) ❼ Ayrton Senna (Brazil, 28 yrs 7 mths) ❽= James Hunt, Nelson Piquet (UK/Brazil, 29 yrs 2 mths) ❿ Mike Hawthorn (UK, 29 yrs 6 mths)

CART MONEY WINNERS OF ALL TIME

	Driver	Total prizes ($)			Driver	Total prizes ($)
1	Al Unser Jr.	18,342,156		6	Rick Mears	11,050,807
2	Bobby Rahal	15,900,258		7	Danny Sullivan	8,884,126
3	Michael Andretti	14,704,619		8	Arie Luyendyk	7,732,188
4	Emerson Fittipaldi	14,293,625		9	Raul Boesel	6,971,887
5	Mario Andretti	11,552,154		10	Al Unser	6,740,843

Source: Championship Auto Racing Teams

JACQUES VILLENEUVE

MONEY-WINNERS AT THE INDIANAPOLIS 500, 1998*

	Driver/chassis	Total prizes ($)
1	Eddie Cheever, Dallara-Aurora	1,433,000
2	Buddy Lazier, Dallara-Aurora	483,200
3	Steve Knapp, G Force-Aurora	338,750
4	Davey Hamilton, G Force-Aurora	301,650
5	Robby Unser, Dallara-Aurora	209,400
6	Kenny Brack, Dallara-Aurora	310,750
7	John Paul, Jr., Dallara-Aurora	216,350
8	Andy Michner, Dallara-Aurora	182,050
9	J. J. Yeley, Dallara-Aurora	198,550
10	Buzz Calkins, G Force-Aurora	248,500

* Drivers are ranked here according to their finishing order.
Source: Indianapolis Motor Speedway

DRIVERS WITH THE MOST WINSTON CUP RACE WINS*

	Driver	Years	Wins
1	Richard Petty	1958–92	200
2	David Pearson	1960–86	105
3=	Bobby Allison	1975–88	84
=	Darrell Waltrip#	1972–98	84
5	Cale Yarborough	1957–88	83
6	Dale Earnhardt#	1975–98	71
7	Lee Petty	1949–64	55
8=	Ned Jarrett	1953–66	50
=	Junior Johnson	1953–66	50
10	Herb Thomas	1949–62	48

* *Through March 31, 1998*

Still driving at end of 1998 season

The Winston Cup's a season-long series of races organized by the National Association of Stock Car Auto Racing, Inc. (NASCAR). Races, which take place over closed circuits such as Daytona Speedway, are among the most popular motor races in the US. All the drivers in the Top 10 are from the US.

Source: NASCAR

ALL-TIME LAP LEADERS AT THE INDIANAPOLIS 500

	Driver	Laps led
1	Al Unser	644
2	Ralph DePalma	612
3	Mario Andretti	556
4	A. J. Foyt Jr.	555
5	Wilbur Shaw	508
6	Emerson Fittipaldi	505
7	Parnelli Jones	492
8	Bill Vukovich	485
9	Bobby Unser	440
10	Rick Mears	429

Source: Indianapolis Motor Speedway

TOP 10 CART DRIVERS WITH MOST RACE WINS
(Years/wins)

❶ A. J. Foyt Jr. (1960–81, 67) ❷ Mario Andretti (1965–93, 52) ❸ Al Unser (1965–87, 39) ❹ Michael Andretti (1986–97, 36) ❺ Bobby Unser (1966–81, 35) ❻ Al Unser Jr. (1984–95, 31) ❼ Rick Mears (1978–91, 29) ❽ Johnny Rutherford (1965–86, 27) ❾ Rodger Ward (1953–66, 26) ❿ Gordon Johncock (1965–83, 25)
Source: Championship Auto Racing Teams

FASTEST WINNING SPEEDS OF THE DAYTONA 500

	Driver*	Car	Year	Speed km/h	Speed mph
1	Buddy Baker	Oldsmobile	1980	285.823	177.602
2	Bill Elliott	Ford	1987	283.668	176.263
3	Dale Earnhardt	Chevrolet	1998	277.953	172.712
4	Bill Elliott	Ford	1985	277.234	172.265
5	Dale Earnhardt	Chevrolet	1998	276.921	172.071
6	Richard Petty	Buick	1981	273.027	169.651
7	Derrike Cope	Chevrolet	1990	266.766	165.761
8	A. J. Foyt	Mercury	1972	259.990	161.550
9	Richard Petty	Plymouth	1966	258.504	160.627 #
10	Davey Allison	Ford	1992	257.913	160.256

* *All winners from the United States*

Race reduced to 495 miles/797 km

First held in 1959, the Daytona 500 is raced every February at the Daytona International Speedway, Daytona Beach, Florida. One of the most prestigious races of the NASCAR season, it covers 200 laps of the 2½-mile/4-km high-banked oval circuit.

Source: NASCAR

NASCAR MONEY WINNERS OF ALL TIME*

	Driver	Total prizes ($)		Driver	Total prizes ($)
1	Dale Earnhardt	31,692,650	6	Darrell Waltrip	16,382,260
2	Bill Elliott	18,251,882	7	Mark Martin	15,053,967
3	Jeff Gordon	17,215,112	8	Ricky Rudd	13,803,150
4	Terry Labonte	17,135,662	9	Geoff Bodine	11,833,069
5	Rusty Wallace	16,803,870	10	Dale Jarrett	11,771,762

* *Through March 31, 1998*   *Source: NASCAR*

ICE HOCKEY

TOP 10

POINT-SCORERS IN AN NHL CAREER*

	Player	Seasons	Goals	Assists	Total points
1	Wayne Gretzky#	19	885	1,910	2,795
2	Gordie Howe	26	801	1,049	1,850
3	Marcel Dionne	18	731	1,040	1,771
4	Mark Messier#	19	597	1,015	1,612
5	Phil Esposito	18	717	873	1,590
6	Mario Lemieux	12	613	881	1,494
7	Stan Mikita	22	541	926	1,467
8	Paul Coffey#	18	380	1,085	1,465
9	Ron Francis	17	428	1,006	1,434
10	Bryan Trottier	18	524	901	1,425

* Regular season only
# Still active 1997–98 season

BEST-PAID PLAYERS IN THE NHL, 1997–98

	Player	Team	Salary ($)
1	Joe Sakic	Colorado Avalanche	17,000,000
2	Chris Gratton	Philadelphia Flyers	10,000,000
3	Eric Lindros	Philadelphia Flyers	7,500,000
4	Wayne Gretzky	New York Rangers	6,500,000
5	Mark Messier	Vancouver Canucks	6,000,000
6 =	Pavel Bure	Vancouver Canucks	5,500,000
=	Paul Kariya	Anaheim Mighty Ducks	5,500,000
8	Jaromir Jagr	Pittsburgh Penguins	5,100,000
9	Steve Yzerman	Detroit Red Wings	5,079,063
10	Pat Lafontaine	New York Rangers	4,800,000

Source: National Hockey League Players Association

WINNERS OF THE HART TROPHY

	Player	Years	Wins		Player	Years	Wins
1	Wayne Gretzky	1980–89	9	8 =	Jean Beliveau	1956–64	2
2	Gordie Howe	1952–63	6	=	Bill Cowley	1941–43	2
3	Eddie Shore	1933–38	4	=	Phil Esposito	1969–74	2
4 =	Bobby Clarke	1973–76	3	=	Bobby Hull	1965–66	2
=	Howie Morenz	1928–32	3	=	Guy Lafleur	1977–78	2
=	Bobby Orr	1970–72	3	=	Mark Messier	1990–92	2
=	Mario Lemieux	1988–96	3	=	Stan Mikita	1967–68	2
				=	Nels Stewart	1926–30	2

Source: National Hockey League

TEAMS WITH THE MOST STANLEY CUP WINS

	Team	Wins
1	Montreal Canadiens	23
2	Toronto Maple Leafs	13
3	Detroit Red Wings	9
4 =	Boston Bruins	5
=	Edmonton Oilers	5
6 =	New York Islanders	4
=	New York Rangers	4
8	Chicago Black Hawks	3
9 =	Philadelphia Flyers	2
=	Pittsburgh Penguins	2

GOALSCORERS IN AN NHL CAREER*

	Player	Seasons	Goals		Player	Seasons	Goals
1	Wayne Gretzky#	19	885	7	Bobby Hull	16	610
2	Gordie Howe	26	801	8	Dino Ciccarelli#	18	602
3	Marcel Dionne	18	731	9	Jari Kurri#	17	601
4	Phil Esposito	18	717	10	Mark Messier#	18	597
5	Mike Gartner#	19	708				
6	Mario Lemieux	12	613				

* Regular season only
# Still active 1997–98 season

During his time as Governor General of Canada from 1888 to 1893, Sir Frederick Arthur Stanley became interested in what is called hockey in the United States, and ice hockey elsewhere, and in 1893 presented a trophy to be contested by the best amateur teams in Canada. The first trophy went to the Montreal Amateur Athletic Association, who won it without a challenge from any other team. The NHA became the National Hockey League (NHL) in 1917.

Source: National Hockey League

TOP 10

ASSISTS IN AN NHL CAREER*

	Player	Seasons	Assists
1	Wayne Gretzky#	19	1,910
2	Paul Coffey#	18	1,090
3	Gordie Howe	26	1,049
4	Marcel Dionne	18	1,040
5	Ray Bourque#	19	1,036
6	Mark Messier#	19	1,015
7	Ron Francis#	17	1,006
8	Stan Mikita	22	926
9	Bryan Trottier	18	901
10	Dale Hawerchuk	17	891

* *Regular season only*

\# *Still active 1997–98 season*

TOP 10

POINT-SCORERS IN STANLEY CUP PLAY-OFF MATCHES

	Player	Total points
1	Wayne Gretzky*	382
2	Mark Messier*	295
3	Jari Kurri*	233
4	Glenn Anderson	214
5	Paul Coffey*	195
6	Bryan Trottier	184
7	Jean Beliveau	176
8	Denis Savard	175
9	Doug Gilmour*	171
10	Denis Potvin	164

* *Still active 1997–98 season*

TOP 10

GOALTENDERS IN AN NHL CAREER*

	Goaltender	Seasons	Games won
1	Terry Sawchuk	21	447
2	Jacques Plante	18	434
3	Tony Esposito	16	423
4	Glenn Hall	18	407
5	Grant Fuhr#	16	382
6	Patrick Roy#	12	380
7	Andy Moog#	17	372
8	Rogie Vachon	16	355
9	Gump Worsley	21	334
10	Harry Lumley	16	333

* *Regular season only*

\# *Still active 1997–98 season*

TOP 10

GOALSCORERS IN 1997–98

	Player	Team	Goals
1=	Peter Bondra	Washington Capitals	52
=	Teemu Selanne	Anaheim Mighty Ducks	52
3=	Pavel Bure	Vancouver Canucks	51
=	John LeClair	Philadelphia Flyers	51
5	Zigmund Palffy	New York Islanders	45
6	Keith Tkachuk	Phoenix Coyotes	40
7	Joe Nieuwendyk	Dallas Stars	39
8	Rod Brind'Amour	Philadelphia Flyers	36
9	Jaromir Jagr	Pittsburg Penguins	35
10=	Jason Alison	Boston Bruins	33
=	Mats Sundin	Toronto Maple Leafs	33
=	Ray Witney	Edmonton Oilers Florida Panthers	33
=	Alexei Yashin	Ottawa Senators	33

Source: National Hockey League

TOP 10

BIGGEST NHL ARENAS

	Stadium/home team	Capacity
1	Thunderdome, Tampa, Tampa Bay Lightning	26,000
2	Forum, Montreal, Montreal Canadiens	21,401
3	United Centre, Chicago, Chicago Blackhawks	20,500
4	Canadian Airlines Saddledrome, Calgary, Calgary Flames	20,200
5	Joe Louis Sports Arena, Detroit, Detroit Red Wings	19,275
6	Kiel Center, St. Louis, St. Louis Blues	19,260
7	General Motors Place, Vancouver, Vancouver Canucks	19,056
8	Meadowlands Arena, East Rutherford, New Jersey Devils	19,040
9	Palladium, Ottawa, Ottawa Senators	18,500
10	Madison Square Garden, New York, New York Rangers	18,200

The smallest arena is the Miami Arena, home of the Florida Panthers, which has a capacity of 14,703.

SOCCER – THE WORLD CUP

THE 10
HIGHEST-SCORING GAMES IN THE FINAL STAGES OF THE WORLD CUP

	Game/year	Score
1	Austria *vs.* Switzerland, 1954	7–5
2 =	Brazil *vs.* Poland, 1938	6–5
=	Hungary *vs.* W. Germany, 1954	8–3
=	Hungary *vs.* El Salvador, 1982	10–1
5	France *vs.* Paraguay, 1958	7–3
6 =	Hungary *vs.* South Korea, 1954	9–0
=	W. Germany *vs.* Turkey, 1954	7–2
=	France *vs.* W. Germany, 1958	6–3
=	Yugoslavia *vs.* Dem. Rep. of Congo, 1974	9–0
10 =	Italy *vs.* US, 1934	7–1
=	Sweden *vs.* Cuba, 1938	8–0
=	Uruguay *vs.* Bolivia, 1950	8–0
=	England *vs.* Belgium, 1954	4–4
=	Portugal *vs.* North Korea, 1966	5–3

Hungary's 8–3 victory over West Germany in 1954 was in the Group games, where for tactical reasons West Germany fielded six reserves. When the two teams met again in the final, West Germany won 3–2.

THE 10
HIGHEST-SCORING WORLD CUP FINALS

	Year	Games	Goals	Average per game
1	1954	26	140	5.38
2	1938	18	84	4.66
3	1934	17	70	4.11
4	1950	22	88	4.00
5	1930	18	70	3.88
6	1958	35	126	3.60
7	1970	32	95	2.96
8	1982	52	146	2.81
9 =	1962	32	89	2.78
=	1966	32	89	2.78

TOP 10
GOAL SCORERS IN THE FINAL STAGES OF THE WORLD CUP

	Player/country/years	Goals
1	Gerd Müller, W. Germany, 1970–74	14
2	Just Fontaine, France, 1958	13
3	Pelé, Brazil, 1958–70	12
4	Sandor Kocsis, Hungary, 1954	11
5 =	Helmut Rahn, W. Germany, 1954–58	10
=	Teófilo Cubillas, Peru, 1970–78	10
=	Grzegorz Lato, Poland, 1974–82	10
=	Gary Lineker, England, 1986–90	10
9 =	Leónidas da Silva, Brazil, 1934–38	9
=	Ademir Marques de Menezes, Brazil, 1950	9
=	Vavà, Brazil, 1958–62	9
=	Eusébio, Portugal, 1966	9
=	Uwe Seeler, W. Germany, 1958–70	9
=	Jairzinho, Brazil, 1970–74	9
=	Paolo Rossi, Italy, 1978–82	9
=	Karl-Heinz Rummenigge W. Germany, 1978–86	9

THE 10
HIGHEST-SCORING WINS BY COUNTRIES ON THEIR DEBUT IN THE FINAL STAGES OF THE WORLD CUP

	Winners/losers	Year	Score
1	Italy *vs.* United States	1934	7-1
2	Germany *vs.* Belgium	1934	5-2
3	France *vs.* Mexico	1930	4-1
4	Hungary *vs.* Egypt	1934	4-2
5 =	Chile *vs.* Mexico	1930	3-0
=	US *vs.* Belgium	1930	3-0
7 =	Romania *vs.* Peru	1930	3-1
=	Spain *vs.* Brazil	1934	3-1
=	Portugal *vs.* Hungary	1966	3-1
=	Tunisia *vs.* Mexico	1978	3-1

TOP 10
HOST COUNTRIES IN THE WORLD CUP

	Host	Year	Final standing
1 =	Uruguay	1930	Winners
=	Italy	1934	Winners
=	England	1966	Winners
=	West Germany	1974	Winners
=	Argentina	1978	Winners
6 =	Brazil	1950	Runners-up
=	Sweden	1958	Runners-up
8 =	Chile	1962	Third
=	Italy	1990	Third
10 =	France	1938	Last 8
=	Switzerland	1954	Last 8
=	Mexico	1970	Last 8
=	Mexico	1986	Last 8

Spain in 1982 (last 12) and the US in 1994 (last 16) are the only two host countries not to have reached the last eight.

THE 10
LEAST SUCCESSFUL COUNTRIES IN THE WORLD CUP

	Country	Tournaments	Games played	won
1	Bulgaria	5	16	0
2	South Korea	4	11	0
3 =	El Salvador	2	6	0
=	Bolivia	3	6	0
5	Republic of Ireland	1	5	0
6	Egypt	2	4	0
7 =	Canada	1	3	0
=	Greece	1	3	0
=	Haiti	1	3	0
=	Iraq	1	3	0
=	New Zealand	1	3	0
=	United Arab Emirates	1	3	0
=	Dem. Rep. of Congo	1	3	0

THE 10

COUNTRIES WITH THE MOST PLAYERS EJECTED IN THE FINAL STAGES OF THE WORLD CUP

	Country	Dismissals
1=	Argentina	7
=	Brazil	7
3	Uruguay	6
4=	Czechoslovakia	4
=	Germany/W. Germany	4
=	Hungary	4
7	Yugoslavia	3
8=	Cameroon	2
=	Chile	2
=	Holland	2
=	Italy	2
=	Soviet Union	2

A total of 60 players have received their marching orders in the final stages of the World Cup since 1930. The South American nations account for 23 of them.

THE 10

HIGHEST-SCORING DEFEATS BY COUNTRIES ON THEIR DEBUT IN THE FINAL STAGES OF THE WORLD CUP

	Losers/winners	Year	Score
1	South Korea vs. Hungary	1954	0-9
2	Dutch East Indies vs. Hungary	1938	0-6
3	Poland vs. Brazil	1938	5-6
4	New Zealand vs. Scotland	1982	2-5
5	Bolivia vs. Yugoslavia	1930	0-4
6=	Mexico vs. France	1930	1-4
=	Turkey vs. W. Germany	1954	1-4
8	Egypt vs. Hungary	1934	2-4
9=	Belgium vs. US	1930	0-3
=	El Salvador vs. Belgium	1930	0-3
=	Iran vs. Holland	1978	0-3
=	North Korea vs. Soviet Union	1966	0-3
=	Paraguay vs. US	1950	0-3

THE 10

COUNTRIES THAT HAVE PLAYED THE MOST GAMES IN THE FINAL STAGES OF THE WORLD CUP

	Country	Tournaments	Games played
1=	Brazil	15	73
=	Germany/W. Germany	13	73
3	Italy	13	61
4	Argentina	11	52
5	England	9	41
6=	Uruguay	9	37
=	Spain	9	37
=	Sweden	9	37
9=	France	9	34
=	USSR/Russia	8	34

WORLD CUP 1994
The 1994 World Cup was held in the United States, playing to packed stadiums. The final, in which Brazil beat Italy, was the first to be decided on penalties.

TENNIS

MARTINA HINGIS

TOP 10

WINNERS OF WOMEN'S GRAND SLAM SINGLES TITLES

	Player/country	A	F	W	US	Total
1	Margaret Court (Australia)	11	5	3	5	24
2	Steffi Graf (Germany)	4	5	7	5	21
3	Helen Wills-Moody (US)	0	4	8	7	19
4=	Chris Evert-Lloyd (US)	2	7	3	6	18
=	Martina Navratilova (Czechoslovakia/US)	3	2	9	4	18
6	Billie Jean King (US)	1	1	6	4	12
7=	Maureen Connolly (US)	1	2	3	3	9
=	Monica Seles (Yugoslavia/US)	4	3	0	2	9
9=	Suzanne Lenglen (France)	0	2	6	0	8
=	Molla Mallory (US)	0	0	0	8	8

A = Australian Open; F = French Open; W = Wimbledon; US = US Open

TOP 10 FEMALE PLAYERS IN THE WORLD*

❶ Martina Hingis ❷ Lindsay Davenport
❸ Jana Novotna ❹ Arantxa Sanchez Vicario
❺ Monica Seles ❻ Venus Williams
❼ Conchita Martinez ❽ Amanda Coetzer
❾ Irina Spirlea ❿ Mary Pierce
* According to WTA rankings June 15, 1998

TOP 10

WINNERS OF MEN'S GRAND SLAM SINGLES TITLES

	Player/nationality	A	F	W	US	Total
1	Roy Emerson (Aus)	6	2	2	2	12
2=	Bjorn Borg (Swe)	0	6	5	0	11
=	Rod Laver (Aus)	3	2	4	2	11
4	Pete Sampras (US)	2	0	4	4	10
5=	Jimmy Connors (US)	1	0	2	5	8
=	Ivan Lendl (Cze)	2	3	0	3	8
=	Fred Perry (GB)	1	1	3	3	8
=	Ken Rosewall (Aus)	4	2	0	2	8
9=	René Lacoste (Fra)	0	3	2	2	7
=	William Larned (US)	0	0	0	7	7
=	John McEnroe (US)	0	0	3	4	7
=	John Newcombe (Aus)	2	0	3	2	7
=	William Renshaw (GB)	0	0	7	0	7
=	Richard Sears (US)	0	0	0	7	7
=	Mats Wilander (Swe)	3	3	0	1	7

A = Australian Open; F = French Open; W = Wimbledon; US = US Open

TOP 10

SHORTEST MEN'S SINGLES FINALS AT WIMBLEDON

	Match	Year	Set scores	Total games
1=	William Renshaw *vs.* John Hartley	1881	6–0 6–1 6–1	20
=	Fred Perry *vs.* Gottfried von Cramm	1936	6–1 6–1 6–0	20
3=	William Johnston *vs.* Frank Hunter	1923	6–0 6–3 6–1	22
=	Donald Budge *vs.* Bunny Austin	1938	6–1 6–0 6–3	22
=	John McEnroe *vs.* Jimmy Connors	1984	6–1 6–1 6–2	22
6=	Lew Hoad *vs.* Ashley Cooper	1957	6–2 6–1 6–2	23
=	Rod Laver *vs.* Martin Mulligan	1962	6–2 6–2 6–1	23
=	John Newcombe *vs.* Wilhem Bungert	1967	6–3 6–1 6–1	23
9=	Ellsworth Vines *vs.* Bunny Austin	1932	6–4 6–2 6–0	24
=	Jack Kramer *vs.* Tom Brown	1947	6–1 6–3 6–2	24
=	Jimmy Connors *vs.* Ken Rosewall	1974	6–1 6–1 6–4	24
=	John McEnroe *vs.* Chris Lewis	1983	6–2 6–2 6–2	24

T O P 1 0

PLAYERS WITH THE MOST US SINGLES TITLES

	Player*	Years	Titles
1	Molla Mallory	1915–26	8
2 =	Richard Sears	1881–87	7
=	William Larned	1901–11	7
=	Bill Tilden	1920–29	7
=	Helen Wills-Moody	1923–31	7
=	Margaret Court#	1962–70	7
7	Chris Evert-Lloyd	1975–82	6
8 =	Jimmy Connors	1974–83	5
=	Steffi Graf (Ger)	1988–96	5
10 =	Robert Wrenn	1893–97	4
=	Elisabeth Moore	1896–1905	4
=	Hazel Wightman	1909–19	4
=	Helen Jacobs	1932–35	4
=	Alice Marble	1936–40	4
=	Pauline Betz	1942–46	4
=	Maria Bueno (Bra)	1959–66	4
=	Billie Jean King	1967–74	4
=	John McEnroe	1979–84	4
=	Martina Navratilova	1983–87	4
=	Pete Sampras	1990–96	4

* All players are from the US unless otherwise stated

Includes two wins in Amateur Championships of 1968 and 1969, which were held alongside the Open Championship

MALE PLAYERS IN THE WORLD*

	Player	Country
1	Pete Sampras	US
2	Marcelo Rios	Chile
3	Petr Korda	Czech Republic
4	Carlos Moya	Spain
5	Greg Rusedski	GB
6	Patrick Rafter	Australia
7	Yevgeny Kafelnikov	Russia
8	Jonas Bjorkman	Sweden
9	Alex Corretja	Spain
10	Cedric Pioline	France

* ATP rankings as of June 22, 1998

LATEST US OPEN WINNERS (MEN)

	Winner	Year
1	Patrick Rafter (Australia)	1997
2	Pete Sampras (US)	1996
3	Pete Sampras (US)	1995
4	Andre Agassi (US)	1994
5	Pete Sampras (US)	1993
6	Stefan Edberg (Sweden)	1992
7	Stefan Edberg (Sweden)	1991
8	Pete Sampras (US)	1990
9	Boris Becker(Germany)	1989
10	Mats Wilander (Sweden)	1988

PETE SAMPRAS

LATEST US OPEN WINNERS (WOMEN)

	Winner	Year
1	Martina Hingis (Switzerland)	1997
2	Steffi Graf (Germany)	1996
3	Steffi Graf (Germany)	1995
4	Arantxa Sanchez Vicario (Spain)	1994
5	Steffi Graf (Germany)	1993
6	Monica Seles (Yugoslavia)	1992
7	Monica Seles (Yugoslavia)	1991
8	Gabriella Sabatini (Argentina)	1990
9	Steffi Graf (Germany)	1989
10	Steffi Graf (Germany)	1988

DAVIS CUP WINNING TEAMS)

	Country	Wins
1	United States	31
2	Australia	20
3	France	8
4 =	Sweden	6
=	Australasia	6
6	British Isles*	5
7	Great Britain*	4
8	West Germany	2
9 =	Germany	1
=	Czechoslovakia	1
=	Italy	1
=	South Africa	1

* England competed separately between 1922 and 1928.

WINTER SPORTS

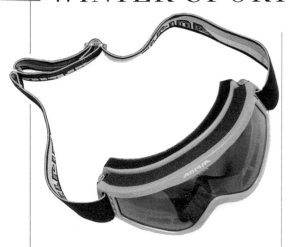

FASTEST WINNING TIMES OF THE IDITAROD DOGSLED RACE

	Winner/year	Day	Time hr	min	sec
1	Doug Swingley, 1995	9	2	42	19
2	Jeff King, 1996	9	5	43	19
3	Jeff King, 1998	9	5	52	26
4	Martin Buser, 1997	9	8	30	45
5	Martin Buser, 1994	10	13	2	39
6	Jeff King, 1993	10	15	38	15
7	Martin Buser, 1992	10	19	17	15
8	Susan Butcher, 1990	11	1	53	28
9	Susan Butcher, 1987	11	2	5	13
10	Joe Runyan, 1989	11	5	24	34

The race, which has been held annually since 1973, stretches from Anchorage to Nome, Alaska, covering 1,158 miles/ 1,864 km. Iditarod is a deserted mining village along the route, and the race commemorates an emergency operation in 1925 to get medical supplies to Nome following a diphtheria epidemic.

Source: Iditarod Trail Committee

ALPINE SKIING WORLD CUP TITLES – MEN

	Name/country	Years	Titles
1	Marc Girardelli (Luxembourg)	1985–93	5
2=	Gustavo Thoeni (Italy)	1971–75	4
=	Pirmin Zurbriggen (Switzerland)	1984–90	4
4=	Ingemar Stenmark (Sweden)	1976–78	3
=	Phil Mahre (US)	1981–83	3
6=	Jean Claude Killy (France)	1967–68	2
=	Karl Schranz (Austria)	1969–70	2
8=	Piero Gross (Italy)	1974	1
=	Peter Lüscher (Switzerland)	1979	1
=	Andreas Wenzel (Liechtenstein)	1980	1
=	Paul Accola (Switzerland)	1992	1
=	Kjetil Andre Aamodt (Norway)	1994	1
=	Alberto Tomba (Italy)	1995	1
=	Lasse Kjus (Norway)	1996	1
=	Luc Alphand (France)	1997	1
=	Hermann Maier (Aus)	1998	1

ALPINE SKIING WORLD CUP TITLES – WOMEN

	Name/country	Years	Titles
1	Annemarie Moser-Pröll (Austria)	1971–79	6
2=	Vreni Schneider (Switzerland)	1989–95	3
=	Petra Kronberger (Austria)	1990–92	3
4=	Nancy Greene (Canada)	1967–68	2
=	Hanni Wenzel (Liechtenstein)	1978–80	2
=	Erika Hess (Switzerland)	1982–84	2
=	Michela Figini (Switzerland)	1985–88	2
=	Maria Walliser (Switzerland)	1986–87	2
=	Kajta Seizinger (Germany)	1996–98	2
10=	Gertrude Gabl (Austria)	1969	1
=	Michèle Jacot (France)	1970	1
=	Rosi Mittermeier (West Germany)	1976	1
=	Lise-Marie Morerod (Switzerland)	1977	1
=	Marie-Thérèse Nadig (Switzerland)	1981	1
=	Tamara McKinney (US)	1983	1
=	Anita Wachter (Austria)	1993	1
=	Pernilla Wiberg (Sweden)	1997	1

DOWNHILL RACER
Ski races have been held since the last century, but have developed as major Olympic and World events in the 20th century along with the international growth of interest in the sport.

WORLD AND OLYMPIC FIGURE SKATING TITLES – MEN

	Skater/country	Years	Titles
1	Ulrich Salchow (Sweden)	1901–11	11
2	Karl Schäfer (Austria)	1930–36	9
3	Dick Button (US)	1948–52	7
4	Gillis Grafstrom (Sweden)	1920–29	6
5 =	Hayes Jenkins (US)	1953–56	5
=	Scott Hamilton (US)	1981–84	5
7 =	Willy Bockl (Austria)	1925–28	4
=	David Jenkins (US)	1957–60	4
=	Ondrej Nepela (Czechoslovakia)	1971–73	4
=	Kurt Browning (Canada)	1989–93	4

OLYMPIC FIGURE SKATING COUNTRIES

	Country	G	S	B	Total
1 =	USSR/CIS/Russia	20	14	6	40
=	US	12	13	15	40
3	Austria	7	9	4	20
4	Canada	2	8	8	18
5	UK	5	3	7	15
6	France	2	2	7	11
7 =	Sweden	5	3	2	10
=	Germany/West Germany	4	3	3	10
=	East Germany	3	3	4	10
10 =	Norway	3	2	1	6
=	Hungary	0	2	4	6

BOBSLED

WORLD AND OLYMPIC FIGURE SKATING TITLES – WOMEN

	Skater/country	Years	Titles
1	Sonja Henie (Norway)	1927–36	13
2 =	Carol Heiss (US)	1956–60	6
=	Herma Planck Szabo (Austria)	1922–26	6
=	Katarina Witt (East Germany)	1984–88	6
5 =	Lily Kronberger (Hungary)	1908–11	4
=	Sjoukje Dijkstra (Netherlands)	1962–64	4
=	Peggy Fleming (US)	1966–68	4
8 =	Meray Horvath (Hungary)	1912–14	3
=	Tenley Albright (US)	1953–56	3
=	Annett Poetzsch (East Gemany)	1978–80	3
=	Beatrix Schuba (Austria)	1971–72	3
=	Barbara Ann Scott (Canada)	1947–48	3
=	Kristi Yamaguchi (US)	1991–92	3
=	Madge Sayers (UK)	1906–08	3

WINNERS OF WORLD ICE DANCE TITLES

	Skater/country	Years	Titles
1 =	Alexsandr Gorshkov (USSR)	1970–76	6
=	Lyudmila Pakhomova (USSR)	1970–76	6
3 =	Lawrence Demmy (UK)	1951–55	5
=	Jean Westwood (UK)	1951–55	5
5 =	Courtney Jones (UK)	1957–60	4
=	Eva Romanova (Czechoslovakia)	1962–65	4
=	Pavel Roman (Czechoslovakia)	1963–65	4
=	Diane Towler (UK)	1966–69	4
=	Bernard Ford (UK)	1966–69	4
=	Jayne Torvill (UK)	1981–84	4
=	Christopher Dean (UK)	1981–84	4
=	Natalya Bestemianova (USSR)	1985–88	4
=	Andrei Bukin (USSR)	1985–88	4
=	Oksana Gritschuk (Rus)	1994-97	4
=	Yevgeniy Platov (Rus)	1994-97	4

TOP 10 OLYMPIC BOBSLEDDING NATIONS
(Total number of medals)

❶ Switzerland (26) ❷ Germany/West Germany (17) ❸ US (14) ❹ East Germany (13) ❺ Italy (11) ❻ UK (4) ❼= Austria (3), Former USSR (3) ❾= Canada (2), Belgium (2)

WINTER OLYMPIC MEDAL-WINNING COUNTRIES

	Country	G	S	B	Total
1	USSR/Russia	108	77	74	259
2	Norway	83	87	69	239
3	US	59	58	43	160
4	Germany/West Germany	57	52	45	154
5	Austria	39	53	53	145
6	Finland	38	49	48	135
7	East Germany	39	36	35	110
8	Sweden	39	28	35	102
9	Switzerland	29	31	32	92
10	Canada	25	26	28	79

THIS SPORTING LIFE

TOP 10

MOVIES WITH SPORTS THEMES

	Film/year	Sport
1	*Days of Thunder* (1990)	Stock car racing
2	*Rocky IV* (1985)	Boxing
3	*Rocky III* (1982)	Boxing
4	*Rocky* (1976)	Boxing
5	*A League of Their Own* (1992)	Baseball
6	*Rocky II* (1979)	Boxing
7	*Tin Cup* (1996)	Golf
8	*White Men Can't Jump* (1992)	Basketball
9	*Cool Running* (1993)	Bobsledding
10	*Field of Dreams* (1989)	Baseball

Led by superstar Sylvester Stallone's *Rocky* series, the boxing ring, a natural source of drama and thrills, dominates Hollywood's most successful sports-based epics. Baseball is a popular follow-up, both in the movies in this Top 10 and others just outside.

RECORD-BREAKER
Although later eclipsed by higher earners, Chariots of Fire (1973) was once the most successful sports movie of all time.

TOP 10

SPORTS REPRESENTED BY THE JAMES E. SULLIVAN AWARD

	Sport	Awards
1	Track and field	37
2	Swimming	9
3	Football	4
4 =	Diving	3
=	Speed skating	3
6 =	Basketball	2
=	Golf	2
=	Sculling	2
=	Wrestling	2
10 =	Baseball	1
=	Figure skating	1
=	Gymnastics	1
=	Tennis	1

The award is made annually to the sportsman or woman who has contributed most to good sportsmanship. The trophy is in memory of James E. Sullivan, the president of the Amateur Athletic Union (AAU) from 1906 to 1914. Recent winners of the award include track-and-field champions Florence Griffith-Joyner, Ed Moses, Mary Decker, and Carl Lewis.

Source: Amateur Athletic Union

THE 10

MOST COMMON SPORTS INJURIES

	Common name	Medical term
1	Bruise	Soft tissue contusion
2	Sprained ankle	Sprain of the lateral ligament
3	Sprained knee	Sprain of the medial collateral ligament
4	Low back strain	Lumbar joint dysfunction
5	Hamstring tear	Muscle tear of the hamstring
6	Jumper's knee	Patella tendinitis
7	Achilles tendinitis	Tendinitis of the Achilles tendon
8	Shin splints	Medial periostitis of the tibia
9	Tennis elbow	Lateral epicondylitis
10	Shoulder strain	Rotator cuff tendinitis

THE 10

CATEGORIES OF ATHLETES WITH THE LARGEST HEARTS*

1	*Tour de France* cyclists
2	Marathon runners
3	Rowers
4	Boxers
5	Sprint cyclists
6	Middle-distance runners
7	Weightlifters
8	Swimmers
9	Sprinters
10	Decathletes

* Based on average medical measurements

The heart of a person who engages regularly in a demanding sport enlarges according to the strenuousness required.

MOST INJURY-CAUSING SPORTS IN THE US

	Sport	No.*
1	Basketball	692,396
2	Bicycle riding	586,808
3	Football	389,463
4	Baseball, softball	366,064
5	Roller skating	175,295
6	Soccer	156,960
7	Swimming	134,022
8	Volleyball	86,551
9	Exercising with equipment	86,157
10	Fishing	80,515

* Injuries treated in hospital emergency departments

Source: National Safety Council/National Sporting Goods Association/Consumer Product Safety Commission

PARTICIPATION ACTIVITIES IN THE US

	Activity	No.*
1	Exercise walking	76,300,000
2	Swimming	59,500,000
3	Exercising with equipment	47,900,000
4	Camping	46,600,000
5	Bicycle riding	45,100,000
6	Bowling	44,800,000
7	Fishing	44,700,000
8	Billiards/pool	37,000,000
9	Basketball	30,700,000
10	Hiking	28,400,000

* Participated more than once during 1997

Source: National Sporting Goods Association

HIGHEST-EARNING ATHLETES IN THE WORLD*

	Name/sport	Income 1997 ($)		
		endorsements#	salary	total
1	Michael Jordan, Basketball	47,000,000	31,300,000	78,300,000
2	Evander Holyfield, Boxing	1,300,000	53,000,000	54,300,000
3	Oscar De La Hoya, Boxing	1,000,000	37,000,000	38,000,000
4	Michael Shumacher (Ger), Motor racing	10,000,000	25,000,000	35,000,000
5	Mike Tyson, Boxing	—	27,000,000	27,000,000
6	Tiger Woods, Golf	24,000,000	2,100,000	26,100,000
7	Shaquille O'Neal, Basketball	12,500,000	12,900,000	25,400,000
8	Dale Earnhardt, Stock car racing	15,500,000	3,600,000	19,100,000
9	Joe Sakic, Ice hockey	100,000	17,800,000	17,900,000
10	Grant Hill, Basketball	12,000,000	5,000,000	17,000,000

* All athletes are from the US unless otherwise stated
# Sponsorship and royalty income from endorsed sports gear.

Used by permission of Forbes Magazine

SPORTS EVENTS WITH THE LARGEST TV AUDIENCES IN THE US

	Event	Date	Rating
1	Super Bowl XVI	Jan 24, 1982	49.1
2	Super Bowl XVII	Jan 30, 1983	48.6
3	XVII Winter Olympics	Feb 23, 1994	48.5
4	Super Bowl XX	Jan 26, 1986	48.3
5	Super Bowl XII	Jan 15, 1978	47.2
6	Super Bowl XIII	Jan 21, 1979	47.1
7=	Super Bowl XVIII	Jan 22, 1984	46.4
=	Super Bowl XIX	Jan 20, 1985	46.4
9	Super Bowl XIV	Jan 20, 1980	46.3
10	Super Bowl XXX	Jan 28, 1996	46.0

Source: Nielsen Media Research

TOYS & GAMES

TOP 10

VIDEO GAMES OF 1997

	Game	Publisher
1	N64 Mario Kart 64	Nintendo
2	N64 Star Fox with Rumble Pack	Nintendo
3	N64 Super Mario 64	Nintendo
4	N64 Diddy Kong Racing	Nintendo
5	N64 Golden Eye 007	Nintendo
6	PSX Final Fantasy VII	Sony Computer
7	PSX NFL Gameday 98	Sony Computer
8	N64 Star Wars : Shadows of Empire	Nintendo
9	PSX Madden NFL 98	Electronic Arts
10	PSX Crash Bandicoot	Sony Computer

Source: The NPD Group – TRSTS

TOP 10

US LOTTERY JACKPOTS

	State/date	Jackpot ($ millions)
1	Wisconsin, May 20, 1998	195.0*
2	Pennsylvania, Apr 26, 1989	115.6
3	California, Apr 17, 1991	111.8
4	Wisconsin, July 7, 1993	111.2*
5	Florida, Sep 15, 1990	106.5
6	California, Apr 8, 1998	104.0
7	Arizona, Mar 4, 1995	101.8*
8	Indiana/ Nebraska, Nov 30, 1994	101.0*
9	New York, Jan 26, 1991	90.0
10	Florida, Oct 26, 1991	89.8

* *The Powerball game is played in 20 states and the District of Columbia*

Source: Multi-State Lottery

TOP 10

MOST EXPENSIVE TOYS EVER SOLD AT AUCTION BY CHRISTIE'S EAST, NEW YORK

	Toy/sale	Price ($)*
1	"The Charles," a fire-hose-reel made by American manufacturer George Brown and Co, c.1875, December 1991	231,000
2	Märklin fire station, December 1991	79,200
3	Horse-drawn double-decker tram, December 1991	71,500
4	Mikado mechanical bank, December 1993	63,000
5	Märklin Ferris wheel, June 1994	55,200
6	Girl skipping rope mechanical bank, June 1994	48,300
7	Märklin battleship, June 1994	33,350
8	Märklin battleship, June 1994	32,200
9=	Bing keywind open phaeton tinplate automobile, December 1991	24,200
=	Märklin fire pumper, December 1991	24,200

* *Including 10 percent buyer's premium*

The fire hose-reel at #1 in this list is the record price paid at auction for a toy other than a doll. Models by the German tinplate maker Märklin, regarded by collectors as the Rolls-Royce of toys, similarly feature among the record prices of auction houses in the UK and other countries, where high prices have also been attained.

Source: Christie's East

BARBIE
The basic Barbie doll, dressed in just a bikini, sells for about $10, while the most expensive, a collector's item, brings in around $1,000.

TOP 10
TOYS OF 1997

	Toy	Manufacturer
1	Tamagotchi Virtual Pet	Bandai America
2	Sesame Street Tickle Me Elmo	Tyco Preschool
3	Holiday Barbie '97	Mattel
4	Giga Pets	Tiger Electronics
5	Star Wars Figure I	Hasbro Toy Group
6	Star Wars Figure II	Hasbro Toy Group
7	Sesame Street Tickle Me Elmo	Tyco Preschool
8	Jeep Wrangler	Fisher-Price
9	Nano Virtual Pet	Playmates Toys
10	Super Talk! Barbie Sun Jammer	Fisher-Price

Source: The NPD Group - TRSTS

TOP 10
MOST VALUABLE CHARACTER STANDEES/SERIAL POSTERS

	Item	Year	Value ($)
1	Superman Fleischer Cartoon Standee	1941	27,000
2	New Adventures of Batman and Robin Three-Sheet	1949	8,000
3=	Adventures of Captain Marvel Six-Sheet	1941	7,500
=	Atom Man *vs.* Superman 6 ft Standee	1950	7,500
5=	Captain America Three-Sheet	1944	6,000
=	Adventures of Captain Marvel One-Sheet	1941	6,000
=	Captain Midnight Three-Sheet	1940s	6,000
=	Phantom Three-Sheet	1940s	6,000
=	Spy Smasher Three-Sheet	1942	6,000
10	The Day the Earth Stood Still 5 ft Standee	1951	5,500

Source: Gemstone Publishing

TREASURE HOUSE
Dollhouses and their miniature contents are highly prized among collectors and often attain substantial prices at auction.

TOP 10
COMPUTER GAMES (MAC)

	Game	Publisher
1	Myst (CD-ROM)	Broderbund
2	Duke Nukem 3D Atomic (CD-ROM)	GT Interactive
3	Civilization 2 (CD-ROM)	GT Interactive
4	Mac Cube (CD-ROM)	Aztech New Media
5	Command and Conquer (CD-ROM)	Interplay
6	Warcraft II (CD-ROM)	Cendant Software
7	More Mac Cube (CD-ROM)	Aztech New Media
8	Dark Forces (CD-ROM)	Lucas Arts
9	Links Pro (CD-ROM)	Access
10	7th Guest (CD-ROM)	Virgin

Source: PC Data

TOP 10
COMPUTER GAMES (PC)

	Game	Publisher
1	Riven: The Sequel to Myst (CD Win95)	Broderbund
2	Myst (CD Win95)	Broderbund
3	Microsoft Flight Simulator (CD Win95)	Microsoft
4	Diablo (CD Win95)	Cendant Software
5	Monopoly (CD Win)	Hasbro
6	Barbie Fashion Designer	Mattel
7	NASCAR II (CD Win95)	Cendant Software
8	Command and Conquer: Red Alert (CD Win95)	Cendant Software
9	Barbie Magic Hair Styler (CD Win95/Win)	Mattel
10	Lego Island (CD Win95)	Mindscape

Source: PC Data

TOP 10 BOARD GAMES IN THE US
(Manufacturer)

❶ Monopoly (Parker Brothers) ❷ Star Wars Trilogy Monopoly (Parker Brothers) ❸ Disney Wonderful World of Trivia (Mattel) ❹ Star Wars Monopoly (Parker Brothers) ❺ Sorry (Parker Brothers) ❻ Deluxe Monopoly (Parker Brothers) ❼ Clue (Parker Brothers) ❽ Life (Milton Bradley) ❾ Taboo (Milton Bradley) ❿ Jenga (Milton Bradley)
Source: The NPD Group – TRSTS

ACKNOWLEDGMENTS

Special thanks to Dafydd Rees, who has taken responsibility for many of the music, video, sports, and other US-specific lists. Thanks also, as always, to Caroline Ash, and to Luke Crampton, Jackie Lane, Ian Morrison, and the late Barry Lazell, who contributed his expertise to most of the previous editions of *The Top 10 of Everything*, and who is greatly missed. Thanks also to the individuals, organizations, and publications listed below who kindly supplied the information necessary to prepare many of the lists.

Carol Anthony, Megaera Ausman, Margaret Barker, Tania Bates, Kim Bloxdorf , Susan Boudreaux, Richard Braddish, Tom Bradley, Cathy Burt, Shelly Cagner, Paul Clolery, Peter Compton, Kaylee Coxall, Gabriella Daley, Bruce Daniel, Claudia Dickens, Tom Doyle, Dr. Stephen Durham, Tracey Eberts, Bonnie Fantasia, Toya Farden, Lynn Fava, Kevin Fearn, Christopher Forbes, Deborah Gangloff, Valerie Geiss, Russell E. Gough, Diane Green, William Hartston, Kim Hazelbaker, Grace Hazzard, Gary Hemphill, Peggy Hendershot, Duncan Hislop, Tony Hutson, Alan Jeffreys, Susan Kjellgvist, Ginger Koloszyc, Robert Lamb, Anthony Lipmann, Dr. Benjamin Lucas, Phil Matcham, Noah Migel, Jerry Mitchell, Dr. Jacqueline Mitton, Thom Moon, Wes Murphy, Sharon Nadelbach, Vincent Nasso, Tim Neely, Rebecca Norris, Tim O'Brien, Tim O'Donovan, Enzo Paci, Mary Ann Porreca, Kate Prager, Rosalind Proctor, Mark Rathbone, Benn Ray, Christiaan Rees, Linda Rees, Adrian Room, Melinda Saccone, Pat Shannon, Josh Sherman, Linda Siniscal, Rocky Stockman, MBE, Tom Stoudt, Paul Svercl, James Taylor, Jonathan Tichler, Alison Wainwright, David Wakefield, Tony Waltham, Arthur H. Waltz, John Weber, Ann Wilkes, Ray Wisbrock.

Academy of Motion Picture Arts and Sciences, Airport Operators Council International, American Automobile Manufacturers Association, Amateur Athletic Union, American Booksellers Association, American Correctional Association, American Forests, American Kennel Club, American Library Association, American Wholesale Marketers Association, American Zoo and Aquarium Association, *Amusement Business*, Amusement and Music Operators Association, Arbitron, Art Sales Index, ASCAP, ASH, Association of American Railroads, Audit Bureau of Circulations, Baby Center, Inc., *Beverage Digest*, Beverage Marketing Corporation, *Billboard*, Boston Athletic Association, *BP Statistical Review of World Energy*, British Library, Bureau of Engraving and Printing, Bureau of Federal Prisons, Bureau of Justice Statistics, Cablevision, Carbon Dioxide Information Analysis Center, Cat Fanciers' Association, Central Intelligence Agency, Championship Auto Racing Teams (CART), Channel Swimming Association, Charities Aid Foundation, Christian Research Association, Christie's East, Christie's London, Christie's South Kensington, *Classical Music*, CocaCola, Congressional Medal of Honor Society, Consumer Information Center, Country Music Association, Cowles/Simba Information, Cremation Society, *Crime in the United States*, *Daily Racing Form*, Death Penalty Information Center, Department of the Army, Corps of Engineers, Diamond Information Centre, Duncan's American Radio, *Editor and Publisher Year Book*, Environmental Protection Agency, Equine Line, Federal Bureau of Investigation, Feste Catalogue Index Database/Alan Somerset, *Flight International*, Food and Agriculture Organization of the United Nations, *Forbes Magazine*, Ford Motor Company,

Fortune, Foundation Center, Friends of the Earth, Gallup Organization, Gemstone Publishing, General Accident, Generation AB, Geological Museum, London, George Foster Peabody Awards, Going for Green, Gold Fields Mineral Services Ltd., *Goldmine*, Hollywood Foreign Press Association, Iditarod Trail Committee, Indianapolis Motor Speedway, Information Resources, Inc., Institute of Sports Medicine, International Atomic Energy Agency, International Civil Aviation Organization, International Cocoa Organization, International Coffee Organization, International Dairy Foods Association, International Game Fish Association, International Ice Cream Association, International Monetary Fund, International Tea Committee, International Union for the Conservation of Nature, International Union of Geological Sciences Commission on Comparative Planetology, *International Water Power and Dam Construction Handbook*, Interpol, IPEDS, Jockey Club, Lloyds Register of Shipping/MIPG/PPMS, Magazine Publishers of America, Major League Baseball, Mansell Color Company, Inc., Metropolitan Opera House, New York, Modern Language Association of America, MORI, Motion Picture Association of America, Inc., MRIB, Multi-State Lottery, NARAS, NASA, National Academy of Popular Music, National Association for Stock Car Auto Racing (NASCAR), National Association of College Bookstores, National Basketball Association (NBA), National Center for Education Statistics, National Center for Health Statistics, National Climatic Data Center, National Council of the Churches of Christ in the USA, National Dairy Council, National Fire Protection Association, National Football League (NFL), National Hockey League (NHL), National Oceanic and Atmospheric Association, National Public Radio, National Safety Council, National Solid Waste Management Association, National Sporting Goods Association, NCAA, New York Drama Desk, New York Road Runners Club, *New York Post*, Niagara Falls Museum, Nielsen Media Research, Nobel Foundation, *NonProfit Times*, NPD Group Worldwide, Nua Ltd., *Oxford English Dictionary*, Patent Office, PBS, PC Data, *People*, Pet Food Institute, Pet Industry Joint Advisory Council, PGA Tour, Inc., Phobics Society, *Playbill*, Popular Music Database, Produktschap voor Gedistilleerde Dranken, Professional Golf Association (PGA), Project FeederWatch/Cornell Lab of Ornithology, Public Lending Right, Public Library Association, *Publishers Weekly*, Pullman Power Products Corporation, *Railway Gazette International*, Recording Industry Association of America (RIAA), Record Research, *Restaurants & Institutions*, Royal Aeronautical Society, Scotch Whisky Association, *Screen Digest*, Siemens AG, Sotheby's, *Spaceflight*, *Sporting News*, *Statistical Abstract of the United States*, STATS Inc., Stubs, Taylors of Loughborough, *Theatre World*, Thoroughbred Racing Communication, *Time*, Tourist Industries, International Trade Administration, Trebor Bassett Ltd., UNESCO, *Uniform Crime Reports*, United Nations, Universal Postal Union, *USA Today*, US Board on Geographic Names, US Bureau of Economic Analysis, US Bureau of Labor Statistics, US Bureau of the Census, USCOLD, US Department of Agriculture, US Department of Agriculture Forest Service, US Department of Justice, US Department of Labor, US Department of the Interior, National Park Service/National Register of Historic Places, US Department of Transportation, Federal Aviation Administration, US Department of Transportation, Federal Highway Administration, US Department of

Transportation, National Traffic Safety Administration, US Fish and Wildlife Service, US Geological Survey, US Immigration and Naturalization Service, US Lighthouse Society, US Mint, US Postal Services, US Social Security Administration, US Trotting Association, *Variety*, Video Scan, Inc., *Video Store*, Ward's, *World Almanac and Book of Facts*, World Bank, World Health Organization, World Intellectual Property Organization, World Resources Institute, World Tourism Organization.

PICTURE CREDITS

t=top, c=center, a=above, b=below, l=left, r=right
© Academy & Motion Picture Arts & Services ® 167tl; Allsport USA/Brian Bahr 228tc/Dave Cannon 245tr/Mark Thompson 236bl; BFI/United International Pictures 148br; Camera Press/N. Diaye 111br; Christie's Images 179tr; Corbis/Bettmann/Everett 70tl, 162t /UPI 163bl; Ecoscene 43br; Mary Evans Picture Library 71br, 126bc, 211br; Ronald Grant Archive 177bl, 177tr, 177tl; Susan Greenhill 6tl; Hulton Getty 56r, 84tr, 219tc; Image Bank 127tr; Liaison 74tr; London Transport Museum 214bl; National Maritime Museum 44cr; National Motor Museum, Beaulieu 82bc, 210tl; Novosti 13tl; Paramount/Courtesy Kobal 149tr; Redferns/David Redfern 180tl; Rex Features 92tl, 105bl, 113tl, 123bc, 128tl, 131bl, 134tl, 136tl, 137bc, 140tr, 159ca, 159cb, 161bl, 164tl, 176bl, 212tl, 220tl, 243tr, 246bl /Jim Graham 145tr /B. Heinrich 169br /Iwasa 94br /Kevin Kolczyn 232tl /Raddaiz 168tr /Tim Rooke 49br, 242tl /Sipa Press 112tr, 139tr, 241b /Richard Sowersby 108tl /Bob Strong 19br /Pierre Suu 130tl /John Webster 85br; Royal Geographical Society 58bl; Science & Society Picture Library 189bl; Science Museum 218tl; Science Photo Library/Nasa 11tl; Frank Spooner Pictures 22b, 40bl, 48tr, 81tc, 89bl, 115tr, 120br, 132cc, 133tr, 135br, 142bl, 143bc, 157tl, 158bl, 160tr, 172tr, 174bl, 175tc, 225br, 226bl, 226tr /Joe Baker 142tr /Alain Benainous 152tl /Liaison 14bl /Singh Spooner 178bl; Sporting Pictures (UK) Ltd 244br; Tony Stone Images 87tl /Ben Edwards 97tr /Bill Heinsohn 194tr /Arnulf Husmo 193tl /Peter Pearson 107bc /Dave Saunder 199tl /Jack Vearey 199br /Baron Wolman 187bc /Herbert Zetti 155bl; Topham Picturepoint 72br, 146tr; Universal/Courtesy Kobal 148tl; Zefa Pictures 25tr, 63bl, 100bc, 109br

Every effort has been made to trace the copyright holders, and we apologize in advance for any unintentional omissions. We would be pleased to insert the appropriate acknowledgments in any subsequent edition of this publication.

ILLUSTRATIONS

Richard Bonson, Mick Loates, Eric Thomas, Richard Ward, John Woodcock

INDEX

Patricia Coward

PUBLISHER'S ACKNOWLEDGMENTS

Dorling Kindersley would like to thank Chris Gordon and Jason Little for administrative and DTP assistance. DK Publishing, Inc., thanks Ray Rogers, Jill Hamilton, and, especially, Mary Sutherland, for her invaluable assistance.

PACKAGER'S ACKNOWLEDGMENTS

GLS would like to thank Terry Burrows, Michael Downey, and Christain Kepps for additional editorial assistance, and Dave Farrow for additional design assistance.